SCHARNHORST AND GNEISENAU

DANIEL KNOWLES

FONTHILL

Fonthill Media Language Policy

Fonthill Media publishes in the international English language market. One language edition is published worldwide. As there are minor differences in spelling and presentation, especially with regard to American English and British English, a policy is necessary to define which form of English to use. The Fonthill Policy is to use the form of English native to the author. Daniel Knowles was born and educated in the United Kingdom; therefore, British English has been adopted in this publication.

Fonthill Media Limited
Fonthill Media LLC
www.fonthillmedia
office@fonthillmedia.com

First published in the United Kingdom and the United States of America 2023

British Library Cataloguing in Publication Data:
A catalogue record for this book is available from the British Library

Copyright © Daniel Knowles 2023

ISBN 978-1-78155-887-4

The right of Daniel Knowles to be identified as the author of this work has been asserted by him in accordance with the Copyright, Designs and Patents Act 1988.

All rights reserved. No part of this publication may be reproduced, stored in a retrieval system or transmitted in any form or by any means, electronic, mechanical, photocopying, recording or otherwise, without prior permission in writing from Fonthill Media Limited

Typeset in 10pt on 13pt Sabon
Printed and bound in England

Acknowledgements

As always, I am grateful to the multitude of people who have been kind enough to provide assistance and advice with regards to information and in providing photographs during the course of writing this book. In the first instance, I wish to extend my thanks to Gary Martin of the HMS *Glorious*, *Ardent*, and *Acasta* Association (GLARAC) along with Kelvin Youngs and Ralph Snape of Aircrew Remembered for their kind assistance with photographs. I must also extend a big thank you to Antonio Bonomi, who was kind enough to provide permission for me to use the illustrations contained in the plate section showing the camouflage schemes of both *Scharnhorst* and *Gneisenau* throughout their respective lifetimes and whose knowledge of the camouflage of the two ships has proved invaluable in establishing timeframes when photographs were taken. Additional thanks must be extended to Michael Emmerich, Simon Matthews, Anil Kumar, Chris Thornton, as well as to Arthur van Beveren and Lenco van der Weel of bunkersite.com, Robert Henderson, Peter Moise, Richard Aitken, and Harco Gijsbers of Beeldbank WO2.

For guidance and assistance with documents and additional photographs, thanks must be extended to the staff of the National Archives in Kew and the staff of the US Naval History and Heritage Command Center. Every effort has been made to trace copyright holders and obtain their permission for the use of copyright material. This has not always been possible. As such, the publisher and author apologise for any errors or omissions in the above list and would be grateful if notified of any corrections that should be incorporated in future reprints or editions of this book.

Thanks should also be extended to Alan Sutton, Jay Slater, Jamie Hardwick, and the other members of the team at Fonthill Media who helped to bring this book to publication.

Finally, I wish to thank my parents Gary and Tracey, my sister Natalie, my grandparents Eddie and Iris, and everyone else in my family along with my friends Jake Dorrell and David Osborne for their continued encouragement and support.

Contents

Acknowledgements		3
Kriegsmarine Ranks		7
Introduction		9
1	In the Shadow of Versailles	11
2	Anatomy of the Scharnhorst-class	23
3	*Gneisenau*: Construction and Sea Trials	43
4	*Scharnhorst*: Construction and Sea Trials	51
5	To War	63
6	Operation Juno	88
7	Operation Berlin	106
8	At Brest	121
9	Operation Cerberus: The Channel Dash	131
10	Deployment to Norway	152
11	The Hunters and the Hunted	160
12	Ostfront	172
13	'*Scharnhorst* Will Ever Reign Supreme'	186
14	'On the Field of Honour'	208
15	The Fate of the *Gneisenau*	215
16	The Wreck of the *Scharnhorst*	221
Epilogue		223
Appendix I: Commanding Officers		225
Appendix II: Ships Sunk by the Gneisenau and Scharnhorst During Operation Berlin		226
Appendix III: Survivors of the Scharnhorst		227
Appendix IV: Scharnhorst Roll of Honour		228
Appendix V: Gneisenau Roll of Honour		240
Endnotes		243
Bibliography		249
Index		252

Kriegsmarine Ranks

Below are ranks of the *Kriegsmarine* during the Second World War and their equivalent ranks in the Royal Navy and the United States Navy:

Großadmiral	Admiral of the Fleet
Generaladmiral	Admiral
Admiral	Admiral
Vizeadmiral	Vice Admiral
Konteradmiral	Rear-Admiral
Kommodore	Commodore
Kapitän zur See	Captain
Fregattenkapitän	Commander
Korvettenkapitän	Lieutenant Commander
Kapitänleutnant	Lieutenant
Oberleutnant zur See	Lieutenant (Junior Grade)
Leutnant zur See	Ensign
Oberfähnrich zur See	Passed Midshipman
Fähnrich zur See	Midshipman
Seekadett	Cadet
Matrosenstabsoberfeldwebel	Master Chief Petty Officer
Matrosenoberfeldwebel	Senior Chief Petty Officer
Matrosenfeldwebel	Chief Petty Officer
Obermaat/Oberbootsmaat	Leading Petty Officer
Maat/Bootsmannsmaat	Petty Officer
Matrosenhauptgefreiter	Leading Seaman
Matrosenobergefreiter	Seaman
Matrosengefreiter	Seaman Apprentice
Matrose	Seaman Recruit

Introduction

After the *Bismarck*, the *Scharnhorst* is probably the most famous capital ship to have seen service with the *Kriegsmarine*. Nevertheless, she and her sister ship *Gneisenau* have been largely overshadowed by the *Bismarck* and *Tirpitz* despite the fact that they played a more proactive role in the prosecution of the Second World War. Referred to alternatively as battleships and battlecruisers, *Scharnhorst* and *Gneisenau* marked the beginning of German naval rearmament following the Treaty of Versailles and were originally intended to be employed in a war against France, which at the time of their construction was considered to be Germany's primary opponent in any conflict.

Almost completely identical, the two ships were referred to in Great Britain as 'the ugly sisters' and 'the Elusive Sisters'.[1] Among some ranks of the Royal Navy, the ships were referred to as 'Salmon' and 'Gluckstein' after a British tobacconist. Despite these names, they were graceful ships with long, slender lines that emphasised their 11-inch guns.

Commissioned in 1938 and 1939 respectively, *Gneisenau* and *Scharnhorst* were the most successful German battleships of the Second World War. The story of these two warships is one of mixed fortunes. During the early years of the Second World War, *Scharnhorst* and *Gneisenau* saw extensive service together operating against the Royal Navy and the Atlantic convoy routes, where, as Stephen Roskill noted in volume one of the official British history of the war at sea, the two ships exerted 'a considerable influence on our [British] naval dispositions and on the allocation of our air effort'.[2]

From 1942, when they participated in one of the most audacious operations of the Second World War by sailing up the English Channel directly under the nose of history's greatest maritime nation to return to Germany, the fortunes of the ships changed. For *Gneisenau*, the war would be as good as over and she would meet an inglorious end, while for *Scharnhorst*, a period of relative inactivity hidden among the fjords of Norway followed before she was cornered on Boxing Day 1943 and went down with her flag flying in the last battleship engagement between British and German naval forces, and what would prove to be the penultimate battleship engagement in history.[3]

The story of the *Scharnhorst* and *Gneisenau* is more than the story of two warships. It is the story of the naval war in the North Sea, the Arctic, the Atlantic, and on the Channel Front.

1

In the Shadow of Versailles

The *Scharnhorst* and *Gneisenau* were the first ships to be officially classified by the *Kriegsmarine* as *Schlachtschiff* (battleships), while other German battleships had been classified as *Linienschiffe* (ships of the line) and *Panzerschiffe* (armoured ships).[1] While the *Kriegsmarine* classified the *Scharnhorst* and *Gneisenau* as battleships, during the course of the Second World War, the Royal Navy classified the two ships as battlecruisers, although the ships were reclassified by the Royal Navy as being battleships after the war.[2] While the Royal Navy classified the *Scharnhorst* and *Gneisenau* as battlecruisers, the 1940 edition of *Jane's Fighting Ships* classified both the Scharnhorst-class and the ships of the Bismarck-class as battleships.[3] In addition to this, the United States Navy classified the ships of the Scharnhorst-class as battleships. As a result, in English language works, the *Scharnhorst* and *Gneisenau* have been referred to on occasion as battlecruisers and on other occasions as battleships.

From the inception of their design, the ships of the Scharnhorst-class were subjected to a number of limitations. First and foremost among these limitations were the provisions and restrictions that the Treaty of Versailles placed on Germany. Under the Treaty of Versailles, Germany was permitted to construct new vessels up to a displacement of 10,000 tons with the treaty stating that 'Germany is forbidden to construct or acquire any warships other than those intended to replace the units in commission'.[4]

The number of ships that Germany could possess was also restricted under the terms of the treaty with Germany being permitted to retain only six pre-dreadnought battleships, six light cruisers, twelve destroyers, and twelve torpedo boats with a further two pre-dreadnought battleships, two cruisers, four destroyers, and four torpedo boats in reserve.[5] U-boats were forbidden under the terms of the treaty along with an air force. Even manpower levels were precisely detailed in the terms of the treaty.

The armistice terms had demanded that the German High Seas Fleet, which was comprised of seventy-four warships, was to deliver itself to Admiral Sir David Beatty, the commander-in-chief of the Royal Navy's Grand Fleet whereupon it was to be interned in British waters pending the signing of the peace agreement that was the Treaty of Versailles. The surrender of the High Seas Fleet was taken on 21 November

1918 with the ships and their skeleton crews sailing to Rosyth before sailing on into internment at Scapa Flow in the Orkney Islands.

Following the armistice, the Allied powers spent much time quarrelling over the final terms of the treaty, which ultimately ran to over 200 pages in length, was composed of 75,000 words, and contained 400 separate clauses. The Germans put up resistance to signing the treaty and held out until the third week of June 1919 when they eventually accepted the terms almost without further negotiation. There was, however, a last-minute delay over the final signing. During this time on 21 June, the entire Grand Fleet (which had been keeping watch over the High Seas Fleet) weighed anchor and departed Scapa Flow in order to conduct exercises in the North Sea, leaving two destroyers and a handful of small patrol vessels to guard the German fleet.

As the Grand Fleet departed Scapa Flow, *Konteradmiral* Ludwig von Reuter, the German admiral in command of the interned fleet, gained the impression that the armistice negotiations had run into trouble, having read of the possibility in a newspaper (or so he would later claim to interrogators). With no agreement possible, his orders commanded him to scuttle the fleet. Claiming that he was unaware on 21 June that the armistice had been extended to allow last-minute changes to be made to the treaty, von Reuter assumed that the departure of the Grand Fleet was somehow connected to the treaty negotiations in Paris. Interrogators would later argue that the reverse of what von Reuter stated was in fact the truth and argued that he believed that the peace treaty was about to be signed and that he had planned that on no account were the Allies to get their hands on his ships. Whatever his motives, von Reuter issued orders for the High Seas Fleet to be scuttled—a decision that was one of the most staggering and spectacular in naval history; it was an event that shook the world.[6] This action left the German navy, then known as the *Reichsmarine*, with only the remnants of the fleet that it had once possessed.

The navy that was provided to Germany under the terms of the Treaty of Versailles and as a result of von Reuter's actions amounted to a coastal force of questionable strength. As a result, it was only natural that Germany's new naval leaders would wish to have the situation with regards to the strength of the *Reichsmarine* improved at the earliest opportunity. In the early 1920s, the first thoughts were given towards replacing the pre-dreadnought battleships and the old cruisers with new vessels. The proposals for the replacement vessels were not, however, easily put into practice.

The Weimar Republic was politically unstable and faced continual changes of government. Between the end of 1918 and 30 January 1933, Germany had twenty cabinets and twelve different chancellors, allowing for little continuity. Financially, Germany was in a desperate state with the reparations demanded by the victorious allied powers serving to virtually ruin the economy, which led to hyperinflation. It was not until the mid-1920s, when the economic situation began to stabilise, that the government began to look more kindly upon the requirements of the navy.

Despite the economic turmoil, some of the *Reichmarine*'s needs were catered for. December 1921 saw the keel laid of the light cruiser *Emden*, which was launched in January 1925 and commissioned in October of that same year as the first major vessel of the navy since the First World War. The first new replacement vessel for a pre-dreadnought was 'Armoured Cruiser A', later named the *Deutschland*. The

Deutschland was a *Panzerschiffe*, a vessel that would come to gain a more infamous name—the pocket battleship. Meanwhile, as Germany struggled economically and slowly turned its attentions towards the renewal of older vessels, the Allied powers began to look towards disarmament and arms limitations.

In the wake of the First World War, the United Kingdom, United States, and Japan all began looking towards modernising their respective fleets by constructing new capital ships. All of the new post-war capital ships proposed by Great Britain, the United States and Japan were heavily armed and heavily armoured. The distinction between each of the proposed ships designed by the three nations was speed: some of the proposed vessel retained the existing standard of the battle fleet of 21–23 knots while other designs were planned to be able to attain a minimum speed of 30 knots. So it was that almost before the smoke of the First World War had cleared, the major world naval powers were planning newer, bigger and more powerful ships than those that had clashed at the Battle of Jutland.[7]

The post-war building programmes that were proposed by these major naval powers amounted to yet another naval arms race, the likes of which had contributed to the First World War. While having planned their respective building programmes, the United States, Japan, and Great Britain all had good reasons for wishing to abandon their programmes, not least of which were financial. Indeed, the First World War had cost Britain approximately £20 billion, and as such, she could ill-afford to become embroiled in an arms race given the exorbitant costs involved. In the United States, an arms race was unwelcomed by the population while Congress had voted down President Woodrow Wilson's 1919 naval expansion programme. The 1920 presidential election campaign also saw American politics return to non-interventionism, as such, little enthusiasm existed for naval expansion.[8]

In late 1921, the US government became aware that plans were afoot in Britain for a conference to discuss the strategic situation in the Pacific and the Far East. In an effort to forestall this conference, President Warren G. Harding convened the Washington conference. During his election campaign, Harding had urged the lowering of defence spending and had been a proponent of disarmament. A US senator called William Borah was the first to propose a conference at which the major naval powers would agree to cut their fleets, an idea that appealed to Harding. Invitations were sent to delegations from Great Britain and the British Empire, Japan, Italy, and France to journey to Washington D.C. to discuss an end to the naval arms race. The conference convened in November 1921.

The main thrust of the proposals that were discussed at the conference concerned the naval might of the United States, Britain, and Japan. At the first plenary session held on 21 November, Hughes presented the proposals of the United States. This proposed a ten-year pause ('holiday') on the construction of capital ships, which included the immediate suspension of all capital ships under construction and the scrapping of all proposed capital ships while also placing a limit on the number and types of vessels that could be constructed. In this, it was proposed to scrap existing or planned capital ships to give a tonnage ratio of 5:5:3:1.75:1.75 to Britain, the United States, Japan, Italy, and France. A ratio of 5:5:3 would also be applied to the tonnage of secondary vessels.

With respect to capital ships, tonnage would be restricted to 500,000 for both Great Britain and the United States, 300,000 tons for Japan, and 175,000 each for Italy and France. Under this proposal, the United States offered to cancel and scrap nine of the ten battleships and all six of the battlecruisers that it then had under construction. In addition to this, all older battleships up to but not including the ships of the Delaware-class were to be scrapped. Under this proposal, Britain would cancel the G3 battlecruisers that had been ordered in October 1921 and would scrap all of her older battleships up to the King George V-class (1911). This proposal would see Japan cancel the No. 13 class battlecruisers and the Kii-class battleships as well as scrap the Kaga-class battleships, the four Amagi-class battlecruisers, and the recently completed *Mutsu*. An additional ten battleships up to but not including the Settsu-class would also be scrapped. In all, the plan called for the scrapping of a total of sixty-six capital ships already in existence or under construction.

The proposals surrounding capital ships were largely accepted by the British delegation, however, they proved controversial with the British public. Under the proposals, it would no longer be possible for Britain to maintain adequate fleets in home waters, the Mediterranean, and in the Far East simultaneously, something which provoked outrage from some sections of the Royal Navy. Nevertheless, there was a huge demand for Britain to agree. Naval spending was unpopular in Britain and the Dominions. Finally, the proposals provided Britain with the opportunity to maintain a prominent naval position while cutting a vast swathe of her naval power, thus cutting expenditure at a time when her government was making major decreases in its budget owing to the recession that followed the war.[9]

The Japanese delegation was divided on the proposal as Japanese naval doctrine of the time required the maintenance of a fleet that was 70 per cent the size of that of the United States. The French delegation initially responded negatively to the idea of reducing the tonnage of its capital ships to 175,000 and demanded an increase to 350,000 tons, above that delegated to Japan. In the end, concessions were made regarding cruisers and submarines, which helped to persuade the French to agree to a limit on capital ships.[10] Another issue that required readdressing from a French point of view was that Italy was to have parity, something which was considered unsubstantiated. Ultimately, pressure from both the British and American delegations led to the French delegation accepting parity. Parity with the French was considered a great success by the Italian government, although it would never actually be attained.

Much discussion was had on the inclusion or exclusion of individual warships. In particular, the Japanese delegation was keen to retain the *Mutsu*, the newest battleship commissioned into service with the Imperial Japanese Navy. After much deliberation, it was agreed to allow Japan to retain the *Mutsu* and provisions were subsequently made to allow the US Navy and the Royal Navy to construct equivalent ships. The United States would retain three of the four ships of the Colorado-class while Britain was permitted to build two new 16-inch gun battleships, displacing 35,000 tons that would become HMS *Nelson* and *Rodney*.

The Washington Naval Treaty was concluded on 6 February 1922 and ratifications were exchanged in Washington on 17 August 1923 before being registered in the

League of Nations Treaty Series on 16 April 1924. The terms of the Washington Naval Treaty stated:

> Construction of new battleships was prohibited for a period of ten years.
> Ships had to be twenty years old before being replaced.[11]
> Battleship tonnage was limited to a maximum of 35,000 tons.
> The main armament of battleships was to be limited to no greater than 16 inches.
> Aircraft carriers were limited to a displacement of 27,000 tons and could carry no more than ten heavy guns of a maximum calibre of 8 inches. As a caveat to this, each signatory was allowed to use two existing capital ship hulls for aircraft carriers with a displacement limit of 33,000 tons each. For the purposes of the treaty an aircraft carrier was defined as a warship displacing more than 10,000 tons designed and constructed exclusively for launching and landing aircraft. Aircraft carriers lighter than 10,000 tons did not count towards the tonnage limits while all aircraft carriers then under construction or in service (HMS *Argus*, HMS *Furious*, the USS *Langley* and the *Hōshō*) were declared 'experimental' and not counted in the tonnage limits.
> All additional warships were to be limited to a maximum of 10,000 tons and were limited to carrying a maximum gun calibre of 8 inches.
> Tonnage was restricted to 500,000 tons for both Great Britain and the United States, 300,000 for Japan, and 175,000 tons for both France and Italy.

Subsequently, to comply with the treaty, Britain sent twenty-two capital ships to the breaker's yard while the United States and Japan despatched four each, leaving the Royal Navy with twenty-two battleships and battlecruisers, the US Navy with eighteen, and the Japanese Navy with ten.

The Washington Naval Treaty achieved a remarkable reduction in existing and proposed battleships. While stipulating that no new battleships could be laid down until November 1931, the Washington Naval Treaty would run until the end of 1936. The 1920s stood out as a period in which the world's naval authorities and their governments appeared to be dedicated to ensuring that the First World War really was the 'War to End All Wars'.

Long before the Washington Naval Treaty expired, and before the 'battleship holiday' came to an end, a disarmament conference was held in Geneva, Switzerland in June 1927. The conference proved to be a spectacular failure. Italy and France did not attend, meanwhile, Britain and the United States became deadlocked on the issue of heavy cruisers while British attempts to place further restrictions on battleships fell on deaf ears. In 1930, a third naval conference was convened, this time in London. Marred by disagreements between France and Italy that saw their delegates withdrawn, Britain, the United States, and Japan agreed on a number of points which impacted on capital ships.

The London Conference was a revival of the efforts that had gone into the 1927 Geneva Naval Conference. Under the agreed treaty, which was signed on 22 April 1930 and commonly referred to as the London Naval Treaty, the standard displacement of submarines was restricted to 2,000 tons with each major power being allowed to keep three submarines up to 2,800 tons and France one. The gun calibre of submarines was restricted for the first time to 6.1 inches, the only exception being the already constructed French *Surcouf*, which mounted 8-inch guns. The restriction on submarine gun calibres put an end to the concept of the 'big gun' submarine which had been pioneered with the design and construction of the *Surcouf* and British M-class.

The treaty also established a distinction between cruisers armed with guns no greater than 6.1 inches, which were deemed light cruisers, and those with guns up to 8 inches— heavy cruisers. The number of heavy cruisers that could be maintained by each navy was limited. Britain was permitted fifteen with a total tonnage of 147,000; the United States eighteen totalling 180,000 tons; and Japan twelve totalling 108,000 tons. No limits were placed on the number of light cruisers that could be maintained by each nation, but tonnage limits were set at 192,200 tons for Britain, 143,500 tons for the United States, and 100,450 tons for Japan. Destroyers were defined as ships of less than 1,850 tons with guns not exceeding 5.1 inches and were limited. Japan was permitted a total destroyer tonnage of 105,500 while Britain and America were permitted destroyers up to 150,000 tons.

On 9 December 1935, a second disarmament conference was convened in London which culminated in the signing of the Second London Naval Treaty on 25 March 1936. Great Britain and the Dominions, the United States, and France were all signatories of the treaty. Japan, which had signed the previous treaties, withdrew from the conference on 15 January while Italy refused to sign the treaty largely as a result of the controversy following its invasion of Abyssinia and the sanctions imposed by the League of Nations. The conference was intended to limit the growth in naval armaments until 1942, however, the absence of Japan prevented an agreement being reached on a ceiling for the number of warships that could be maintained by each nation.

Like previous treaties, the Second London Naval Treaty limited the maximum size of the ships and the maximum calibre of guns that they could be armed with. Under the provisions of the treaty, capital ships were restricted to a displacement of 35,000 tons and could be armed with a maximum gun calibre of 14 inches. At the insistence of the American negotiators, a so-called 'escalator clause' was included in the treaty in case any of the countries that had previously signed the Washington Naval Treaty refused to adhere to the new limitations. The 'escalator clause' allowed the United States, Britain, and France to raise the limits on gun calibres from 14 to 16 inches if Japan or Italy still refused to sign the treaty after 1 April 1937.[12]

Meanwhile, in Germany, design work on the *Panzerschiffe* had begun in 1923 before a temporary halt in the design and development work was forced by the collapse of the economy in 1924. The then commander-in-chief of the *Reichsmarine*, Admiral Hans Zenker, pushed hard for the resumption of the design work, resulting in three proposals being drafted in 1925. In total, the *Reichsmarine* ended up with five potential designs for the new armoured ships. The designs varied from ships capable of 32 knots and armed with eight 8-inch guns to ships capable of 22 knots and armed with 15-inch guns. Eventually, the design that was selected by the *Reichsmarine* for the vessel that would become the *Deutschland* (which would have two sister ships, the *Admiral Graf Spee* and *Admiral Scheer*) was for a vessel armed with 11-inch guns. The decision to arm the new vessels with this calibre of gun was a conscious one in order to avoid provoking the Allied powers and to ease the pressures on design staff.[13]

The *Panzerschiffe Deutschland* in 1934.

A postcard image of the three *Panzerschiffe* during a fleet parade. From left to right: *Admiral Graf Spee*, *Admiral Scheer*, and *Deutschland*. (*Author's Collection*)

The pocket battleship was a revolutionary type of vessel and was a hybrid built within the specifications of the Washington Naval Agreement. In terms of the calibre of her main armament, the *Deutschland* was a capital ship, yet owing to her relatively light displacement of 14,520 tons, she was a heavy cruiser. It is worth noting that while the *Deutschland* adhered strictly to the limitations placed on Germany under the Treaty of Versailles, the *Admiral Scheer* and *Admiral Graf Spee* were heavier, carrying additional armour to improve their defensive capabilities.

Nevertheless, there was significant political opposition to the construction of the new ships at the time. The *Reichsmarine* was, therefore, forced to delay placing an order for the *Panzerschiffe* until after the 1928 *Reichstag* elections during which questions over whether or not to build the new ships had been a point of contestation among the election campaigns.

While being a hybrid vessel that was half capital ship, half heavy cruiser, the *Panzerschiffe* was significantly more powerful than the heavy cruisers possessed by the Royal Navy, the French *Marine Nationale*, and the United States Navy. There was hope within German naval circles that the construction of ships that were more powerful than the heavy cruisers of the Allied nations would force the Allies into admitting Germany to the Washington Naval Treaty, thereby circumventing the limitations imposed by the Treaty of Versailles in exchange for the cancellation of the *Deutschland*. The French, however, vehemently opposed any concessions to Germany and any weakening of the Versailles settlement.

In 1932, the *Reichstag* passed the *Schiffbauersatzplan* (replacement ship construction programme), which called for two separate phases of naval construction. The first phase, which was to last from 1930 to 1936, was to be followed by the second, which was to last from 1936 to 1943. The second phase of the plan was intended to break the limitations of the Treaty of Versailles in secret. The *Schiffbauersatzplan* came into effect in November 1932 under the overall control of Reich Defence Minister Kurt von Schleicher in response to the doomed Geneva Disarmament Conference from which Germany finally took her leave on 14 October 1933.

France, long considered as being Germany's principal potential enemy, reacted promptly to the appearance of the *Deutschland* and the construction of her two sister ships by placing orders for two larger battleships: the *Dunkerque* and *Strasbourg*. Displacing 26,000 tons and armed with eight 13-inch guns in two quadruple turrets, the Dunkerque-class could attain a speed of 30 knots. The *Dunkerque* was launched on 2 October 1935 and commissioned on 1 May 1937 while the *Strasbourg* was launched on 12 December 1936 and commissioned in April 1939. Undoubtedly, other neutral powers noticed the construction of the Deutschland-class vessels but looked on with less alarm than the French did. The construction by France of the *Dunkerque* and *Strasbourg* was closely watched by the Germans and prompted a review of German naval planning.[14]

On 30 January 1933, President Hindenburg appointed Adolf Hitler as chancellor of Germany. A purge of the political establishment followed, which eliminated opposition to the National Socialist German Workers Party and cleared the way for Hitler to achieve his objectives. Although initially hesitant, by March 1935, Hitler had declared

The French battleship *Dunkerque* in 1937. (*Author's Collection*)

Germany's sovereignty in defence matters and initiated a rearmament programme. It is highly likely that the foundations were laid in April 1934 when the *Deutschland* embarked upon a goodwill cruise to Norway carrying Hitler, Chief of the Naval Staff Admiral Erich Raeder, Supreme Commander of the German Army *Generaloberst* Werner von Fritsch, and Reich War Minister *Generaloberst* Werner von Blomberg.

Since 1933, Raeder had argued for an increase in the defensive qualities of the *Panzerschiffe* and for an increase in the offensive power of the main battery with the addition of a third triple turret.[15] The navy, which in 1935 had been renamed the *Kriegsmarine*, maintained that the design would become unbalanced.[16] Hitler agreed to an increase in armour protection and internal subdivisions to assist with damage control, but he refused to permit an increase in the ship's armament. Finally, in February 1934, Hitler acquiesced over the additional third turret.[17]

This led to contracts being approved for the two armoured ships, 'D' and 'E', which were to be constructed in response to the Dunkerque-class. Displacing 20,000 tons, the ships were to be larger than the Deutschland-class at 754 feet (230 metres) long and 84 feet (25.5 metres) wide. In the design of ships 'D' and 'E', emphasis had been laid on an improved protection scheme with an 8.6-inch (220-mm) armoured belt, a citadel of 2 inches (50 mm), and a upper deck with a thickness of 3.1 inches (80 mm). The main armament was set as being 11-inch guns with some thought given to equipping the new ships with eight guns in two quadruple turrets similar to the arrangement on the Dunkerque-class as opposed to six guns in two turrets as on the Deutschland-class, however, this would have required a completely new design. The traditional 5.9-inch (15 cm) gun was retained for the secondary armament alongside 3.9-inch, 1.5-inch, and 0.7-inch (10-cm, 3.7-cm, and 2-cm) anti-aircraft guns. The installation of torpedo tubes was also envisaged.

Lengthy discussions were subsequently held concerning the desirability of matching the 13-inch main armament of the French ships. Consideration was also given to 14- and 15-inch guns, but as had been the case with the quadruple turret idea, a completely new design would have been required in order to mount them. Furthermore, Hitler would not have given this proposal approval since for some time he had been making overtures to Great Britain. It is reasonably certain that Hitler was anxious at the time for reconciliation with the world's leading naval power and that by opting for a calibre of gun larger than 11 inches it would have been likely that the negotiations which led to the Anglo-German Naval Agreement would have been jeopardised.

On 26 March 1935, during a meeting with British Foreign Secretary Sir John Simon and his deputy Anthony Eden, Hitler stated his intention to reject the naval disarmament section of the Treaty of Versailles but claimed that he was prepared to discuss a treaty regulating the scale of German naval rearmament.[18] In a speech in Berlin on 21 May 1935, Hitler formally offered to discuss a treaty limiting Germany to a navy 35 per cent the size of the Royal Navy. Disavowing any intention of engaging in a pre-1914-style naval arms race with Britain, Hitler stated:

> The German *Reich* government recognises of itself the overwhelming importance for existence and thereby the justification of dominance at sea to protect the British Empire, just as, on the other hand, we are determined to do everything necessary in protection of our own continental existence and freedom.[19]

The following day, the British cabinet voted to formally take up Hitler on his offer. Talks between the British delegation headed by Simon and the German delegation led by Joachim von Ribbentrop began on 4 June 1935. It was agreed that Germany could construct a navy on the ratio of 35:100 with the German delegation conceding that this ratio would be expressed in ship tonnage with Germany building her tonnage up to whatever the British tonnage was in various warship categories.

For two weeks, talks continued in London on technical issues that mainly related to how tonnage ratios would be calculated in the various warship categories. Desperate for success, Ribbentrop agreed to almost all of the British demands.[20] On 18 June 1935, the Anglo-German Naval Agreement was signed in London by Ribbentrop and Sir Samuel Hoare, the new British foreign secretary. Believing that the signing of the treaty marked the beginning of an Anglo-German alliance, Hitler, at the time, referred to 18 June 1935 as 'the happiest day of his life'.[21]

Five months after they were ordered, the keels of the two D-class cruisers were scrapped on the stocks to make way for two new vessels; these would become the *Scharnhorst* and *Gneisenau*. The provisional names of the two D-class vessels—*Ersatz Elsass* and *Ersatz Hessen* were reallocated to new ships, the contracts for which were awarded to the Kriegsmarineweft Wilhelmshaven and Deutsche Werke in Kiel. In cancelling the D-class it was decided that the new vessels should be enlarged so as to counter the Dunkerque-class. Work was, however, delayed for fourteen months in order to allow Hitler to secure the Anglo-German Naval Agreement before work commenced.[22] In addition to this, work was partly delayed due to numerous design changes that were implemented after the ships were ordered.[23]

Under the Anglo-German Naval Agreement, the maximum gun calibre that was permitted was 16 inches. With this, Hitler soon had second thoughts about the calibre of gun to be used on the new ships and ordered that they should be armed with 15-inch guns. However, 15-inch guns would take years to develop. At the same time, Hitler wanted capital ships as soon as possible in order to fulfil his political ideals. Hitler was also reminded that despite the allowances of the Anglo-German Naval Agreement, Britain had historically been sensitive about increases in the main armament of German capital ships.[24] A compromise was therefore sought. Hitler decreed that the ships would be armed with 11-inch guns but that the ships would carry nine guns in three triple turrets and that the ships would be up-gunned to 15 inches at the earliest opportunity. The 15-inch gun would eventually be used to arm the *Bismarck* and *Tirpitz*.

In enlarging the design of ships 'D' and 'E' to counter the Dunkerque-class, the size of these two ships increased officially to 26,000 tons. Thicker armour was envisaged in order to offer protection against 15-inch shells. An effort was also made to provide the best possible protection against bombs and torpedoes. Owing to a shortage of space amidships, single-barrelled 5.9-inch gun houses were to be sited, although elsewhere the secondary armament would be sited in twin turrets.

Difficulties existed over the choice of the main plant for the new vessels, and controversy gave rise to lively discussions between naval architects and engineers. Eventually, the architectural and engineering departments were brought together under a single controlling authority which lead to steam turbine drive being decided upon. While arguments still persisted, further delay was deemed to be unjustifiable. That the final decision favoured steam turbine propulsion was due principally to the fact that the equivalent diesel plant was not available because the problems that the plant suffered had not been fully addressed. Further to this, a euphoric atmosphere surrounded the newly introduced high-pressure steam plant that was being used by merchant vessels and inshore installations with many believing it to be the final word in marine drive.

Another reason that lay behind the decision to install steam drive had been the ship testing committee's criticism of the construction method of the diesel installation in the ships of the Deutschland-class. The criticism was, however, only partly justified as the lightness of the unit had been a basic contractual specification laid down by the *Reichsmarine*. In order to comply with the specifications, the foundations were built lightly, and, as was later discovered, weakly. This was mainly an architectural flaw. Subsequently, the *Deutschland* had to ship extra ballast in order to increase her stability. If some of this additional weight had been allowed to the diesel manufacturer, the problems that existed with the foundations would not have arisen.

From a political perspective, the construction of battleships 'D' and 'E' was a clear breach of the Treaty of Versailles. So too was the declaration of military sovereignty, which was made on 16 March 1935. The tonnage of the armoured cruisers 'B' and 'C', which would become the pocket battleships *Admiral Scheer* and *Admiral Graf Spee*, also amounted to an infringement of the Treaty of Versailles, however, the culpability for this infringement lay with the pre-Hitler German governments and *Reichstag*. The building of battleships 'D' and 'E' was sanctioned retroactively by the Anglo-German Naval Agreement.

Following the First World War, the post-war German navy had been torn over what direction its future should take; Poland was viewed by the army as the future potential enemy. The navy therefore assumed that in a conflict with Poland, France would come out in support of the Poles. It was expected that in such a conflict, Great Britain would remain neutral and that, as a result, the Royal Navy would not constitute a threat. By 1938, however, Hitler's foreign policy was increasing the likelihood of a conflict with Britain. Against this backdrop, the head of the *Kriegsmarine*, Admiral Erich Raeder ordered the completion of the *Bismarck* and *Tirpitz* to be expedited. Despite Hitler's posturing, the *Führer* assured Raeder that war would not break out until at least 1948.

In the meantime, Raeder began planning for war with Britain and believed that Britain could be defeated through a surface raider strategy attacking commerce. According to Raeder's plans, this would force the Royal Navy to use its naval might to defend the convoy routes permitting German ships to operate in the North Sea. The first draft of this plan was called Plan 'X' and was followed by a paired-down version known as Plan 'Y'. Plan 'Y' was in turn followed by a final version known as Plan 'Z'. Initially rejected by Hitler, Plan 'Z' was remodelled and accepted on 1 March 1939. Under the revised plan Germany would deploy battleships and aircraft carriers in task forces in support of *Panzerschiffe* and light cruisers which would attack British commerce.

Plan 'Z' as approved by Hitler called for a surface fleet of 230 vessels including battleships, battlecruisers and aircraft carriers. The below table offers an illustration of what Plan 'Z' called for in contrast to the true strength of the *Kriegsmarine* at the outbreak of war on 1 September 1939.

Vessel type	Projected Number	Number Completed
Battleships	10	4
Battlecruisers	3	0
Aircraft Carriers	4	0
Panzerschiffe	15	3
Heavy Cruisers	5	3
Light Cruisers	13	6
Escorts	22	0
Destroyers	68	30
Torpedo Boats	90	36

The above table included the two Bismarck-class battleships under construction, the *Scharnhorst* and *Gneisenau*, the three Deutschland-class *Panzerschiffe* and the six light cruisers that were already in service. The five vessels of the Admiral Hipper-class fulfilled the plan's mandate for heavy cruisers while the M-class of light cruisers was to fulfil the mandate for light cruisers. On 27 July 1939, Raeder revised Plan 'Z' and cancelled all twelve of the P-class *Panzerschiffe*.[25]

Despite the assurances of Hitler that war would not break out until at least 1948, following the German invasion of Poland on 1 September 1939, 3 September found Germany at war with both Great Britain and France. Less than a year after it was approved, Plan 'Z' was cancelled, its positive effects on German naval construction being minimal. Following the outbreak of war, all of the major warships authorised under the plan were cancelled with only the major ships which pre-dated the plan being completed.

2
Anatomy of the Scharnhorst-class

The *Scharnhorst* and *Gneisenau* were both Scharnhorst-class battleships and were the second largest warships built for the *Kriegsmarine* after the *Bismarck* and *Tirpitz*. It is the purpose of this chapter to outline the different characteristics and features of the Scharnhorst-class and to highlight the differences that existed between the two ships as well as between the ships of this class and other ships which saw service with the *Kriegsmarine*.

General Characteristics

At the waterline, the *Scharnhorst* and *Gneisenau* were 741 feet 6 inches (226 metres) long. Despite this, the *Scharnhorst* had an overall length of 771 feet 8 inches (234.9 metres) while *Gneisenau* had a slightly shorter overall length of 753 feet 11 inches (229.8 metres). Both vessels had a beam of 98 feet 5 inches (30 metres) and were designed to displace 35,540 tons, which would have given the ships a draught of 29 feet 10 inches (9.1 metres). With a standard displacement of 32,600 tons, the draught of the ships was reduced to 27 feet 3 inches (8.3 metres) while when at full load, the ships displaced 38,100 tons, draught increased to 32 feet 6 inches (9.9 metres).

The *Kriegsmarine* considered the ships of the Scharnhorst-class to be poor sea boats; they were bow-heavy while fully loaded and very 'wet' as high as the bridge. The problem of being wet ships was something that was mitigated to an extent by the replacement of the straight stem with an 'Atlantic bow', though it is worth noting that the use of 'A' turret would remain restricted while in heavy seas. The stern of the *Scharnhorst* and *Gneisenau* was also frequently wet and the ships were somewhat sluggish in entering a turn. In shallow waters, so poor was their respective handling that the ships almost always required the assistance of tugboats. With hard rudder, the ships lost over 50 per cent speed and heeled over more than ten degrees. In some instances during sea trials, the ships heeled over as much as thirteen degrees with hard rudder.[1]

The *Scharnhorst* and *Gneisenau* had a crew of between fifty-six and sixty officers and between 1,613 and 1,780 enlisted men. The crews of the respective ships were augmented by another ten officers and sixty-one men when they served as squadron flagships.

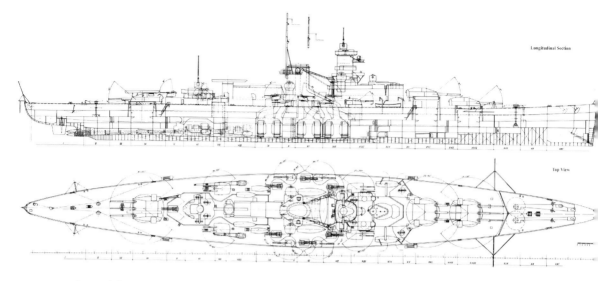

Plans of the Scharnhorst-class.

	General Details	
	Scharnhorst	*Gneisenau*
Building Costs	143.5 million Reichsmarks	146.2 million Reichsmarks
Measurement (Net Registered Tons)	19,401	19,401
Displacement (Full Load)	38,100	38,100
Length (Overall)	771 ft, 8 in (234.9 m)	753 ft, 11 in (229.8 m)
Length (Waterline)	741 ft, 6 in (226 m)	741 ft, 6 in (226 m)
Maximum Draught	32 ft, 6 in (9.9 m)	32 ft 6 in (9.9 m)
Speed (knots)	31.5	31.3
Range (at 19 knots)	8,200 miles (13,100 km)	7,100 miles (11,500 km)
Bunker Capacity (Tons)	6,200	6,200
Ship's Company	60 officers 1,908 men (1943)	56 officers 1,613 men (1939)

Armament

The ships of the Scharnhorst-class were armed with nine 11.1-inch SK C/34 quick-firing guns in three triple turrets arranged two forward and one aft known from bow to stern as 'Anton', 'Bruno', and 'Caesar'.[2] The SK C/34 was effectively an improved version of the 11-inch SK C/28 guns which were mounted on the ships of the Deutschland-class and possessed a longer barrel. While the SK C/34 was a smaller calibre than the main battery armaments of the capital ships of other navies, this weapon was preferred by a number of gunnery officers within the *Kriegsmarine* owing to the higher rate of fire that it offered.[3]

The guns were equipped with three different types of shell including a 727.5-lb (330-kg) armour-piercing shell, and two 694.4-lb (315-kg) high explosive shells. All three types of shell used the same propellant charges: an RPC/38 93.7-lb (42.5-kg) fore charge and an RPC/38 168.8-lb (76.5-kg) main charge. The SK C/34 that armed the *Scharnhorst* and *Gneisenau* had a rate of fire of three shells per minute and each gun was expected to fire 300 rounds before enough wear had been incurred on the barrel to warrant replacement.

The guns were mounted in three Drh LC/34 turrets. Similar to most other German installations, the turrets had an electric system of rotation while all other operations were performed hydraulically. The turrets could be traversed at a speed of 7.2-degrees per second. The main turrets were so designed that once installed, the guns in turrets 'Anton' and 'Caesar' could be elevated to 40 degrees and depressed to minus 8 degrees while the guns of turret 'Bruno' could be elevated to 40 degrees and depressed to minus 9 degrees. At maximum elevation, the SK C/34 guns were capable of hitting a target at a range of 25 miles (40 km).

The secondary armament of the Scharnhorst-class consisted of twelve 5.9-inch (15-cm) SK C/28 L/55 quick-firing guns. The guns were mounted in four Drh L. C/34 twin turrets and four MPL/35 pedestal mounts. The SK C/28 was designed as a smaller and lighter version of the SK C/25 6-inch gun, which had been used as the main armament of the Königsberg- and Leipzig-class cruisers. The SK C/28 shared

Taken on board either *Scharnhorst* or *Gneisenau* during the winter of 1939–40 at Kiel, the gun turret 'Anton' can be seen a maximum elevation. (*NH 101571, US Naval History and Heritage Command Center*)

The forward 11-inch guns of the *Gneisenau*. *Scharnhorst* is on the left. (*NH 97538, US Naval History and Heritage Command Center*)

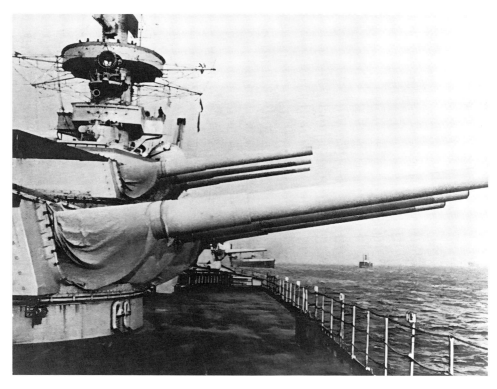

The 11-inch forward guns of the *Gneisenau, c.* 1940. Note the bloomers on the guns. (*NH 81941, US Naval History and Heritage Command Center*)

The rangefinder hood on the starboard side of turret 'Caesar' aboard either *Scharnhorst* or *Gneisenau*. (NH 102531, US Naval History and Heritage Command Center)

11-inch ammunition being hoisted aboard either the *Scharnhorst* or *Gneisenau*. (*Richard Aitken*)

the design of the SK C/25 with a loose barrel, jacket, and breech-piece with a vertical sliding breech block.[4] The guns were capable of being elevated to an angle of 40 degrees and depressed to minus 10 degrees. Firing shells with a weight of 100 lb (45.3 kg), at maximum elevation the SK C/28 had a maximum range of just over 14 miles (23 km). Each turret was capable of firing six shells per minute.[5] These guns were also mounted aboard the *Bismarck* and *Tirpitz* as a secondary armament.

Anti-aircraft defence was provided by fourteen 4.1-inch (10.5-cm) C/33 L/65 guns, sixteen 1.5-inch (3.7-cm) L/83 guns and a number of 0.7-inch (2-cm) guns. The SK C/33 used by the *Kriegsmarine* was related to the Flak 38 anti-aircraft gun used by the *Wehrmacht*. Mounted on the ships of the Scharnhorst-, Bismarck-, Deutschland- and Admiral Hipper-classes, the guns were mounted in pairs on electrically powered tri-axial mountings that were designed to compensate for the movement of the ship and thus help maintain a lock on the intended target. The mounts were open to the weather and sea swell. Not correctly waterproofed, as a result, the SK C/33 proved to be a high-maintenance burden. The maximum firing range of the SK C/33 was 7.08 miles (11.39 km), however, the effective range of the weapon was 5.87 miles (9.44 km).

After 1942, six 21-inch (53.3-cm) deck-mounted torpedo tubes were taken from the light cruisers *Leipzig* and *Nürnberg* and installed on the *Scharnhorst* and *Gneisenau*. The tubes were supplied with eighteen torpedoes. The torpedoes were 23 feet, 7 inches (7.18 metres) long and carried a 661-lb (300-kg) Hexanite warhead. The torpedoes could be set for three speeds: 30 knots, 40 knots or 44 knots. At 30 knots, the torpedoes had a range of 8.69 miles (13.9 km). At 40 knots, the range fell considerably to 4.97 miles (8km) while at 44 knots, the range was reduced still further to 3.7 miles (5.9km). It was later found that 44 knots caused the engine of the torpedoes to overheat after which point this speed setting was discontinued.

The port forward 5.9-inch turret of the *Scharnhorst* or *Gneisenau*. Behind, single-mounted 5.9-inch guns can be seen with 4.1-inch guns above. (NH 97507, US Naval History and Heritage Command Center)

Likely taken from the superstructure aboard either *Gneisenau* or *Scharnhorst*, two of the ship's 4.1-inch batteries can be seen along with one of the single 5.9-inch mounts. (*Beeldbank WO2*)

Crewmen loading one of the 4.1-inch guns of the *Gneisenau*. (*NH 81940, US Naval History and Heritage Command Center*)

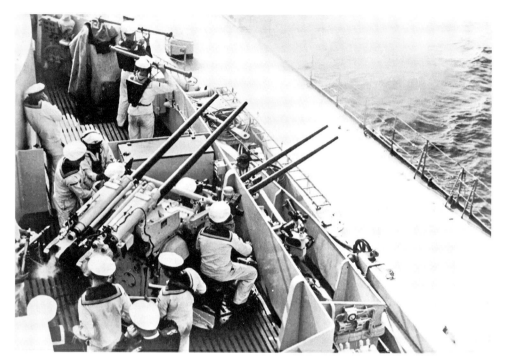

One of the 1.5-inch L/83 guns of the *Gneisenau* in action during firing exercises off Rügen Island, August 1939. (*Beeldbank WO2*)

Armour

The ships of the Scharnhorst-class were equipped with Krupp armour. The hulls of the ships were constructed from longitudinal steel frames over which the outer hull plates were welded. The hulls of the *Scharnhorst* and *Gneisenau* contained twenty-one watertight compartments while for approximately 80 per cent of their length, the ships possessed a double bottom. The ships had an armoured deck, which measured 2 inches (50 mm) in thickness, which was in turn backed by the main armour deck. The main armour deck was 0.79 inches (20 mm) thick at the bow and increased to 2 inches in the central portion of the ship which contained the machinery spaces and magazines before decreasing to 0.79 inches aft.

This deck was supported by 4.1-inch (105-mm) thick slopes on either longitudinal side.[6] These slopes connected to the lower edge of the main belt and served to significantly increase the armour protection over the critical areas of the ships. This arrangement was referred to as the 'turtle deck'.[7] The vital areas of the Scharnhorst-class were well-armoured against any calibre of shell fired by battleships of the time at ranges where the shell would have to penetrate both the main belt and sloping deck. At long ranges, however, the deck armour of the ships could easily be penetrated by heavy calibre shells.[8] All of the above-mentioned sections of the ship were composed of hard Wotan steel.[9]

The belt armour of the Scharnhorst-class was composed of Krupp cemented steel and was 14 inches thick in the central portion of the ship where the vital areas were located. Forward of turret 'Anton', the belt armour tapered to 5.9 inches before tapering to zero at the bow. Aft of turret 'Caesar' the belt armour decreased to 7.9 inches and tapered to nothing at the stern. The central portion of the belt was backed by 6.7-inch-thick shields. The forward conning tower had 13.7-inch-thick sides and a roof that was 7.9 inches thick. The rear conning tower of the ships was considerably less well armoured with sides which were only 3.9 inches thick and a roof that was 2 inches thick.[10]

The barbettes that housed the main battery turrets were also heavily armoured. The sides of the barbettes were 13.7 inches thick and tapered to 7.9 inches on the centreline where they were shielded by the gun turrets above.[11] All of the turret and barbette armour was Krupp cemented steel.

The underwater protection systems of the ships were designed to withstand a direct hit from a 550-lb explosive warhead. The *Kriegsmarine* conducted several full-scale underwater explosion tests with sections of armour cut from the old pre-dreadnought *Preussen*. The tests revealed that welded steel construction better withstood the impact of a 550-lb warhead than riveted steel plates. The torpedo bulkhead, which was composed of Wotan *Weich* (Wotan soft) steel, placed behind the armour belt, was riveted.[12] This was done because plate joints which had been incorrectly welded would not sufficiently withstand the explosive shocks of a torpedo impact.

The underwater protection system was constructed out of several layers: The outer layer which varied between 0.47 and 2.6 inches in thickness was located directly underneath the main armoured belt and was designed to detonate a torpedo warhead. Behind the outer plate was a large void that had been incorporated so as to allow gasses from the explosion to expand and dissipate. Beyond this void was a fuel bunker with a 0.31-inch-thick outer wall which would absorb any remaining explosive force. The fuel bunker was supported by longitudinal stiffeners and transverse bulkheads.[13]

The underwater side protection system did, however, have numerous faults. While it was extremely strong amidships, at either end of the citadel, it was significantly weaker, with the result that while amidships a 550-lb warhead could be withstood, at either end of the citadel the protection system would only stop a 440-lb warhead. A further significant weakness in the design was the arrangement of the torpedo bulkhead. The torpedo bulkhead was connected to the lower portion of the sloped deck at an angle of 10 degrees and was held in place by two riveted angled bars. The bars were constantly placed under a significant amount of stress owing to the bending forces of the hull. When combined with the explosive force of a torpedo warhead, the bars could not withstand the increased pressure and were likely to fail. Finally, the beam of 98.5 feet (30 metres) meant that the protection system had to be weaker around the main battery turrets as a significant amount of hull space around the main armament was taken up by the barbettes and magazines.[14]

Radar

Both the *Scharnhorst* and *Gneisenau* were equipped with two sets of Seetakt radar. During the late 1920s, Hans Hollmann began work in the field of microwaves which was to become the base for most radar systems. In 1935, he published *Physics and Technique of Ultrashort Waves* which was picked up by researchers across the globe. At the time that he published this work, Hollmann had been interested in the use of microwaves for communication. At the same time, however, he and his partner, Hans-Karl von Willisen, also began work on radar-like systems.

In 1928, Hollmann, von Willisen, and Paul-Günther Erbslöh had set up a company called *Gesellschaft für elektroakustische und mechanische Apparate* (GEMA). In the autumn of 1934, GEMA constructed the first commercial radar system which could be used for detecting ships. This initial system only provided a warning that a ship was in the general vicinity of the direction that the antenna was pointing and did not provide an accurate direction of travel or any information related to the range of the vessel. The purpose of this early radar system was to help avert a collision at night or in times of poor visibility.

In the summer of 1935, on orders from the *Kriegsmarine*, GEMA developed a pulse radar with which the cruiser *Königsberg* was detected at a range of 5 miles (8 km), and had an accuracy of up to 54.6 yards (50 metres). The military implications of the system were not lost and construction began on land- and sea-based versions of the system. The land-based variant was known as Freya radar while the sea-based variant was designated Seetakt. The priority of the *Kriegsmarine* for the system was ranging. Detecting targets and objects at night or in poor visibility was of secondary importance. Even gun-laying using radar was not an initial priority. The first operational model was installed on the pocket battleship *Admiral Graf Spee* in January 1938 and operated on 500 MHz while the maximum range at which a ship-sized target could be detected was 100 miles (220 km) under perfect conditions, although more typically the detection range was around half that. The early model Seetakt systems were followed in 1939 by a modified version known as Dete 1, which operated between 368 and 390 MHz.

On the *Scharnhorst* and *Gneisenau*, one Seetakt set was mounted on the forward gun director, which was mounted on top of the bridge while a second radar set was mounted on the rear main battery director. The Seetakt sets fitted to the ships of the Scharnhorst-class operated initially at 368 MHz at 14 Kw though the sets were later upgraded to operate at 100 Kw on 375 MHz.[15]

Propulsion

Initially, diesel propulsion was planned for use aboard *Scharnhorst* and *Gneisenau* as a diesel system had been used in the three *Panzerschiffe*. It was, however, decided to use a superheated steam propulsion system in the Scharnhorst-class because the required total output for the desired speed of the class was three times that of the *Panzerschiffe*. In the case of a triple-screw ship this could have meant more than twice the shaft horsepower per shaft of the *Panzerschiffe*, and in the case of a quadruple-screw ship this would have amounted to more than 40,000hp per shaft. This was a requirement which was beyond the diesel technology then available and devising engines which could have met this demand would have taken an unforeseen amount of time. As high-pressure superheated steam had already proved a successful method of propulsion, it was considered the most suitable choice for high-power machinery.[16]

The *Scharnhorst* was powered by three Brown, Boveri & Co.-geared steam turbines while *Gneisenau* was powered by three Germania-geared turbines. The turbines drove three bladed screws each of which was 15 feet, 9 inches (4.8 metres) in diameter. Steam was provided to the turbines by twelve Wagner ultra-high-pressure oil-fired boilers. The ships had a designed speed of 31 knots and during trials, both vessels would exceed this speed: *Scharnhorst* would attain a speed of 31.5 knots while *Gneisenau* would attain 31.3 knots.

To feed the boilers, the ships carried 2,800 tons of fuel oil as designed though additional storage areas including hull spaces between the belt armour and the torpedo bulkhead increased the capacity of the ships to 6,200 tons. At maximum fuel load, the ships were expected to sail 9,300 miles (15,000 km) at a cruising speed of 19 knots. In practice, however, *Scharnhorst* was capable of sailing 8,200 miles (13,100 km) at 19 knots while *Gneisenau* could only manage to sail 7,100 miles (11,500 km) at the same speed.[17]

All types of engine have pros and cons attached. Diesel engines are instantly ready to provide drive; they can be put at once to maximum output from zero. With steam systems, like that which was fitted to the Scharnhorst-class, much more time is required. From cold, when all of the boilers have been shut down and none of the

A crew member at work in the engine room of the *Scharnhorst*. (Peter Moise)

turbines have been pre-heated, the process can take around two hours. Furthermore, diesel systems tend to be more economical. For this reason, the *Admiral Graf Spee* was able to target merchant shipping in the South Atlantic and sail as far afield as the Indian Ocean between rendezvous with her supply ship *Altmark*, while the *Scharnhorst* and *Gneisenau* with their steam engines were confined to the North Atlantic. In terms of maximising space, a steam plant is more advantageous when compared to a diesel system. The high output required of diesel turbines demands several motors which take up a significant amount of floor space, whereas the turbines of the high-pressure steam turbines of the Scharnhorst-class required less space.

Electrical power was supplied to the ships by five electricity plants. Each plant consisted of four diesel generators and eight turbo-generators. The four diesel generators were divided into pairs: two supplied 300 Kw each while the other pair produced 150 Kw each. The eight turbo generators were also of a mixed capacity. Six of the turbo generators supplied 460 Kw each while the remaining two each produced 230 Kw. The total power output was 4,120 Kw at 220 volts.[18]

Aircraft

When constructed, *Scharnhorst* and *Gneisenau* were equipped with two catapults for the launching of aircraft. One catapult was located atop the hanger behind the ship's funnel while the second catapult was installed atop turret 'Caesar'. The catapult atop turret 'Caesar' was later removed leaving just one catapult.

Each of the ships was capable of carrying a maximum of three aircraft. Initially, Heinkel He 114 aircraft were carried aboard *Scharnhorst* while *Gneisenau* carried both He 114s and Arado Ar 95s before they were replaced with Arado Ar 196 seaplanes. From ships like the *Scharnhorst* and *Gneisenau*, the aircraft could be launched by catapult but then had to land on the water to be brought back aboard by crane. In the armed forces of Germany at the time, all air activities were the responsibility of the Luftwaffe. This included the development, procurement, operation and maintenance of all ship-borne aircraft.

There was never a separate German naval air arm as in the Royal Navy, US Navy or Imperial Japanese Navy. Indeed, even the aircraft that would have been operated from the never-to-be-completed aircraft carrier *Graf Zeppelin* would have been manned by, and the responsibility of, the Luftwaffe.

Right: The catapult atop turret 'Caesar' of the *Scharnhorst*. (NH 102536, US Naval History and Heritage Command Center)

Below: The port-side crane lifts an Arado Ar 196 back on board. (*Author's Collection*)

Heinkel He 114

Constructed as a replacement to the Heinkel He 60, the He 114 made its first flight in 1936 and was introduced into service in 1939. The fuselage of the He 114 and the flotation gear of the aircraft were conventional, however, its wing arrangement was highly unusual. The upper set of wings was attached to the fuselage by a set of cabane struts as in a parasol wing monoplane while the lower wings were of a much lesser span while having the same chord. Such aircraft are known as sesquiplanes, essentially biplanes with smaller lower wings. The He 114 was not a great success and was not built in large numbers. The He 60 had handled very well on the water but had been sluggish in the air, the He 114 meanwhile had poor handling on the water and in the air was scarcely better than the He 60. With a maximum speed of 208 mph (335 km/h) and a range of 571 miles (920 km), the He 114 was armed with one 7.92 mm (0.312 in) MG15 machine gun in a flexible mount beside the observer and could carry two 110-lb (50-kg) bombs loaded one under each wing.[19]

Heinkel He 114 Specifications	
Crew	Two (pilot and observer)
Length	38 ft, 2.5 in (11.65 m)
Wingspan	44 ft, 7.5 in (13.6 m)
Height	17 ft, 2 in (5.23 m)
Engine	1 × BMW 132K 9-cylinder radial engine 960hp
Speed	208 mph (335 km/h)
Maximum Service Ceiling	16,075 ft (4,900 m)
Range	571 miles (920 km)
Empty Weight	5,070 lb (2,300 kg)
Armament	One 7.92-mm (.312-in) MG15
	Two 110-lb (50-kg) bombs

Arado Ar 95

The Arado Ar 95 was designed in 1935 as a two-seat seaplane for coastal patrol, reconnaissance and light attack purposes. The first prototype was powered by a BMW 132 radial engine and took to the skies in 1936. A second prototype was constructed which was equipped with a Junkers Jumo 210 liquid-cooled engine. The two prototypes were evaluated against the Focke-Wulf Fw-62 after which the BMW-powered prototype was considered worthy of further study with an order for six aircraft being placed which were sent for further evaluation with the Condor Legion during the Spanish Civil War.

The Ar 95 was not ordered by the German armed forces, though a handful of the type did see service on board the *Gneisenau*. Instead, the aircraft was offered as an export as both a floatplane and land-based aircraft. Six land-based variants of the aircraft were ordered by the Chilean Air Force and were delivered prior to the outbreak of war. Turkey also placed an order for the Ar 95 in the floatplane capacity, however, these were taken over by Germany at the outbreak of the war whereupon they were used for training and coastal reconnaissance in the Baltic.

A Heinkel He 114 seaplane on the catapult of the *Gneisenau*. (NH 83614, US Naval History and Heritage Command Center)

Gneisenau seen from astern. On the forward catapult, a Heinkel He 114 can be seen while an Arado Ar 95 sits on the catapult atop turret 'Caesar'. (NH 80977, US Naval History and Heritage Command Center)

Arado Ar 95 Specifications	
Crew	Two (pilot and observer)
Length	36 ft, 5 in (11.10 m)
Wingspan	41 ft (12.5 m)
Height	11 ft, 10 in (3.60 m)
Engine	1 × BWM 132De air-cooled 9-cylinder radial 880hp
Speed	193 mph (310 km/h)
Maximum Service Ceiling	24,000 feet (7,300 m)
Range	684 miles (1,100 km)
Empty Weight	2,450 lb (1,111 kg)
Armament	1 × fixed forward-firing 7.92-mm (.312) MG17
	1 × flexible 7.92-mm MG15 in rear cockpit
	1 × 1,764-lb (800-kg torpedo or 1,102 (500-kg bomb)

Arado Ar 196

The Arado Ar 196 was designed to meet a requirement for an overwater reconnaissance aircraft which could operate from ships, shore bases on the coast, rivers, and lakes. The Ar 196 was a low-wing monoplane powered by a nine-cylinder air-cooled BMW 132K radial engine, which drove a three-bladed variable pitch propeller. This gave the aircraft a maximum speed of 194 mph (312 km/h). The variant that was carried aboard both the *Scharnhorst* and *Gneisenau* was the A-3 variant with a range of 665 miles (1,070 km) and a service ceiling of 23,000 feet (7,020 m). With regards weaponry, the Ar 196A-3 was equipped with two 20-mm MG FF cannon (one in each wing), a 7.92-mm MG17 in the cowling, and a 7.92-mm MG15 on the rear seat. In addition to this, beginning with the A-2 variant, the Ar 196 was equipped with a bomb rack under each wing which enabled the aircraft to carry 110-lb bombs. The crew of the aircraft numbered two: a pilot and an observer.[20]

Arado Ar 196A-3 Specifications	
Crew	Two (pilot and observer)
Length	36 ft (11m)
Wingspan	41 ft (12.4m)
Height	14 ft (4.4m)
Engine	BMW 132K radial engine 947 hp
Speed	194 mph (312 km/h)
Maximum Service Ceiling	23,000 feet (7,020 m)
Range	665 miles (1,070 km)
Empty Weight	6592 lb (2,990 kg)
Maximum take-Off Weight	8,200 lb (3,720 kg)
Armament	2 × 20-mm MG FF cannon
	1 × 7.92-mm MG17
	1 × 7.92-mm MG1
	2 × 110-lb (50-kg) bombs

Anatomy of the Scharnhorst-class

Raising an Arado Ar 196 from the hanger of one of the ships. (*Author's Collection*)

The wings are assembled on the aircraft prior to being lifted onto the catapult. This photograph was taken while *Scharnhorst* was at Brest, hence the camouflage netting to the side of the hanger. (*Author's Collection*)

Above: An Arado Ar 196 on the catapult of the *Gneisenau*, c. 1940. (NH 83610, US Naval History and Heritage Command Center)

Left: An Ar 196 moments before being launched from the catapult of the *Gneisenau*, c. 1940. (NH 82411, US Naval History and Heritage Command Center)

Scharnhorst-class v. Other Battleships

Ship	Scharnhorst	Tirpitz	HMS King George V	HMS Rodney	USS Washington	Littorio	Richelieu
Class	Scharnhorst-class	Bismarck-class	King George V-class	Nelson-class	North Carolina-class	Littorio-class	Richelieu-class
Length	771 ft (234.9 m)	823.6 ft (251 m)	745 ft (227 m)	710.2 ft (216.5 m)	729 ft (222 m)	780.1 ft (237.76 m)	813 ft (247.9 m)
Beam	98 ft (30 m)	118.1 ft (36 m)	103 ft (31 m)	106 ft (32.3 m)	108 ft (33 m)	107.7 ft (32.82 m)	108 ft (33 m)
Draught	32 ft (9.8 m)	30.6 ft (9.3 m)	32.6 ft (9.9 m)	31 ft (9.4 m)	38 ft (12 m)	31 ft (9.6 m)	32 ft (9.7 m)
Displacement (Full Load)	38,100 tons	52,600 tons	42,200 tons	38,030 tons	46,100 tons	45,236 tons	47,548 tons
Speed (Knots)	31	30	28	23	28	30	30
Main Armament	9 × 28 cm (11-inch) SK C/34	8 × 38 cm (15-inch) SK C/34	10 × BL 14-inch Mk VII Naval Gun	9 × BL16-inch (406 mm) MK I Gun	9 × 16-inch/45 caliber Mark 6 Gun	9 × 381 mm (15-inch) Cannone da 381/50 Ansaldo M1934	8 × 380 mm (15-inch)/45 Modèle 1935
Maximum Main Armament Range	25.4 miles (40.9 kilometres)	22.69 miles (36.51 kilometres)	20.73 miles (33.36 kilometres)	22.6 miles (36.37 kilometres)	21 miles (33.7 kilometres)	22 miles (35 kilometres)	25.9 miles (41.7 kilometres)
Complement	1,669	2,065	1,314 to 1,631	1,314 (1,361 as flagship)	1,880	1,830	1,620
No. of Aircraft Carried	3	4	4	2	3	3	3

Above left: The forward control tower of the *Scharnhorst* seen from abreast the funnel looking forward. Atop the control tower is the 34-foot (10.5-m) rangefinder. (*NH 102544, US Naval History and Heritage Command Center*)

Above right: The view from the foretop of the *Scharnhorst* looking down at the base of the funnel. Note the crewmen working on what appears to be a paravane at the bottom of the image. (*NH 102545, US Naval History and Heritage Command Center*)

The bridge of the *Scharnhorst*. (*Peter Moise*)

3

Gneisenau: Construction and Sea Trials

The building contract for *Panzerschiffe* 'E' (*Ersatz Hessen*) was placed at the Deutsche Werke, Kiel on 25 January 1934. At the time that the contract was placed for the construction of the ship final approval for the design had yet to be received. Nevertheless, on 14 February, the keel was laid. Construction work on the hull was suspended on 5 July and the work was subsequently scrapped as the original plans were modified. Under the designation Construction Number K235 a new keel was laid afresh on Slipway One of the Deutsche Werke on 6 May 1935.

The hull was launched on 8 December 1936. At the launching ceremony, a speech was delivered by the commander-in-chief of the army, *Generaloberst* Werner von Fritsch, before the christening of the vessel was undertaken by the widow of *Kapitän zur See* Julius Maerker, who had lost his life commanding SMS *Gneisenau* during the Battle of the Falkland Islands on 8 December 1914. The hull thundered down the slipway and into the water, however, on entering the water, the progress of the hull was not fully arrested with the result that the stern collided with the quay of the Kiel Seegarten Bridge located on the opposite side of the launching basin.[1]

Following being launched, the *Gneisenau* underwent fitting-out work before being commissioned into the *Kriegsmarine* under the command of *Kapitän zur See* Erich Förste on 21 May 1938. When the ship was commissioned, part of the complement of the *Gneisenau* was shipped in from the light cruiser *Karlsruhe*, which was paid off at Wilhelmshaven for a refit.

Shortly after being commissioned, the *Gneisenau* departed Kiel to undergo sea trials. During this time, the sea trials took the form of a maiden voyage for the ship in northern waters. On 22 August 1938, the *Gneisenau* was at Kiel for the launching of the heavy cruiser *Prinz Eugen*, where she also took part in the *Kieler Förde*, the last great German naval review. During the course of the *Kieler Förde*, Hitler paid a visit to the future fleet flagship along with the Hungarian regent Admiral Miklós Horthy de Nagybánya. The home port of the *Gneisenau* was to be Wilhelmshaven, however, on 20 September 1938, as she tried to enter the port for the first time, she collided with the Entrance III lock wall, which led to the ship being taken into dry dock. As a result

Above: The hull of the *Gneisenau* shortly before being launched on 8 December 1936. The christening was undertaken by the widow of *Kapitän zur See* Julius Maerker, who had lost his life commanding SMS *Gneisenau* during the Battle of the Falkland Islands twenty-two years earlier. (*NH 110878, US Naval History and Heritage Command Center*)

Left: The forecastle of the *Gneisenau* while being fitted out. When this photograph was taken, the ship was nearing completion. (*Author's Collection*)

Gneisenau seen during builders' trials off Kiel, April 1938. (*NH 81104, US Naval History and Heritage Command Center*)

Gneisenau at Kiel, 1938. Behind the *Gneisenau* is the pocket battleship *Admiral Graf Spee*. (*Author's Collection*)

Left: Gneisenau during 1938. (NH 110877, US Naval History and Heritage Command Center)

Below: Gneisenau underway, 1938. (World War Photos)

Gneisenau leading the *Admiral Graf Spee*, *Admiral Scheer*, *Deutschland*, and several cruisers during the *Kieler Förde*, the last great German naval review. (NH 80978, US Naval History and Heritage Command Center)

Gneisenau taken from astern during the *Kieler Förde*. (NH 81105, US Naval History and Heritage Command Center)

of this, the decision was taken to base the ship at Kiel while Wilhelmshaven was made the home port of the *Admiral Graf Spee*.[2]

In October, *Gneisenau* was taken in hand for a refit that saw her original straight stem replaced by an 'Atlantic bow', a new raked funnel cap fitted, and the main mast moved aft. This work was completed by the end of December 1938, which allowed for a second round of sea trials to be undertaken in the spring of 1939.

On 12 June 1939, *Gneisenau* weighed anchor and departed Kiel for a six-week trial cruise into the mid-Atlantic for target practice exercises to be undertaken and for the ship to be fully shaken down. Departing Kiel, the ship transited the English Channel and headed into the Atlantic, around Spain and Portugal to Las Palmas, where she arrived on 1 July. Departing Las Palmas the following day, *Gneisenau* set a course for Madeira and then the Azores before heading back through the English Channel to return to Kiel on 26 July.

Gneisenau in early 1939 undergoing sea trials following having her 'Atlantic stem' fitted. (*Michael Emmerich*)

Gneisenau during early 1939. (*NH 83609, US Naval History and Heritage Command Center*)

Gneisenau underway, 1939. (*World War Photos*)

Above left: Gneisenau in 1939. (NH 110875, US Naval History and Heritage Command Center)

Above right: Gneisenau at anchor in Madeira. (*Author's Collection*)

(World War Photos)

Above left: Members of the ship's crew cleaning the guns of turret 'Caesar' during the summer of 1939. (*Author's Collection*)

Above right: Gneisenau at various points throughout 1939. (NH 110876, US Naval History and Heritage Command Center)

4
Scharnhorst: Construction and Sea Trials

The building contract for *Panzerschiffe* 'D' (*Ersatz Elsass*), as the ship was intended to be called, was placed with the Marinewerft, Wilhelmshaven on 25 January 1934. As with the *Gneisenau*, at the time that the contract was placed, final approval for the design of the ship had yet to be received. The keel of the ship was laid on the slipway on 14 February 1934 with work proceeding on the hull until 5 July when construction was halted and the decision was taken to scrap the work already completed as the original plans were modified in order to accommodate the new specifications of the ship. From 1935, the Marinewerft was renamed the *Kriegsmarinewerft* and it was here that the keel was laid afresh on 15 June 1935 under the designation Construction Number 125.

The ship spent almost sixteen months on the slipway before finally being launched on 3 October 1936. The hull of the new ship was christened *Scharnhorst* by the widow of *Kapitän zur See* Felix Schultz, who had commanded the armoured cruiser SMS *Scharnhorst* and lost his life during the battle of the Falkland Islands.[1] Also in attendance of the launching ceremony were Hitler and the minister for war, *Generalfeldmarschall* Werner von Blomberg. The *Scharnhorst* would spend the next twenty-seven months undergoing fitting-out work, which saw the installation of her deck, armament, and upper works.[2]

With the fitting-out work completed, on 7 January 1939, *Scharnhorst* was commissioned into the *Kriegsmarine* under the command of *Kapitän zur See* Otto Ciliax before beginning her sea trials two days later.[3] The trials were conducted from January through to April and indicated that a number of adjustments and alterations were necessary. One problem that was highlighted by the sea trials was the dangerous tendency to ship considerable amounts of water in heavy seas, which caused flooding in the bow and damaged electrical systems in the forward turret.

The hull of Construction Number 125 during assembly on the slipway at the *Kriegsmarine Werft*.

The hull of the *Scharnhorst* on the slipway prior to being launched. (*Chris Thornton*)

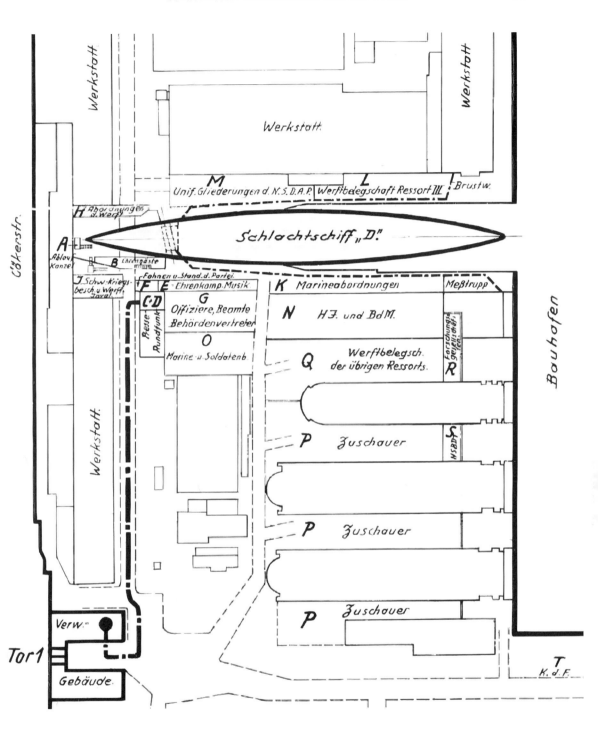

One of the press cards issued prior to the launch of the *Scharnhorst* showing a map of the area.

Scharnhorst on the slipway prior to being launched. (*Chris Thornton*)

The christening platform ahead of the launch of the *Scharnhorst* at Wilhelmshaven. Among those on the platform, just to the right of Hitler, are *Generalfeldmarschall* Werner von Blomberg and Admiral Raeder. (*306-NT-99098, US Naval History and Heritage Command Center*)

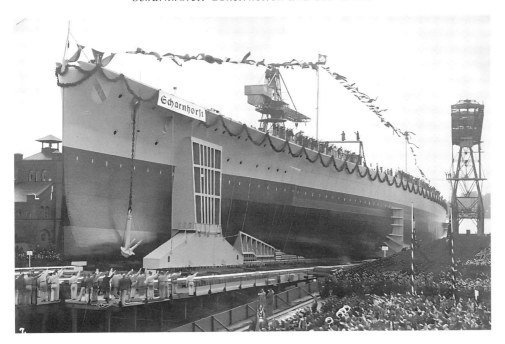

(*World War Photos*)

The launch of *Scharnhorst*, 3 October 1936. Prior to being launched, the hull spent sixteen months on the slipway. (*World War Photos*)

Above left: (*World War Photos*)

Above right: Scharnhorst shortly after entering the water having been launched. (*Author's Collection*)

The hull following being launched. (*Author's Collection*)

Above left: This photograph was taken in 1937 while the ship was being fitted out. Turret 'Anton' has been mounted. Behind, the barbette of turret 'Bruno' can be seen along with the raw structure of the armoured bridge. (*Author's Collection*)

Above right: The commissioning ceremony on the aft deck, 7 January 1939. (*NH 97536, US Naval History and Heritage Command Center*)

Members of the crew boarding the ship shortly before the commissioning ceremony. (*Author's Collection*)

Scharnhorst during her commissioning ceremony, 7 January 1939.

Scharnhorst at anchor at Wilhelmshaven shortly after being commissioned, January 1939. (*NH 59670, US Naval History and Heritage Command Center*)

During the period in which she was undergoing her sea trials, *Scharnhorst* returned to Wilhelmshaven as the flagship of the *Kriegsmarine* for the launching of Germany's latest and largest battleship the *Tirpitz*. Following the launch of the *Tirpitz*, Hitler and a cluster of generals and admirals made their way to the *Scharnhorst* where on the ship's quarterdeck a ceremony was held as Raeder was promoted to the rank of *Großadmiral*, becoming the first individual to hold the rank since Alfred von Tirpitz.

Scharnhorst continued on her trials until the beginning of July when she was taken in hand at the *Kriegsmarinewerft* to be refitted, which would see an extensive modification to the bow. Manoeuvred into the 40,000-ton floating dry dock at the Westwerft, the original straight stem was replaced by an 'Atlantic bow'. This work proceeded until around early August 1939, when the work was completed allowing the ship to be re-floated. In addition to the modification of the bow, the refit also saw the installation of an enlarged aircraft hangar and, as with the *Gneisenau*, the installation of a raked funnel cap while the main mast was moved further aft.

On 2 September 1939, the day following the German invasion of Poland, *Scharnhorst* undertook sea trials to test the modifications that had been made. The trials revealed that work was required on the ship's superheated tubes as they did not function as designed. The following day, a new chapter began for the ship as Britain and France declared war on Germany.

Scharnhorst tied to a mooring buoy in Wilhelmshaven harbour as men in one of the ship's boats pushes off. The ship's badges can be clearly seen on the bow. (*NH 102537, US Naval History and Heritage Command Center*)

Above left: Scharnhorst seen from the dockside at the launch of the *Tirpitz*.

Above right: Scharnhorst at Wilhelmshaven for the launch of the *Tirpitz*. (*World War Photos*)

Hitler on board *Scharnhorst* following the launch of the *Tirpitz*. (*Beeldbank WO2*)

Scharnhorst during early 1939. (*Beeldbank WO2*)

Scharnhorst (left) and *Gneisenau* (right) alongside in a German port during the spring or early summer of 1939. At the time that this photograph was taken, *Gneisenau* had been refitted with an Atlantic bow while *Scharnhorst* was yet to be similarly fitted. (*NH 97537, US Naval History and Heritage Command Center*)

Scharnhorst in port with her crew manning the rail during 1939 after having been fitted with the Atlantic stem. (*NH 97504, US Naval History and Heritage Command Center*)

Scharnhorst during the early autumn of 1939 following the completion of her refit. (*NH 101558, US Naval History and Heritage Command Center*)

(*NH 101559, US Naval History and Heritage Command Center*)

5
To War

On 3 September 1939, Britain and France declared war on Germany following the failure of German forces to withdraw from Poland. At the time that war was declared, both the *Gneisenau* and *Scharnhorst* were to be found at Brunsbüttel. While 3 September was a curiously quiet day for the men aboard the German ships, on 4 September, they received their first taste of war when fourteen Wellington bombers of 3 Group and fifteen Blenheims of 2 Group, RAF Bomber Command, carried out the first in a series of attacks against the ships of the *Kriegsmarine* at its anchorages. The Blenheims attacked the pocket battleship *Admiral Scheer* in the Schillig Roads at low level and succeeded in scoring four hits. Fortunately for the crew of the *Admiral Scheer*, none of the bombs exploded. Five Blenheims were lost on the raid. At 6.03 p.m., the Wellingtons arrived over Brunsbüttel and attacked the *Scharnhorst* and *Gneisenau* from an altitude of approximately 5,000 feet (1,500 m). No hits were scored by the bombers, which lost two of their number.[1]

By November 1939, the refit work and the subsequent sea trials of the *Scharnhorst* were complete making the ship fully operational.[2] By this time, *Kapitän zur See* Ciliax had been succeeded as commanding officer of the *Scharnhorst* by *Kapitän zur See* Kurt Hoffmann. On 26 November, the *Gneisenau* also received a new commanding officer in *Kapitän zur See* Harald Netzbrandt.

On 7 October 1939, in the company of the light cruiser *Köln* and the destroyers *Wilhelm Heidkamp*, *Friedrich Ihn*, *Diether von Roeder*, *Karl Galster*, *Max Schulz*, *Paul Jacobi*, *Bernd von Arnim*, *Erich Steinbrink*, and *Friedrich Eckoldt*, *Gneisenau* put to sea for her first sortie of the war. Sailing into the North Sea, this force aimed to draw heavy units of the Royal Navy's Home Fleet over a line of U-boats that had been assembled and to draw the Royal Navy's ships into the range of Luftwaffe units. The mission failed in both of its goals and the ships returned to anchor on 9 October, but not before a force of twelve Wellingtons was launched by the RAF which failed to score hits on any of the German warships.[3]

When war was declared on Germany, the Royal Navy sought to enact and enforce a blockade of Germany as it had done during the First World War. Under the name of the Northern Patrol, British forces sought to prevent trade to and from Germany

Left: *Kapitän zur See* Kurt Hoffmann.

Below: Taken on 23 October 1939, this photograph shows the crew of *U-47* receiving a salute from the *Scharnhorst* as she returns to Kiel. Commanded by Günther Prien, *U-47* was returning to harbour following sinking HMS *Royal Oak* inside Scapa Flow. (*NH 97503, US Naval History and Heritage Command Center*)

A Heinkel He 111 flying past the *Gneisenau* in the North Sea, 1939. (*Author's Collection*)

by checking merchant ships and their cargoes. In addition to this, the Northern Patrol was to stop German warships and raiders from leaving the North Sea and entering the Atlantic and *vice versa*, protect the Shetland Islands from invasion, and gather intelligence from intercepted neutral ships.[4] The Northern Patrol had previously existed between 1904 and 1917.

Three days after Britain declared war on Germany in 1939, the force was reactivated. The reactivated Northern Patrol was given a more extensive area of operations than during the First World War, which included the areas north of Scotland and Ireland, between the north of Scotland and Norway, around the Shetlands, the Faroe Islands, Iceland, and the Denmark Strait.[5] As in the First World War, older cruisers from the Reserve Fleet made up the original units of the Northern Patrol, however, these were soon supplanted and replaced by armed merchant cruisers.

It was against this backdrop that, flying the flag of Admiral Wilhelm Marschall, at 2 p.m. on 21 November, the *Gneisenau* departed Wilhelmshaven in the company of the *Scharnhorst*. The intention of Marschall was to break through to the Iceland–Faroes gap and to then move into the waters where the patrol lines of the Northern Patrol were thought to be whereupon a feint would be made into the North Atlantic to draw off the ships of the Northern Patrol and to dislocate British shipping movements. Finally, Marschall intended to sail into the mists of the far north whence, making use of the long nights, he would select his opportunity to slip back to Germany at high speed.

While this was not a very aggressive plan for two of Germany's most powerful vessels since nothing other than a brush with the Northern Patrol was likely and a chase through the North Sea, it is probable that Raeder, on whose direction the orders were framed, felt that only small, limited risks should be taken in the first venture by the *Kriegsmarine*'s largest and newest ships. Following departing Wilhelmshaven, the two ships sailed through the North Sea and passed to the north of the Shetland and Faroe Islands before conducting a patrol in the Iceland–Faroes gap.

On 22 November, *Gneisenau* and *Scharnhorst* encountered a heavy storm that forced a reduction in speed to 20 knots. The following day found much-improved weather conditions, and the wind had dropped significantly, allowing for the use of all weapons without any issues. At around noon on 23 November, a ship was sighted, which turned out to be an Icelandic fishing vessel. At 3.30 p.m., smoke was once more sighted on the horizon. On this occasion, the smoke was from the armed merchant cruiser HMS *Rawalpindi*. Built for P&O, the *Rawalpindi* had been in service on the Britain to India route until shortly before the outbreak of war when she had been requisitioned by the Admiralty. Now, with a crew of 276 under the command of Captain Edward Kennedy, she was patrolling the waters between Iceland and the Faroe Islands. Earlier in the day, the *Rawalpindi* had stopped a Swedish freighter. A boarding party was left in charge of the merchant vessel while the *Rawalpindi* returned to her patrol duties. At 3.30 p.m., lookouts aboard the *Rawalpindi* reported to Captain Kennedy that a ship had been sighted on the horizon to starboard.

Looking through his binoculars, Kennedy identified the ship as being either the pocket battleship *Deutschland*, which had been reported in the area, or the *Scharnhorst*. Kennedy had been ordered not to engage the *Deutschland* if he stumbled upon the pocket battleship, but was instead to radio her position to the Home Fleet. A call to action stations rang out throughout the *Rawalpindi* as the ship's course was altered to port at full speed in order to make for the cover afforded by a bank of fog as a contact report was transmitted. Smoke floats were deployed in the water to help obscure the ship, but they failed to ignite. Subsequently, Kennedy ordered another change of course, on his occasion to starboard where an iceberg approximately 4 miles away offered better protection.

The German ship, which turned out not to be the *Deutschland* but the *Scharnhorst*, was now closing on the merchant cruiser in an effort to cut off her escape route. A signal to 'heave to' was flashed to the *Rawalpindi*, which was followed by a warning shot across the bow. On the bridge, Kennedy did not respond to the orders from the German raider. As the *Scharnhorst* closed on the *Rawalpindi*, Kennedy ordered a second report to be made to the Admiralty, giving the position of the armed merchant cruiser as 60° 40' north, 11° 29' west.

It is now known that Kennedy was wrong in his identification of the German vessel. The *Deutschland* had departed Wilhelmshaven on 24 August, before war was declared, and that she had passed through the Denmark Strait into the Atlantic before returning by the same route on 8 November. By 15 November, the *Deutschland* was at Kiel but no intelligence to that effect had been received by the Admiralty at the time of the *Rawalpindi*'s contact with the *Scharnhorst*. The error in identification by those aboard the *Rawalpindi* helped to confuse the intelligence picture of the Admiralty as to the movements and dispositions of the *Kriegsmarine*'s main units for some

The *Rawalpindi* shortly after her conversion from a liner to an armed merchant cruiser. (*Author's Collection*)

time. Indeed, it would not be until mid-December that the Admiralty would begin to understand what had occurred on 23 November.[6]

As noted above, when the enemy vessel was first sighted, Kennedy identified the ship as the *Deutschland* or *Scharnhorst* before issuing a second signal confirming the identification of the ship as the *Deutschland*. This begs the question as to why the *Scharnhorst* was incorrectly identified as being a pocket battleship. To identify an unknown vessel in northern waters towards dusk is likely to be difficult in any case. With major German warships, however, the difficulty in identification was compounded by the fact that the ships of the Deutschland-class, Scharnhorst-class, and even in some respects the Bismarck-class had similar silhouettes. This is particularly the case when no means were available of comparing the relative sizes of the ships or at distances where fairly pronounced details such as the placing of the main battery turrets could not be distinguished. In the case of the second report from the *Rawalpindi* confirming that she had sighted the *Deutschland*, it was a perfectly reasonable assumption to make given that the *Deutschland* was believed to be at sea and was expected to attempt to return to Germany via the northern passages during November.

Whether or not the enemy was the *Deutschland* or the *Scharnhorst*, with her eight 6-inch guns, the *Rawalpindi* was hopelessly outgunned. The German raider now flashed a second signal from her bridge calling on the armed merchant cruiser to 'heave to'. This instruction was also ignored by Captain Kennedy, largely because by this time, a second ship had been sighted off to starboard which Kennedy at first took to be another vessel of the Northern Patrol. The signal officer of the *Rawalpindi* soon identified the second vessel as the *Gneisenau*. Trapped between powerful German forces and hopelessly outgunned, Kennedy was heard to say: 'We'll fight them both, they'll sink us and that will be that. Goodbye'.[7]

Aboard the *Scharnhorst*, *Kapitän* Hoffmann ordered that a third signal be flashed to the *Rawalpindi* whereupon the signal 'Abandon your ship' was made. Hoffmann was somewhat stunned when this signal was also ignored; twice more the signal to abandon the *Rawalpindi* was made, and twice more Kennedy ignored the instruction. Hoffmann now believed that the commander of the *Rawalpindi* had to be mad as the First World War-era 6-inch guns of the merchant cruiser were no match for the eighteen 11-inch guns of the two German battleships.

With his signals calling for Kennedy and his crew to abandon ship having been continuously ignored, Hoffmann was left with no alternative but to order the merchant cruiser to be sunk. Just as Hoffmann prepared to issue the order for the *Scharnhorst* to open fire he received a reply to his signals in the form of a salvo of 6-inch shells which were directed at the *Gneisenau* before a second salvo was fired at the *Scharnhorst*.

At 3.45 p.m., *Scharnhorst* opened fire. Her first salvo struck the boat deck just below the bridge where it killed almost everyone on the bridge with the exception of Captain Kennedy and destroyed the radio room. A second salvo from the *Scharnhorst* destroyed the main gun control station and served to knock out one of the *Rawalpindi*'s starboard guns. A third salvo slammed in to the *Rawalpindi*'s engine room, knocking out the dynamos which provided electrical power to the ship's systems. Unable to operate the shell hoists, Kennedy ordered Chief Petty Officer Humphries to pass the order on to the seven remaining gun commanders to continue to fire independently as the main fire control system was out of action. Humphries was also ordered to enlist all available hands in the task of carrying 6-inch shells from the magazines to the guns.

German shells continued to rain down, and one by one, the guns of the *Rawalpindi* were gradually silenced. By now the *Rawalpindi* was burning from stem to stern. With live shells and sticks of cordite freely rolling on the deck next to burning debris, Kennedy and two other men went to the stern to lay a smokescreen. Soon thereafter, they were reported dead. The *Rawalpindi* was now dead in the water.

The time had come for those members of the *Rawalpindi*'s crew who could do so to abandon ship. One lifeboat containing forty wounded men was lowered but overturned, depositing the men into the freezing water. At approximately 4 p.m., while other lifeboats were being lowered, shells from the *Scharnhorst* found the forward magazine of the *Rawalpindi*. The armed merchant cruiser exploded, broke in two, and sank. Those in the lifeboats were swamped as the *Scharnhorst* swung about to avoid the sinking ship before returning to pull survivors from the water.

During the course of the engagement, the *Rawalpindi* succeeded in scoring one hit on the *Scharnhorst*, causing only minor splinter damage. Some 238 men, including Captain Kennedy, were killed. Thirty-seven men would be pulled from the water by the *Scharnhorst* and taken prisoner while a further eleven would later be picked up by HMS *Chitral*, which was another armed merchant cruiser. For his action, Captain Kennedy was posthumously Mentioned in Dispatches, while the engagement made the crew members of the *Scharnhorst* and *Gneisenau* eligible for the High Seas Fleet badge.⁸

At the time that the *Rawalpindi* was engaged by the *Scharnhorst*, the commander-in-chief of the Royal Navy's Home Fleet, Admiral Charles Forbes, and his flagship HMS *Nelson* were on the river Clyde. At 3.51 p.m., he received the reports from the *Rawalpindi* that she was under attack from the *Deutschland* whereupon he immediately ordered all of the ships at his disposal to raise steam with all dispatch and to head out into the North Sea to intercept the German raider. At his disposal on the Clyde, Forbes had his flagship HMS *Nelson* along with HMS *Rodney*, the cruiser *Devonshire*, and seven destroyers of the 8th Destroyer Flotilla. The battlecruiser HMS *Hood*, which was at Devonport for a refit, received orders to prepare for sea, while at Rosyth were the light cruisers *Southampton*, *Edinburgh*, and *Aurora* along with two destroyers.

On patrol, Forbes could count on the light cruiser HMS *Newcastle*, two C-class cruisers, and a Danae-class cruiser (HMS *Delhi*) which were on station between the Faroe Islands and Iceland and the heavy cruisers *Norfolk* and *Suffolk* supported by three armed merchant cruisers in the Denmark Strait. HMS *Sheffield* and three other Danae-class cruisers were at Loch Ewe while HMS *Glasgow* and two destroyers were at sea to the north-east of the Shetlands attempting to intercept the German liner *Bremen*. Meanwhile, a convoy bound for Norway was just leaving the Firth of Forth escorted by three destroyers while five submarines were on patrol in the North Sea.

As orders were issued for the ships to sail to intercept the slayer of the *Rawalpindi*, the convoy and its escorts were given orders to join the *Glasgow* and her consorts off the Shetlands where they would sail northwards to their destination. HMS *Newcastle* and *Delhi*, the two ships closest to the *Rawalpindi*'s position, were ordered to close and shadow the enemy. Meanwhile, all ships then at anchor proceeded to sea to expand the search area. Submarines from the Forth and Tyne were ordered to patrol on a westward line from the Lister Light while others were stationed off Horns Reef, the Skaw, and the Naze. Having redisposed his forces to maintain contact with the enemy and to cover all likely return routes, Forbes hurried north towards a central position 60 miles off the Norwegian coast.⁹ Air searches were implemented as all armed merchant cruisers were temporarily withdrawn from the patrol lines.

Meanwhile, the Admiralty ordered additional changes in the dispositions of the Royal Navy's resources for the greater safety of merchant shipping already at sea and to strengthen the searching forces. HMS *Warspite* was ordered to detach from the convoy bound for Halifax that she was escorting and was ordered to proceed to the Denmark Strait while HMS *Repulse* and *Furious* sailed east from Halifax. On 25 November, HMS *Hood* was finally cleared for sea and weighed anchor to assist with the hunt whereupon she joined forces with the French battleship *Dunkerque* before heading to a position from which the North Atlantic trade routes could be covered. It now only remained to keep in contact with the *Gneisenau* and *Scharnhorst* until they could be brought to battle with the heavy units of the Home Fleet.

Two hours after having received the sighting reports from the *Rawalpindi*, HMS *Newcastle* had closed on the last reported position of the armed merchant cruiser.

First, a searchlight and then gun flashes were sighted by the crew of the cruiser. At the time that the searchlight and gun flashes were sighted, visibility was approximately 8 miles with several rain squalls lingering in the vicinity, which may at any time have closed and served to reduce visibility. It has since been revealed that when the *Newcastle* first sighted *Scharnhorst*, the battleship had stopped and was picking up survivors and that having picked up one boat containing twenty-one survivors, she got underway once more following a signal from the *Gneisenau*.

At 6.15 p.m., lookouts aboard the *Newcastle* sighted a darkened ship at 6.5 miles distance, and then two minutes later, a second ship was sighted to the right of the first which was signalling via signal lap to her consort. At 6.22 p.m., the range between the *Newcastle* and the German ships was closing rapidly, prompting *Newcastle* to reduce speed and alter course away.

The British cruiser had, in fact, been sighted by the German ships at the time that she turned away. To the *Newcastle* fell the traditional role of a cruiser in contact with heavy enemy units, namely that of shadowing and maintaining contact. Those aboard the *Newcastle* knew that there were two enemy vessels that they were shadowing and that at least one of them, the slayer of the *Rawalpindi*, was heavily armed and armoured. For the *Newcastle* to have engaged a heavily armed enemy and an unknown one with her 6-inch guns would have courted disaster for the cruiser. As to why Marschall who knew that the presence of his ships had been reported and that no friendly units were in the vicinity did not engage the *Newcastle* upon sighting the cruiser cannot be easily explained.

The task of the *Newcastle* in shadowing the *Gneisenau* and *Scharnhorst* was made all the more difficult by a rain squall which interposed itself between the battleships and the cruiser greatly reducing visibility. At 6.54 p.m., *Newcastle* emerged from the rain squall into an area of moderate visibility to find neither of the German ships in sight. HMS *Newcastle*, joined by HMS *Delhi*, would continue to search to the north-east and then north-west until dawn on 24 November, never to regain contact.[10] Like the majority of ships in the Royal Navy at the time, *Newcastle* did not possess radar. Had radar been fitted, she would almost certainly have been able to maintain contact for a significant period of time.

Following the engagement and the sighting of the *Newcastle*, Marschall decided to abandon the feint to the west owing to 'the rapid approach of darkness and [the] time lost in picking up survivors', thus further reducing the already limited scope of his operational orders.[11] These reasons do not, however, offer credible arguments for Marschall making a hasty withdrawal. In the first instance, the coming of darkness would have served to provide cover for the feint while the time lost in the sinking of the *Rawalpindi* and the recovery of one boat full of survivors was only approximately two and half hours.

A far more probable reason for the withdrawal is that Marschall knew that his position had been reported and that the Home Fleet would already be searching for him and his ships. Heavy units of the Home Fleet were likely already being directed his way and the admiral anticipated intensive British air patrols the following day. Marschall was not to know that no unit of the Royal Navy that was capable of matching the *Gneisenau* and *Scharnhorst* on anything approaching equal terms

HMS *Newcastle*, the Town-class light cruiser that shadowed the *Gneisenau* and *Scharnhorst* following the sinking of the *Rawalpindi* before losing them in a rain squall. (*Author's Collection*)

was within a few hundred miles of his position, nevertheless, discretion advocated a prompt withdrawal.

Following shaking off HMS *Newcastle* by sailing eastwards at high speed, Marschall proceeded to act with great circumspection. At approximately midnight on 24 November, he ordered an alteration of course to the north-east reaching a potion of 65° 40' north, 06° 00' east by the following evening. The *Gneisenau* and *Scharnhorst* remained in this general area until 11 a.m. on 25 November in order to re-enter the North Sea. Entering the North Sea that evening, Marschall found the visibility to be too good for his liking and elected to reverse course northwards until midnight. The following morning, in poor weather which brought with it low visibility, Marschall resumed his southerly course and by daybreak had reached a point parallel to Stadtlandet, 20 miles off the Norwegian coast.

As the German ships continued south, as a result of the atrocious weather conditions, the *Gneisenau* sustained severe sea damage. In addition to this, during the course of the day a ship, likely one of the cruisers or destroyers established in a patrol line by Forbes, was sighted which appeared not to sight the German battleships. Marschall's anxieties were almost over for the poor weather continued until his two ships finally docked at the Roadstead in Wilhelmshaven at 1 p.m. on 27 November.[12]

Meanwhile, Forbes had been at sea furiously hunting the German battleships. On the evening of 24 November, he redisposed his cruisers in order to improve the chances of sighting the enemy if they made a dash towards Germany. The lack of an aircraft carrier to work with the Home Fleet served to deprive Forbes of the ability to conduct his own air searches, forcing him to rely solely on the efforts of Coastal Command. On 29 November, following a fruitless search, Forbes ordered the normal movement of shipping to be resumed on 1 December.

Having returned to Germany, *Scharnhorst* remained at Wilhelmshaven to have her damage repaired, while on 29 November, *Gneisenau* weighed anchor and departed Wilhelmshaven to transit the Kiel Canal before dropping anchor at Kiel where she had her own damage repaired. *Gneisenau* would remain at Kiel until February 1940. As she underwent her repair work in Wilhelmshaven, the *Scharnhorst* had a *Magnetischer Eigenschultz* (magnetic self-protection system), a system designed to reduce the magnetic signature of the ship in an effort to help prevent the detonation of magnetic mines and torpedoes, installed. The ship also had a new FuMo22 radar set mounted on the foretop platform while the ship's boilers were overhauled. Following completing repairs, *Scharnhorst* departed Wilhelmshaven for the Baltic by way of the Kiel Canal in order to conduct gunnery training. Heavy ice in the Baltic would keep the ship, along with the *Gneisenau*, at Kiel until 5 February 1940 when she returned to Wilhelmshaven.

All of the events covered in the chapter so far occurred during the period known as the Phoney War when Germany, Britain, and France found themselves at war with little actual fighting occurring. In 1940, however, the Phoney War became much more real and the *Scharnhorst* and *Gneisenau* would play prominent roles.

Accompanied by the heavy cruiser *Admiral Hipper* and the destroyers *Wolfgang Zenker*, *Wilhelm Heidkamp*, and *Karl Galster*, under the command once more of Admiral Marschall, on 18 February 1940 *Gneisenau* and *Scharnhorst* departed Wilhelmshaven and embarked upon Operation Nordmark. In this, the ships were to sail between the Shetland Islands and Norway to attack British merchant shipping. British aerial reconnaissance gave warning of the departure of the German ships with the result that the only convoy at sea in the area was recalled as a cordon of submarines was disposed to intercept the likely route of the German vessels while the heavy units of the Home Fleet put to sea so as to be in the general area to intercept. During the night of 18 February, the *Wolfgang Zenker* was forced to detach from the squadron and to return to Germany having suffered severe ice damage which caused her to begin to take on water.

As Marschall's ships put to sea, the destroyers *Paul Jacobi*, *Theodor Riedel*, *Hermann Schoemann*, and *Leberecht Maass* of the 2nd Destroyer Flotilla under *Fregattenkapitän* Rudolf von Pufendorf, preceded by the torpedo boats *Luchs* and *Seeadler*, escorted additional ships through the Skagerrak before being detached to search independently for Allied merchant traffic. Additional support for Operation Nordmark was provided by U-boats, three of which were to operate between the Shetlands and Norway, two in Fair Isle Channel, with another three off the Pentland Firth. A further three U-boats were also held in reserve near the coast of Scotland.

Hampered by a lack of aerial reconnaissance, *Gneisenau* and *Scharnhorst* came across no targets which prompted a return to Wilhelmshaven. Owing to the severity of the winter of 1939-40, icebreakers had to be used to clear the estuaries of the Jade and Weser Rivers before Wilhelmshaven could be re-entered. While the surface units failed to come across and sink any merchant shipping, the U-boats had a much more fruitful hunt.

Above: *Scharnhorst* alongside undergoing repair work. (*World War Photos*)

Below: View from the forward superstructure of the *Scharnhorst* underway during the winter of 1939–40. (*NH 102529, US Naval History and Heritage Command Center*)

Scharnhorst's boatswain of the watch at his duty station amidships during the winter of 1939–40. One of the ship's 5.9-inch guns is in the background. (*NH 102533, US Naval History and Heritage Command Center*)

Members of the crew of the *Scharnhorst* standing on the quarterdeck with a Christmas tree, December 1939. At the time, the ship was under repair at Wilhelmshaven. (*NH 102535, US Naval History and Heritage Command Center*)

The main battery guns of the *Scharnhorst* being fired during the winter of 1939–40. (*NH 102530, US Naval History and Heritage Command Center*)

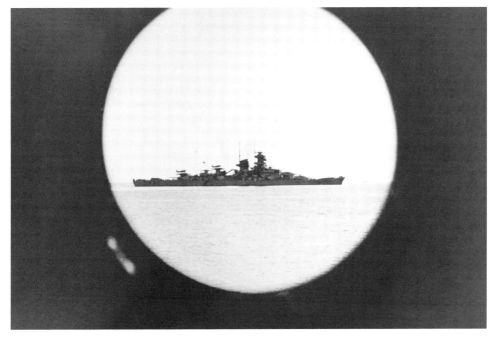

Gneisenau photographed through a porthole on the *Scharnhorst* sometime during the winter of 1939–40. It is likely that this photograph was taken when *Scharnhorst* arrived in the Baltic to undertake gunnery trials. (*NH 101577, US Naval History and Heritage Command Center*)

Above left: A member of *Scharnhorst*'s crew on deck by one of the ship's main battery turrets during the winter of 1939–40. (*NH 102532, US Naval History and Heritage Command Center*)

Above right: Two crewmembers of the *Scharnhorst* standing on the ice in Kiel harbour during the winter of 1939–40. (*NH 101562, US Naval History and Heritage Command Center*)

Scharnhorst amongst the ice in Kiel harbour during the winter of 1939–40. (*NH 101560, US Naval History and Heritage Command Center*)

Photographed from *Scharnhorst*, the pre-dreadnought battleship *Hessen* (which had been relegated to a target ship) is pictured during January 1940 acting as an icebreaker in the western Baltic. Heavy ice in the Baltic forced the cancellation of planned target practice by *Scharnhorst*. (NH 101568, US Naval History and Heritage Command Center)

Taken from the *Scharnhorst*, two Type 24 torpedo boats are making their way through the frozen waters of the western Baltic in late January 1940. (NH 102541, US Naval History and Heritage Command Center)

The pre-dreadnought battleship *Schlesien* photographed from *Scharnhorst* underway in the Baltic near Kiel during late January 1940 ahead of the gunnery exercises that were ultimately cancelled owing to the unusually thick ice that winter. (NH 102540, US Naval History and Heritage Command Center)

Above left: A close-up of the main bow anchor and forecastle of *Scharnhorst* during the winter of 1939–40. (*NH 101563, US Naval History and Heritage Command Center*)

Above right: The ice-covered foredeck, main armament, and superstructure. (*NH 101561, US Naval History and Heritage Command Center*)

View of the forward guns of the *Scharnhorst* showing the accumulation of ice overnight during the winter of 1939–40. (*NH 102526, US Naval History and Heritage Command Center*)

Ice on the main deck of the *Scharnhorst* during the winter of 1939–40. The photograph was taken looking forward up the port side from amidships. The rear of the port forward SK C/28 gun turret is in the foreground. (*NH 101570, US Naval History and Heritage Command Center*)

The ice-encrusted lifelines along the side of the main deck of the *Scharnhorst*. (*NH 101566, US Naval History and Heritage Command Center*)

Crewmen cleaning one of the 11-inch guns of the *Scharnhorst*. (NH 102527, US Naval History and Heritage Command Center)

Above left: A close-up photograph of crewmen cleaning one of the 11-inch guns of the *Scharnhorst*. Note the sleeve around the muzzle of the gun. (NH 102528, US Naval History and Heritage Command Center)

Above right: Kapitän zur See Kurt Hoffmann addressing the officers and men of the *Scharnhorst* from a platform erected by turret 'Caesar', early 1940. Part of the aircraft catapult is visible atop the turret. (NH 102534, US Naval History and Heritage Command Center)

Above left: Scharnhorst and *Gneisenau* (just visible on the horizon) framed in the torpedo elevator compartment of the *Admiral Hipper* during Operation Nordmark. (042673, Australian War Memorial)

Above right: Looking north-east from the Hipperhafen with Kaiser Wilhelm Bridge in the distance, taken from aboard the *Scharnhorst* during the winter of 1939–40, *Gneisenau* can be seen ahead with a floating crane alongside. (NH 102543, US Naval History and Heritage Command Center)

Oberleutnant Wolfgang Luth's *U-9* sank the 1,213-ton Estonian vessel *Linda* while *U-14* under *Oberleutnant* Herbert Wohlfarth sank the 1,066- and 1,064-ton Danish merchant vessels *Sleipner* and *Rhone* along with the Swedish merchantmen *Liana* and *Osmed*. *U-61* sank two vessels while *U-63* sank the 3,840-ton Swedish *Santos*. *U-57* under the command of *Kapitänleutnant* Claus Korth sank the 10,191-ton British merchant liner *Gretafield* and damaged the *Loch Maddy* whose destruction was completed by *U-23*, which also sank the destroyer HMS *Daring*, which was forming part of the escort to convoy HN-12 approximately 40 miles to the east of the Pentland Firth.

Two days before Operation Nordmark was launched, a force of British destroyers led by Captain Philip Vian aboard HMS *Cossack* intercepted the German supply vessel *Altmark* in Norwegian waters. The *Altmark* had been the supply vessel to the *Admiral Graf Spee* during her raiding sortie through the South Atlantic prior to the battle of the River Plate and her subsequent scuttling in Montevideo harbour in December 1939. The crews from the merchant vessels sunk by the *Graf Spee* were transferred to the *Altmark* before the supply ship sailed back to Germany. The interception of the *Altmark* by HMS *Cossack* and the other destroyers of Vian's command freed 299 British seamen but violated Norwegian neutrality. The so-called *Altmark* incident is regarded as one of the reasons behind Hitler's final decision to invade Denmark and Norway.

Denmark and Norway had not originally featured in Hitler's designs for the conquest and domination of Europe. The *Kriegsmarine*, however, smarting from having been bottled up in Wilhelmshaven and Kiel during the First World War, began to press for an operation to secure the Norwegian ports, namely Narvik and Trondheim shortly after the conquest of Poland.[13] With the full realisation that Germany was once more at war with Great Britain and with that, at war with the world's most powerful naval power,

Admiral Rolf Carls, the third highest-ranking officer of the *Kriegsmarine*, began to promote the idea of securing the Norwegian ports as operational bases to *Großadmiral* Raeder. Impressed by the proposal, Raeder ordered the proposal to be studied by the *Seekriegsleitung* (naval war staff) and thought enough of the idea to mention it to Hitler.

The notion of invading Norway was further encouraged by the former Norwegian foreign minister Vidkun Quisling, who requested German support for his proposed coup and a peaceful occupation to guard against British interference. Unsure of the prospects of invading Norway, it was the *Altmark* incident, which finally helped to settle the matter. The resolve of the British amid the outcry from the Norwegian government demonstrated to Hitler and his staff that the Norwegians could do little more than offer protests and that this demonstrated just how powerless they were to ward off Allied action, or for that matter, to defend against a pre-emptive attack by Germany to secure this open flank. Furthermore, the securing of Denmark and Norway would secure the route of the shipments of iron ore from Sweden that Germany was so dependent upon.[14] Five days following the *Altmark* incident Hitler ordered detailed planning for the invasion of Norway, which was to proceed with urgency under the code name Operation Weserübung.

The final plan was based on daring actions and surprise execution in order to simultaneously deliver light elements of three army division carried in the crew compartments of almost every vessel of the *Kriegsmarine* at Norway's five primary seaports of Oslo, Bergen, Narvik, Trondheim and Kristiansand, while a further two divisions crossed the undefended border into Denmark. The greatest threat to the opening moves of the invasion were expected to come from the Royal Navy supported by the Royal Air Force and was expected to be directed against the two assault groups bound for Narvik and Trondheim. It was decided therefore that the two most powerful ships in the *Kriegsmarine*—*Gneisenau* and *Scharnhorst*—should therefore be deployed to protect the two groups.[15]

The operation began on 3 April when covert supply vessels slipped out of German ports in advance of the main elements of the *Kriegsmarine*. The following day, 4 April, sixteen Allied submarines were ordered to the Skagerrak and Kattegat, the two straits between southern Norway and eastern Denmark to serve as a screen to, and to provide advanced warning of, a German response to Operation Wilfred. Operation Wilfred was the codename given to the operation undertaken by the Royal Navy to mine the channel between mainland Norway and her offshore islands aimed at preventing the transport of Swedish iron ore through Norwegian waters. Operation Wilfred was launched on 5 April when Vice-Admiral William Whitworth, flying his flag in the battlecruiser HMS *Renown*, accompanied by twelve destroyers, departed Scapa Flow and set a course for the Vestfjord.

On 7 April, as bad weather developed over the North Sea causing rough seas and blanketing the area with thick fog, flying the flag of *Vizeadmiral* Günther Lütjens, *Gneisenau* and *Scharnhorst* weighed anchor and departed Wilhelmshaven to provide cover to the Trondheim and Narvik assault forces.[16] Joined by the *Admiral Hipper*, at approximately 2.30 p.m., following being sighted by a British reconnaissance aircraft, the three ships were subjected to an attack by a group of RAF bombers that failed to score any hits. The reconnaissance flight had reported the German ships as being one

Above left: Vizeadmiral Günther Lütjens.

Above right: HMS *Renown*. (*Author's Collection*)

cruiser and six destroyers, however, the crews of the bombers reassessed the strength of the German ships as being one battlecruiser, two cruisers, and ten destroyers. Owing to the enforcement of strict radio silence, this fact was not reported by the aircrews until 5 p.m.

On learning of the German naval movements, the Admiralty quickly came to the conclusion that the Germans were attempting to break the blockade that had been placed on Germany and that the *Kriegsmarine* was going to attempt to disrupt the Atlantic trade routes. Admiral Forbes was notified of the German movements and was ordered to sail to intercept the *Kriegsmarine* at 8.15 p.m. During the course of the evening of 7 April, as the Home Fleet put to sea, the rough seas and high winds in the North Sea caused structural damage to *Scharnhorst* with flooding contaminating some of the ship's fuel stores.[17]

Meanwhile HMS *Renown* had arrived off Vestfjord and as the 20th Destroyer Flotilla conducted its minelaying operation, *Renown* and the destroyer *Greyhound* patrolled the area 30 miles of the west of Vestfjord, 100 miles from the minefield. During the course of the night, the remaining elements of the German invasion force departed Germany.

On 8 April, the first contact between the *Kriegsmarine* and the Royal Navy occurred during Operation Weserübung. At around 8 a.m., the destroyer HMS *Glowworm* (which had sailed with the *Renown* but had detached from the battlecruiser to search for a member of her crew who had been swept overboard) came across the German destroyers *Bernd von Arnim* and *Hans Lüdemann* in heavy fog. The German destroyers turned away, pursued by the *Glowworm*. Sailing through the murk HMS *Glowworm* suddenly found herself confronted by the *Admiral Hipper*. The *Hipper* opened fire, hitting the destroyer several times. Knowing that his ship was doomed, Lieutenant-Commander Gerard B. Roope, the commanding officer of the *Glowworm*, decided to ram the heavy cruiser, tearing away side armour and causing damage that would force her to put into Trondheim for repairs. Shortly thereafter, *Glowworm* sank but not before a signal had been made detailing her contact with the German forces. As the *Admiral Hipper* engaged

HMS *Glowworm*, the *Gneisenau* and *Scharnhorst* provided distant cover to the edge of the Vestfjord before detaching in order to take up their patrol station further north.

The destroyers of Operation Wilfred were ordered to re-join *Renown* before Whitworth received orders to concentrate on preventing any German force from proceeding to Narvik. Most of the night of 8–9 April was spent to the west of the Lofoten Islands before a course south-eastwards was set at 2.30 a.m. on 9 April. Frequent snow squalls made visibility variable, but the coming of the dawn twilight at around 3.25 a.m. began to improve the situation.

At 3.37 a.m., when sailing on a course of 130 degrees at 12 knots, lookouts aboard the *Renown* sighted a darkened ship emerging out of a snow squall with another ship sailing astern. Sighted in a position of 67° 20' N, 09° 40' E, some 50 miles west of Stromvaer Light, when first sighted, the ships were identified as being one Scharnhorst-class vessel accompanied by a cruiser of the Admiral Hipper-class. The two ships lay broad on the port bow about 10 miles distant, steering north-west on a course opposite to that of *Renown* and her escorts.[18] The ships were in fact the *Gneisenau* and *Scharnhorst*. The Seetakt radar of the two battleships had in fact picked up a radar contact at 3.30 a.m., which prompted the crews of both ships to go to action stations.[19] Those aboard the *Gneisenau* had at first been unsure of the identity of the radar contact. Astern of the flagship, it would fall to the *Scharnhorst* to make the first positive identification of the *Renown*.

Lütjens had a significant firepower advantage over Whitworth, nevertheless, he had no intention of pressing this advantage; indeed, his only concern was to put as much sea between the elderly British battlecruiser and his own battleships as possible. *Renown* maintained her course for approximately ten minutes before altering course to 80 degrees, whereupon she increased speed at first to 15 and then to 20 knots. At 3.59 a.m., *Renown* hauled around so that she was roughly parallel with the two German ships with her A-arcs just open. At 4.05 a.m., when she was abaft the beam of the *Gneisenau*, at a range of 10.56 miles (17 km), the 15-inch guns of the battlecruiser thundered into action. Six minutes later, at 4.11 a.m., *Gneisenau* returned fire. The German battleship had not returned fire earlier as the identity of the ship was undetermined.

The *Scharnhorst* made the first positive identification of *Renown*, however, those aboard the *Scharnhorst* did not sight the British battlecruiser until she opened fire against the flagship.[20] Deep inside the *Renown* was Chief Petty Officer Bill Kennelly. From his action station, Kennelly could not see anything of the engagement but felt the roaring of the guns through the ship and the smashing effect of the sea against the hull.

> We were closed up and nattering quietly when the intercom crackled and—'This is the Captain speaking. Two unidentified warships have been sighted and we are closing'. Next came: 'We are about to open fire and increase to full speed'. The weather of course was, as usual, lousy, very heavy seas and snow squalls. We left our destroyer escorts far behind as they couldn't cope with the seas and in every sense it was all ours.[21]

From his position on the bridge of the *Renown*, Signal Boy A. V. Herbert could see little of the two German ships save the flashes of their guns. Meanwhile, *Gneisenau* and *Scharnhorst*, returning fire against the British battlecruiser, scored two hits on the *Renown* recalled by Henry Shannon:

> They had two remarkable hits on us, one 11-inch shell passed through *Renown* just above the water line and went out through the other side without bursting. One compartment was flooded through this hit and one engine room rating was trapped in the compartment underneath. Damage control was of a high standard and the compartment was watertight. He was rescued later after the action when the holes were blocked and the upper compartment pumped out.
>
> The second hit went through our foremast right in line with the 15-inch and 4.5-inch spotting tops, they sure knew what they were aiming for. That shell carried away the main wireless aerial so we were out of touch with the Admiralty for a while, but it was repaired during the action by the wireless officer; he was decorated for this deed later, and well deserved it. We didn't have a single casualty on *Renown* but our own fire from the forward 15-inch guns shook the rivets so much off our starboard bulge forward that 40 feet of it stuck out at the angle of 90° and this caused a terrible, second, bow wave. Our forward messdeck was flooded but the damage control party again pumped it out and erected a false bulkhead, which did the job for a time.[22]

A third shell passed through the gunroom bathroom on the starboard side and out of the port side above the waterline without exploding. This was fortunate as it was above the steering compartment and rudder head. Bill Kennelly and his Double Bottom Party were busily employed as a result of the damage incurred from the German fire:

> One shell drilled hole in our mainmast, the second clipped the funnel, while the third penetrated close aft of Y magazine, into and out through the bottom of the Admiral's wine store. Never have I seen so many volunteers to help the DB Party pump out the compartment, all arriving with the suck-sacks, toolbags and what have you and all subsequently gliding away forrard with their loot! I don't know how the Admiral managed for wine but we all did very well thank you, our DB section looked more like an off-licence.[23]

While the *Renown* took slight punishment at the hands of the *Gneisenau* and *Scharnhorst*, she was more than equally dishing it out. At 4.17 a.m., *Gneisenau* sustained a hit on her foretop that destroyed her main fire control equipment and temporarily disabled her main armament.[24] In addition to this, turret 'Caesar' sustained slight damage from a shell hit.[25] *Scharnhorst*, meanwhile, was facing her own difficulties. The ship's radar malfunctioned with the result that she was not able to efficiently engage the *Renown*.

At 4.18 a.m. with no means of using the main armament of the *Gneisenau* effectively, Lütjens altered course to 30 degrees with the intention of breaking off the engagement. To cover the flagship, *Scharnhorst* crossed the stern of the *Gneisenau* and began to make smoke. *Renown* shifted fire in order to target *Scharnhorst*. For around the next hour and a half, there ensued a chase to windward. As the ships thundered on, the swell became increasingly heavier. All the while *Renown* continued to fire at *Scharnhorst*, which managed to manoeuvre to avoid being hit, and occasionally loosed off a salvo directed at the *Gneisenau*. Both German ships continued to return fire in kind. The aft turret of *Gneisenau* was brought back into action, but at 4.34 a.m., the ship sustained a hit on turret 'Anton' near the left hood of the rangefinder. The watertight hood was wrecked allowing in water which flooded the turret putting it out of action. An additional hit was sustained which struck the aft anti-aircraft position on the port side.

Shortly before 5 a.m., the two German ships vanished into a rain squall. Aboard the *Renown*, speed had been increased to the maximum at the beginning of the engagement, however, in an effort to keep the forward guns firing, speed had been gradually reduced, as was explained by Captain A. W. Gray, the head of the ship's engineering department:

> *Renown* had to maintain a maximum of 24 knots to avoid the two foremost turrets being submerged by the high seas; it was found that when she had worked up to steam at 28 knots it was impossible in those conditions for the turrets to fire.[26]

Speed therefore was reduced to 24 knots, and then 23 knots before finally 20 knots was adopted. At that speed, in the heavy seas, *Renown* could barely maintain the range. *Gneisenau* and *Scharnhorst*, firing astern were not so affected by the heavy seas preventing them from firing and could maintain a high speed thus allowing them to slowly increase the range. When the German ships entered the squall, *Renown* turned on to an easterly course and increased speed to 25 knots. At around 5.20 a.m., the German ships emerged from the squall and the range had increased further. *Renown* turned once again to bring the enemy on to her bows before opening fire once more. No hits were observed.

Further squalls of rain and sleet served to obscure the enemy from view and although *Renown* managed to work up to 29 knots for a few minutes, she was unable to close the range to the German ships, which were last observed at 6.15 a.m., by which time they were well out of range of the *Renown*'s main armament.[27] *Renown* would maintain her northerly course until around 8 a.m., when she altered course westward so as to be in a position to intercept the German ships again if they altered course and attempted to break back to the south towards Germany.

Scharnhorst was, meanwhile, suffering from mechanical trouble. A large amount of water was shipped forward, which put her forward turret out of action.[28] In addition to this, following running at high speed to increase the range to the *Renown*, problems had developed with the ship's starboard turbines, which prompted a reduction of speed to 25 knots.[29]

By 12 p.m. on 9 April, *Gneisenau* and *Scharnhorst* had reached a point north-west of the Lofotens. Having reached this point, they altered course west for twenty-four hours in order to effect temporary repairs. The temporary repair work completed, the two ships sailed south where on 12 April they rendezvoused with the *Admiral Hipper*. During the course of the day, the three ships were sighted by a RAF reconnaissance aircraft, which prompted an air attack. Poor visibility served to shield the German ships from the RAF and allowed them to safely reach Germany. *Scharnhorst* sailed to the Deutsche Werke in Kiel where she had her damage repaired and the aircraft catapult that had been installed atop turret 'Caesar' was removed.[30]

Gneisenau, meanwhile, had her battle damage repaired at Wilhelmshaven. With her battle damage repaired, she was taken into dry dock in Bremerhaven between 26 and 29 April in order to undergo periodic maintenance.[31] Following being undocked, *Gneisenau* was to sail into the Baltic for a brief series of trials, however, on the morning of 5 May, while sailing at 22 knots off the Elbe estuary, she detonated a magnetic mine approximately 69 feet off the port rear quarter, 79 feet below the hull. The explosion caused significant damage to the hull and flooded several compartments, which caused the ship to take on a half-degree list to port. The concussion from the detonation damaged many internal and topside components, including the starboard low-pressure turbine and rear rangefinder. Repair work was effected in a floating dry dock in Kiel between 6 and 21 May. Following a brief shakedown cruise in the Baltic, by 27 May, the ship was back at Kiel at full combat readiness.

Scharnhorst alongside at Wilhelmshaven March 1940. While engineering ratings receive a lecture on machinery, atop turret 'Caesar', with the assistance of a floating crane, the catapult is removed from the turret. (*Simon Matthews*)

6

Operation Juno

Having returned to Wilhelmshaven on 4 June, *Gneisenau* and *Scharnhorst* sortied once more to Norway where they were joined by the *Admiral Hipper* and the destroyers *Hans Lody, Erich Steinbrink, Karl Galster,* and *Hermann Schoemann*.[1] Under the command of Admiral Marschall, the operation had been under discussion since 14 May and was conceived as a raid into the fjords of Norway to provide relief for the garrison at Narvik, but this was extended at Hitler's behest to include the guarantee of seaborne supplies to the German forces fighting in Norway, an addition that was recognised as turning what had at first been conceived as a brief sortie into a commitment of weeks, possibly even months.[2] It was the protracted nature of the operation, combined with Raeder's desire for a spectacular naval operation, that had justified the use of the battleships.[3] Trondheim, as it was fully stocked and well protected, was designated as the base of operations for the sortie.

Sortieing northwards, on 7 June, the squadron rendezvoused with the tanker *Dithmarschen* so that the *Admiral Hipper* and the destroyers could take on fuel.[4] Aboard *Gneisenau*, Marschall spent 7 June attempting to assess enemy strengths in the northern area of operations with a view to mounting an attack on Harstad during the night of 8–9 June. Intelligence passed to Marschall established the presence of the battleship HMS *Valiant* and the aircraft carriers *Ark Royal* and *Glorious*, but Group West assured him that there was nothing in the patterns of the British signals to suggest that the British were aware of his presence. Marschall now turned to aerial reconnaissance in order to add to his understanding of what lay between himself and his ships, and their objective. Marschall was informed of a convoy comprised of seven vessels 100 miles to the south-east of his position, which the admiral assumed were empty of their respective cargos and were returning home. Aside from this, information remained sparse, with Marschall noting: 'Air reconnaissance in the northern area is, as previously, not available'.[5]

Late that evening, during a conference with his commanding officers, a report reached Marschall that pointed to significant naval activity off the mouth of Andfjord. Shortly after midday, an aircraft had sighted a light cruiser, two destroyers, and two large ships on a westerly course. The two large ships that were sighted were HMS *Ark Royal* and

Scharnhorst (left) and *Gneisenau* (right) in a German port, possibly Wilhelmshaven, *c.* 1939–40. (NH 42203, US Naval History and Heritage Command Center)

Above left: Gneisenau taken from astern, *c.* 1940. (NH 82410, US Naval History and Heritage Command Center)

Above right: Scharnhorst at sea in June 1940 during the Norwegian campaign. The ship has been cleared for action with the deck edge stanchions and lifelines having been taken down. (NH 83982, US Naval History and Heritage Command Center)

Glorious. In addition to these, two destroyers, which appeared to have stopped, were also sighted. When this report reached Marschall, it prompted him to record: 'It occurs to me that the noticeable westward movement may indicate a British evacuation of Norway and that the westbound convoys will now offer valuable targets'.⁶

Subsequently, at 3 a.m. on 8 June, Marschall informed Group West that he intended to operate against the westbound convoys. He was, however, instructed to 'proceed with main task Harstad' and to leave the convoys to the *Admiral Hipper* and destroyers, an order which was later amended at the insistence of the naval staff to the simple statement: 'The main objective is, as before, the destruction of enemy naval forces in the area of Harstad-Narvik'. It was an order that seemed to allow Marschall a measure of discretion in how he acted.⁷

In light of this order, Marschall spread his ships out in a search formation and swept across the convoy routes between Harstad and the Scottish coast. The wind was light to moderate, blowing north-westerly with clear skies. As they searched, Marschall's squadron stumbled upon the minesweeping trawler HMT *Juniper* which was escorting the tanker *Oil Pioneer*, the empty troopship *Orama* and the passenger liner *Atlantis* which had been pressed into service as a hospital ship. The *Juniper* was sunk by gunfire from the *Admiral Hipper* along with the *Oil Pioneer* and *Orama*.⁸ The *Atlantis*, meanwhile, was allowed to proceed on her way unmolested.

It is worth noting that the *Orama* was returning virtually empty, carrying only 100 German prisoners of war when she was sunk. A total of 275 survivors from the ships were pulled from the water. Following the sinking, Marschall was certain that the British must now be aware of his presence and that he would likely have no other opportunity to refuel his escorts undisturbed. So it was that the *Admiral Hipper* and the destroyers were detached to Trondheim to refuel while he proceeded to the Harstad area with *Gneisenau* and *Scharnhorst*. Following replenishing their fuel the *Admiral Hipper* and destroyers were to then support supply convoys on the route to Bodø.

Marschall sailed north to rendezvous once more with the *Dithmarschen* in order to warn the tanker to clear the area before operating against the aircraft carriers that had been reported off the Norwegian coast. Sailing north at 18 knots, *Gneisenau* was leading the *Scharnhorst* when at 3.46 p.m., *Fähnrich zur See* Goos and W. Schulte in the foretop control platform of *Scharnhorst* identified smoke on the horizon 60 degrees to the east off the starboard side. A signal was immediately sent to the *Gneisenau* where it was passed to Marschall. At 3.58 p.m., another signal was sent from *Scharnhorst* to *Gneisenau* reporting the contact to be at a distance of 21.6 miles (40 km). Marschall elected to investigate and ordered the two ships to work up to 30 knots and to turn on to a course of 330 degrees. Unknown to anyone aboard the German ships at that moment in time, they had sighted the aircraft carrier HMS *Glorious*.

Glorious had arrived off the Norwegian coast on 2 June to provide support to Operation Alphabet, the evacuation of Allied forces from Norway. The role of *Glorious* was to evacuate the RAF fighters from Norway and to ferry them back to Britain. During the afternoon of 7 June, ten Gloster Gladiators of 263 Squadron were flown aboard the carrier and were followed in the early evening by the Hawker Hurricanes of 46 Squadron. During the early hours of 8 June, the commanding officer of the *Glorious*,

Officers on the bridge of the *Scharnhorst* look out towards the smoke on the horizon identified by *Fähnrich zur See* Goos and Schulte. *Kapitän zur See* Hoffmann is in the centre. (*Gary Martin*)

Captain Guy D'Oyly-Hughes was granted permission to proceed independently with the destroyers *Acasta* and *Ardent* to Scapa Flow in order to hold a court martial for the carrier's air commander, J. B. Heath, who had been left behind at Scapa Flow for his refusal to carry out an attack against shore targets on the grounds that the targets were at best ill-defined and that his aircraft were unsuited to the task being requested of them.[9]

Shortly after 4 p.m., two unidentified vessels were sighted whereupon HMS *Ardent* under the command of Lieutenant-Commander J. F. Barker, the closest destroyer to the unidentified vessels, was dispatched to investigate while HMS *Acasta* (Lieutenant-Commander C. E. Glasford) was ordered to remain close to the aircraft carrier and to transition from the starboard side to the port side of the carrier.

At the time that the as of yet unidentified *Scharnhorst* and *Gneisenau* were sighted, *Glorious* was at the fourth degree of readiness (cruising stations). Twelve out of her eighteen boilers were active, no lookout was in the crow's nest while no combat air patrols were being flown, and no aircraft were arranged on the deck to enable a swift take off. As *Ardent* went to investigate the unidentified ships, a pipe was made for five Swordfish to be ranged on the flight deck. Meanwhile, the crews of the *Scharnhorst* and *Gneisenau* were ordered to action stations before, at 4.07 p.m., the radar was switched on for gunnery aid. Three minutes later, the gunnery officer of the *Scharnhorst*, *Fregattenkapitän* Wolf Löwisch, reported that from his position he could see a vessel with a thick funnel and a mast, as well as that the vessel possibly had a flight deck. At 4.13 p.m., Löwisch reported more precisely that he could see an aircraft carrier that he believed to be HMS *Ark Royal* escorted by two destroyers. At 4.15 p.m., *Ardent* began to make a series of light signals to the German ships requesting an identification signal. Five minutes later, action stations rang out across the British ships.

Ardent began to turn to port to avoid closing further with the two approaching German ships and started to run parallel to them at a distance of 8 miles as *Glorious* executed her own turn to port while *Acasta* started to produce a smokescreen to cover the aircraft carrier. Orders were given to the main armament crews of the German ships to target the aircraft carrier while the secondary armament crews were issued orders to engage the *Ardent*. At 4.27 p.m., *Gneisenau* opened fire against *Ardent*, hitting the destroyer with her first salvo in boiler room I, causing a reduction of speed. In response, the destroyer opened fire with her 4.7-inch guns and commenced zig-zagging. As she took evasive action, *Ardent* fired a volley of torpedoes against the German ships, one of which was seen to pass close ahead of *Scharnhorst*. Three minutes after the flagship, at 4.30 p.m., permission was granted for the secondary armament of the *Scharnhorst* to open fire against *Ardent*. A further two minutes would pass before permission was granted for the ship's main battery to open fire against *Glorious*.

The first salvo from the main battery of the *Scharnhorst* dropped short while the second salvo was just too far over before the third salvo found its mark. A shell from this first salvo hit *Glorious* and cut off the transmission of the contact report which was, in reality, far too late to save the aircraft carrier and her crew. How much of a contact report *Glorious* succeeded in transmitting is open to debate. Historian John Asmussen has claimed that *Glorious* transmitted a report stating 'Two battlecruisers bearing 308° distance 15 mile on course 030°: My position 154° from 69'N 04°E'.[10] Robert Elkington was in the communications room of HMS *Ark Royal* wearing a pair of headphones probing for either an unguarded signal, the dots and dashes of a Morse signal that may have provided warning of a lurking submarine, and transmission from aircraft. He recalled:

> Suddenly there was this burst of noise, '2PB' in Morse. Well, I knew what that meant—two pocket battleships—but that was all there was. It didn't last long enough for me to get a fix. I took the signal pad to the Petty Officer in charge, but there was no position, nothing.[11]

Another salvo from *Scharnhorst* slammed into the *Glorious*, which hit the flight deck and burst in the upper hanger where it started a large fire. The hit destroyed two Swordfish which were being prepared for take-off while the hole in the flight deck served to ensure that no aircraft could take off from the carrier.[12] As a pall of smoke hung above the carrier's wake, splinters penetrated the boiler casing causing a temporary loss of steam pressure. At 5.33 p.m., owing to interference with the main armament firing at *Glorious*, the secondary armament of the *Scharnhorst* was ordered to cease firing. Seven minutes later, these guns once more opened fire against *Ardent*. Barker manoeuvred the destroyer well, however, the ship was still hit by accurate German fire. As the secondary armament opened fire against *Ardent*, *Acasta* now opened fire against the two battleships.

The sea breaks over the bow of the *Scharnhorst* as the ship's forward guns begin to be traversed to engage HMS *Glorious*, *Ardent*, and *Acasta*. (*Gary Martin*)

Taken from aboard *Scharnhorst*, ahead *Gneisenau* can see seen firing her main armament at HMS *Glorious*. (*Gary Martin*)

Scharnhorst firing at HMS *Glorious*. (NH 83612, US Naval History and Heritage Command Center)

Scharnhorst during the engagement with the British ships. This photograph was taken seconds after the preceding image. (*Gary Martin*)

Gneisenau firing against HMS *Glorious*. (NH 83981, US Naval History and Heritage Command Center)

Scharnhorst seen from *Gneisenau* during the engagement with HMS *Glorious*. (NH 82409, US Naval History and Heritage Command Center)

The smokescreen produced by HMS *Acasta* as seen from *Scharnhorst*. (*Gary Martin*)

By 5.41 p.m., the smoke screen produced by *Acasta* was becoming very effective in hiding *Glorious* and served to also provide a screen into which *Acasta* herself could dive in and out of. Around this time, the decision was made aboard the *Gneisenau* to cease firing against the *Ardent* and to concentrate fire against *Glorious*. As *Gneisenau* concentrated her fire against *Glorious*, *Ardent* launched a second torpedo attack against *Scharnhorst*. Alarms rang out across the battleship at the sight of the torpedoes in the water. Sharp alterations of course were made to avoid the torpedoes as *Ardent* continued to dive in and out of her own smoke screen, all the while her guns blazing away.

Around 5.44 p.m., *Ardent* succeeded in hitting *Scharnhorst* with a 4.7-inch shell and launched a third spread of torpedoes, which prompted the battleship to make another sharp turn to avoid being hit. By this time, *Glorious* was ablaze and listing heavily to starboard. At 5.56 p.m., an 11-inch shell struck the bridge, killing D'Oyly-Hughes and almost all of the other bridge personnel. In the wake of this, the ship's executive officer, Commander Ted Lovell, assumed command of the ship. Just before 6 p.m., the main battery of the *Scharnhorst* ceased firing against *Glorious* while *Gneisenau* continued to engage the carrier until around two minutes later, when she too ceased fire owing to visual contact being lost as the blazing ship was obscured by smoke.

Still, the secondary guns of the two ships continued to engage the destroyers. As the engagement continued, *Scharnhorst* began to suffer from issues with her engines while one boiler ceased to function as a result of a split tube. As *Ardent* launched what amounted to her fifth torpedo attack against *Scharnhorst*, she sustained another hit from the battleship. Having been hit, *Ardent* began to list heavily to port as her speed dropped to 15 knots. It was only now that a signal was made by the German ships to the Naval High Command informing them that they had engaged enemy ships. Having been battered, at 6.10 p.m., *Glorious* finally sank with the loss of all but forty-three of her crew.[13]

With the destroyer reduced to a blazing wreck, around the time that *Glorious* sank, *Gneisenau* ceased firing at the *Acasta*, which sank stern first around 6.20 p.m. Before she sank, *Acasta* launched a series of torpedo attacks against *Scharnhorst*. Suddenly, the crew of the *Acasta* saw a flash and a large column of water erupted on the starboard side of the German ship as a torpedo found its mark. A torpedo struck the *Scharnhorst* in the vicinity of turret 'Caesar', knocking the position out of action. Thick black smoke belched from the vicinity of the impact as seawater flooded in. The magazine to the turret was flooded while the starboard engine room was also put out of action. The ship began to list to starboard and went down 9 feet at the stern. Two officers and forty-six ratings were killed by the impact and detonation of the torpedo.

Meanwhile, at 6.11 p.m., the heavy anti-aircraft guns of the *Scharnhorst* were trained on the *Ardent* and opened fire. The anti-aircraft guns pummelled the destroyer for four minutes until a signal was received from the *Gneisenau* ordering her gunners not to waste any more ammunition. In spite of this order, a few more rounds from the *Scharnhorst* were fired at the *Ardent* before the destroyer finally sank at 6.25 p.m.

With *Glorious* and the two destroyers sunk, *Gneisenau* and *Scharnhorst* made a hasty escape from the area, unaware that the *Glorious* had not been in contact with other Allied ships and that their presence was unknown. As such, the two German ships did not stop to pick up survivors. Survivors of the *Glorious* estimated that around 900 men

HMS *Glorious* burning and listing heavily. (*Gary Martin*)

Smoke from the *Glorious* and *Acasta* seen from *Scharnhorst*. (*Gary Martin*)

Above left: HMS *Acasta* sinking stern first following being reduced to a blazing wreck. (*Gary Martin*)

Above right: Smoke from the sinking British ships taken at the end of the engagement. (*Gary Martin*)

Shell cases on the deck of the *Scharnhorst* following the engagement. (*Gary Martin*)

managed to abandon the aircraft carrier. Of these, forty-two men survived the ordeal, while the others all succumbed to their injuries and/or the perishing cold of the water. The Royal Navy, meanwhile, remained unaware of the loss of HMS *Glorious*, *Ardent* and *Acasta* until their sinking was announced on German radio. The Norwegian ship *Borgund*, on passage to the Faroe Islands, arrived at the scene of the sinking on 10 June and picked up thirty-seven survivors who were landed at Thorshaven, where two later died. Another Norwegian vessel, the *Svalbard II*, which was also sailing to the Faroes, picked up a further five men from the *Glorious* but was sighted by a German aircraft and forced to return to Norway where the survivors became prisoners of war.

Most of those who abandoned the *Acasta* died from exposure with the result that of the crew of 163, only two men were picked up by the *Borgund*.[14] Out of *Ardent*'s crew of 154, all but two died of their wounds and exposure; those survivors were picked up by a German seaplane five days after the sinking. One of the two survivors later died from exposure while the other was eventually repatriated to Britain in 1943 on account of ill health.[15]

While a coup had been achieved over the Royal Navy with the sinking of HMS *Glorious*, significant damage had been inflicted on the *Scharnhorst*. One boiler was out of action and issues were being suffered with one engine room. A torpedo hit had been sustained that knocked turret 'Caesar' out of action, the radar was put out of action, and flooding had occurred. As the ships retired, a damage assessment was conducted on board the battleship; this revealed that the shell plating had borne the brunt of the detonation and that a section of hull plating 19 × 45 feet (6 × 14 m) had been blown out. The explosion had been deep enough that a major portion of the energy from the detonation had been vented into the ship where it tore the torpedo bulkhead from the armour deck. Two transverse bulkheads, the battery deck, and the first platform deck were all damaged while the armour shelf and some of the adjacent structure were slightly damaged. The torpedo had struck the ship where the propeller shafts passed through the torpedo bulkhead. As a result of the inadequate connection of the torpedo bulkhead to the armoured deck, extensive flooding of the inboard compartments was permitted. As such, four of the twenty-two main watertight compartments had some flooding, totalling 2,500 tons of water, creating a 3-degree list to starboard and causing the ship to be 9 feet (3 m) down by the stern.

The flooding and general damage affected the ship's propulsion. The starboard shaft which passed through the lower part of the underwater side protection system abreast turret 'Caesar' was destroyed and the shaft alley flooded. A seaman was trapped in the alley and when one of his crewmates opened a watertight door in a rescue attempt, the aft engine room, which supplied power to the centreline shaft, began to flood rapidly. So rapid was the flooding that it was impossible to properly secure the plant. One of the turbines, under maximum load, cooled so rapidly that the housing came into contact with the turbine blades and had to be stopped. All steam connectors in this area were shut down and with the starboard engine room secured, the ship was left with only one shaft in operation.

Turret 'Caesar' was knocked out of operation. Compartments below the magazine were flooded while electrical and other equipment in the magazine was damaged. The aft starboard 5.9-inch twin turret was put out of action as a result of the flooding of sub-turret compartments and damage to the electrical systems while the fire-control system for the aft guns was damaged. Collision mats were rigged by the damage control party in an effort to prevent further structural damage being inflicted on the ship, however, the attempt to rig the mats was abandoned when they could not be secured.

Limited by the maximum speed of the *Scharnhorst*, the two ships proceeded at 20 knots to Trondheim where they arrived at around noon on 9 June. During the afternoon of 9 June, divers ascertained the scale of the damage to the hull while repairs began to be enacted from the repair ship *Huascaran* and the salvage ship *Parat*. At the same time, ammunition was replenished from the supply ship *Alsteror*. On 10 June, an aircraft of RAF Coastal Command sighted the *Scharnhorst* at Trondheim. Marschall meanwhile had put to sea in the *Gneisenau* with the *Admiral Hipper* and four destroyers and would return to anchor later that day. Meanwhile, the storm of Operation Juno was beginning to break. Marschall received few plaudits for sinking HMS *Glorious* or her escorts which was dismissed as being 'an extraordinary stroke of luck'. Rather, in place of this, he faced censure for what was viewed as his mishandling of the operation and for the tactical error which resulted in damage to the *Scharnhorst*. He reported sick ten days after the sinking of HMS *Glorious* and was relieved by *Vizeadmiral* Gunther Lütjens, who had previously flown his flag in *Gneisenau* during Operation Weserübung.[16]

On 11 June, following the sighting of the *Scharnhorst* at Trondheim by the aircraft from Coastal Command, twelve Hudson bombers flew to Trondheim where they launched an attack against the *Scharnhorst*, *Gneisenau* and *Admiral Hipper*. Thirty-six 220-lb armour-piercing bombs were dropped, all of which missed the targets. The Royal Navy joined the RAF in attacks against the German ships at Trondheim.

Elements of the Kriegsmarine at Trondheim, June 1940. From left to right, the ships are *Gneisenau*, *Scharnhorst*, and the *Admiral Hipper*. (NH 82407, US Naval History and Heritage Command Center)

Accompanied by HMS *Rodney*, HMS *Ark Royal* was ordered to Trondheim to exact revenge for the loss of the *Glorious*. On 12 June, one of *Rodney*'s junior ratings, E. L. Brown, noted: '10pm, in position outside Trondheim. Midnight, planes from *A. Royal* to bomb German fleet there. We are to back them up. Expecting bombers and air raids. No sleep tonight, curse them'.[17]

In using the Fleet Air Arm to attack the *Scharnhorst* as she lay at anchor, the Admiralty hoped to repeat the Fleet Air Arm's brilliant feat in managing to sink the cruiser *Königsberg* which had been sunk at anchor at Bergen on 10 April.[18] Fifteen Blackburn Skuas were to take part in the attack. Nine of the aircraft were drawn from 803 Squadron while six came from 800 Squadron. Ron Jordan, an armourer from 800 Squadron, knew that something was afoot when he and his fellow armourers were ordered to arm the Skuas with 500-lb armour-piercing bombs, a bomb load not normally carried for a combat air patrol or when conducting attacks against shore installations:

> To get two squadrons ranged together, we knew that it was exceptional. You see, we normally ranged three aircraft at a time on the flight deck. And of course with the 500-lb armour-piercing bombs, you only use that against a warship. There was a feeling that this was going to be a very stiff job.[19]

At midnight on 13 June, the Skuas took off from the flight deck of the *Ark Royal*, formed up and headed to Trondheim. A diversionary raid by the RAF on Vaernes was scheduled to take place at the same time that the Skuas attacked the *Scharnhorst* but the RAF bombers arrived over Vaernes before the *Ark Royal*'s aircraft arrived over Trondheim. Led by Lieutenant-Commander John Casson, the formation of Skuas approached Trondheim at 2.43 a.m. in clear skies and the broad daylight typical of the northerly latitude and time of year. Rather than distracting the Luftwaffe fighters or preventing them from taking off, the Skua crews found that the premature arrival of the RAF Beauforts over Vaernes served only to alert the German fighter defences with the result that the Bf-109Es and Bf-110s were already airborne.[20] In addition to the Luftwaffe fighters, as the aircraft of 803 and 800 Squadrons winged over the fjord at an altitude of 10,000 feet (3,050 m), anti-aircraft fire from the ships below and shore batteries rose into the sky to greet them.

Lieutenant-Commander Casson led 803 Squadron around to attack *Scharnhorst* from stern to bow while Captain R. T. Partridge led 800 Squadron around to attack the ship from bow to stern. As he led the squadron into their diving attack, Casson's Skua and three others were shot down by the marauding Messerschmitts. Partridge led the aircraft of 800 Squadron into their attack. Partridge and three other Skuas from 800 Squadron were also shot down with Partridge managing to bail out of his blazing aircraft to become a prisoner of war. Partridge did succeed in releasing his bomb, however, it missed the target. Partridge's wingman, Lieutenant Kenneth V. Spurway followed his leader down and, releasing his bomb, succeeded in striking *Scharnhorst* on the starboard side abaft the funnel. Fortunately for the crew of the battleship, the bomb failed to detonate.[21]

The seven aircraft that survived the attack returned to the *Ark Royal* where they landed around 3.45 a.m. Ron Skinner recalled the increasing despondency as the crew of the *Ark Royal* waited for the Skuas to return and land:

> We waited until the planes, if they were still flying, would have run out of fuel. I think we slowly realized that sixteen of our aircrew were not going to return. It was a great blow, I think particularly for those involved in the flying operations. It affected us for days. We called it Black Thursday.[22]

With the aircraft recovered *Ark Royal*, *Rodney* and their destroyers set a course for Scapa Flow in fog so thick that two of the destroyers collided and were severely damaged. For the Blackburn Skua, the attack on the *Scharnhorst* at Trondheim was its last hurrah. Owing to high attrition rates, it was withdrawn from frontline service shortly after the raid.

The raid by the Skuas from *Ark Royal* and the one bomb which struck the *Scharnhorst* and failed to explode did little to hamper the repair work for within ten days of arriving at Trondheim the turbine of the centreline shaft had been repaired. Nevertheless, the damage to the starboard shaft was deemed to be serious and could only be surveyed in dry dock as it was feared that the shaft had been severed by the explosion. As a precaution, the propeller was lashed to the hull. On 18 June, *Scharnhorst* embarked upon engine trials in Trondheimsfjord and the following day, the ship was declared seaworthy enough to make 24 knots.

On 20 June, two shafts were operational and the damage had been sufficiently repaired to allow the ship to weigh anchor and to make for Kiel, escorted by three vessels of the 1st Minesweeping Flotilla, the destroyers *Hans Lody*, *Hermann Schoemann*, *Karl Galster*, and *Erich Steinbrink* and the torpedo boats *Kondor* and *Greif*. As the *Scharnhorst* and her escorts set a course for Kiel the *Gneisenau* and *Admiral Hipper* were to attempt a break out into the North Atlantic, thus drawing the attention of the British away from the *Scharnhorst*. At 10.09 p.m. on 20 June, while approximately 46 miles (74 km) north-west of Halten, Lütjens' ships were sighted by the submarine HMS *Clyde* under the command of Lieutenant-Commander David Ingram.

The *Clyde* launched a torpedo attack and succeeded in hitting the *Gneisenau* in the bow just forward of the splinter belt, which caused serious damage. A significant amount of water poured into the two forward watertight compartments and the ship was forced to return to Trondheim at the reduced speed of 19 knots where she arrived the following day.[23] At Trondheim, the repair ship *Huascaran* was moored alongside the *Gneisenau* to effect temporary repairs.

Meanwhile, *Scharnhorst* was at sea sailing south towards Germany. During the course of 21 June, an aircraft from Coastal Command sighted the *Scharnhorst* and her consorts off the isle of Utsire. This information was relayed back to Britain, whereupon plans were quickly made to attack the battleship. At around 3 p.m., six Fairey Swordfish torpedo bombers attacked *Scharnhorst* but they were beaten back by heavy anti-aircraft fire. The Swordfish were followed at around 4.30 p.m. by a group of nine Bristol Beauforts armed with 500-lb (227-kg) armour-piercing bombs. The Beauforts were also unsuccessful in

Gneisenau in a Norwegian port, likely Trondheim, *c.* 1940. (*NH 82408, US Naval History and Heritage Command Center*)

Gneisenau seen from the *Admiral Hipper*, June 1940. (*Author's Collection*)

Gneisenau seen in the North Sea. In the background is an Admiral Hipper-class cruiser. It is likely that this photograph was taken on 20 June 1940 when Lütjens took the *Gneisenau* and *Admiral Hipper* and attempted to break out into the Atlantic to draw the attention of the British from *Scharnhorst* as she returned to Kiel. (*NH 110872, US Naval History and Heritage Command Center*)

Crew members of the *Gneisenau* being taken ashore at Trondheim following the torpedoing of the ship by HMS *Clyde*. (*Author's Collection*)

their attack, being driven off by anti-aircraft fire and German fighters. Shortly after the attack by the Beauforts, the Germans intercepted signals indicating that a significant portion of the Home Fleet was at sea in an effort to intercept the battleship, whereupon the decision was taken to put in at Stavanger. When the decision was made to put in at Stavanger, elements of the Home Fleet were within 35 miles of the *Scharnhorst*. *Scharnhorst* anchored that evening in the Skudenesfjord before moving to an anchorage in Dusavik Bay at 4 a.m. the next morning. At around 5.30 a.m. on 22 June, *Scharnhorst* departed Stavanger for Kiel. The southern part of the Green Belt was reached at 5.30 p.m. on 23 June, and at 10.26 p.m., the ship moored alongside buoy A12 in Kiel.

During the afternoon of 24 June, *Scharnhorst* was taken into dry dock 'C' whereupon work to fully repair her damage began. That night, the flooded stern compartments were cleared and the bodies of crewmen were recovered before funerals were held on 27 June. The repair work on the ship would last for around six months.[24] On 21 November, with the repair work completed, *Scharnhorst* sailed to Gotenhafen to conduct a series of sea trials in the Baltic.

Meanwhile, *Gneisenau* was sufficiently repaired at Trondheim to permit her to weigh anchor and sail to Kiel. Accompanied by the *Admiral Hipper* and the destroyers *Friedrich Ihn*, *Hans Lody*, *Paul Jacobi*, and *Karl Galster*, *Gneisenau* departed Trondheim on 25 July and arrived at Kiel two days later. At Kiel, *Gneisenau* was taken into dry dock at the Howaldtswerke dockyard to undergo five months' worth of repairs.[25] *Gneisenau* remained at Kiel until 21 October when she too sailed into the Baltic to undertake a series of sea trials.

Above left: *Scharnhorst* at Scheerhafen during the autumn of 1940 while undergoing sea trials in the Baltic. (*World War Photos*)

Above right: Following being repaired in October 1940, *Gneisenau* was painted in Baltic camouflage and proceeded into the Baltic to conduct a series of trials. The ship is seen here while undergoing trials. (*NH 110874, US Naval History and Heritage Command Center*)

7
Operation Berlin

On 19 December 1940, both the *Gneisenau* and *Scharnhorst* left the Baltic and sailed to Kiel in preparation for Operation Berlin. Commanded by Lütjens, who once more flew his flag in the *Gneisenau*, Operation Berlin called for the two battleships to break out into the North Atlantic whereupon they would seek out Allied merchant convoys and commence commerce raiding. On 28 December, the two ships weighed anchor before making an attempt to break out into the Atlantic, however, before they could do so, they encountered severe storms that caused damage to the *Gneisenau* necessitating a postponement of the operation and a return to port. *Gneisenau* returned to Kiel where she underwent repair work while *Scharnhorst* proceeded to Gotenhafen.

By early January 1941, the repairs had been completed, and on the 22nd, the two ships once more embarked on Operation Berlin. Although every effort had been made to enforce secrecy, the two ships were sighted by a British agent as they transited the Skagerrak whereupon a report was transmitted to the Admiralty in London. The Admiralty, in turn, passed the sighting report on to the commander-in-chief of the Home Fleet, Admiral John Tovey, who immediately put to sea with a force comprised of three battleships, eight cruisers, and eleven destroyers in the hope of intercepting the two German ships in the Iceland–Faroes gap. Tovey had assumed correctly that Lütjens had planned on using this passage to break out into the Atlantic. As Lütjens sailed northwards, the radar on the *Gneisenau* reported two contacts, which turned out to be British cruisers, prompting the German admiral to take his ships further northwards to attempt a break-out via the Denmark Strait located between Greenland and Iceland.

One of the cruisers that had been picked up on the radar of the German ships was HMS *Naiad* whose lookouts had also glimpsed the battleships through a rain squall, however, the cruiser did not make any attempt to shadow the German ships with the result that Tovey came to the conclusion that the sighting report had been erroneous and returned to Scapa Flow with the Home Fleet.

Having decided to enter the North Atlantic by way of the Denmark Strait, Lütjens decided that before entering the Atlantic it would be wise for his ships to replenish their fuel stocks. A rendezvous was made with the tanker *Adria* on 30 January. Bad weather hampered the refuelling process with the result that it was not completed until

Gneisenau during the early stages of Operation Berlin before the tops of her main and secondary turrets were painted yellow. (*NH 110869, US Naval History and Heritage Command Center*)

2 February, by which time both ships had taken on 3,400 tons of fuel. Immediately after having refuelled, the battleships began their journey through the Demark Strait. On 3 February, the ships had broken through the Denmark Strait, and southern Greenland was reached the following day.[1] On 5 February, *Gneisenau* and *Scharnhorst* rendezvoused with the tanker *Schlettstadt* to the south of Cape Farewell, from where they both took on 1,500 tons of fuel. The refuelling was completed on 6 February.

Having made it into the Atlantic and refuelled his ships, Lütjens was presented with a choice of two hunting grounds. The first lay to the north, where convoys designated HX and SC crossed the Atlantic between Britain and Canada. The designation HX was given to eastbound convoys and originated in Halifax, Nova Scotia, from where they sailed to ports in Britain. While *en route* to Britain, the HX convoys absorbed the BHX convoys which originated from Bermuda. Later in the war HX convoys would also originate from New York. The HX convoys were initially considered fast convoys, comprised of ships which could attain between 9 and 13 knots. SC convoys ran in parallel to the HX convoys and were considered slow convoys, being comprised of vessels that could make 8 knots or less.[2]

The second hunting ground was to the south where convoys designated SL and OG sailed between Britain, Gibraltar, and Freetown, Sierra Leone. The designation SL was given to convoys comprised of merchant ships that sailed independently from South America, various African countries, and countries in the Indian Ocean to

Gneisenau partially obscured from view by a high wave as she sails through the North Atlantic during Operation Berlin. It is likely that this photograph was taken during the bad weather and heavy seas that hampered refuelling from the tanker *Adria*. (NH 110868, US Naval History and Heritage Command Center)

Gneisenau in the North Atlantic following transiting the Denmark Strait. The large wave places this photograph around the time that the ship's sailed through rough weather between 30 January and 2 February. (NH 110870, US Naval History and Heritage Command Center)

Above: A wave breaks across the foredeck of the *Scharnhorst* somewhere in the Atlantic during Operation Berlin. (*Author's Collection*)

Right: *Scharnhorst* wallowing in the Atlantic during Operation Berlin. (*Author's Collection*)

Freetown where they were formed into a convoy before sailing on to Liverpool. OG convoys were convoys destined to sail to Gibraltar from Britain, the OG standing for 'outbound to Gibraltar'. Lütjens decided that in the first instance, his efforts would be concentrated on the convoy route between Canada and Britain.

On 30 January, forty-one ships comprising convoy HX-106 departed Halifax bound for Liverpool.[3] Providing escort to the convoy was a force comprised of the battleship HMS *Ramillies*, five destroyers, three corvettes, and two anti-submarine warfare trawlers. Having refuelled his ships and decided to concentrate on Allied merchant convoys between Britain and Canada, Lütjens received intelligence from *B-Dienst*, which saw him order an alteration of course to the south on the report that HX-106 had departed Halifax at the end of January. Officially called the *Kriegsmarine Beobachtungsdienst* (naval radio monitoring service) and more commonly referred to and known as *B-Dienst*, this service was responsible for the interception and monitoring of enemy communications and for cracking any codes encountered. Members of the *B-Dienst* were civilian specialists who were employed by the *Kriegsmarine*.[4]

At 8.30 a.m. on 8 February, lookouts aboard the *Scharnhorst* and *Gneisenau* sighted the smoke of HX-106 on the horizon.[5] At 9.47 a.m., the range to the convoy was approximately 17.3 miles (28 km), and Lütjens manoeuvred his ships to attack from the north and south in a pincer move. Shortly thereafter, the vague outline of what appeared to be a capital ship began to loom out of the haze on the horizon. Eleven minutes later, the capital ship was identified as being HMS *Ramillies*. *Kapitän zur See* Hoffmann offered to use *Scharnhorst* to draw off the *Ramillies* so that *Gneisenau* could engage the merchant ships. This strategy, if successful, would have entailed little risk to the *Scharnhorst* as she was 11 knots faster than the veteran British battleship and her more modern 11-inch guns outranged the 15-inch guns of the *Ramillies*. Lütjens elected not to engage, and indeed, his orders forbade him to do so, as he had been ordered not to engage enemy capital ships unless absolutely necessary and he was not to risk unnecessary damage to his ships. Instead, Lütjens broke off the interception and the two German ships slipped away.[6]

Lütjens was certain that the British had sighted the *Gneisenau* and *Scharnhorst* and was not happy with the tactical situation as his presence would likely be reported thus making it difficult to achieve success against merchant convoys. At the same time, it heightened the risk of a confrontation with enemy capital ships as the Royal Navy would begin a systematic hunt for him and his two ships. Fortunately for Lütjens, however, the British lookouts had only sighted one of his ships, and even then, the lookouts had mistakenly identified the Scharnhorst-class battleship as the heavy cruiser *Admiral Hipper*. A reason for this misidentification was most likely the fact that the British knew that the *Admiral Hipper* was at large in the Atlantic, while, since Admiral Tovey had discounted the reports from HMS *Naiad*, it was believed that the *Gneisenau* and *Scharnhorst* were still in Germany.

Subsequently, Lütjens took *Gneisenau* and *Scharnhorst* north-west to a position between Greenland and Canada, where the battleships were refuelled from the tankers *Esso Hamburg* and *Schlettstadt*. The German ships resumed their patrol on 17 February with Lütjens hoping to intercept convoy HX-111. The convoy eluded the German raiders and prompted a westward hunt for merchant traffic.

On 22 February, lookouts aboard the *Gneisenau* reported sighting a feather of smoke on the horizon. Action stations rang out across the ships as speed was increased in order to intercept. As *Gneisenau* and *Scharnhorst* closed the range, a slightly disappointing sight greeted the crews as while the ships had stumbled upon a group of five unescorted merchant vessels, the ships were riding high in the water, an indicator that they were not laden with essential war materials, but were in fact empty. As such, the ships, returning to the United States, would hardly be worth the trouble of an attack. Lütjens quickly realised, however, that he had no alternative other than to order an attack. As soon as the merchant ships sighted the sleek grey hulls of the approaching battleships, they began to scatter. At the same time, the air became a hive of radio signals. A warning shot was fired in the direction of the merchant ships, to which the captains appeared to pay no attention, remaining on their respective courses as the transmissions increased. The time was almost 11 a.m. and Lütjens decided that it was now time to fire the guns of his ships in anger.

At 10.55 a.m., the passenger-cargo ship *Kantara* fell victim to the guns of the *Gneisenau* and *Scharnhorst*. At 1.12 p.m., *Gneisenau* sank a second passenger-cargo ship, the *Trelawny*, while *Scharnhorst* sank the tanker *Lustrous*. At 4.23 p.m., as *Scharnhorst* sailed in pursuit of a tanker that ultimately escaped, *Gneisenau* claimed another victim in the form of the merchantman *A. D. Huff*. In addition to these vessels, another merchant vessel, the *Harlesden*, was known to be approximately 50 miles away. Lütjens realised that something had to be done about this merchant vessel also, if only to put her wireless out of action in an effort to prevent his location from being betrayed.

The task of neutralising the wireless of the *Harlesden* was given to the crew of one of the *Gneisenau*'s Ar 196 seaplanes. The seaplane returned around an hour after having been launched to report that the wireless aerial of the ship had been destroyed, but that in the process, the aircraft had been subjected to machine gun fire. Time was short for the *Harlesden* as having recovered the Arado, the German ships set off in pursuit of the merchantman, sinking the ship at 11.08 p.m.

In a period of just over twelve hours, five merchant vessels amounting to 25,431 gross registered tons was sunk.[7] The cost in ammunition had, however, been high. Following the engagement, Lütjens decided to move to a new area as one tanker had escaped while distress signals had been made by the other merchant vessels revealing the presence of his ships. During the night of 22–23 February, Lütjens used his radio for the first time since 8 February when he made two transmissions. The first transmission reported his success in sinking five merchant vessels while the second ordered the tankers *Esso Hamburg* and *Schlettstadt* to rendezvous at a point near the Azores.

On 26 February, *Gneisenau* and *Scharnhorst* rendezvoused with the tankers *Ermland* and *Friedrich Breme* whereupon they began to take on fuel. At the same time, 180 prisoners taken from the merchant vessels sunk on 22 February were transferred to the *Ermland*. The refuelling was completed by 7 a.m. on 28 February, at which point the battleships resumed their sortie. By the beginning of March, the two ships had covered 11,000 miles, almost half the distance around the world.

On 1 March, Lütjens took the opportunity to inform the sailors under his command: 'I take this opportunity of expressing my complete satisfaction with the performance of the personnel, and especially the engine room ratings'. Those aboard the *Scharnhorst* were especially entitled to Lütjens' praise as they had been hard at work throughout the operation hitherto keeping the ship's superheated boilers operational as the steel tubes proved once more to be unable to withstand the high temperatures of operational service. *Gneisenau* appears not to have suffered similar trouble to her sister ship.

Now operating against the SL and OG convoys, on 3 March, the ships arrived in the vicinity of the Cape Verde Islands. On 5 March, one of the Arado seaplanes from the *Scharnhorst* was launched in order to conduct a search for merchant vessels in the vicinity. After a period of four hours, the aircraft had still not returned to the ship. Sailing in the general direction that the aircraft had flown, it was eventually found riding on the water having run out of fuel. The following day, the two ships met *U-124*, which was on its fourth patrol of the war during which it would sink eleven merchant ships.

The *Scharnhorst* and *Gneisenau* were now sailing up and down a line between the Cape Verde Islands and the coast of Africa at 12 knots in an effort to conserve fuel as they searched for another convoy. At 9.20 a.m. on 7 March, a lookout in the foretop of the *Scharnhorst* sighted a mast on the horizon. A closer examination revealed the mainmast to be that of a battleship that was subsequently identified as being HMS *Malaya*. Where there was a battleship it was reasonable to assume that a convoy would almost certainly be in the immediate vicinity. *Gneisenau* worked up speed in preparation to conduct a reconnaissance. Two hours later, her lookouts picked out the masts of twelve merchant ships sailing due south. Again, as a result of his orders not to become embroiled in an engagement with enemy capital ships, Lütjens refused to authorise an attack.

Lookouts aboard the *Malaya* also sighted the German ships, prompting the battleship to alter course and to close within 14 miles (23 km) of the *Gneisenau* and *Scharnhorst*, well within gunnery range of the two German ships. Refusing to be drawn into an engagement Lütjens withdrew, before reversing course to shadow the convoy while directing two U-boats (*U-124* and *U-105*) on to the convoy.[8] At 1.42 a.m., *U-124* sighted the convoy and an hour later *U-105* did likewise. Between 2.45 and 3 a.m., the two U-boats sank six merchant ships totalling 28,488 gross registered tons.

Having directed the U-boats onto the convoy, *Scharnhorst* and *Gneisenau* headed back out towards the mid-Atlantic to rendezvous with the tankers *Uckermark* and *Ermland*. During the course of 9 March, while sailing to the rendezvous point with the takers, the Greek freighter *Marathon*, loaded with coal bound for Alexandria, was stumbled upon before being sunk, almost causally, by the *Scharnhorst*. Two days later, the battleships met the tankers where they began to replenish their fuel stocks and take on additional supplies. From this point, the *Ermland* and *Uckermark* would sail with the battleships and would assist in the search for Allied merchant vessels. Operating on the western part of the convoy route between 39° N and 46° W, the four ships would sail abreast of one another with an interval of 30 miles (56 km) between each ship. Given reasonable visibility, such a formation allowed for a distance of 120 miles (220 km) to be searched. The order of the line was the *Uckermark*, *Gneisenau*, *Scharnhorst*, and *Ermland*.

At 9 p.m. on 11 March, a long signal from Navy Group West reached Lütjens. The signal ordered Lütjens to cease operations against the convoys sailing between Canada and Britain from 18 March as the *Admiral Hipper* and *Admiral Scheer* were due to break out into the North Atlantic during the period of the new moon. The

Gneisenau seen from *Scharnhorst* during Operation Berlin. (NH 110871, US Naval History and Heritage Command Center)

Scharnhorst seen during Operation Berlin from *U-124*. The photograph was taken when the battleships met the U-boat, which was on its fourth war patrol on 6 March. (*Author's Collection*)

Gneisenau seen during the course of Operation Berlin. The photograph was printed on to postcards used by the ship's company. (*Michael Emmerich*)

signal went on to state that *B-Dienst* had reported that a force comprised of the battlecruiser *Repulse*, the aircraft carrier *Furious*, and a number of destroyers had departed Gibraltar and were sailing a westerly course. The sailing of the *Furious* and *Repulse* from Gibraltar was not in response to the potential breakout of the *Admiral Hipper* and *Admiral Scheer*, nor was it a response to Lütjens' ships being at large in the Atlantic, rather, at the time *Furious* was involved in operations ferrying aircraft to Takoradi. Nevertheless, the presence of the *Repulse* and *Furious* concerned Naval Group West to the point where Lütjens was ordered to use the *Gneisenau* and *Scharnhorst* as a diversion while the *Hipper* and *Scheer* broke out into the Atlantic. According to the signal to Lütjens, the best way for *Gneisenau* and *Scharnhorst* to create a diversion was for the two ships to make for Brest on the French Atlantic coast.

Lütjens still had seven days before his orders to cease operations against Allied merchant convoys had to be executed so the hunt for Allied merchant shipping continued. On 15 March, the *Uckermark* sighted a group of six unescorted merchant vessels. Moving to intercept, *Scharnhorst* sank the tankers *Athelfoam* and *British Strength* while *Gneisenau* sank a third tanker, the *Simnia*. In addition to sinking three tankers, the other three tankers were captured. The *Bianca* was captured by the *Gneisenau* at 10.20 a.m. and was followed by the *San Casimiro* at 1.40 p.m. and *Polykarb* at 5.50 p.m. Prize crews were placed on board the three tankers with orders to sail to Bordeaux.

At 1 a.m. on 16 March, signals were picked up aboard the *Gneisenau* and *Scharnhorst* from the *Uckermark* that the silhouettes of merchant vessels had been sighted on the horizon. At dawn, it became clear that another convoy (HX-114) had been located. The first merchant vessel of HX-114 to fall victim to the German guns was the 4,500-ton *Rio Dorado*, which was sunk at 4.28 a.m. The *Rio Dorado* was followed to the bottom of the Atlantic by the *Empire Industry* at 8.55 a.m., and then the *Granli*, *Mangkai*, *Myson*, *Royal Crown*, *Silverfir*, *Demerton*, and *Sardinian Prince*.

At the time, the battleship HMS *Rodney* was in the vicinity of HX-114 with HMS *Malaya*. Distress signals were picked up by those aboard the *Rodney* from the *Rio Dorado* and the other merchant vessels whereupon the battleship altered course in order to investigate. *Rodney* arrived on the scene too late to save any of the victims, by which time *Gneisenau* and *Scharnhorst* had made good their escape.

HMS *Rodney* had not been the only vessel to pick up the distress signals from the *Rio Dorado* and other merchantmen. The 1,831-ton *Chilean Reefer*, which was sailing independently to Newfoundland with a cargo of bacon, had also picked up the signals. The *Chilean Reefer* was a Danish-flagged vessel that was re-registered under the Red Ensign at Singapore following the German invasion of Denmark. Having picked up distress signals from the merchant vessels under attack, the captain of the *Chilean Reefer*, Thomas Bell, decided to clear the area as quickly as he could. During the course of the afternoon, however, lookouts aboard the merchant vessel sighted the silhouette of a warship cresting over the horizon, the sight of which was followed by gun flashes. As giant spouts of water erupted around the *Chilean Reefer*, a raider distress signal giving an accurate position was made.[9] The distress signal from the *Chilean Reefer* was picked up by HMS *Rodney*, which worked up to full speed and set a course for the reported position of the merchantman.

Meanwhile, the *Chilean Reefer* made smoke in an effort to hide herself while trying to evade the fall of shot from the *Gneisenau*. *Gneisenau* had opened fire on the merchant ship from a range of 12 miles, and despite maintaining her onslaught until she closed to within 1,000 yards, she still could not sink the merchant vessel. During the course of the day, the weather had closed in, changing from a light mist to being overcast with thick black clouds and drizzle. With the change in weather, the sea began to whip up.

As *Gneisenau* closed the range, the merchantman opened fire with a single 4-inch gun and stubbornly refused to surrender. Lütjens, and the commanding officer of the *Gneisenau*, *Kapitän zur See* Otto Fein were left somewhat perplexed. The defiance of the merchant vessel was something they had not experienced hitherto, which led them to begin to suspect that the *Reefer* was perhaps a carefully disguised armed merchant cruiser potentially armed with torpedo tubes. Other questions were raised, such as if the vessel was an armed merchant cruiser, could she be working in conjunction with a battleship or heavy cruiser by acting as a scout? The decision was therefore taken to edge away and finish off the cargo vessel from a safer distance.

As *Gneisenau* opened the range to her victim and continued her bombardment, Bell issued the order to abandon ship as the vessel began to blaze from bow to stern. Even so, shells continued to be poured into the *Chilean Reefer*. By the time *Gneisenau* ceased fire, a total of seventy-three rounds had been expended, much more than the total expended on any other target during the course of the cruise.

As the lifeboat from the *Chilean Reefer* was ordered to come alongside the *Gneisenau* with the intention of her crew being interned into captivity alongside the crewmembers from other merchant vessels sunk, the thoughts held by Lütjens and Fein that the *Reefer* was perhaps an armed merchant cruiser operating as a scout to heavier forces began to be supported by the appearance of a blip on the ship's radar screen at a range of 11 miles and closing. Fifteen minutes later, the large bulk of HMS *Rodney* loomed large on the horizon. Lookouts aboard the British battleship had sighted a large ship and a blazing merchant vessel at a range of 15 miles.

From his position manning the periscope of 'X' turret, Sub-Lieutenant Eryk Sopocko of the *Rodney* saw a glow on the horizon and thought it was the moon rising. He soon realised

The merchant ship *Chilean Reefer* on fire following being engaged by *Gneisenau*. (*Author's Collection*)

(*Author's Collection*)

Ablaze, the *Chilean Reefer* is hidden behind a pall of smoke. Moments after this photograph was taken a blip appeared on the radar screen of the *Gneisenau* at a range of 11 miles as HMS *Rodney* approached. (*Author's Collection*)

that it was a ship ablaze, reflecting orange-red on the underside of the clouds.[10] *Rodney* was frustrated by the rapidly fading light combined with the blazing *Chilean Reefer* which made it extremely difficult to see what was lurking beyond the merchantman. Marine Len Nicholl was another of the ship's company who was closed up in his action station in one of the ship's 6-inch turrets: 'I could see the *Chilean Reefer* on fire. I also saw a little light in the sea, so I reported it and it turned out to be one of the merchant ship's lifeboats'.[11]

As lookouts aboard the *Gneisenau* watched with dread as the *Rodney* crested over the horizon, the British battleship signalled a challenge via signal lamp: 'What ship?' Lütjens knew that he would have to flee rather than fight, with the nine 16-inch guns of the *Rodney* providing the British battleship with a significant weight of shell advantage over his own nine 11-inch guns. In an effort to buy time, *Gneisenau* flashed a reply that she was the cruiser *Emerald*. Understandably, those aboard the *Rodney* were perplexed. HMS *Emerald* was a light cruiser that had been commissioned in 1926, displaced 9,435 tons at full load, and had three funnels. Under any circumstances, she could not be mistaken for the *Gneisenau*. Having replied to the challenge from *Rodney* that his ship was HMS *Emerald*, Fein ordered the ship to work up to 32 knots. As she showed the older *Rodney* a clean pair of heels, *Gneisenau* made a signal to the *Uckermark* to also leave the area with utmost speed.

The German battleship departed so swiftly once challenged that her rudder damaged one of the lifeboats from the *Chilean Reefer*. From one of the 6-inch gunnery director positions Sub-Lieutenant Peter Wells-Cole 'saw the shadowy *Gneisenau* pushing off'. The commanding officer of the *Rodney*, Captain Frederick Dalrymple-Hamilton, now had a decision to make—whether or not to pursue. He was, however, left with no alternative course of action. With the first of the Royal Navy's next generation of battleships, HMS *King George V*, having only been completed in December 1940 and still being worked up to fighting efficiency, the *Rodney* and her sister ship, HMS *Nelson*, remained the most experienced and powerful units in the Royal Navy. Approaching the blazing *Chilean Reefer*, Dalrymple-Hamilton therefore needed a cool head as he was responsible for the preservation of a precious national asset and the likelihood of achieving a good result over the much faster *Gneisenau* in the darkness which now descended was almost nil. As such, rather than dash off in pursuit of the much faster enemy, Dalrymple-Hamilton issued orders to pick up survivors from the *Chilean Reefer*.

The searchlights of the *Rodney* swept over the wave tops finding only large patches of burning oil at first before picking up a small boat rigged with a sail rising on peaks and sliding into troughs. The lifeboat contained twenty-seven men of British, Danish, and Chinese nationality and included Captain Bell, the chief officer, and two dead seamen. Taken aboard the battleship, the survivors explained that they believed that it was the *Gneisenau* that had attacked their ship.

Ten more of the *Chilean Reefer*'s crew were believed to be in another lifeboat, of which there was no immediate sign. As *Rodney* began to leave the scene, the second lifeboat was spotted, its position given away by a small light. *Rodney* reversed course and approached the lifeboat but there were no signs of life. There has since been speculation that the lifeboat was occupied but that on seeing *Rodney* begin to sail away, the occupants lost all hope of being rescued and threw themselves into the water, preferring to drown rather than endure a long agonising death adrift in the Atlantic. Having sunk both lifeboats, *Rodney* finally departed, leaving behind only burning oil slicks and bobbing corpses somewhere in the darkness.

To Sub-Lieutenant Wells-Cole, the *Chilean Reefer* incident revealed the perils faced by the merchant navy, 'It illustrated to use how fortunate we were in *Rodney*, a 35,000-ton battleship, compared with the poor, wretched merchant seamen. It brought home to us the reality of what they were going through'.[12] Paymaster-Lieutenant Allen conveyed the frustration that descended throughout *Rodney* following the incident:

> There was much controversy in the messes round the ship. Perhaps if we had been ten minutes earlier, or the sun had set in the east for a change, or we had been eight knots faster, or had an aircraft carrier—perhaps we might have brought her [*Gneisenau*] to action.[13]

Sub-Lieutenant Eric Walton, who was down in the engineering spaces of the *Rodney* during the *Chilean Reefer* incident, later observed:

> It was one of the most disheartening, sad moments of that early part of the war. The whole ship was disconsolate. There we were loaded up with 16-inch and 6-inch and the loud hailer had actually announced 'there is the old bastard' or words to that effect. So, we knew she was in the sights. We just waited and, after an hour in which nothing was broadcast at all. I finally came on deck and there was a star shell in the air and we were picking up survivors …[14]

According to Junior Rating G. Conning, the reasons for not opening fire on the *Gneisenau* were perfectly reasonable and understandable:

> As we approached dark was falling and [there were] rainsqualls. We could not get a range on the raider as the burning ship was blinding our range takers and she fled behind it. We had her supply ship or tender [the *Uckermark*] right in our sights but Captain Dalrymple-Hamilton would not fire as she no doubt had seamen prisoners aboard…. I would say that the *Chilean Reefer* spoiled our chance of getting the raider as she was bound to attack the convoy that night.[15]

The *Gneisenau* made good her escape and rejoined the *Scharnhorst*, and on 18 March, the two battleships refuelled once more from the *Uckermark* and *Ermland*. During the early morning of 19 March, the battleships fell into line and, at a speed of 23 knots, set a course for Brest. Lütjens now faced the problem of reaching the French port. As far as he was aware, HMS *Malaya* was in the vicinity of the Cape Verde Islands, HMS *Rodney* was lurking somewhere in the Atlantic, and British forces from Gibraltar were at sea. Even *B-Dienst* could offer the admiral little by way of information. As such, the best that Lütjens could hope to do was to make the final, most dangerous stage of the journey by night, where the darkness would afford his ships some measure of protection. With this, he hoped to reach the approaches to Brest at dawn on the 22nd.

If Lütjens was uncertain as to the disposition of the Royal Navy, the British were equally unsure as to the whereabouts of the German raiders, with the Admiralty setting in train a wide range of movements in an effort to head them off. Nothing was heard of the German ships until 20 March. HMS *Renown* was by now in the company of the aircraft carrier *Ark Royal* and was sailing towards the Bay of Biscay as part of the Admiralty's movements to cut off the German raiders. During the course of 20 March, a patrolling aircraft from the *Ark Royal* sighted the tankers *Polykarb*, *San Casimiro*, and *Bianca*, which had been captured by *Gneisenau* and *Scharnhorst* five days earlier. *Renown* altered course and soon intercepted two of the tankers (the *Bianca* and *San Casimiro*) both of which immediately scuttled when the *Renown* came into view. William Cain was a member of the *Renown*'s crew who was hastily assembled into a boarding party, which was mustered in the hope of recapturing the tankers:

> The Germans, unfortunately, had this habit of scuttling their ships and had done so much of it in two wars that they were very proficient at it. The boarding parties were trained in what to do; the engine room section makes its way down to the boiler and engine rooms and shuts off the sea cocks if they have not been damaged. To scuttle a ship one method is to open the sea cocks wide and snap the wheels off with a hammer. It is then impossible to close them so the sea rushes in until she sinks. Another method, though not commonly used by the Germans, is explosive charges with which a hole is blown in the ship's bottom.[16]

In both cases, the German prize crews were too fast for the boarding parties and there was no hope of reclaiming the two tankers. Nevertheless, the boarding parties did achieve the rescue of British prisoners and captured the German crews. A total of forty-six British merchant seamen were rescued along with their erstwhile captors, many of whom were from the *Scharnhorst*. From the interrogation of the German prize crews, those aboard the *Renown* were at last able to learn first-hand why the two German ships had fled during their encounter a year earlier off Narvik. According to the head of the engineering department aboard the battlecruiser, Captain A. W. Gray, 'On interrogation the sailors from *Scharnhorst* replied that the Germans imagined that the other two battle-cruisers, *Hood* and *Repulse*, would obviously be in company with us and they did not appreciate [that] *Renown* was by herself'.[17] The third tanker, *Polykarb*, evaded recapture and succeeded in reaching Bordeaux.

While the transfer of merchant men and prize crews from the tankers to the *Renown* was underway a Fairey Fulmar from *Ark Royal* appeared overhead with its radio out of action and began to flash an urgent message. At 6.30 p.m., Admiral James Somerville, the commander of Force H, reported to the Admiralty that an aircraft from the *Ark Royal* had sighted the *Gneisenau* and *Scharnhorst* at 5.30 p.m. at 46° 50'N, 21° 25'W and that the two ships were sailing on a course of 000° at 20 knots. At the time, *Renown* was 120 miles south-east of the reported location and had less than half of her full fuel capacity remaining. Having already sent his destroyers back to Gibraltar to refuel, Somerville decided to press on in the forlorn hope of closing the distance between the *Renown* and the German ships.

The hopes of another aircraft from *Ark Royal* establishing contact with the battleships was poor as darkness was descending, nevertheless, an attempt was made when Lieutenant-Commander Tillard and Lieutenant Somerville argued that as they had first spotted the *Scharnhorst* and *Gneisenau* then they should be the ones to take a Fulmar and to search the sea once more and try to re-establish contact. After an hour on patrol, nothing was sighted and the Fulmar landed back on the *Ark Royal*.[18]

Throughout the night, Force H pressed on into the Bay of Biscay, but dawn on 21 March would bring disappointment. The Admiralty ordered three destroyers of the 5th Flotilla at Plymouth to rendezvous with Force H, but the coming of daylight saw thick fog descend on the area of operations, nullifying any hopes of re-establishing contact with the German vessels. With this, the Admiralty ordered Force H to return to Gibraltar.

While the fog of 21 March nullified the hopes of the British regaining contact with the *Gneisenau* and *Scharnhorst*, the fog was not exactly welcomed by those aboard the German ships either. A Luftwaffe escort was scheduled to arrive over the battleships at noon but the fog prevented the aircraft from getting airborne. It was not until 4.30 p.m. that visibility improved sufficiently for three Heinkel He 115s to provide an escort. At 7 p.m., the torpedo boats *Jaguar* and *Iltis*, having sailed from Brest, rendezvoused with the battleships whereupon they provided an anti-submarine escort. The remainder of the voyage proceeded without incident, and at 3 a.m. on 22 March, the escort provided by the *Iltis* and *Jaguar* was bolstered by destroyers from the flotilla stationed at Brest. Four hours later, the entrance of the port finally loomed into sight. Entering the harbour, *Scharnhorst* berthed alongside the Quai de la Ninon where the battleship *Dunkerque* had once moored. Meanwhile, the *Gneisenau*, in need of minor repair work, was installed in the No. 8 dry dock.

Operation Berlin was at an end. The cruise had lasted sixty days and saw the battleships cover 17,800 miles, a record for German capital ships. During the course of the operation, twenty-two merchant vessels totalling 113,690 gross registered tons were sunk or captured. Two days following the arrival of the battleships, the *Uckermark* and *Ermland* docked at La Pallice, an outer port of La Rochelle that had been constructed to accommodate large oceangoing passenger liners. Following arriving at Brest, aboard *Gneisenau*, Lütjens and his staff set about packing their bags in preparation for a return to Germany where they had orders to join the battleship *Bismarck* for a new operation.

Above left: Weather-beaten, *Gneisenau* entering Brest. (*Author's Collection*)

Above right: *Gneisenau* entering Brest at the conclusion of Operation Berlin. (*Author's Collection*)

8
At Brest

Having arrived at Brest and docked alongside the Quai de la Ninon, all aboard the *Scharnhorst* was not well, particularly with regards the ship's super-heaters. Although her engineers had kept the ship going throughout the two months that the ship had spent in the Atlantic, a great deal of work was required to keep them operational. At the same time, it was proposed that the *Kriegsmarine*'s newest battleship, the *Bismarck*, would break out into the Atlantic in order to raid Allied merchant shipping and that she should be joined by *Scharnhorst* and *Gneisenau*. The proposed time for the sortie of the *Bismarck* was mid-April. On this timeline, owing to the timescale anticipated to enact repairs on the super-heaters, *Scharnhorst* would not be ready to join the *Bismarck* with the result that for the first time, *Gneisenau* and *Scharnhorst* would be separated as *Gneisenau* would join *Bismarck* on her raiding sortie known as Operation Rheinübung, leaving *Scharnhorst* at Brest.

On 28 March, an RAF photo-reconnaissance Spitfire overflew Brest, revealing to the British the presence of the two German battleships in the French port. Brest was favourably located on the French Atlantic coast for air attacks from Great Britain, and the two ships were now exposed to a continual onslaught from bombers and torpedo aircraft. The first attack commenced on the night of 30–31 March and was launched by more than 100 aircraft, but they failed to score any hits. A similar-sized force returned four nights later but found it difficult to locate the ships.

On the night of 4–5 April, fifty bombers returned to Brest. On this occasion, the Continental Hotel where the German naval staff and many of the ship's officers were quartered was hit just as the evening meal was being served. There are no records of the casualties that were inflicted, although the casualty figures are thought to have been considerable. Again, like on the previous occasion, most of the bombs that were dropped missed the port and fell on the town of Brest. During the course of the raid, however, one 500-lb armour-piercing bomb narrowly missed the *Gneisenau* but caught the dry dock in which the ship was lying. As a result of this, the ship was taken out of dry dock and was subsequently anchored in the harbour.[1]

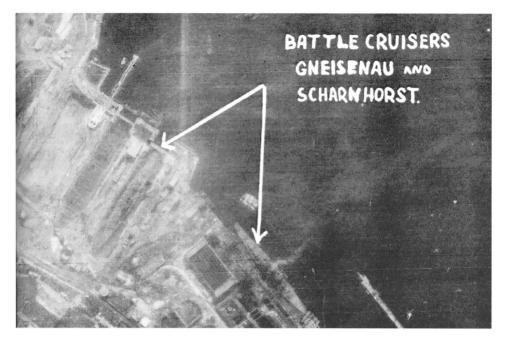

A RAF reconnaissance photograph showing *Scharnhorst* and *Gneisenau* at Brest. (*Author's Collection*)

(*Author's Collection*)

Above left: A weather-beaten *Scharnhorst* alongside in Brest following Operation Berlin. (*Author's Collection*)

Above right: Gneisenau in a dry dock at Brest. (*Author's Collection*)

In terms of resources, these attempts by RAF Bomber Command to sink the ships proved costly. During a week-long campaign against the ships, more than 250 sorties had been flown and four aircraft were lost for the result of one bomb landing close to *Gneisenau*. The onus now shifted from Bomber Command to Coastal Command. While they were at Brest, the two ships were subjected to regular overflights by reconnaissance aircraft. So it was that the movement of the *Gneisenau* from the No. 8 dry dock into the harbour was noticed. Reconnaissance overflights showed *Scharnhorst* to be moored alongside the harbour quay and to be well protected by anti-torpedo nets. *Gneisenau*, however, moored in the inner harbour, was considered vulnerable to a torpedo attack.

An attack was immediately ordered for the following day, 6 April, shortly after dawn. The task of carrying out the raid fell to 22 Squadron flying Bristol Beauforts. The squadron was operating a detachment of aircraft from St. Eval having moved to the southwest from its home airfield at North Coates in Lincolnshire. Only six aircraft were available to conduct a torpedo attack against the battleship, and only three of the aircrews were torpedo-trained. The plan which was therefore decided upon was that an attack would be launched in which the aircraft would attack in two formations of three; three aircraft would bomb the anti-torpedo nets before the second wave carrying torpedoes would conduct the main attack against the *Gneisenau*.[2]

The three pilots chosen to conduct the torpedo attack were Flying Officer John Hyde, Sergeant H. Camp, and Flying Officer Kenneth Campbell. The crew of the Beauforts knew that Brest was well defended and that the harbour benefitted from the natural protection of the surrounding hills. Reconnaissance photographs showed *Gneisenau* to be moored 500 yards from the harbour mole, which meant that the crews would have to deliver their torpedoes with extreme accuracy and, following releasing their weapons, the pilots would have to conduct a steep turn away from the surrounding high ground.

The raid got off to an inauspicious start. The six aircraft were scheduled to take off around 4.30 a.m. but heavy overnight rain at St Eval turned the airfield into a swamp and prevented two of the bomb-carrying Beauforts from getting airborne. The one bomb-carrying aircraft that did manage to get airborne became disorientated in the poor weather conditions with the aircrew's navigation not helped by the fact that it was still dark meaning that landmarks, which would have been used for navigation were extremely difficult to locate.

The torpedo-carrying aircraft fared little better; one aircraft became lost in the heavy rain while the other two lost contact with each other in the misty conditions over the sea. Unaware of the issues being faced by the other aircraft, the Beaufort piloted by Campbell, and crewed by Sergeant Jimmy Scott (observer), Sergeant William Mulliss (wireless operator), and Flight Sergeant Ralph Hillman (air gunner), pressed on towards the planned rendezvous point a short distance from Brest harbour.[3]

Campbell's aircraft reached the rendezvous point as it was starting to become light. With no signs of the other Beauforts, Campbell decided to circle at the rendezvous point and watch for visible signs of the bomb explosions from the first wave. As 6 a.m. approached, there was still no sign of any other aircraft. Knowing that he and his crew would soon lose the cover afforded by the murky dawn as the sky became lighter with each passing minute, and not knowing what had happened to any other aircraft, Campbell decided to press on with the attack alone.

Inside the harbour, *Gneisenau* was well protected. The ship was secured alongside the wall on the north shore of the harbour, protected by the stone mole that curved around from the west. On the rising ground behind the battleship stood a battery of anti-aircraft guns with additional batteries clustered thickly across the surrounding landscape, which encircled the outer harbour. In the outer harbour, near the mole, three heavily armed anti-aircraft ships were moored. It was against this gauntlet of defences that Campbell and his crew pressed home their attack.

As Campbell took the Beaufort down to sea level, the aircraft was greeted by a wall of anti-aircraft fire as the gunners sighted the lone torpedo bomber approaching at low level. As it crossed the mole, the Beaufort passed the three anti-aircraft ships below the height of their masts as Campbell hugged the waves as closely as he dared. The seconds that ticked by felt like an eternity as the aircraft ran in towards its target. In the final seconds of the run-in, Campbell climbed to 50 feet, just high enough to release the torpedo at minimum range. As soon as the torpedo had been released, the Beaufort embarked on a steep banking turn to port towards the safety of the cloud base above. The run-in and torpedo release had been textbook, however, as the Beaufort banked away and gained height in an effort to avoid the high ground and to seek the shelter of the clouds, it presented an easy target to the German gunners.[4] The aircraft was bracketed by anti-aircraft fire and heavily pummelled whereupon it plummeted into the harbour. The four airmen stood no chance of escaping and were all killed in the impact.

As the Beaufort crashed into the harbour, the torpedo found its mark, hitting *Gneisenau* where it caused severe damage below the waterline and damaged the starboard propeller shaft. In the wake of the attack, the ship was taken back into dry dock to have the damage repaired. Nine months would pass before the damage was fully repaired. In the wake of the attack, the bodies of Campbell, Scott, Mulliss, and Hillmann were retrieved from the harbour and buried with full military honours. When news of the lone attack filtered through to London by way of the French Resistance, it was announced that Campbell was to be posthumously awarded the Victoria Cross, Britain's highest award for gallantry.[5]

Despite the damage inflicted on *Gneisenau* by Campbell and his crew, the raids by the RAF against the two ships at Brest continued. Between April and September, on average, 100 sorties per month were launched against the two ships. Between October and the end of the year, this figure dropped to seventy-five. The number of bombs dropped also fell. In August 1941, Bomber Command dropped 4,242 tons of bombs against the two ships at Brest. By February 1942, this figure had decreased to 1,011 tons.[6] Nevertheless, the sorties against *Scharnhorst* and *Gneisenau* amounted to 10 per cent of Bomber Command's efforts, tying up three squadrons for bombing operations and a fourth for mine-laying operations.

Daylight raids against the ships, it was estimated, incurred 20 per cent losses while losses at night were negligible, but so too were the results. While night after night Bomber Command returned to Brest to bomb *Scharnhorst* and *Gneisenau*, referred to as 'Salmon' and 'Gluck' by the airmen, Sir Richard Persie, the commander-in-chief of Bomber Command protested to Sir Charles Portal, the chief of the air staff, that his pilots were wasting hundreds of tons of explosives on a task for which his aircrews were not trained, nor equipped, to undertake. Yet air attacks on enemy warships had always been an obvious, vital strategic role for Bomber Command to fulfil.[7]

Flying Officer Kenneth Campbell, VC.
(*Aircrew Remembered*)

Despite this, however, the journey from the bomber bases in Britain to Brest was relatively short and, in conducting operations against *Scharnhorst* and *Gneisenau*, aircrews gained experience of being subjected to anti-aircraft fire and searchlights; this experience, alongside the small casualties incurred, meant these operations proved useful training. The argument against the operations was that for little return, the sorties diverted precious aircraft from what was viewed as the more important mission of bombing Germany. The damage inflicted on Germany at this stage of the war by Bomber Command was relatively small in any case.

Unknown to the crews of the *Scharnhorst* and *Gneisenau* was that they were part of an inter-service battle between the RAF and Royal Navy. Throughout the course of the war, the Royal Navy waged an unceasing battle against the Air Ministry for the largest share of Britain's industrial resources and for the greatest possible number of long-range aircraft that were being constructed. While the RAF wanted longer-range aircraft in order to be able to strike targets deeper inside the Third Reich, the Royal Navy lobbied for aircraft for reconnaissance and anti-submarine operations. In this inter-service struggle, both parties to the dispute stooped to unseemly depths in the pursuit of their cases.

By insisting that Bomber Command should waste effort against the *Scharnhorst* and *Gneisenau* and then against the impenetrable U-boat pens of the French ports, the Royal Navy diminished its credibility as a judge of the effective use of air power. Such was the dispute that Admiral Whitworth would write at the height of the controversy, 'Our fight with the Air Ministry becomes more and more fierce as the war proceeds. It is a much more savage one than our war with the Huns, which is very unsatisfactory and such a waste of effort'.[8]

The request of the Admiralty that Bomber Command be employed against German naval forces was not one which had been well received at the Air Ministry with Portal writing on 1 March 1941, 'A very high proportion of [our] bomber effort will be required to pull the Admiralty out of the mess they have got into…'[9] Nevertheless, the air raids continued.

Faced with the almost daily attacks by the RAF, the Germans went to a great deal of trouble to deceive the British as to where the battleships were. The battleships were draped with camouflage netting in what was perhaps an obvious defensive measure. More ingenious was the notion of constructing a decoy village on the roofs of some buildings to deceive the bombers as to their location while the French training cruiser *Jeanne d'Arc* was embellished with wood and canvas until from the air, she assumed a passable likeness to *Scharnhorst*. In addition to these measures, devices were installed to create artificial fog to blanket the area hiding the ships from view.

While *Scharnhorst* and *Gneisenau* were holed up at Brest, late May 1941 saw the *Bismarck* accompanied by the heavy cruiser *Prinz Eugen* embark on Operation Rheinübung, under the command of Lütjens. The sortie was to have seen *Bismarck* and *Prinz Eugen* raid Allied commerce as *Scharnhorst* and *Gneisenau* had done during Operation Berlin. Sighted as they transited the Kattegat, the two ships were spotted by a RAF reconnaissance flight as they lay at anchor in a Norwegian fjord before being intercepted in the Denmark Strait during which the *Bismarck* was damaged. Lütjens detached the *Prinz Eugen* to conduct commerce raiding while she, harried by the Royal Navy, attempted to make for Saint

Gneisenau draped with camouflage netting while in dry dock at Brest. (*Author's Collection*)

Nazaire. Finally cornered by the Royal Navy, the *Bismarck* was sunk on 27 May 1941. *Prinz Eugen*, meanwhile, ventured out into the North Atlantic but before any merchant shipping was located, defects developed in the ship's engines forcing a curtailment of the operation. At 7.30 p.m. on 1 June, the ship entered Brest harbour and was taken into dry dock.[10] A month after having arrived at Brest, the *Prinz Eugen* sustained considerable damage when she was struck by a bomb. Such was the damage inflicted on the ship that she was put out of commission for the remainder of the year.

As a result of the continual air raids, it was found prudent to quarter as many crew members ashore as could be spared, first in a hotel at Roscoll and later in barracks at Landerneau, La Roche. Quartered away from the ships, these crew members were comparatively safe from the bombing. As an added bonus for would-be leave-goers, the main railway line to Paris passed nearby.

While she was undergoing repairs, miraculously it would seem, *Scharnhorst* had emerged from all of the air raids unscathed. With the repairs to the ship's machinery completed in July, the decision was taken to move the ship from Brest as her luck would not hold and eventually she would be hit. Consequently, it was decided to move her to La Pallice with the move scheduled for 21 July; that day, the ship weighed anchor and departed Brest. Responding perfectly to the helm, the ship worked up to 30 knots without any issues and conducted satisfactory gunnery trials before anchoring at La Pallice.

La Pallice had been chosen as an anchorage because of the shoals offshore which offered a measure of protection and reduced the number of escort vessels required to protect the ship at anchor. Conversely, the port was disastrously lacking in anti-aircraft defences. For *Scharnhorst*, trouble arrived on 24 July as she lay at anchor. Commendably, it had taken the RAF a very short time to locate the ship at her new anchorage. At noon,

Two Halifaxes over the naval dockyard towards the dry docks where *Scharnhorst* and *Gneisenau* are berthed (top right) harbour during a daylight raid on the port during 1941. A smokescreen can be seen to be developing over the dry docks. Middle right, a stick of bombs can be seen to have exploded inland from their intended target, the *Prinz Eugen*.

several squadrons of RAF bombers arrived over the French coast to target the German ships at anchor. Fifteen Handley Page Halifax bombers of Nos 35 and 76 Squadrons flew to La Pallice to attack *Scharnhorst* at her moorings while the other squadrons flew to Brest as planned to attack *Gneisenau* and *Prinz Eugen*. Arriving over La Pallice, the fifteen Halifaxes commenced bombing from altitudes of between 10,000 and 12,000 feet.[11] Five bombs hit the starboard side of the ship simultaneously in an almost straight line parallel to the centreline. Two of the bombs that struck the ship were 500-lb high-explosive bombs while the other three were 1,000-lb semi-armour-piercing bombs.

One 500-lb bomb detonated abeam the conning tower just forward of the starboard 5.9-inch turret. The bomb passed through the upper and middle decks before

Inside a Drh LC/34 turret looking towards the three guns from the back of the turret. (*bunkersite.com*)

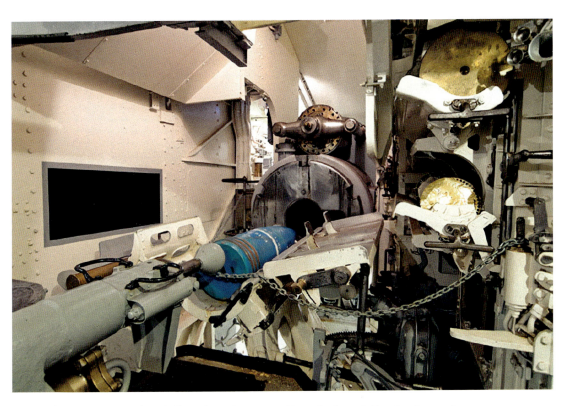

The centre gun with a shell ready to be rammed into the barrel. (*bunkersite.com*)

The position of one of the turret's observers nestled between two gun barrels in the front of the turret. (*bunkersite.com*)

The turret commander's position, a risen platform with different lines of communication to the gun operators and various other positions. (*bunkersite.com*)

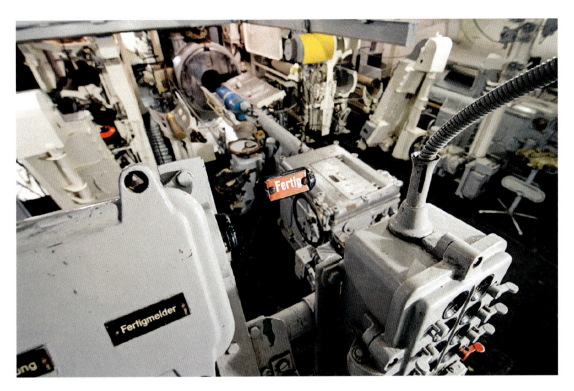

The view of the turret from the commander's platform. (*bunkersite.com*)

The inside of a SK C/28 turret.

Gneisenau   Scharnhorst

The crests of the *Scharnhorst* and *Gneisenau*. (*Author's Collection*)

Taken in July 1939, *Gneisenau* is seen here refuelling from the tanker *Westerwald* off the coast of Madeira during her cruise into the Atlantic. (*Author's Collection*)

Above: Scharnhorst photographed quite possibly on 20 April 1939, with the ship decorated for Hitler's birthday. (*Author's Collection*)

Right: Looking down from the bridge of the *Scharnhorst* from the bridge while the ship is at Wilhelmshaven. (*Author's Collection*)

Above left: Hitler's motorcade in front of the *Scharnhorst*, 1 April 1939 while the ship is at Wilhelmshaven for the launch of the *Tirpitz*. (Chris Thornton)

Above right: (Chris Thornton)

Scharnhorst amidships, 1 April 1939. (*World War Photos*)

Taken at Wilhelmshaven on the day of the launch of the *Tirpitz*, this photograph shows the ceremony held on board the *Scharnhorst* in which Hitler bestowed the rank of *Großadmiral* upon Raeder, making him the first individual to hold the rank since Alfred von Tirpitz. A *Panzerschiffe* can be seen in the background. (*Author's Collection*)

Above: Hitler aboard *Scharnhorst*. (*Chris Thornton*)

Right: Hitler and *Kapitän zur See* Otto Ciliax on board the *Scharnhorst*. (*Chris Thornton*)

Hitler aboard the *Scharnhorst* surveying the view out over Wilhelmshaven from the rear of the superstructure. (*Chris Thornton*)

At the beginning of July 1939, *Scharnhorst* was taken in hand and manoeuvred into the 40,000-ton floating dry dock at the *Westwerft* for a refit that saw her straight stem replaced by an Atlantic bow. (*Author's Collection*)

Gneisenau at anchor in October 1939. Note that the tops of the main battery turrets have been painted red in an effort to facilitate identification by friendly aircraft. (*Author's Collection*)

Scharnhorst at Kiel during the spring of 1940. (*Simon Matthews*)

Above: Scharnhorst during the autumn of 1940. Note the unusual Baltic camouflage scheme that adorns the ship. (*Author's Collection*)

Gneisenau during Operation Berlin. One of the ship's 5.9-inch turrets is in the foreground. (*NH 83099-KN, US Naval History and Heritage Command Center*)

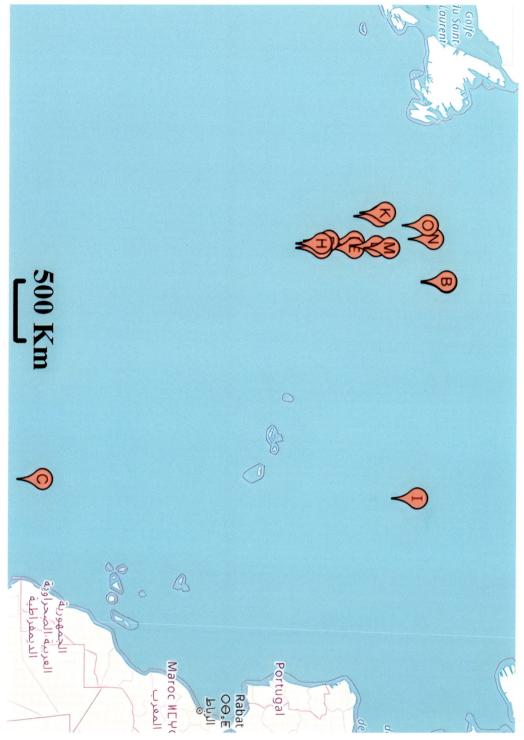

The location of ships sunk during Operation Berlin. Key: A: *Kantara, Trelawny, Lustrous, A.D. Huff*. B: *Harlesden*. C: *Marathon*. D: *Athelfoam*. E: *British Strength, Rio Dorado*. F: *Simnia*. G: *Bianca*. H: *San Casimiro*. I: *Polykarp*. J: *Empire Industry*. K: *Granli*. L: *Mangkai*. M: *Myson, Royal Crown, Silverfir, Sardinian Prince*. N: *Demeterton*. O: *Chilean Reefer*. (*Author's Collection*)

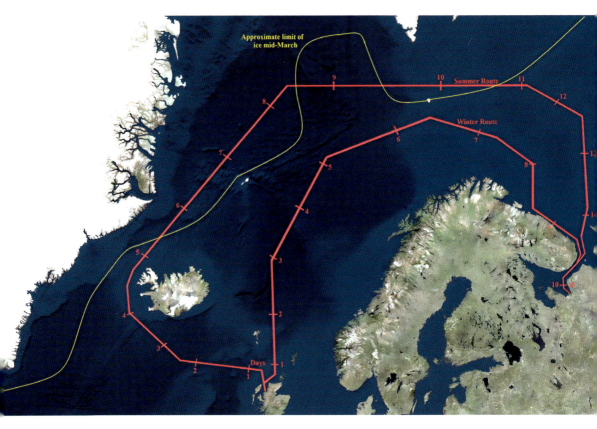

The route taken by the Arctic Convoys. (*Author's Collection*)

Turret 'Caesar' as it stands today on the site of the Austrått fortress. Now a museum following being decommissioned in 1968, the site is one of the most complete examples of Second World War German coastal batteries in existence. (*Lars Erik Brattås*)

A SK C/28 gun turret from the *Gneisenau* in position at the Stevnsfort, which was closed in 2000 and reopened in 2008 as a museum.

Above left: The signalman's position on the main mast.

Above right: A single SK C/28 gun of the starboard side. The position of the gun shows that it was not trained on any of Fraser's ships when *Scharnhorst* sank.

Above: The ship's torpedo tubes with torpedoes still in place.

Below: The port rudder.

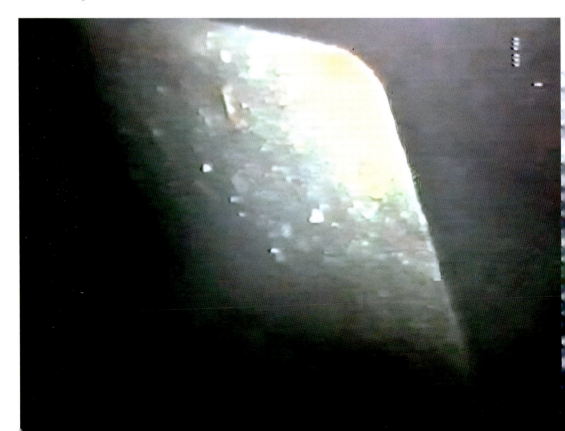

The stern anchor still in position.

The memorial stone to the *Scharnhorst* located just outside of Wilhelmshaven. (*Philipp Jakob*)

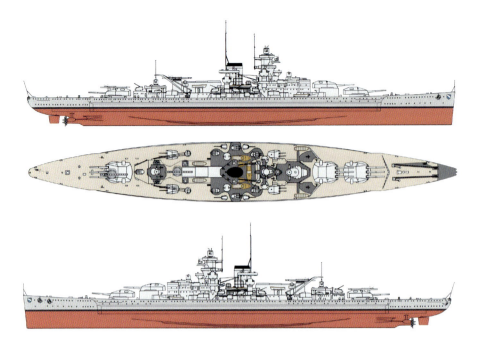

Scharnhorst as she looked on the day of her commissioning, 7 January 1939. Note that at the time the ship had been completed with a straight stem and the mainmast on the funnel. In addition to this, the ship was completed with a catapult atop turret 'Caesar'. (*Antonio Bonomi*)

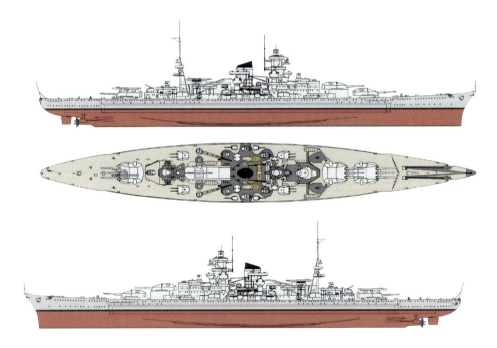

Scharnhorst as she appeared in August 1939 following undergoing modifications at the *Kriegsmarinewerft*, which saw the straight stem replaced by an 'Atlantic bow'. The anchors were repositioned on the deck, while the mainmast was moved further aft as a raked funnel cap was installed. An enlarged hanger was also fitted. (*Antonio Bonomi*)

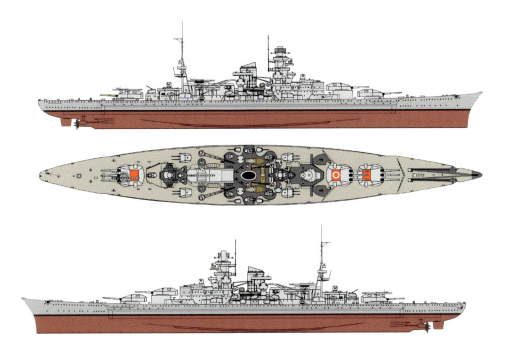

Scharnhorst as she appeared during her second round of sea trials, conducted after being re-floated from the *Kriegsmarinewerft*, which began on 2 September 1939. (*Antonio Bonomi*)

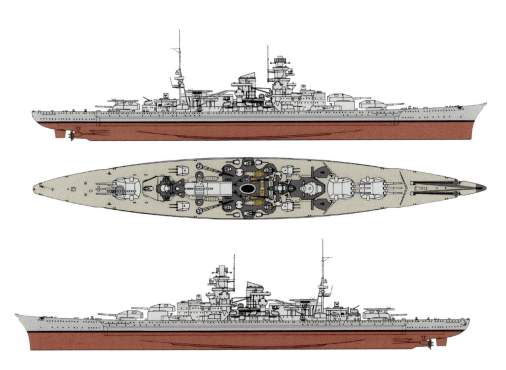

Scharnhorst as she appeared during her first war patrol in late November 1939 during which HMS *Rawalpindi* was sunk. (*Antonio Bonomi*)

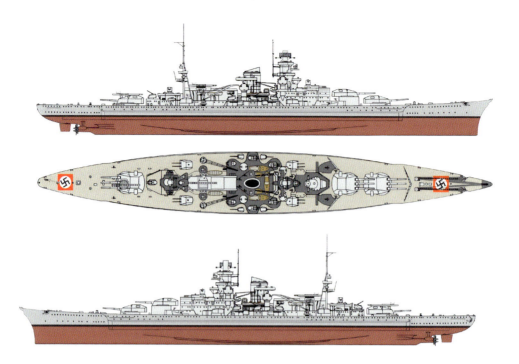

Scharnhorst as she appeared in February 1940 when she participated in Operation Nordmark. (*Antonio Bonomi*)

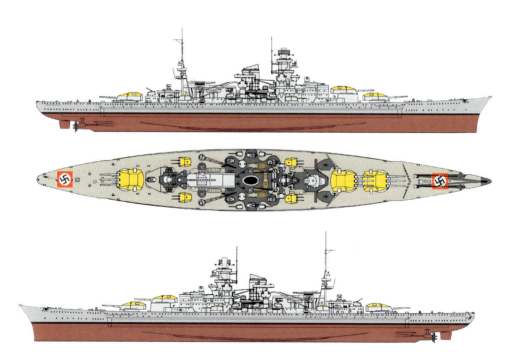

Ahead of Operation Weserübung in April 1940, the tops of the main battery and secondary armament turrets were painted yellow as a means of recognition from the air. (*Antonio Bonomi*)

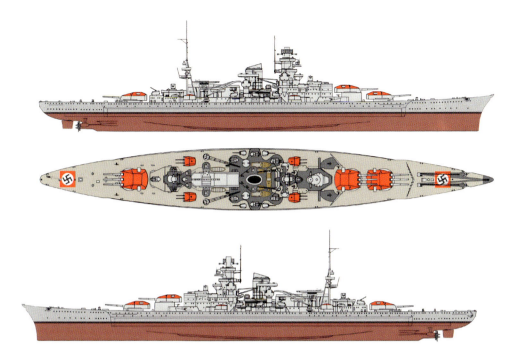

The yellow air recognition marks (*Fliegersichtzeichen*) on the tops of the turrets were painted red by the launch of Operation Weserübung. (*Antonio Bonomi*)

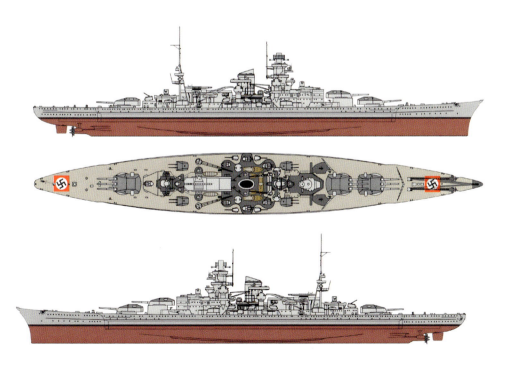

By the time of Operation Juno, which resulted in the sinking of HMS *Glorious* in June 1940, the red *Fliegersichtzeichen* had been replaced with dark grey. (*Antonio Bonomi*)

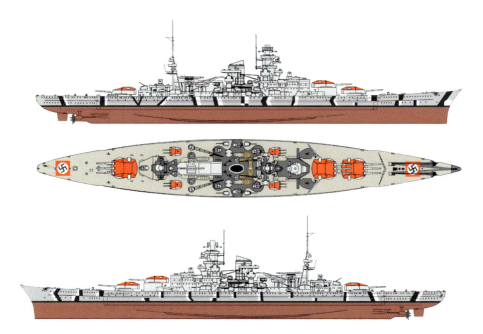

Having returned to Kiel following being damaged during Operation Juno, *Scharnhorst* underwent six months of repairs. On 21 November 1940, with the repair work completed, the ship sailed to Gotenhafen to conduct a series of sea trials in the Baltic, where *Scharnhorst* was repainted with an almost unknown Baltic camouflage scheme. (*Antonio Bonomi*)

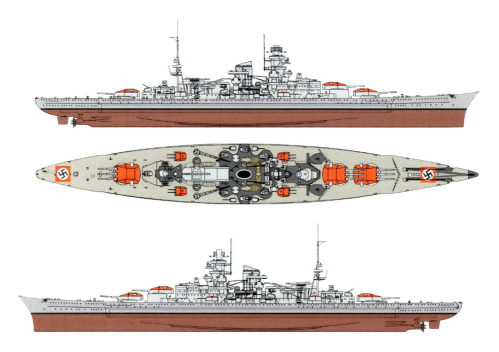

Scharnhorst as she appeared in December 1940 when she left the Baltic and sailed to Kiel in preparation for Operation Berlin. With *Gneisenau* damaged by severe storms, the operation was postponed whereupon *Scharnhorst* sailed to Gotenhafen. The Baltic camouflage on the hull had been painted over with outboard grey while the ship retained red *Fliegersichtzeichen* on her turrets. (*Antonio Bonomi*)

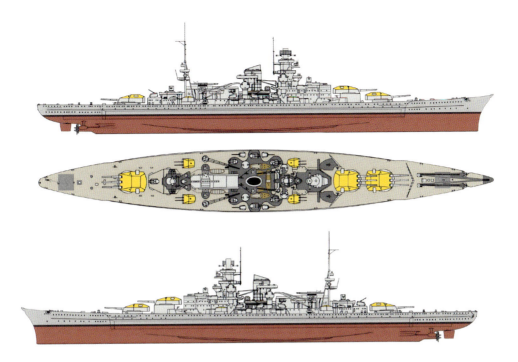

Scharnhorst as she appeared when she embarked upon Operation Berlin in January 1941. Note the *Fliegersichtzeichen* on the turrets have been painted yellow. (*Antonio Bonomi*)

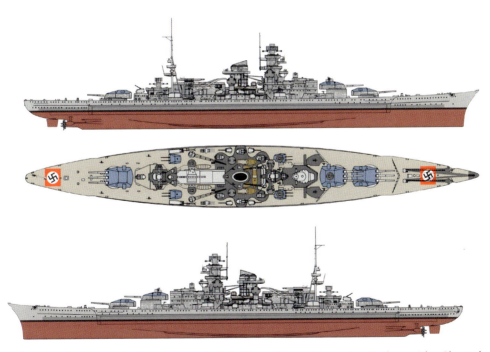

Following the long period spent at anchor at Brest, during Operation Cerberus (the Channel Dash), *Scharnhorst* was given an irregular paint scheme. Note the dark grey mottle scheme on the upperworks while the turret tops have been painted blue-grey. (*Antonio Bonomi*)

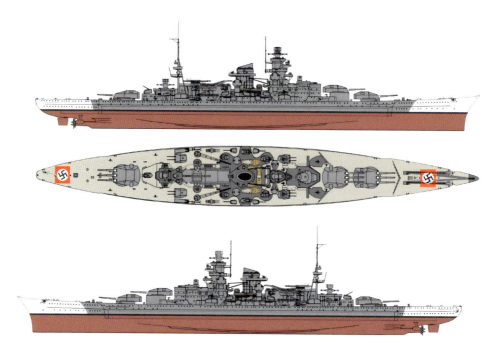

Following returning to Germany during Operation Cerberus, *Scharnhorst* underwent a period of repair and refitting in the Baltic before being deployed to Norway in March 1943, where she joined other German units including the *Tirpitz*. This scheme shows how *Scharnhorst* appeared between March and July 1943. (*Antonio Bonomi*)

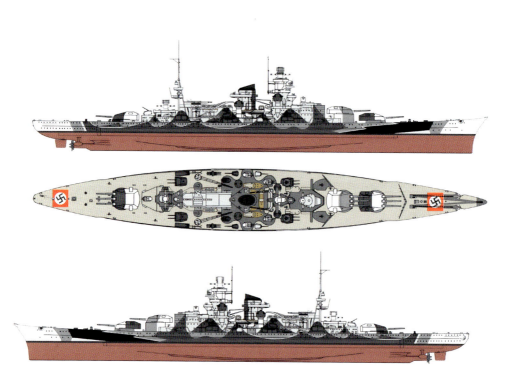

From July 1943 through to her sinking at the Battle of North Cape on Boxing Day 1943, *Scharnhorst* was painted with this 'dazzle' camouflage scheme intended to break up the outline of the ship and allow her to blend in with the surrounding landscape when at anchor. (*Antonio Bonomi*)

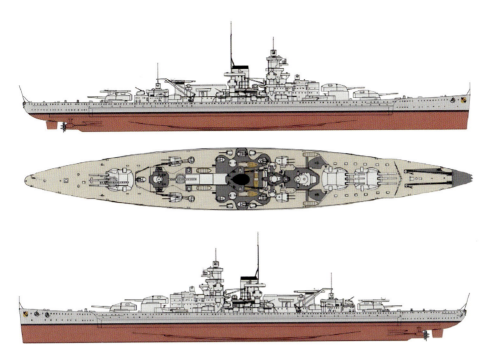

Gneisenau as she appeared on the day of her commissioning, 21 May 1938. Note that the ship has been completed with a straight stem and a straight funnel cap. The mainmast was fixed to the funnel while a catapult was installed atop turret 'Caesar'. Note the ship's crest on the bow. (*Antonio Bonomi*)

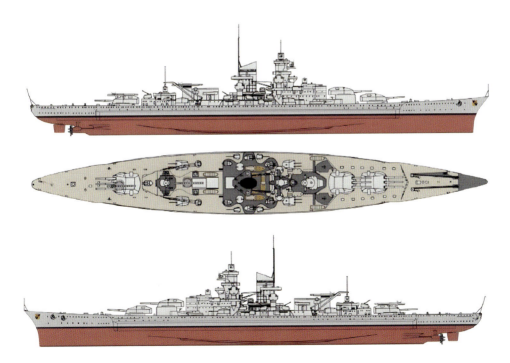

Gneisenau as she appeared by the end of December 1938 ahead of her second round of sea trials in the spring of 1939. In October 1938, the ship was taken in hand for a refit, which saw the straight stem replaced by an 'Atlantic bow', while a new raked funnel cap was fitted while the mainmast was moved aft. (*Antonio Bonomi*)

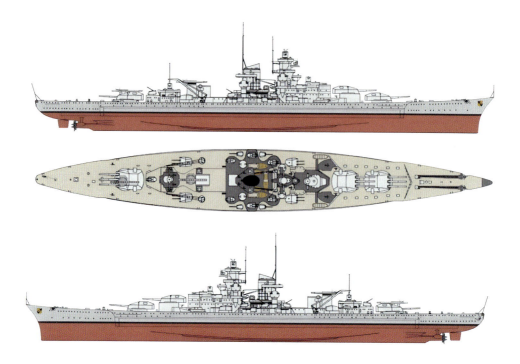

Gneisenau as she appeared at the time of her Atlantic cruise in June–July 1939. In this configuration, it is worth noting that the funnel cap has been reduced in size and that the anchors have now been placed on the main deck. (*Antonio Bonomi*)

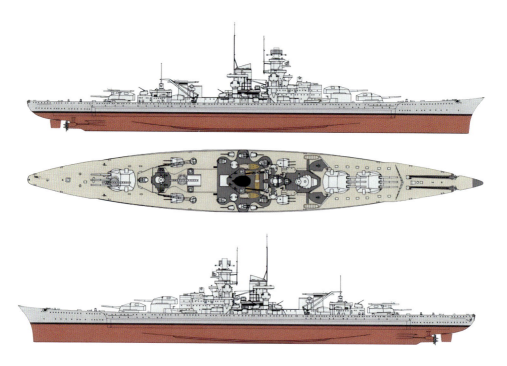

Gneisenau as she appeared at the outbreak of war in September 1939. Note the radar atop the forward superstructure. (*Antonio Bonomi*)

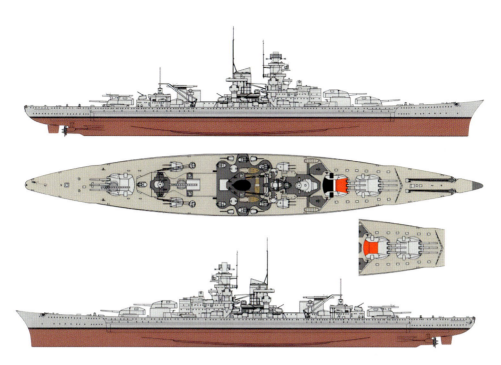

At the end of 1939, trials were conducted to enable the identification of friendly vessels by Luftwaffe aircraft. At first, thought was given to painting the top of turret 'Bruno' with the national flag's colours as had occurred at the end of the First World War and during the Spanish Civil War. This scheme shows turret 'Bruno' painted first with the black, white, and red of Imperial Germany, while the inset shows the turret roof and back painted red in reference to the Swastika. (*Antonio Bonomi*)

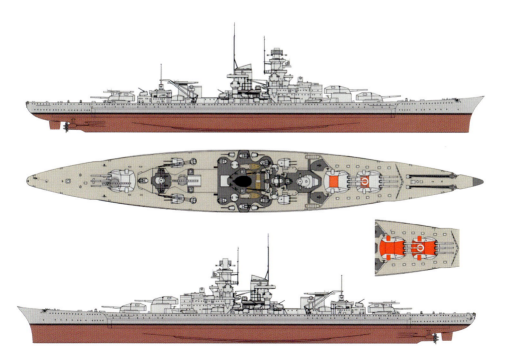

Another image showing the efforts to enable the identification of friendly vessels by the Luftwaffe. In this scheme, turrets 'Anton' and 'Bruno' have both been painted with air recognition markings as a means of identification. (*Antonio Bonomi*)

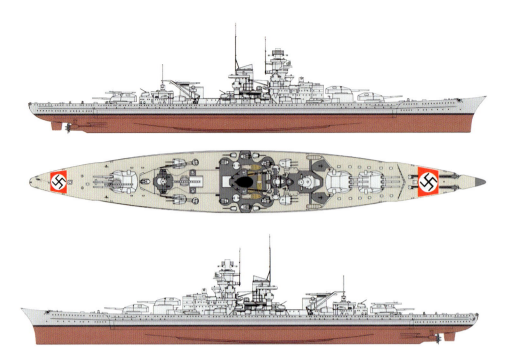

Gneisenau as she appeared at the beginning of 1940. At the time, the admiral's bridge had not been enclosed. The main battery turrets have been repainted grey while Swastikas have been painted on the forecastle and quarterdeck to aid recognition from the air. (*Antonio Bonomi*)

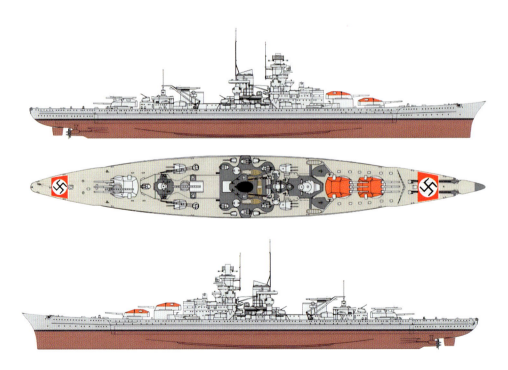

Gneisenau as she appeared in February 1940 when she partook in Operation Nordmark. Note that turrets 'Anton' and 'Bruno' have been painted red in order to aid recognition. (*Antonio Bonomi*)

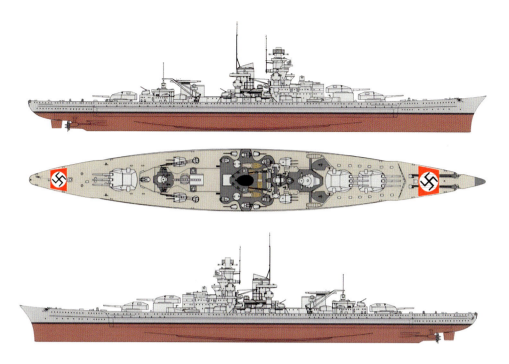

Following Operation Nordmark, in March 1940, the catapult atop turret 'Caesar' was removed. (*Antonio Bonomi*)

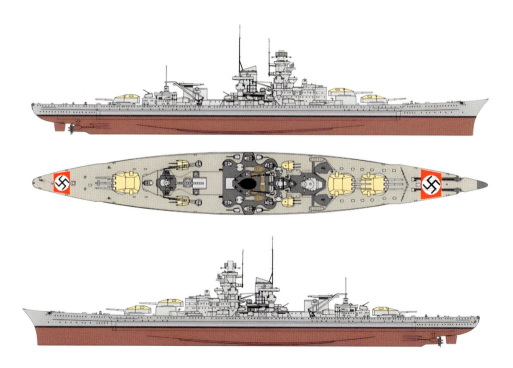

Gneisenau as she appeared in April 1940 at the beginning of Operation Weserübung. Ahead of the launching of the operation, the top of main battery turrets and those of the secondary armament were painted yellow. (*Antonio Bonomi*)

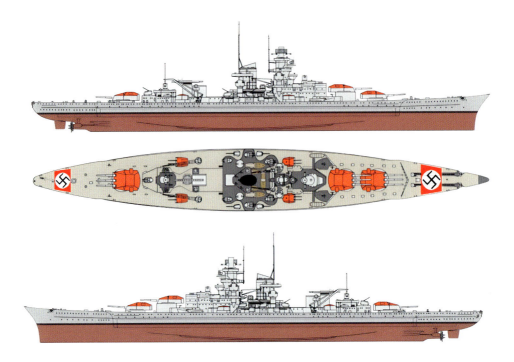

During the course of Operation Weserübung, the roofs of the main and secondary armament turrets were repainted red. This was a strategic move as red more readily allowed Luftwaffe aircrews to identify the ship as friendly as it was noted at the time that some vessels of the Royal Navy had the tops of their turrets painted yellow. (*Antonio Bonomi*)

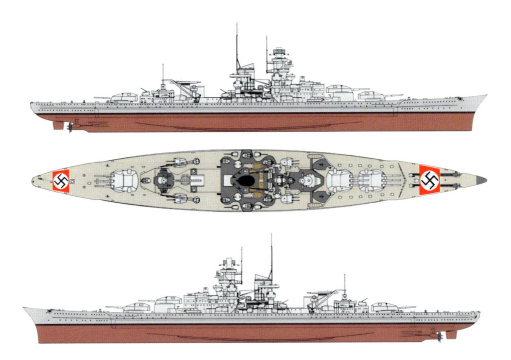

Following Operation Weserübung, *Gneisenau* had her battle damage repaired at Wilhelmshaven. While undergoing repairs, the turrets reverted to grey while the eagle was removed from the stern. (*Antonio Bonomi*)

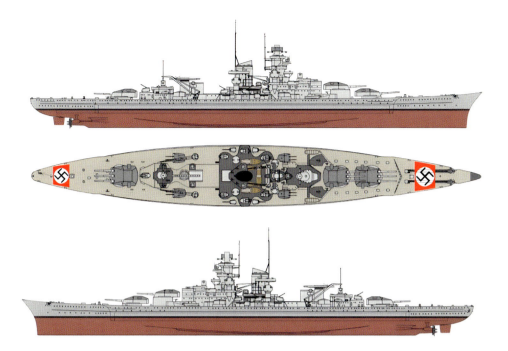

Gneiseau as she appeared during Operation Juno between 4 and 10 June, during which time HMS *Glorious*, *Ardent*, and *Acasta* were sunk. Note the main and secondary battery turrets were painted dark grey. (*Antonio Bonomi*)

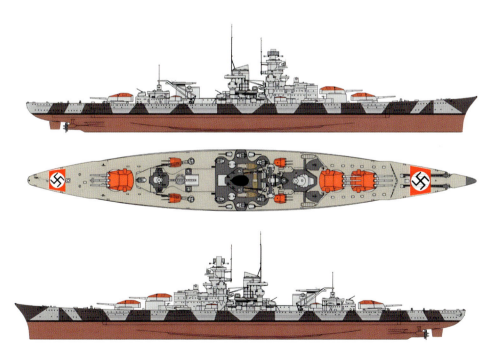

On 20 June, *Gneisenau* was torpedoed by HMS *Clyde*. The torpedo struck the ship just forward of the splinter belt and caused a significant amount of water to pour into the two forward watertight compartments. *Gneisenau* then returned to Trondheim, where she arrived on 21 June. Temporary repairs were conducted ahead of a return to Germany, during which the ship was painted in the camouflage scheme shown, which she carried during her return to Kiel where she arrived on 27 July. (*Antonio Bonomi*)

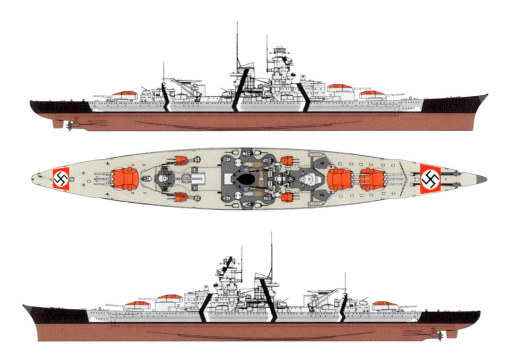

Following undergoing repairs at the *Howaldtswerke* dockyard, on 21 October 1940, *Gneisenau* sailed into the Baltic to conduct a series of sea trials, where the ship was painted with Baltic camouflage. Note how this Baltic camouflage scheme, typical of that which other *Kriegsmarine* vessels were painted, contrasts with that which *Scharnhorst* sported. (*Antonio Bonomi*)

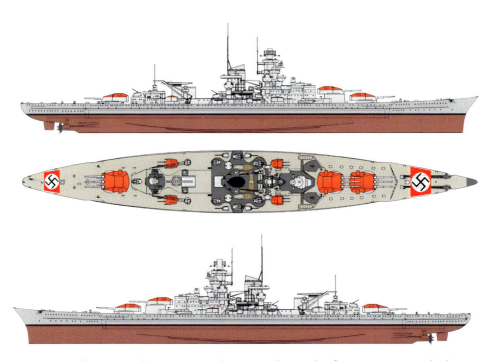

Gneisenau as she appeared on 28 December 1940 during the first attempt to embark upon Operation Berlin. Damage to the ship caused by severe storms resulted in a postponement to the operation while repairs were conducted. (*Antonio Bonomi*)

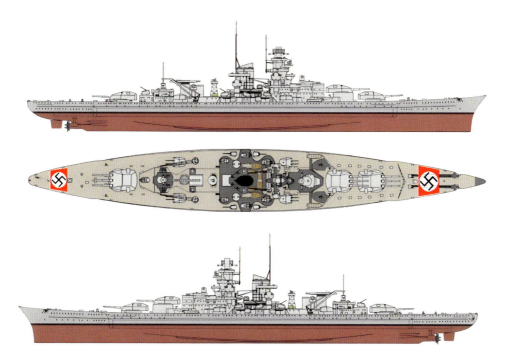

Gneisenau as she appeared on 22 January 1941 when she embarked upon Operation Berlin. Note the 20-mm *Flakvierling* tower which has been fitted between the funnel and hanger. (*Antonio Bonomi*)

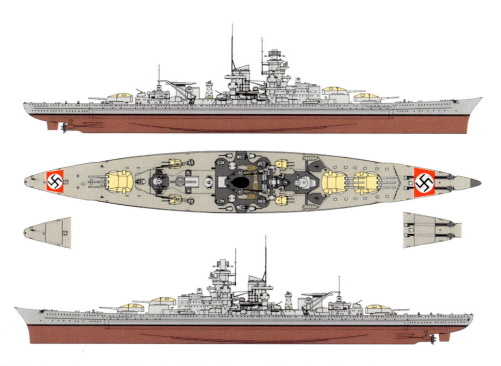

During the early stages of Operation Berlin, the tops of the main and secondary armament turrets were painted yellow while the swastikas fore and aft were covered over. (*Antonio Bonomi*)

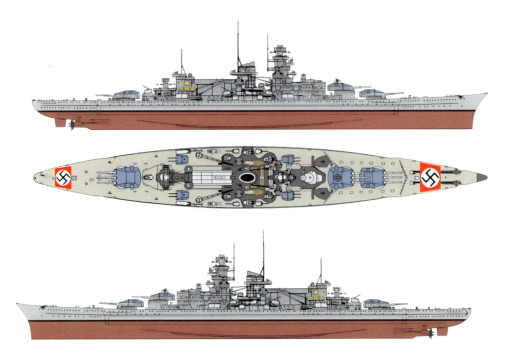

At the conclusion of Operation Berlin, *Gneisenau* and *Scharnhorst* dropped anchor at Brest. *Gneisenau* was taken into the No. 8 dry dock to undergo minor repair work, where she was fitted with an enlarged hanger while the upperworks were painted in a mottled fashion and the turret tops a blue-grey. This is how *Gneisenau* appeared when she was moved from the dry dock on 5 April 1942 and into the harbour. The following day, she would be torpedoed by a Beaufort piloted by Flying Officer Kenneth Campbell. (*Antonio Bonomi*)

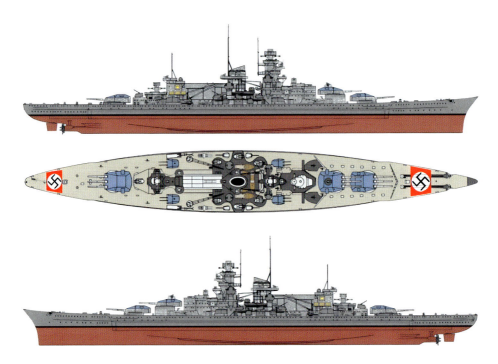

Immediately prior to embarking upon Operation Cerberus, *Gneisenau* was given an adjusted camouflage scheme. The ship retained the mottled upperworks and the blue-grey turrets while the light grey that adorned the hull was overpainted with a dark grey. (*Antonio Bonomi*)

exploding on the armour deck, which remained intact. The first platform deck was torn and buckled significantly in the area of the explosion. The side armour in the vicinity was deflected half an inch with a small hole being punched in it. Rivets that joined the armoured torpedo bulkhead to the main deck were loosened sufficiently to allow water to seep into the ship. The second 500-lb bomb landed just forward of turret 'Caesar' around 10 feet (3 metres) from the edge of the deck on the starboard side. The bomb penetrated two decks before exploding against the main armour deck which was punctured. Several frames suffered splinter damage while the joint between the deck and the torpedo bulkhead also suffered damage. In addition to this, the bomb put the ammunition hoists to the 1.4-inch anti-aircraft guns out of action, heating and plumbing piping beneath the battery and middle decks were damaged and some flooding was observed in the outboard spaces.

Meanwhile, two 1,000-lb bombs struck the starboard side between the 5.9-inch and 3.9-inch guns around 11.5 and 8.5 feet respectively from the edge of the deck. The two bombs penetrated the upper deck before crashing through the lower armour deck and the first platform deck. One of the two bombs was then deflected downward along the torpedo bulkhead and out through the double bottom without exploding while the second passed through the armour belt without exploding. The third 1,000-lb bomb struck the ship slightly abaft turret 'Caesar', where it tore a hole in the upper deck, and passed through the side plating before burying itself in the seabed to be recovered later.

The three 1,000-lb bombs caused a respectable amount of damage despite failing to explode. The restraining walls of the ship's wing tanks were holed by splinters, the number four generator room was flooded, and there was also flooding in the magazine of turret 'Caesar'. The starboard shaft alley, ten watertight spaces, and five additional spaces over the length of 33 feet were flooded. Ammunition hoists for turret 'Caesar' were put out of action, several electrical installations were inoperable, lights extinguished, cabling damaged, and operations in the fire control stations were disrupted.

As a result of the flooding, the ship took on an 8-degree list to starboard, and most of the void tanks used for counter flooding were flooded. Had the 1,000-lb bombs exploded, the damage would have been far more extensive. Trim by the stern increased as a result of the flooding. In all, two members of the ship's company were killed while fifteen others were injured. Subsequently, *Scharnhorst* would undergo work for a period of four months to repair the damage.

While *Scharnhorst* was undergoing repair work, a new radar was installed on the ship while the output for the forward radar was increased to 100 kW. In an effort to increase their efficiency as commerce raiders, *Scharnhorst* and *Gneisenau* were fitted with two triple 20.9-inch torpedo tubes on rotatable mountings from the light cruisers *Leipzig* and *Nürnberg*, which were installed on the upper deck between the aft 4.1-inch and 5.9-inch turrets. No attempt was made, however, to link the torpedo tubes with the fire control system of the ships, rather, a leading torpedo-man used the aiming apparatus on the battery itself to aim the weapon. Furthermore, the anti-aircraft armament of the *Scharnhorst* was considerably increased as additional 0.79-inch anti-aircraft guns were installed.

On 23 December 1941, the British chiefs of staff sat down at a meeting to consider whether the destruction of the major naval units at Brest could be considered primary objectives. Air Commodore Albert Durston, who was in charge of Bomber Command's co-operation with the Royal Navy, subsequently wrote, 'We cannot continue ad infinitum to waste our bomber effort on these ships, nor yet to allow a large part of our bomber force to be held idle at the mere whisper of the departure of one of them'.[12]

To compound matters, on 7 December, Japan entered the war. With the Japanese assault in the Pacific, the resources of the Royal Navy were stretched to their limits. As such, to allow the escape of the *Scharnhorst*, *Gneisenau*, *Prinz Eugen*, and any other German units from Brest would be a strategic disaster. Durston went on to write that 'It is imperative that these ships be reduced to twisted masses of metal, or very severely damaged, in the shortest possible time'. To achieve this, Durston proposed an intensive effort against the ships in which the entire resources of Bomber Command would be used.

Beginning at 7 p.m. one evening, the port of Brest would be attacked continuously throughout the night. In this, waves of thirty aircraft would fly over Brest at thirty-minute intervals until one hour before dawn. All told, 300 aircraft were to be used in the operation dropping 3,413 tons of bombs on the port. By comparison, 20,202 tons of bombs had been dropped on the whole of Germany hitherto with Bomber Command incurring the loss of 127 aircraft in the process. Ultimately, Durston's plan was never implemented as while the RAF was pondering how to destroy the ships at Brest, the German high command was pondering how to return the ships to Germany.

Handley Page Halifax bomber of 35 Squadron during a raid over Brest to attack *Scharnhorst* and *Gneisenau* during December 1941.

9

Operation Cerberus: The Channel Dash

At 7.39 a.m. on 27 December 1941, as the ice-covered rooftops glistened in the moonlight, the sleepy fishing port of Vågsøy began to stir into life. Some 4 miles offshore, the cruiser HMS *Kenya*, flying the flag of Rear Admiral Harold Burrough, and six other ships crept slowly towards the harbour mouth. Aboard the ships, 550 commandos—the British Army's new elite fighting force—checked their equipment one final time before climbing up the decks of the two troop ships and clambering into landing craft. As the men embarked in silence, the minutes were counting down to the launch of Operation Archery.[1]

The objectives of Operation Archery were fivefold:

1. To destroy and/or capture enemy equipment and troops;
2. To destroy enemy industrial plants;
3. To seize documents, codes and instruments;
4. To arrest Norwegian collaborators known as Quislings;
5. To evacuate Norwegian volunteers for the Free Forces.[2]

At 8.48 a.m., Burrough gave the order to open fire. Seconds later the silence of the Arctic dawn was shattered as HMS *Kenya* immediately opened fire with her 6-inch guns against German shore batteries. Aircraft droned overhead, attacking German anti-aircraft guns as landing craft carrying the commandos made their run into the shore. The German forces were taken by surprise. On the small island of Måløy, the landings were virtually unopposed. At Vågsøy, things were not as straightforward with the commando landings coinciding with experienced German mountain troops enjoying a period of leave from the eastern front in the town.[3] Nevertheless, the commandos were successful in their mission and by the afternoon were back on board the landing craft returning to the troopships with almost 100 German prisoners, four quislings, and over seventy new recruits for the Norwegian Army of Liberation.

The raid had an effect out of all proportion to the forces embarked. In the aftermath of the raid, Hitler became convinced that the war would be won or lost in Norway and that the Allies may attempt to mount a large-scale invasion from Britain. Some

30,000 troops were diverted to Norway and coastal defences in the region were strengthened. For Hitler, Operation Archery confirmed his thoughts that Scandinavia and in particular Norway, was his 'zone of destiny'.

From August 1941, in the wake of the German invasion of the Soviet Union, convoys laden with supplies of food and war materials including tanks and aircraft had sailed from Britain, Iceland and ports in North America to ports in the Soviet Union (primarily Murmansk and Archangel) under the Lend-Lease programme. The convoys were escorted by ships of the Royal Navy and Royal Canadian Navy initially before some escorts were provided by ships of the US Navy from 1942. The first convoy to the Soviet Union, the 'Dervish' convoy, was comprised of six merchant vessels and departed Hvalfjord on 21 August, arriving at Archangel ten days later. Following the 'Dervish' convoy, the PQ series of convoys, which took their name from Philip Quellyn Roberts who was a planning officer at the Admiralty, began to sail. Outbound convoys to the Soviet Union were given the designation PQ while homeward-bound convoys were designated QP, a reversal of the PQ designation.

Convoy PQ-1 departed Hvalfjord on 29 September and reached Archangel on 11 October.[4] It was followed by PQ-2, which departed Liverpool on 13 October 1941, through to PQ-7B, which departed Hvalfjord on 31 December. In all, between August 1941 and the end of December, nine convoys were sent to the Soviet Union while five made the journey from the Soviet Union back to Britain.[5] The Arctic convoys to the Soviet Union sailed along what has been alternatively called 'the Arctic route' and 'the northern route', which was essentially the shortest and most direct route for Lend-Lease aid to reach the Soviet Union. It was, however, at the same time, the most dangerous route owing to the presence of German airfields and naval forces in Norway.

As the Arctic convoys sailed to the Soviet Union during the autumn and early winter of 1941, Hitler began to discuss with Raeder the potential advantages of the heavy units of the *Kriegsmarine* surface fleet—the *Scharnhorst*, *Gneisenau*, and *Tirpitz*—being sent north to Norway. Hitler felt that such a move would compel the British to retain a strong force of Royal Navy vessels in home waters, which could otherwise be put to better use in the Mediterranean, and that the presence of these ships in northern waters would prevent the feared interdiction of Swedish iron ore trade that was so crucial to German industry while also providing an outlet to attack the convoy route to the Soviet Union. Attacks on the Arctic convoys would prove important as they could serve to reduce the capabilities of the Red Army.

On 13 November 1941, Raeder met with Hitler at the *Wolfschanze*, his East Prussian headquarters where they discussed transferring the newly completed *Tirpitz* from the Baltic to Norway. During the course of the meeting, Hitler pushed forward his opinion that 'every ship which is not stationed in Norway is in the wrong place'.[6] So it was that Hitler came to view Norway as the decisive theatre. The question now was raised of what to do with the ships at Brest. There was no immediate likelihood of them putting out into the Atlantic to embark on another sortie, and with Norway now the focus, Hitler decided that the ships at Brest had to be brought back to Germany as soon as circumstances allowed.

The question also existed of how exactly the units at Brest would return to Germany. Two possible routes existed: the first, northwards towards Iceland and then through one of the gaps between Greenland and the north of Scotland and into the North Sea; second, the far more direct route through the English Channel to a German North Sea port. Both routes were fraught with danger. The northern route passed close to Scapa Flow, the base of the Royal Navy's Home Fleet. Once the departure of the ships had been noticed, it would be relatively easy for the Home Fleet to range its assets around Iceland to engage and destroy the ships. The route through the English Channel, a mere 22 miles wide at its narrowest, would take the ships within touching distance of the English coast and would force the ships to run the gauntlet of coastal artillery and aircraft based at airfields along the southern English coast. Furthermore, owing to the narrowness of the Channel, the ships would be confined to a stretch of sea where manoeuvre was almost impossible. Both routes, it would appear, were suicidal.

Raeder was appalled at Hitler's decision and the view held by the *Führer* that the capital ships of the *Kriegsmarine* were a costly extravagance. To Hitler's mind, the ships—while great for their propaganda value, and while their occasional victories were causes of celebration for the Nazi cause—were otherwise a waste of resources. Raeder still maintained that the capital ships should use their strength as commerce raiders in the Atlantic, and as such, he tried to put off the return of the *Scharnhorst* and *Gneisenau* to Germany as long as he could. The Japanese attack on Pearl Harbor and the sinking of HMS *Prince of Wales* and *Repulse* by Japanese aircraft highlighted how vulnerable capital ships were to air attack and Hitler did not wish to see the ships of the *Kriegsmarine* suffer a similar fate.

Although the decision to return the ships to Germany was one that was difficult to argue with, Raeder maintained great reservations. Neither route, he reasoned, offered hope of the vessels making a return to Germany intact. Nonetheless, on Hitler's orders, he issued instructions to Naval Group West and to *Vizeadmiral* Otto Ciliax, who had succeeded Lütjens as fleet commander on 1 July 1941, to consider how the ships would return to Germany. It is worth noting that since she had been commissioned, with the exception of the time she spent undergoing shipyard work, *Gneisenau* had always been the ship in which admirals had flown their flag. Ciliax had been the first commanding officer of the *Scharnhorst*, and for doubtless sentimental reasons, he decided to transfer the role of flagship to his old command.

The planners in France went to work on the issue of returning the ships to Germany and discussed every issue at length. Hitler became annoyed with Raeder and the head of Naval Group West, Admiral Alfred Saalwächter, along with the delays caused by the discussions and so pre-empted the decision, decreeing that the ships would take the direct route through the English Channel to return to Germany, relying on surprise and overwhelming air cover to make the breakthrough.[7] Seeing no more need for further discussion, Hitler instructed his admirals to proceed with planning for a breakthrough via the Channel and went so far as to bluntly inform Raeder that if he rejected the proposal for a dash through the Channel then the *Scharnhorst*, *Gneisenau*, and *Prinz Eugen* would be decommissioned and their guns dismantled for use as shore artillery.

Vizeadmiral Otto Ciliax, the man who succeeded Lütjens on 1 July 1941 and was tasked with considering how the ships at Brest were to return to Germany. Ciliax had been the first commanding officer of the *Scharnhorst*. (*Anil Kumar*)

On 22 January 1942, Hitler convened a special conference at his headquarters at Rastenburg to discuss the operation. Proceedings were pessimistically opened by Raeder before he handed over to Ciliax, who outlined to Hitler the plan that had been produced. Ciliax proposed that the ships would depart Brest under the cover of darkness and would make the passage through the narrowest part of the Channel in daylight, allowing the maximum amount of air cover to be provided at the most critical part of the voyage. Ciliax warned that the volume of fighter aircraft that would be required to provide cover to the ships and to ward off British aircraft was great: 250 fighters were proposed. He also warned that anything short of that required number would lead to certain disaster. Hitler agreed with the plan and promised that the required number of aircraft would be available, although the Luftwaffe raised doubts over whether they could comply with the directive owing to their considerable commitments on the Eastern Front.[8]

At the same time, the British were planning for a dash up the Channel by the ships based at Brest. Both the Admiralty and the RAF began to consider that the Germans may realise that to keep the ships at Brest under continuous bombardment was likely to end in disaster and that they could decide to gamble on making a passage through the Channel to Germany and thus to relative safety. The Admiralty and the RAF also concluded that if the Germans elected to sail their heavy units through the Channel then they would choose to transit the Strait of Dover at night when the ships would be afforded some protection by the darkness. This would mean that a significant portion of the journey from Brest would have to be made in daylight and would mean that the ships could be easily spotted by vigilant air patrols. The British thoughts that the Germans would consider a dash up the English Channel was not a mere assumption, however, for they were aided by ULTRA intelligence gleaned from German Enigma decrypts.[9] Indeed, intelligence gained from reading German Enigma signals would inform the Admiralty that the Germans may consider an attempt to sail the *Scharnhorst* and *Gneisenau* up the English Channel between 10 and 15 February 1942.[10] The British operation to be implemented if the German ships made a dash up the Channel was given the codename Operation Fuller.

Prior to the operation, the Germans began minesweeping operations in the Channel while six destroyers—the *Richard Beitzen*, *Paul Jacobi*, *Hermann Schoemann*, *Friedrich Ihn*, *Z25*, and *Z29*—plus a number of torpedo boats were moved to Brest. These preliminary manoeuvres led the Admiralty to issue a forecast at the beginning of February relating to a German operation to sail up the Channel. This was followed by a signal to Nore Command ordering that six destroyers be maintained at readiness on the Thames and that the command prepare to send six torpedo boats to reinforce those stationed at Dover. Meanwhile, the RAF alerted the forces that it had assigned to Operation Fuller and ordered the squadrons to indefinite readiness on 3 February. Having been brought to indefinite readiness, 19 Group Coastal Command began conducting night reconnaissance operations with Lockheed Hudsons in an effort to detect the movement of the ships from Brest.[11] With the coming of daylight, the Hudson patrols were replaced by Spitfires from Fighter Command.

With it becoming increasingly likely that the German ships would be ready to sail from Brest and that this would likely occur in mid-February, the Admiralty became concerned for the security of a large troop convoy that was due to leave Britain for Sierra Leone on 14 February in case the Germans did decide to venture out into the Atlantic. Escort to the convoy was to be provided by the battleship *Malaya*, the cruiser *Hermione*, and a number of destroyers but now, fearing interception from the German ships, HMS *Rodney* was ordered north from Gibraltar to bolster the escort and offer additional cover.

At noon on 11 February, Ciliax called a conference of senior officers aboard the *Scharnhorst*. At the meeting, he told his captains that both the weather and tides were favourable that night for the launching of Operation Cerberus. Lying 6 miles off the mouth of Brest harbour was the submarine *Sealion* under the command of Lieutenant-Commander G. R. Colvin, which was tasked with monitoring activity around the harbour. At 2 p.m., on the ebb tide, the submarine slipped away from its patrol station in order to surface at a point thirty miles away to recharge its batteries safe in the knowledge that the German ships were at anchor. At 6.27 p.m., a Hudson of 224 Squadron took off from St Eval to begin a night patrol off Brest to maintain a watch for the ships. At 7.15 p.m., as the aircraft was halfway to its patrol area, the wireless operator reported a blip 7 miles to starboard on the anti-surface vessel (ASV) radar. The pilot banked away to investigate and two minutes later was engaged by a Junkers Ju 88 night fighter. Evasive action was taken, which shook off the night fighter. Having shaken off the night fighter, it was then found that the ASV set had stopped working, which prompted the Hudson to return to base.

Just as the Hudson was withdrawing from its watch over the waters off Brest, the crews of the *Scharnhorst*, *Gneisenau*, and *Prinz Eugen* were casting off from their moorings. As they did so, however, the air raid sirens in the port began to wail. As searchlights probed the sky, anti-aircraft batteries opened fire against RAF bombers overhead. As the port was enveloped by artificial fog to cover the ships, Ciliax gave the order to halt the sailing and sat impotently aboard the *Scharnhorst* as flights of Wellingtons droned overhead. Eventually, after some ninety minutes, the last of the bombers departed and the all-clear sounded. With this, Ciliax issued the order for the ships to cast off once more. One by one, the battleships and the heavy cruiser were pulled clear of their berths and swung around towards the entrance of the harbour. Having edged their way clear of the breakwater the destroyers moved into formation beside the large warships and the force moved out into the open sea. The time was 9.30 p.m. The Channel Dash had begun.

Meanwhile, another Hudson had taken off from St Eval to resume the patrol off Brest. It did not arrive on station until 10.38 p.m., by which time Ciliax and his fleet had departed undetected. Around midnight, Ciliax's ships were off Ushant sailing at 27 knots where they started to make up some of the time they had lost during the air raid. The fleet rounded Breton Island and altered course into the English Channel. At 1.25 a.m., the ships altered course north-east to sail a course that would take them just to the north of the German-occupied Channel Islands. This was a crucial moment for the ships as once they entered the English Channel, they would reach the point of no return. Having reached this point, the crews of the ships were told that their destination was Germany. Hitherto they had been kept in the dark as security was imperative, but now the secret was out. As Ciliax's ships sailed on, Coastal Command continued flying search operations off Brest but nothing was sighted on the ASV sets.

The first light of dawn began to show around 7.45 a.m. and almost another hour would elapse before full daylight graced the ships. On board the *Scharnhorst* action stations sounded sending the crews to their battle positions in preparation to fend off the British attacks that everyone knew would come at some point. On the admiral's bridge, *Oberst* Max Ibel joined Ciliax and made contact with his two fighter controllers aboard the *Gneisenau* and *Prinz Eugen* via signal lamp, making sure that they were ready to liaise with the Luftwaffe air umbrella.

At 7.50 a.m., the first Luftwaffe fighters, led by fighter ace *Oberst* Adolf Galland wheeled in from astern of the ships, firing recognition flares to herald their arrival. Roaring low over the ships, the fighters dipped their wings in salute before climbing up to their operational altitude where they began circling above the fleet ready to commence the showdown with the massed strength of the Royal Navy and RAF that they believed could be gathering just over the horizon. At the time, however, nothing could have been farther from the true situation as the British remained blissfully ignorant of the presence of the German ships in the Channel.[12]

At 8.35 a.m. with no sighting of the German ships having been made, Vice Admiral Bertram Ramsay sent a signal from his headquarters at Dover for all units to revert to four hours readiness. As far as the British were concerned, the German heavy units had not attempted to force a passage through the Strait of Dover during the cover of darkness, therefore the threat was over until night descended once more. Out in the Channel meanwhile, Ciliax was receiving warnings of a new minefield that the Royal Navy had laid during the course of the night.

Scharnhorst seen from one of the escorting torpedo boats during the Channel Dash. *Gneisenau* can be seen astern. (*Author's Collection*)

Gneisenau seen during the course of the Channel Dash. (*Beeldbank WO2*)

Operation Cerberus, the Channel Dash. Taken from the *Prinz Eugen*, this photograph shows the German ships during their journey through the English Channel. The ship directly ahead is the *Gneisenau* with *Scharnhorst* visible in the distance. (*NH 69744, US Naval History and Heritage Command Center*)

On this subject, Ciliax received a signal from Naval Group West that the minefield lay directly across the path of the battle fleet and that although minesweepers were at work attempting to clear a passage, their work may not be complete by the time the fleet arrived in the area. Ciliax had to make a decision. To stop and wait around for a path to be cleared would be fatal for his ships while a detour around the minefield would be both hazardous and time-consuming. He therefore decided to trust luck and to proceed through the minefield, albeit at a reduced speed. By 8.30 a.m., the danger zone had been crossed and the ships were once more making 27 knots.

At 8 a.m., Corporal Jones started his shift in charge of the Beachy Head Range and Detection Finding Station. Manning the radar screen was Aircraftsman Gubbins. At 8.24 a.m., Gubbins reported to Jones that a number of enemy aircraft were off the French coast. 'They were mostly circling around and we reported them to Fighter Command's Filter Room via Pevensey. The aircraft did not seem to be moving much, they just kept circling around,' recalled Jones. Around 9.20 a.m., radar interference increased making the plots more difficult to see. At around this time, Gubbins was replaced on watch by Aircraftsman Adams.

> Just before ten o'clock Adams remarked that there was something in the middle of the aircraft which looked like shipping. I took a look myself and came to the conclusion that there were about six vessels with the aircraft. At 1014 and 1016 hours two more plots were made each of which had three ships in it at ranges of 44 and 46 miles. I then passed this information through to Dover Command.[13]

It should be noted that Beachy Head was an RAF station and that it only reported aircraft plots through Fighter Command, with reports of enemy shipping movements being passed to the naval command in whichever command area they were spotted. Beachy Head was not the only station to notice the circling aircraft and Fighter Command Headquarters at Uxbridge received several reports of circling aircraft and persistent interference. In light of these reports, a special reconnaissance flight was ordered by 11 Group at 10.20 a.m.

Two Spitfires of 91 Squadron from Hawkinge took off and overflew the Channel. Approximately 7 miles off Boulogne, two lines of E-boats were sighted sailing eastwards through the Channel. Some 3 miles behind the E-boats, the two pilots, through the murk, noticed approximately twenty-five ships surrounding larger vessels. The two pilots dived their aircraft to take a closer look and veered away moments later when they sighted Bf-109s above them. Pulling out of their dives, the Spitfires pulled up into the clouds and set a course for Hawkinge where they landed at 10.50 a.m. and made their reports, believing that the ships were a large German convoy. Aboard *Scharnhorst*, Ciliax saw the two Spitfires and they peeled away and realised immediately that his fleet had been spotted at last. It was inevitable that the British would vector all of their resources to intercept his ships. No one aboard the German ships was left in any doubt that the main battle would shortly begin.

Two more Spitfires from Kenley were also airborne when the two aircraft from Hawkinge were over the German fleet. The two aircraft from Kenley, flown by Group Captain Victor Beamish and Wing Commander Boyd, saw the ships surrounded by around twelve destroyers and a ring of E-boats around 5 miles off Le Touquet. Pulling into a sharp turn, Beamish and Boyd were greeted by anti-aircraft fire. Continuing their sharp turns, the two pilots managed to briefly open fire on the E-boats and observed some hits. Pulling up, the two Spitfires disappeared into the cloud and, maintaining radio silence as their orders demanded, returned to Kenley. Upon landing, the two pilots made their reports, which filtered to the command headquarters of both the RAF and Royal Navy. Based on this latest information, the code word 'Fuller' was flashed along the south coast of England.

The *Scharnhorst*, *Gneisenau*, *Prinz Eugen*, and their escorts were now in the waters off Cap Griz Nez and would soon be within range of the Channel guns sited near Dover. At Dover, there were a number of fortress guns, mainly of 6-inch calibre, the range of which was too short to reach the German ships. Two 15-inch guns were sited in a battery known as Wanstone, just outside St Margaret's at Cliffe for cross-Channel bombardment but the guns had a slow rate of fire and a limited traverse, making them almost useless against fast-moving ships. The only guns capable of being used offensively against the German ships were contained within one battery of four 9.2-inch guns at South Foreland. With an effective range of 17.9 miles (28.8 km), there would only be a short window when the guns would be able to target the ships.

It was now noon and the ships were beginning to pass through the Strait of Dover. At Dover, every observation post was crammed with officers armed with field glasses probing the murk for signs of the ships. At 12.15 p.m., the radar set of the South Foreland battery picked up the leading target, however, an accurate bearing was hard

The German fleet altering course off Le Touquet. Photographed from *Prinz Eugen*, *Gneisenau* is in the centre with *Scharnhorst* in the distance to the left. (NH 69748, US Naval History and Heritage Command Center)

The Germans ships sailing up the English Channel. One of the escort vessels can be seen to the right of *Scharnhorst*. (NH 69749, US Naval History and Heritage Command Center)

to come by owing to the lack of target discrimination as a result of the *Scharnhorst* being surrounded by a fleet of ships. With visibility down to only 5 miles, at 12.19 p.m., the battery opened fire marking the first British response to the ships since they had departed Brest. The ships were, at the time, passing 2 miles off the French coast, yet despite the murk, to all crew members who had a vantage point, the flash of the guns at South Foreland as they opened fire was clearly visible.

There followed an anxious wait before the shells splashed down harmlessly more than 1 mile to the port of the rear of the nearest escort ship. As E-boats began to produce a smokescreen to help screen the fleet from the British shoreline, the battery opened fire once more. The rumble of explosions could be heard but for those manning the battery, the comforting sounds of further explosions indicating a hit were not forthcoming. The battery continued to fire until 12.36 p.m., when it fired its last salvo at a range of 17 miles (27.4 km), the shells falling well astern of the *Prinz Eugen*. No hits were scored, the efforts of the battery had been a dismal failure, which achieved little other than attracting counter-battery fire from German guns sited at Cap Griz Nez.

On the admiral's bridge of the *Scharnhorst*, Ciliax quietly congratulated himself as his ships had manoeuvred through the choke point of the Dover Strait, which had been recognised as being the most hazardous part of the operation and all that had been thrown against the ships under his command was sporadic gunfire.

At 11.15 a.m., five Motor Torpedo Boats (MTBs) had departed Dover harbour to attack the German fleet, which now numbered approximately sixty vessels. Approximately thirty minutes later, the enemy was sighted. At a range of half a mile, the MTBs began to exchange fire with the E-boats. The flotilla leader, Lieutenant-Commander Pumphrey, decided that for the attack to be a success, he had to close the range to the main German ships, the range to which stood at approximately 2.8 miles (4.5 km).

Suddenly, one of the engines of Pumphrey's MTB faltered and speed dropped away. A signal was sent to the other boats to carry on. Pumphrey was able to turn his MTB to get one of the battleships (believed to have been the *Scharnhorst*) into his sights just long enough to be able to launch two torpedoes. The other MTBs soon found that their speed was insufficient to overhaul the E-boats and as they closed to make their attack, they attracted increasingly heavy fire from the German fleet. The intensity and accuracy of the fire against the MTBs was soon added to by a number of Luftwaffe fighters which dived down and conducted strafing attacks. Torpedoes were launched at a range between 2.8 and 1.7 miles but no hits were scored.[14] As Pumphrey's MTBs commenced their attack, three other MTBs under the command of Lieutenant Long put to sea from Ramsgate. Long's force of MTBs would pass astern of the E-boat screen with the main portion of the German squadron having passed ahead of his flotilla to the north-east.

At 12.25 p.m., 825 Squadron of the Fleet Air Arm was ordered to take off and enter the attack. Under the Command of Lieutenant-Commander Eugene Esmonde, 825 Squadron had acquainted itself well the previous year in the hunt for the *Bismarck* when one of its Swordfish had torpedoed the German battleship from the aircraft carrier *Victorious*. Under Esmonde's leadership, six Swordfish took off from Manston expecting to rendezvous upon taking off with five squadrons of Spitfires that were to act as top cover to keep the Luftwaffe fighters off the torpedo bombers as they commenced their attack runs. The Swordfish took off, but their fighter escort was nowhere to be seen. The first fighters arrived seven minutes later at 12.32 p.m. from Squadron Leader Brian Kingcome's 72 Squadron. The formation continued circling Manston until 12.34 p.m., but no additional fighters arrived. Deciding that he could not delay any longer, Esmonde felt it was time to go and led his six Swordfish north-east into battle.

No. 401 Squadron arrived over Manston at 12.36 p.m., two minutes after the Swordfish and 72 Squadron had departed. No. 124 Squadron, commanded by Squadron Leader Raymond Duke-Woolley, was also detailed to provide top cover and crossed the coast at Deal, 6 miles south of Manston and proceeded along the Channel hoping to catch a glimpse of the Swordfish. No. 124 Squadron had only received the order to take off at 12.20 p.m. Kingcome later recalled events:

> We followed them [the Swordfish] out, and between, I should say, about ten and fifteen miles due east of Dover we found the *Prinz Eugen*. We had to go as slowly as possible, but we kept in touch with the Swordfish until we reached the German ships. I saw one large battleship and between twenty and thirty smaller vessels. The squadron was then broken up by enemy fighters and there was a general fight after that. They were Focke-Wulf 190s and they were operating in pairs. It was impossible to keep in contact with the Swordfish after that, partly due to the enemy fighters and partly due to the visibility which was very poor.[15]

At 12.50 p.m., Esmonde's Swordfish sighted their quarry. Dropping down to 50 feet above the waves, soon tracer from the anti-aircraft guns of the destroyers rose up to greet them as Fw-190s and Bf-109s began to swoop down to be engaged by the Spitfires. Fresh groups of Luftwaffe fighters swooped down and strafed Esmonde's squadron with machine gun and cannon fire, which passed through the lumbering canvas-covered biplanes. Esmonde led the first sub-flight of three aircraft while the second sub-flight was led by Lieutenant Thompson. Sub-Lieutenant Lees, the observer in Swordfish *W5983*, described the run-in towards the German ships as follows:

> Lieutenant Cdr Esmonde was shot up in the first attack, but continued on in a badly damaged aircraft, the port wing being shot to shreds. The other two aircraft in the subflight were also badly damaged, in particular Sub Lieutenant Kingsmill's aircraft, the engine and port wing of which were alight. We flew in over the destroyer screen and sighted two warships slightly on the port bow. Lieutenant Cdr Esmonde altered course and closed in towards the warships, the rest following.[16]

Suddenly, a shell struck the lower part of Esmonde's Swordfish, setting the tail alight. Moments later the Swordfish was struck again and crashed into the Channel killing all on board. At around a distance of 1.5 miles, Swordfish *W5983* launched its torpedo at one of the German ships. Heavily damaged by fighters and anti-aircraft fire, as the aircraft banked away to head back to Manston it lost height forcing the crew to ditch. *W5907* flown by Sub-Lieutenant Kingsmill was heavily damaged also and released its torpedo approximately 1 mile from the *Prinz Eugen*. Hit by more anti-aircraft fire as it banked way, Kingsmill and his crew were also forced to crash land in the Channel.

Of the second sub-flight led by Thompson, little is known as all of the crewmembers of the three Swordfish were killed during the attack. What is known is that their attacks were as resolute as those of the first sub-flight.[17] The torpedoes that were released caused little discomfort for those aboard the German ships as each was easily avoided by a slight alteration of course. Aboard the German ships, all had been amazed to see aircraft appearing out of the murk as if belonging to a by-gone era flying steadily through the barrage of fire. To all, it seemed amazing that the fabric-covered biplanes were all that Britain could send against them. On the bridge of the *Scharnhorst*, *Kapitän zur See* Hoffmann was heard to remark, 'The English are now throwing their mothball Navy at us' and exclaimed, 'poor fellows, they are so very low, it is nothing but suicide for them to fly against these big ships'. Of the attacks by the Swordfish Ciliax would later record that the 'attack of a handful of ancient planes piloted by men whose bravery surpass[ed] any other action by either side that day'.[18]

For the Germans, things were going to plan. They had now exited the Dover Strait and entered the North Sea. No damage or injuries had been suffered and no disasters had befallen the fleet. With events not going at all according to plan for the British, Coastal Command and Bomber Command now entered the fray. The attacks by Bomber and Coastal Commands came late in the day. Beauforts and Hudsons from Coastal Command rendezvoused with a fighter escort over Manston at 2.50 p.m. As the aircraft headed out over the North Sea, contact was lost with the result that all aircraft proceeded independently. When the Beauforts located their quarry, a full-scale dogfight was raging between the Luftwaffe and RAF fighters. Through poor visibility, enemy fighters and heavy anti-aircraft fire, some of the aircraft managed to launch attacks but no hits were made against the German ships. Another group of Beauforts from Thorny Island flew out over the North Sea at 5.05 p.m. In the poor visibility and with a low cloud base, this formation, led by Wing Commander Flood, sighted only three German minesweepers.

Bomber Command launched four waves of aircraft against the German fleet. Composed of Wellingtons, Blenheims, and Manchesters, the first attack by Bomber Command against the German fleet got underway as planned and the aircraft arrived over the estimated position of the German ships at around 2.30 p.m. Unfortunately for the aircrews, the cloud cover was 10/10ths and simply locating the ships proved to be extremely difficult. With the cloud ceiling at 600 feet and visibility at approximately half a mile, pilots suffered issues caused by freezing windscreens. None of the aircraft from the first wave that returned to base reported sighting the German ships. Nevertheless for such a disappointing attack, casualties were high. Five aircraft out of seventy-three dispatched were lost. Some aircraft flew too low and appear to have hit the sea while others are believed to have been shot down.

Some 100 aircraft comprised of Wellingtons, Manchesters, Stirlings, Halifaxes, and Bostons comprised the second wave. The aircraft of the second wave arrived over the target at 4.30 p.m., but the results were even worse than those of the first wave. Again, the ships were not sighted and nine aircraft were lost. A third wave composed of Stirlings, Halifaxes, and Wellingtons numbering forty-one aircraft arrived over the target area at 5.45 p.m. as the stragglers from the second wave were beginning to depart. Few aircraft of the third wave succeeded in locating the enemy ships while those that did had difficulty in bombing effectively. Only one bomber was lost in this last effort.

On board the German ships, the crews could hear the bombers overhead but rarely saw them. Those that were seen swooping through the clouds were greeted by a heavy anti-aircraft barrage and were driven away. *Kapitän* Hoffmann was not sure during the period in which Bomber Command launched its effort whether the aircraft that passed overhead were from different waves or if they were the same bombers simply circling in an attempt to locate his ship and the others in his company.

Meanwhile, while the Fleet Air Arm, Coastal Command and Bomber Command launched their respective waves of aircraft, at 11.45 a.m. Captain Mark Pizey of the 21st Destroyer Flotilla based at Sheerness was at sea conducting exercises when he received a signal stating that the German ships were off Boulogne. Owing to the confusion of the different reports that reached Pizey and the initial underestimation of the speed of the German squadron, it was eventually decided that the destroyers of the 21st Flotilla would attempt to intercept the German squadron off the mouth of the River Maas. The issue with this was that between his then-present location and the River Maas, a minefield stood in Pizey's path. Pizey decided that his ships would sail directly across the mine barrier and simply hope for the best. Increasing speed to 28 knots, it was expected that the 21st Destroyer Flotilla would make its interception around 3.30 p.m. At 2.30 p.m., the flotilla cleared the mine barrier without mishap. At the same time, some distance away to the south-west, the German ships were ploughing their way steadily through the gathering seas.

At 2.32 p.m., the good fortune that had followed Ciliax and his fleet since their departure from Brest came to an abrupt halt in the shallow waters off the mouth of the River Scheldt when the *Scharnhorst* was suddenly rocked by an explosion. All lights on board the battleship failed as it began to lose way. The ship had struck a mine that had been dropped by the RAF sometime previous. The noise of the explosion was so great that *Kapitän* Fein of the *Gneisenau* at first believed that the explosion had occurred aboard his own ship. Looking around, he, along with those aboard the *Prinz Eugen*, were shocked to see *Scharnhorst* sheer off to starboard belching black smoke and leaking oil.[19]

For those aboard the *Gneisenau* and *Prinz Eugen*, there was no question of stopping to see what had occurred as they and the rest of the fleet had to sail on. A young engineering officer, *Leutnant* Timmer, was tasked with delivering the first damage report to Hoffmann. The mine had exploded against Compartment XVI, producing a large hole in the starboard side of the hull. Two double bottom compartments were flooded. As Hoffmann listened to the damage that had been sustained to his ship, Ciliax grew impatient. To him, there seemed no point in remaining on board. As the fleet sailed on, the destroyer Z29 was signalled to come alongside the stricken battleship. Ciliax proposed to transfer his flag to the destroyer and to set off in pursuit of the *Gneisenau* and *Prinz Eugen*. It seemed, to him, to be the only way in which he could maintain control over the fleet.

With the heavy swell and the two ships pitching and rolling heavily, the task of transferring Ciliax and his staff to the destroyer was a difficult one. In the heavy swell,

Taken from *Prinz Eugen*, *Scharnhorst* can be seen in the background dead in the water off the mouth of the River Scheldt after hitting a mine. (*Author's Collection*)

Z29 crashed into the side of the *Scharnhorst* which severely damaged her superstructure leaving the destroyer's captain, *Kapitän zur See* Erich Bey, counting his blessings that the damage was not more severe. Somehow, Ciliax, his chief of staff, and three officers on loan from the Luftwaffe managed to jump from the quarterdeck of the *Scharnhorst* on to what remained of the bridge of Z29. With the transfer complete, the destroyer then proceeded away at 30 knots to catch up with the *Gneisenau* and *Prinz Eugen*. Four torpedo boats remained behind with *Scharnhorst* to offer some protection, yet despite this, it was the rain and the mist that were perhaps the more useful ally to the helpless battleship.

This was a situation that the crews of all of the German ships had dreaded since they departed Brest. As she lay dead in the water, *Scharnhorst* was at the mercy of any British aircraft that might appear in the sky above. Fortunately for those on board the battleship, as described in the previous pages, Coastal and Bomber Command faced extreme difficulty in locating the ships owing to the weather. The ship's chief engineer, Walther Kretzschmar, immediately set to work in the wake of the explosion, and eight minutes after the progress of the *Scharnhorst* had been abruptly halted, Kretzschmar reported that all of the ship's boilers were back in operation.

At 3.05 p.m, he informed Hoffmann that the port engine was operational, and thirty minutes after this, the lights had been brought back into action. With this, *Scharnhorst* was able to resume her journey. There was, nevertheless, a good deal of water in the refrigeration room and the echo-sounder, and the direction finders were out of action, but there was no reason why the ship should not proceed at full speed.

During this time of crisis, Hoffmann betrayed no sign of what must have amounted to a considerable strain. With two of the ship's navigational aids damaged, sandbanks to one side and a minefield off the other, guided by the torpedo boat *T13*, *Scharnhorst* worked up to 27 knots. In the chart room, the navigating officer, Helmuth Giessler, was uncomfortably aware that they were now sailing up a channel 27 miles (43 km) wide flanked by minefields and the Dutch coast. Giessler mentioned his fears to Hoffmann who conceded the danger but informed the navigating officer that there was no question of reducing speed. Giving Giessler a wry smile, Hoffmann remarked, 'Only God and courage can help us now!'

As frantic work was underway to repair the *Scharnhorst* and as the remainder of the German fleet proceeded on, Pizey's 21st Destroyer Flotilla sailed on towards the River Maas. At 3.15 p.m., HMS *Campbell* detected two large echoes on her Type 271 radar at a range of 9.5 miles. Two minutes passed, during which the appearance of additional echoes confirmed that Pizey's command had located the enemy fleet. Visibility through the mist and rain squalls was 4 miles, allowing Pizey to estimate that he would have cover for the first half of his approach. Pizey decided that his ships would conduct torpedo attacks against the enemy fleet and that they would attack in two divisions. The destroyers *Campbell*, *Vivacious*, and *Worcester* would form the first division while HMS *Mackay* and *Whitshed* would form the second division. As the destroyers approached, aircraft swooped down from out of the clouds. The arrival of the destroyers coincided with attacks by Coastal Command and Bomber Command. In the confusion of battle, some of the German pilots who engaged the incoming RAF aircraft believed that Pizey's destroyers were friendly ships and fired off recognition flares while some of the RAF aircrews believed that the destroyers were hostile and attempted to attack.

At 3.42 p.m., gun flashes and anti-aircraft fire were sighted off to starboard at a distance of 4 miles, which was quickly followed by a sighting of the *Gneisenau* and *Prinz Eugen*, which were proceeding in line ahead with their destroyer escort off to port. The British destroyers immediately turned to attack. As they increased speed to close on the German fleet, all of the enemy vessels opened fire with their main armament. As the German salvos began to land, Pizey issued orders to commence zig-zagging. Pizey later described the attack:

> At 3,500 yards I felt that our luck could not hold much longer. Ships were being well straddled and we were closing fast, gradually losing our bearing. At 3,300 yards I saw a large shell, which failed to explode or ricochet, dive under the ship like a porpoise and I felt this was time to turn and fire our torpedoes. *Vivacious* on my starboard quarter turned and fired at the same time.[20]

Having released their torpedoes, *Campbell* and *Vivacious* turned away and retired from the battle as *Worcester* fired her torpedoes. By now, *Gneisenau* and *Prinz Eugen* were themselves taking evasive action, turning away from the torpedoes so that they all missed finding their mark. As *Worcester* turned away to retire, she was struck by shells from either the *Gneisenau* or *Prinz Eugen* in boiler rooms I and II, causing her to stop dead in the water. Drifting with her port side exposed to the enemy, *Worcester*

Gneisenau firing her main battery guns as Luftwaffe fighters secure the airspace during Operation Cerberus. (*Martin Fairbanks*)

was subjected to four salvos from the two capital ships. As fires broke out across the ship as shells slammed into the hull, Lieutenant-Commander Coats, the destroyer's commanding officer, issued the order to abandon ship.

Meanwhile, HMS *Mackay* and *Whitshed* were sailing directly towards the *Prinz Eugen*. As the destroyers approached the heavy cruiser without attracting fire from any of the German ships, Brinkmann was left unsure if the approaching destroyers were friend or foe. At a range of just over 2 miles, HMS *Mackay* fired her torpedoes, clarifying for Brinkmann the identity of the destroyers. *Prinz Eugen* undertook a hard turn to starboard to avoid being hit. Lieutenant-Commander Juniper of HMS *Whitshed* closed the range to a little over 1.5 miles before firing all of his torpedoes, none of which found their mark.

The German fleet regained station and thundered on not wishing to remain and fight. The damaged *Worcester*, much to everyone's surprise, remained afloat prompting HMS *Campbell* and *Vivacious* to reverse course to render assistance. The wounded were taken off as a damage control team set about extinguishing the fires and making the destroyer seaworthy. Lieutenant-Commander Coats refused the offer of a tow from Pizey as one of the ship's boilers was brought back into operation. Raising steam, in company with the other destroyers, the *Worcester* set a course for Harwich.[21]

The attack by the destroyers, like the other attacks conducted during the course of the day, failed. The retirement of the destroyers brought an end to Operation Fuller. The operation had been a complete shambles from the start and now, with daylight fading, the German ships had as good as escaped their pursuers. The British attempt to stop the *Gneisenau*, *Prinz Eugen*, and *Scharnhorst* was over. For the Germans, however, Operation Cerberus was still very much ongoing.

Accompanied by the torpedo boats *T13*, *T15*, *T16*, and *T17*, *Scharnhorst* continued on her way. At 6.16 p.m., the men on deck had their last look at a British aircraft for the day as a Beaufighter was seen circling way off the stern. For Giessler, the ordeal was just beginning. He would later describe the next few hours as 'the longest night of my life' as the darkness concealed navigational hazards and mines. Shortly before dark, *Scharnhorst* was off the Hook of Holland where suddenly, ahead, two of the fleet's destroyers were sighted. The destroyers, one of which was the *Z29*, were hove to. A shell misfire caused major damage to an oil line aboard the destroyer, which caused the ship to come to a halt. The damage to the *Z29* forced Ciliax to seek to transfer his flag for the second time that day to another ship, on this occasion to the *Hermann Schoemann*. Meanwhile, in the rapidly descending darkness, *Gneisenau* and *Prinz Eugen* became detached from one another prompting the two ships to proceed independently.

From the *Scharnhorst*, the destroyers disappeared into the gloom, before, suddenly, at 7.15 p.m., the *Hermann Schoemann* appeared and signalled the battleship to follow. Somewhere ahead of the two ships in the murk was a marker buoy which heralded the entrance to the channel between the Frisian Island and the offshore banks. A rain squall descended upon the *Schoemann* and the *Scharnhorst* into which the marker buoy and destroyer vanished from view. With the echo-sounder out of action, it fell to Giessler to use dead reckoning to guide the battleship to the channel. Speed was reduced as the ship groped its way through the water. Suddenly, a lookout reported something off the starboard quarter; it turned out to be the buoy. At last, the crew could relax. At 7.30 p.m., Hoffmann ordered a partial stand down. Hot meals began to be served on the mess decks as the ship began to sail past the island of Texel.

Gneisenau continued to forge ahead at 27 knots, however, her progress was interrupted at 7.55 p.m., when the ship was rocked by an explosion off the island of Terschelling as she set off a mine. The central shaft was put out of action almost immediately as a result of the explosion. *Kapitän* Fein subsequently ordered the other shafts to be shut down while engineers went to inspect the damage. As the ship drifted 6 miles (10 km) off the coast, the first officer reported a hole in the starboard side of the ship and that the damage was not serious. A steel collision mat was erected to block the hole and to stop the inrush of water while the central shaft was nursed back into life. As with the *Scharnhorst*, the detonation of the mine also damaged the navigational equipment of the *Gneisenau*. Within thirty minutes of the detonation, *Gneisenau* was underway once more. As much as he would have liked to have ordered full speed, Fein recognised that he had to be cautious. Navigating through waters littered with sandbanks, *Gneisenau* crept forward with a leadsman taking soundings at regular intervals.

Behind the *Gneisenau*, *Prinz Eugen* was also navigating the shallow channel. The heavy cruiser was more fortunate than the two battleships for she succeeded in making the passage through to German waters unscathed, even if the journey through the Terschelling banks was made at 8 knots. Approximately ninety minutes elapsed without incident before at 9.35 p.m., just off Terschelling, *Scharnhorst* detonated a second mine. Hoffmann was flung across the bridge as the helm jammed, the gyro compass ceased functioning, the engines stopped and all of the lights went out once more. Some 200 tons of water rushed in, flooding several compartments on the starboard side, causing the ship to take on a list of 7 degrees.

The detonation was heard by the crew of the *Hermann Schoemann*, which immediately reversed course to render assistance. Ciliax ordered a signal be flashed to the battleship, which went without reply. As Ciliax's anxiety began to mount, five minutes elapsed before a terse signal—'Have hit mine'—was seen to be flashed from *Scharnhorst*. The battleship had been unable to reply to Ciliax's signal sooner owing to damage being sustained to the signal lamp.

Kretzchmar once more set to work repairing the damage to get the ship underway. Thirty-seven minutes after hitting the mine, during which time the ship drifted 2 miles (3 km) towards the coast, the starboard shaft was sufficiently repaired to allow the ship to make 14 knots while the centre shaft was sufficiently repaired to make 16 knots.

Aboard the *Hermann Schoemann*, Ciliax was being tormented by confusion and worry. The two ships had once more lost contact with one another. The searchlight of the *Herman Schoemann* was swept across the water looking for the battleship but with the ship not sighted, Ciliax became convinced that she had sunk and that the hunt was now on for survivors. Copious amounts of oil could be seen on the surface of the water but no wreckage that provided encouragement and prompted Ciliax to eventually form the conclusion that the *Scharnhorst* may still be afloat, although he was still under the impression that she was unable to proceed under her own power.

At 10.46 p.m., he transmitted a coded signal to a shore station stating that the *Scharnhorst* was in urgent need of assistance and tugs. The night dragged on and the minutes ticked by before at 11 p.m., the destroyer's searchlight picked up the grey bulk of the *Scharnhorst* sailing towards them at 10 knots. The battleship was back in operation once more. The cost had been light: only one member of the crew suffered injuries.

Just after midnight, *Gneisenau* and *Prinz Eugen* made contact with one another in the vicinity of Heligoland and proceeded in company to Brunsbüttel at the southern end of the Kiel Canal. The two ships arrived at Brunsbüttel shortly before dawn and waited for daylight before attempting to transit the Elbe. *Scharnhorst*, meanwhile, trundled on towards Wilhelmshaven. When Fein decided that it was sufficiently light for the *Gneisenau* to enter the Elbe followed by the *Prinz Eugen* a strong south-westerly gale was blowing. With an air raid siren sounding and with the flooding tide having two more hours to run, the two ships proceeded up the mouth of the Elbe encouraged by the sight of a tug some distance ahead.

As *Gneisenau* entered the Elbe, a number of things went wrong. In the first instance, the tug, the sighting of which had encouraged *Kapitän* Fein to enter the river now seemed to avoid the battleship. As the ship approached the mole at Brunsbüttelkoog, the current caught the stern and swung it around, seeming to make a collision with the mole inevitable. Fein ordered the engines into reverse whereupon *Gneisenau* drew back from one hazard and promptly ran into another. A few feet from the entrance to the harbour, the fairway was obstructed by a wreck. The astern movement which carried the ship clear of the breakwater smashed the ship into this obstacle. Water immediately surged into the starboard shaft as the tugs stood by. Eventually, using only the centre and port engines, Fein brought *Gneisenau* alongside.

The *Scharnhorst* meanwhile, continued on her way and arrived off Wilhelmshaven during the mid-morning. With the River Jade covered with ice, the tug masters and harbour pilots had stayed at home. At 7 a.m., Ciliax boarded the *Scharnhorst*, and for the next four hours, the battleship sat idle in the approaches to the river. Eventually, Hoffmann's patience ran out, prompting him to turn to Giessler whom he ordered to guide the ship slowly into harbour without the assistance of tugs. Slowly *Scharnhorst* crept into harbour. By noon, they were in sight of the docks. The journey was over— Operation Cerberus had been successfully completed.

In occupied Europe and across the world, the Channel Dash was viewed as a great German victory. It had been a bold and carefully planned operation. In Germany, the returning sailors were feted as heroes. Many decorations were forthcoming as a result. Ciliax and Hoffmann were both awarded the Knight's Cross, one of Germany's highest awards. Helmuth Giessler was awarded the German cross in gold while Iron Crosses were lavishly handed out. It is worth noting that for a mysterious reason *Kapitän* Fein did not receive any decorations for the part that he played in the operation.

The success of the operation also proved Hitler correct in his thinking that the British were incapable of reacting quickly enough to stop the ships from transiting the English Channel. The success also reinforced Hitler's own belief in himself as a great military commander. While the operation succeeded in its primary objective, it must also be viewed as a defeat. Indeed even the German naval staff summarised the outcome of the operation as being 'a tactical victory, but a strategic defeat'.[22] In moving the ships from Brest to Germany in preparation for a deployment to Norway, Hitler ultimately exchanged the threat to British Atlantic convoys for a defensive deployment against a threat that never materialised and which at the time was only ever a faint possibility.[23]

From Brunsbüttel, *Gneisenau* was moved to Kiel to undergo repairs. She was joined at Kiel on 15 February by *Scharnhorst*, which also underwent repair work at the Deutsche Werke shipyard.[24] Having returned to Germany, a new chapter in the respective careers of the *Scharnhorst* and *Gneisenau* was to begin.

Operation Cerberus: The Channel Dash

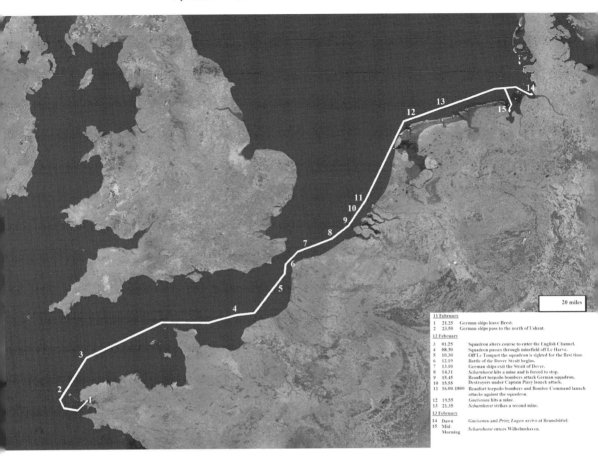

The route of Operation Cerberus. (*Author's Collection*)

Above left: A reconnaissance photograph of Kiel taken by the RAF between February and June 1942. The arrow to the right of centre marks the position of the *Scharnhorst* undergoing repair work following Operation Cerberus. (NH 97505, US Naval History and Heritage Command Center)

Above right: A second reconnaissance photograph of Kiel. The arrow lower centre marks the position of the *Scharnhorst*. (NH 97506, US Naval History and Heritage Command Center)

10
Deployment to Norway

Early August 1942 found the *Scharnhorst* in the Baltic conducting exercises with several U-boats. During one exercise, the battleship suffered the misfortune of colliding with *U-523*. According to those aboard the U-boat, *Scharnhorst* had been lying stopped when an order to surface was given. Just after that, *Scharnhorst* began to get underway. *U-523* surfaced too close to the battleship with the result that the two collided with *Scharnhorst*, suffering considerable damage to her bow.[1]

In the wake of this, *Scharnhorst* departed the exercises and made for a dry dock to undergo repair work. Further indignation was in store for the battleship as the day after colliding with *U-523*, *Scharnhorst* rammed a buoy in the harbour. According to one individual from *U-523*, the collision with the U-boat followed by the ramming of the buoy resulted in the captain being relived.[2] The Admiralty document which records this story, however, includes the following note:

> *Kapitän Zur See* Kurt Hoffmann was in command of *Scharnhorst* from 1940 to 1942. He was promoted to Rear Admiral in April, 1942, but it is not known at what date he actually relinquished his command. This story may refer to a subsequent captain.[3]

Hoffmann relinquished command of the *Scharnhorst* in April 1942 to *Kapitän Zur See* Friedrich Hüffmeier, who ultimately commanded the ship until October 1943, therefore, on this occasion, the testimony from the crewmember of *U-523* is incorrect as Hüffmeier was not relieved of his command and the ship had no other commanding officers between April 1942 and October 1943.[4]

The repair work on the ship was completed in September 1942 whereupon *Scharnhorst* ventured into the Baltic to conduct further training. In late October, *Scharnhorst* sailed to Gotenhafen where she was taken into dry dock and fitted with a new rudder, the design of which was based on the lessons learned from the torpedoing of the *Prinz Eugen* and *Lützow* earlier in the year. Troubles with her boilers and turbines kept the ship in Germany for the remainder of 1942. By December, only two of the ship's three boilers were operational and a complete overhaul of the propulsion system was required.

Taken from a torpedo boat, *Scharnhorst* is seen here in the Baltic, 1942. (*Beeldbank WO2*)

While *Scharnhorst* was in Germany, the Arctic convoys to the Soviet Union continued to sail. The *Tirpitz*, which had sailed to Norway in February 1942, put to sea on 6 March in an attempt to intercept convoys PQ-12 and QP-8. *Tirpitz* failed to intercept and destroy the convoys and was sighted and harried back to Norway by aircraft from HMS *Victorious*. In the wake of PQ-12 and QP-8, the Arctic convoys went through a period where losses began to mount. The convoys that followed in the wake of PQ-12 were the outward-bound PQ-13 and the homeward bound QP-9. PQ-13 was comprised of nineteen vessels, five of which were lost during the journey to the Soviet Union. In addition to the five merchant ships lost, two of the escorting warships were damaged. PQ-14 followed. Twenty-four vessels made up the convoy, sixteen of which reversed course and returned to Iceland when the convoy ran into heavy ice. Of the eight ships that continued on to the Soviet Union, one was lost to a U-boat.

The homeward convoy, QP-10, numbered sixteen ships and lost four of its number to German activity. The next convoys, PQ-15 and QP-11, were composed of twenty-five and thirteen vessels respectively. A large force of two battleships, an aircraft carrier, six cruisers, twenty destroyers, four corvettes, three minesweepers, five trawlers, and an anti-aircraft ship was assembled to provide the convoys with an escort. Luftwaffe bombers succeeded in sinking two merchant vessels from PQ-15 and damaged a third, which was later sunk by *U-251*. QP-11 lost one merchant vessel to German destroyers while the actions of *U-456* and the destroyer *Z25* combined to sink HMS *Edinburgh*. PQ-16, when it sailed, was subjected to no fewer than 108 aerial attacks, which sunk four merchant vessels and damaged two others.[5]

The single largest convoy disaster of 1942 was PQ-17, which was ordered to scatter when it was believed that a powerful German surface force which included the *Tirpitz* had put to sea to intercept the merchant vessels. The result was the loss of twenty-four of thirty-four merchant ships, which prompted the suspension of the convoys during the summer months of perpetual daylight. September 1942 saw the Arctic convoys resume with the sailing of PQ-18, which departed Loch Ewe on 2 September. One-third of PQ-18, thirteen ships, were lost to Luftwaffe and U-boat attacks. The homeward-bound QP-14 lost six vessels. While PQ-18 and QP-14 were not dealt the crippling losses that had been inflicted on PQ-17, the statistics did not make for good reading. Indeed, the combined losses from PQ-18 and QP-14 meant that the probability of a merchant vessel surviving a voyage to and from one of the Soviet ports was less than 50 per cent.

Between 29 October and 2 November, at approximately twelve-hour intervals, alternating British and American merchant vessels and a single Soviet merchant ship set out alone. The merchant vessels sailed independently and relied on submarine patrols to the north of Bear Island and trawlers along the general line of their sailing for protection. The independent sailings betrayed a degree of misgiving but 'were more successful than some people had expected'.[6] Three of the merchant ships dispatched—the *Briarwood*, *Daldorch*, and *John H. B. Latrobe*—were recalled as a result of the sinking of the *Empire Gilbert* by *U-586*. The American Liberty ships *John Walker*, *Richard H. Alvey*, and *Hugh Williamson* made the journey unscathed, along with five Soviet vessels that were sent westward during the same period to Iceland.[7]

QP-15 was composed of thirty vessels and departed the White Sea on 17 November. Three days after setting sail, the convoy was struck by the first in a succession of gales that scattered the merchant ships. One vessel was lost to U-boat activity with the gales and atrocious sea conditions causing severe damage to the other ships. Following QP-15, for security reasons, the designations given to the convoys were changed—JW began to be used for outbound convoys while RA was used for homeward bound convoys. On New Year's Eve 1942, under the command of *Vizeadmiral* Oskar Kummetz, the pocket battleship *Lützow* and the heavy cruiser *Admiral Hipper* along with an assortment of destroyers engaged JW-51B in the Barents Sea. The *Admiral Hipper* engaged the convoy escorts while *Lützow* unsuccessfully attempted to engage the convoy, firing eighty-seven 11-inch shells and seventy-five 6-inch shells at the merchant ships without scoring a direct hit. The arrival of the cruisers HMS *Sheffield* and *Jamaica* forced Kummetz to break off the engagement and return to Norway. The battle was tactically insignificant but was a strategic victory for the Royal Navy, which had far-reaching consequences.[8]

Hitler waited with 'delighted impatience' for news of the battle following a report from a U-boat that reported that JW-51B was being engaged. As he retired to Norway, Kummetz maintained radio silence. To compound matters for the admiral, a breakdown in the teleprinter line from Norway prevented his report of the engagement from reaching Berlin before Hitler learned of the battle's outcome from the BBC. Flying into a rage, Hitler assumed that he had been kept in the dark about the failure of the operation and expressed his view of the uselessness of the capital ships of the *Kriegsmarine*. Hitler immediately summoned Raeder to his headquarters who managed to delay meeting the *Führer* until 6 January 1943 when the two met at the *Wolfschanze* (Wolf's Lair). When Raeder arrived, it soon became apparent that the views that Hitler had expressed on 31 December had not softened as the *Großadmiral* was subjected to a lecture that lasted more than an hour and constituted an attack on the *Kriegsmarine* in which Hitler came close to accusing his commanders of cowardice.

Continuing, Hitler proclaimed that with the exception of the U-boat arm, he could not find a good word to say about the German navy throughout its entire history. He also went on to inform Raeder that not only did the capital ships of the *Kriegsmarine* not do anything, they required almost constant protection for the Luftwaffe and that in the event of an Allied invasion of Norway, the Luftwaffe would be better employed attacking the invasion fleet than defending the *Kriegsmarine*.[9] Hitler then came to an extraordinary conclusion—that the capital ships of the *Kriegsmarine* had no further role to play in the war and would therefore be taken out of commission and scrapped with their guns being pressed into service as coastal batteries.

Following this lecture by Hitler, Raeder decided that he no longer wished to serve as the commander-in-chief of the *Kriegsmarine*, citing the fact that he clearly no longer enjoyed the *Führer*'s confidence. Hitler attempted to qualify his previous observations but Raeder was determined. A few days after his meeting with Hitler, Raeder drafted a memorandum in which he made two recommendations as to who should succeed him: the commander of Naval Group North, Admiral Rolf Carls, and the commander of the U-boat arm, Admiral Karl Dönitz. At the end of January, Dönitz was promoted to the rank of *Großadmiral* and appointed as the new commander-in-chief of the *Kriegsmarine*. At his first meeting with Dönitz, Hitler reaffirmed his determination to scrap the surface fleet. Dönitz replied that he did not concur with the proposal but stated that he needed time to study the details.[10]

Having undergone an overhaul, amid the political fallout from the Battle of the Barents Sea, on 11 January, the *Scharnhorst* and *Prinz Eugen* put to sea and attempted to sail north to Norway. Sighted off the Skaw by a reconnaissance aircraft from Coastal Command, the two ships reversed course as the commander-in-chief of the Home Fleet, Admiral Tovey, ordered six submarines to take up patrolling stations off the Norwegian coast while ordering a destroyer flotilla supported by two cruisers to sweep the waters to the south of Stadlandet. Meanwhile, the heavy units of the Home Fleet prepared for sea in case the sighting of the *Scharnhorst* and *Prinz Eugen* was a prelude to the two ships attempting a breakout into the Atlantic. A fortnight later the two ships attempted once more to sail to Norway but they were sighted once more off the Skaw. Poor weather concealed the ships from the efforts of the RAF and they once more returned to Germany unscathed.[11]

On 8 February, Dönitz met with Hitler at the *Wolfschanze* with a set of detailed proposals regarding the future of the *Kriegsmarine*. Under the proposals, a large number of vessels that made up the surface fleet were to be paid off while a request was made that U-boat production become the complete priority of German industry. Dönitz also asserted his sole right to order those surface units of the *Kriegsmarine*, which were not paid off out on operations. Dönitz also laid down the principle that when in action, commanders should be left to their own devices, to make decisions as they saw fit without interference.

As he talked through his proposals, Dönitz had before him a memorandum that had been drawn up by Raeder as his last action as commander-in-chief, in which he maintained that despite their relative inactivity, the capital ships stationed in Norway were making valuable contributions to the German war effort. As Raeder saw it, so long as the main body of the surface fleet was stationed in Norway, the Allies were obliged to maintain an equal number of capital ships in and around the British Isles and Iceland, which could have been put to more effective use in other theatres of operations, ready to react to any potential Atlantic breakout or challenge to the Arctic convoy route.

Dönitz advocated more rigorous action by the surface fleet and believed that Hitler had handicapped the surface units of the *Kriegsmarine* by insisting that the capital ships could only venture out on operations when there was no aircraft carrier among the Allied naval forces. Seeing the potential for future success by the surface fleet when conditions were right, Dönitz wrote that 'withdrawing these ships from service would not result in any appreciable increase in either manpower or material, and that the implementation of the project could not but react politically and militarily to our disadvantage'.[12] Dismantling the surface fleet as Hitler proposed was 'an even less attractive solution [than maintaining the ships in service] for it made considerable claims on labour and technical resources'—something that Germany could ill-afford.[13]

On 26 February, Dönitz travelled to Vinnitsa where another of Hitler's headquarters was located in order to put forward his case. Beginning by informing Hitler that the *Admiral Hipper*, *Köln* and *Leipzig* had outlived their usefulness and that they would be decommissioned alongside the antique battleships *Schleswig-Holstein* and *Schlesien*, Dönitz proceeded to inform Hitler that he considered the Allied convoys to the Soviet Union ideal targets and that it was his duty to attack them in an effort to reduce the pressure on Germany's forces in the Soviet Union. He therefore announced his proposal to send the *Scharnhorst* north to Norway where she would join the *Tirpitz* and *Lützow*. These ships, Dönitz argued, accompanied by six destroyers would prove to be a formidable menace to the Arctic convoys. Hitler was caught off-guard and flew into a rage in which he denounced the crews of Germany's surface fleet before grudgingly agreeing to his new commander-in-chief's proposal.

So it was that on 8 March, *Scharnhorst* weighed anchor and departed Gotenhafen for Norway. A reconnaissance aircraft found the *Scharnhorst* missing from Gotenhafen, which caused the new commander-in-chief of the Home Fleet, Admiral Bruce Fraser, to move to Hvalfjord while other elements of the Home Fleet prepared to put to sea. Poor weather prevented the searching aircraft from locating the *Scharnhorst* and her escorting destroyers as they sailed north. Off Bergen, the ships encountered a severe storm which forced the destroyers to seek shelter as the battleship pressed on at a reduced speed.[14]

On 11 March as *Scharnhorst* sailed north, the *Tirpitz* departed Trondheim and proceeded to Bogen Bay near Narvik where she joined the *Lützow* and *Nürnberg* during the night of 12–13 March. At 4 p.m. on 14 March, the *Scharnhorst* arrived at the anchorage and dropped anchor. Also at anchor at Bogen Bay alongside the *Tirpitz*, *Scharnhorst*, *Lützow*, and *Nürnberg* were the destroyers *Theodor Riedel*, *Karl Galster*, *Erich Steinbrink*, *Paul Jacobi*, *Z28*, and *Z29* and the torpedo boats *T20* and *T21*. This force of ships remained at Bogen until midnight on 22 March when, under the command of Admiral Kummetz, they weighed anchor and moved north to Altaford, a large inlet that pierced the coast of Finnmark. The voyage to Altafjord passed without incident, the only items of note being a handful of drifting mines. On 24 March, the ships arrived at Altafjord and proceeded through the fjord system to drop anchor in a narrow spur known as Kåfjord.

Heavy units of the Kriegsmarine at anchor at Bogen Bay. From left to right, the ships are the *Tirpitz*, *Scharnhorst*, and *Lützow*. Between *Tirpitz* and *Scharnhorst*, a destroyer can be seen. (*World War Photos*)

Scharnhorst would spend the spring and summer months of 1943 in and around Altafjord. Owing to the suspension of the Arctic convoys during the summer months by the Allies, the time spent at Altafjord was largely uneventful. As *Scharnhorst* gently swayed at anchor in Altafjord, the Battle of the Atlantic was reaching its climax. In this climatic battle, it was not the capital ships of the *Kriegsmarine* that arduously fought the convoy system but the U-boat wolf packs.

In a break to the relative inactivity, exercises were undertaken. At the beginning of April, the *Scharnhorst* and accompanying destroyers sailed out into the Arctic Ocean into the vicinity of Bear Island on a training sortie. On 8 April, *Scharnhorst* suffered a serious internal explosion in the aft auxiliary machinery space above the armour deck. The explosion killed and injured thirty-four members of the crew and prompted the flooding of the magazines which served turret 'Caesar' as a precaution against a magazine explosion. When *Scharnhorst* returned to Altafjord, a repair ship was brought alongside and within two weeks the damage was repaired.[15]

Having been repaired, on 17 May, an exercise was conducted by Kummetz's ships before they returned to their moorings that evening. Shortages of fuel greatly curtailed the activities of the ships, forcing them to spend the majority of their time behind anti-torpedo and anti-submarine nets. It was probably with great relief that at 8 p.m. on 4 July, Kummetz, for the first time since his arrival as commander of the German fleet, issued the order for the entire battle fleet to prepare for sea. With a south-easterly wind blowing which brought with it a welcome rise in the temperature, *Tirpitz*, *Scharnhorst*, *Lützow*, and the destroyers departed Altafjord and set a course for Bear Island to partake in exercises in which *Scharnhorst*, *Tirpitz* and half of the destroyers would attack a British escort force represented by the *Lützow* and the other destroyers. The exercise had to be broken off after four hours owing to a critical

Scharnhorst (left) and *Tirpitz* (right) sometime between March and July 1943 prior to Operation Sizilien. (*Author's Collection*)

shortage of fuel, nevertheless, Kummetz felt reasonably satisfied with the results when the ships slipped back into their mooring on the night of 6 July.[16]

In the aftermath of the exercise, neither the *Scharnhorst*, *Tirpitz*, nor any of the other ships that comprised Kummetz's squadron would leave Altafjord throughout the remainder of July nor during August.[17] In the wake of the exercise, Kummetz wrote:

> This exercise in the open sea gave the Group a boost of sorts, but it also made clear how essential training of this nature is. It cannot be expected that a group penned up in a narrow fjord, and only able to carry out brief exercises involving one or two ships at a time, should act as a coordinated whole and perform tactically correct in whatever situations may arise … such exercises must therefore be regularly carried out.[18]

Given the way in which the events of the war had seen Allied forces turn the tide against Germany, Kummetz most likely knew that this was nothing more than wishful thinking. Indeed, owing to the strict rationing of oil, the ships of Kummetz's squadron were forced to sit idle at their moorings with their engines shut down. Power and heating had to be provided by auxiliary vessels equipped with electric generators and coal-fired steam engines. Even the auxiliary vessels did not come without problems. In July, the generators on board the *Wilhelm Bremen* and *Karl Junge* broke down. With no spare parts to conduct repair work, it was not until another vessel, the *Watt*, was summoned from Narvik that the *Scharnhorst* and *Tirpitz* had their power restored.[19]

In Altafjord, for the crews of the *Scharnhorst* and other vessels at anchor, the days of perpetual daylight dragged by as officers struggled in vain to starve off the boredom that descended. Various expeditions ashore to gather berries and mushrooms were undertaken while ashore in Kåfjord, athletics tournaments and polar championships were held on a gravel playing field. *Kapitän zur See* Hüffmeier would later recall how in August, in an effort to stave off the boredom, 'We set up a stage on the afterdeck and put on eleven variety shows for the men of the big ships, the destroyers, torpedo boats, supply ships, tugs and Army detachments in the neighbourhood. They were greeted with considerable enthusiasm and produced encouraging results'.[20] None of these activities, however, were likely to fight off the blanket of boredom for long.

The heavily censored news from the continent was gloomy. The offensive at Kursk had ground to a halt, while Allied landings in Sicily had precipitated the fall of Mussolini. Over Germany, the Allied air offensive was gaining momentum with aircraft of the United States Army Air Force bombing the Reich by day before RAF Bomber Command returned at night. Men who returned to the ships anchored in Kåfjord following returning from leave brought with them heart-rending accounts of the suffering of the civilian population. Despite all of the activities that were laid on to occupy the crews of the ships, the news from the home front did little to help those stationed aboard the ships. Hüffmeier, who was nothing if not a realist, went so far as to note:

> The uncomfortable feeling we have that up here in the north we are much safer than are our loved ones, exposed as they are to constant bombing attacks, especially in the Ruhr, where many of the men are from. The desire to avenge these attacks on families and friends with the aid of the ships, or in some other way, is very widespread.[21]

In Berlin, Dönitz too was equally aware that the crews of Germany's most powerful capital ships were spending their days idle, tucked away in the fjords inside the Arctic Circle while the war raged around them and wished to provide the crews with the opportunity to feel like they too were hitting back.

Scharnhorst behind anti-submarine and anti-torpedo nets in Altafjord, 1943. (*NH 81939, US Naval History and Heritage Command Center*)

11

The Hunters and the Hunted

The mountainous island of Spitsbergen is the largest island of the Svalbard archipelago in Northern Norway, bordering the Arctic Ocean, Norwegian Sea, and the Greenland Sea. Spitsbergen covers an area of some 15,075 sq. miles (39,044 sq. km), which makes it the largest island in Norway and the thirty-sixth largest island in the world. The first recorded sighting of the island by a European was made by Willem Barnetsz who came across the island while searching for the Northern Sea route in June 1596. The archipelago may have been known to Russian Pomor hunters as early as the fourteenth or fifteenth centuries, although solid evidence pre-dating the seventeenth century is lacking.

During the seventeenth century, Spitsbergen became a whaling base and continued to act as one through the eighteenth century after which it was abandoned. Towards the end of the nineteenth century, the island began to be mined for coal which saw several permanent communities established. The Svalbard Treaty (also known as the Spitsbergen Treaty) of February 1920 recognised the full and absolute sovereignty of Norway over the archipelago while the Svalbard Act of 1925 made the archipelago a part of Norway (between 1920 and 1925, it had dependency status). The treaties established the archipelago as a free economic zone and permitted signatory nations an equal right to engage in commercial activities on the islands while also regulating the demilitarisation of the archipelago.

When the Second World War broke out, many of the inhabitants of Spitsbergen were Russian. As a result of the Molotov–Ribbentrop Pact, there was a limited danger of Germany invading the island, despite the fact that it was a Norwegian territory until the launching of Operation Barbarossa, the invasion of the Soviet Union, on 22 June 1941. With the commencement of hostilities between Germany and the Soviet Union, the island's coal mines were abandoned. On 25 August 1941 members of the Royal Canadian Corps, Royal Engineers, and Free Norwegian Forces, supported by ships of the Royal Navy, landed on Spitsbergen to deny the archipelago to the Germans and to destroy the coal mines along with stores and associated equipment. The Russian inhabitants who numbered 1,969 people, were also evacuated from the islands and taken to Archangel.[1]

In April 1942, Norwegian forces landed at Barentsburg on the island to establish a permanent military presence on the islands. The Norwegian forces were well established by the summer of 1943. In the meantime, in late 1941, following the evacuation of the island, the Germans established a meteorological station on Spitsbergen in the Krossfjorden. The Germans established a network of meteorological stations throughout the Arctic in order to improve their weather forecasting for launching attacks against the Arctic convoys. On 23 August 1942, however, the six-man detachment from the weather station was evacuated by U-boat as the station was vulnerable to Allied attacks during the summer months owing to the recession of ice.

In the wake of the landings on the island by Norwegian forces, an Allied meteorological station was established at Barentsburg which monitored not only the weather but also ice formations and the sea temperatures which were transmitted back to Britain. In September 1943, Spitsbergen was garrisoned by a force comprised of 134 Norwegian soldiers, nine officers from the Royal Norwegian Navy, five British ratings and a liaison officer from the Royal Navy Volunteer Reserve. The garrison force had been told that in the event of a German attack on the island they would receive ample warning as it would be impossible for a major German seaborne operation to go undetected. In the event that the Germans did launch an attack and landed on Spitsbergen, the garrison forces had been issued with instructions to destroy any sensitive equipment and to then retreat into the interior of the island. With a raid by U-boat thought to be a far more likely occurrence than a full-scale landing supported by capital ships, the garrison was provided with a 4-inch naval gun, eight Bofors anti-aircraft guns, and an Oerlikon anti-aircraft gun for defence.[2]

Unknown to the Allies, plans were being drawn up by the Germans to send the *Scharnhorst* and *Tirpitz* to attack the Allied installations on Spitsbergen. The distance from Altafjord to Svalbard is approximately 621 miles (1,000 km)—a distance that could be covered by *Tirpitz* and *Scharnhorst* in under twenty-four hours if they sailed between 20–25 knots. In essence, the plans that were drawn up envisaged the *Tirpitz* and *Scharnhorst*, accompanied by a group of destroyers sailing from Altafjord to Svalbard where, under the codename Operation Sizilien, they would attack the settlements of Barentsburg and Longyearbyen. The operation would be one of the most northerly operations conducted by German forces during the course of the Second World War. The final plans for the operation were issued on 19 August with the only detail left to be settled being the attack date.

At 12 p.m. on 6 September, a rather cryptic message was transmitted by lamp and flags between the ships at anchor stating: 'Will not put to sea for unit exercises according to number 2831. Individual exercises permitted. Report intentions for tomorrow at 22.30'.[3] This was the order to initiate Operation Sizilien. An almost leisurely afternoon was spent preparing the ships to put to sea and it was not until 10 p.m. that the ships began to unshackle from their moorings and began to proceed down Altafjord. It was, of course, impossible to disguise the fact from the local populace that the *Scharnhorst* and almost the entire squadron anchored in the fjord networks were raising anchor; the cryptic message, therefore, was an attempt to convince those members of the local population who paid attention to the movement of the German forces that something other than a concerted operation was about to occur.

The ships proceeded independently through the fjords to the rendezvous point where in the darkness off Altafjord they assembled. The *Scharnhorst* took up a position behind the *Tirpitz* while the destroyers *Karl Galster*, *Theodor Riedel*, and *Hans Lody* sailed at the head of the formation to offer protection against lurking submarines. Meanwhile, the destroyers *Erich Steinbrink*, *Z27*, and *Z30* sailed on the starboard side of the capital ships while *Z29*, *Z31*, and *Z33* sailed on the port side. Shortly before 11 p.m., Kummetz's ships sailed through Stjernsundet and into the Barents Sea. Sailing north-westerly at 19 knots, the squadron had covered half the distance to Bear Island by 8 a.m. on 7 September. Cloud cover concealed the formation from above while visibility on the surface varied between 6.2 and 12.4 miles (10 and 20 km), meaning favourable conditions.

During the course of the afternoon, a British reconnaissance aircraft overflew Altafjord. Two hours later, Kummetz was alerted to the overflight by a signal from admiral commanding Northern Water, Otto Klüber, in Narvik: '16.45 Alta anchorage overflown by Spitfire'.[4] The news was received by Kummetz and the commander officer of the *Tirpitz Kapitän zur See* Hans Meyer with equanimity. At 4.45 p.m., when the Spitfire overflew Altafjord, Kummetz's ships were 248 miles (400 km) from Svalbard. Even if the British realised that the ships had put to sea for the first time in months, no British naval forces could intercept them before they reached their intended destination. Even if the Home Fleet departed Scapa Flow immediately upon receiving the reconnaissance report (something it was unlikely to do based on one report), then it would have to sail at full speed for over fifty hours to reach Svalbard. The German plans did not, however, intend for the squadron to linger for long enough to allow the Royal Navy to react.

The southern parts of Svalbard were reached at 22.00 on 7 September. In an effort to preserve the element of surprise for as long as possible, as the ships approached the archipelago, Kummetz ordered all of the ships to run up the White Ensign as a *ruse de guerre*. The deception was hardly necessary for the garrison was hardly in a position to resist the *Scharnhorst* and *Tirpitz*. As the ships sailed into Isfjord huge glaciers dominated the visions of the German sailors as spirits ran high. On the southern shore of Isfjord lay the targets of the operation: Barenstburg and Longyearbyen. The ships reduced speed to better navigate the fjord as the crews cleared for action. Aboard both the *Tirpitz* and *Scharnhorst*, the Ar 196 floatplanes were armed with bombs and made ready for action.[5]

At approximately 2.43 a.m., Norwegian lookouts on Cape Heer spotted the silhouettes of the ships on the horizon and raised the alarm. Shortly thereafter the Allied radio station known as Green Harbour began to transmit a signal stating that three cruisers and seven destroyers had been sighted. Aboard the *Tirpitz*, as Green Harbour began transmitting, jamming efforts were initiated but it was unclear if the efforts were successful or if the transmission had succeeded in getting through. The jamming efforts by those aboard the *Tirpitz* were unsuccessful as the signal from Green Harbour was picked up by a British station in Reykjavik, which, at 4 a.m., relayed the message to Scapa Flow. As the radio jamming efforts were initiated one of the Ar 196s from the *Tirpitz* was launched the reconnoitre Spitsbergen and, if necessary, to attack Allied strongholds.

At around 4 a.m., the secondary armament of the *Tirpitz* roared into life. Thirty rounds were fired against Green Harbour, after which no further transmissions were noted. The attack was now fully in motion. The destroyers that had provided an anti-submarine screen to the *Tirpitz* and *Scharnhorst* as they sailed to Spitsbergen had carried 600 soldiers of Grenadier-Regiment 349, part of 230. Infanterie-Division who were to put ashore and destroy various facilities on the island. As the destroyers disembarked the troops, the main battery of the *Tirpitz* engaged the garrison anti-aircraft guns before opening fire on the coal mine at Heerodden. Within minutes devastation reined at Barentsberg as dense oily smoke rose into the sky.[6] The *Tirpitz* then manoeuvred and stood off the Gronfjord where her main battery of 15-inch guns paralysed the opposition.

Meanwhile, Kummetz had ordered the *Scharnhorst* to proceed down Isfjord into the Adventfjord to Longyearbyen. This would prove to be a sore point for a significant number of crewmembers of the *Scharnhorst* who disliked seeing their ship ordered into the Adventfjord 'as though she were and ordinary minesweeper' while *Tirpitz* lay off Gronfjord.[7] Resistance was much weaker at Longyearbyen than at Barentsburg with the result that there was little call for the main guns of the *Scharnhorst* to be brought into action.

By 5.12 a.m., Kummetz was receiving reports that all opposition at Longyearbyen and Barentsburg had ceased allowing the men of 230. Infanterie-Division to go about their task of destroying the installations. While the operation had gone smoothly thus far, Kummetz was concerned about the radio transmission from Green Harbour. If the Home Fleet was at Scapa Flow or if elements of the Royal Navy were at anchor in an Icelandic port then they would have to sail for around two days to reach the area between Svalbard and Norway, where they could intercept his squadron by which time Kummetz planned to be back at anchor. If, however, elements of the Home Fleet were already at sea, then they might serve to constitute a real threat to his ships.

By 9 a.m., the men of 230. Infanterie-Division had accomplished their tasks and had re-embarked on the destroyers, permitting the ships to begin their retreat. Shortly after 9.30 a.m., Kummetz issued an order for all ships to close on his flagship. When the order from Kummetz was received, *Scharnhorst* was engaged in shelling a weather station. Before complying with the order to close on the *Tirpitz*, Hüffmeier decided to re-embark the ship's Arado seaplane. As the aircraft attempted to land, the wind increased markedly, causing the waters in the fjord to whip up which served to make landing the Arado difficult.

On the third attempted landing, the aircraft was damaged, which served to further delay *Scharnhorst*'s departure. All the while Hüffmeier neglected to inform Kummetz of what was occurring. It was not until 11.30 a.m. that *Scharnhorst* reached the assembly point, by which time *Tirpitz* and the destroyers had been waiting for an hour and a half. Hüffmeier's failure to inform Kummetz of the delay in recovering the Arado 'resulted in a most unsatisfactory situation … The Squadron Commander had no idea of what the ship was doing between half-past nine and half-past eleven … a delay which in an operational context might have had most regrettable consequences'.[8] Having eventually formed up, Kummetz's squadron left Isfjord and proceeded into the Arctic Ocean at 19 knots.

During the course of the operation, sixteen sailors were wounded, one of them mortally, while seventy-four prisoners were taken. The voyage back to Altafjord was uneventful. Convinced that Allied radio stations had received the transmission from Green Harbour, strict vigilance was required during the course of the journey back to Norway with radio operators aboard the two battleships monitoring all possible frequencies for any indications of Allied activity in response to the attack. Nothing was heard as the ships continued on at 19 knots. The speed chosen by Kummetz suggests that he did not perceive his ships to be in immediate danger and also indicated a desire to conserve fuel.

An Ar 196 was launched to fly above the ships and to search the surrounding area for any Allied activity. No Allied warships were sighted although at 11 a.m. on 9 September a submarine alarm roused the crews though no attack materialised. Kummetz subsequently ordered speed to be increased to 25 knots so as to reach safety quicker. At 3 p.m., Kummetz's ships reached the entrance of Altafjord and were back at their respective moorings by 5.30 p.m.

Operation Sizilien was not the most significant operation to be conducted during the Second World War and provoked no Allied countermeasures. In the aftermath of the raid, British and Norwegian forces would re-establish their positions on Spitsbergen while the Germans would not make any other attempts to destroy the Allied positions on the island. On 10 September, an Ultra decrypt revealed that the *Tirpitz* and *Scharnhorst* had returned to Altafjord. During the time that the two ships were absent from their berths, the Allies had no idea as to why the ships had weighed anchor. A number of reasons for the absence of the ships had been considered, including the capture of agents in Norway, that the Germans were making preparations for a sortie into the Atlantic, and that the ships were preparing for a return to Germany. It was not until two days after the attack on Spitsbergen that the Admiralty in London learned what had transpired which led to the Home Fleet immediately putting to sea, by which time it was already too late to intercept Kummetz's squadron.

The return to Altafjord was a blessing for Rear Admiral Claude Barry, the commander of the Royal Navy's submarine arm for plans had been formulated to attack the *Tirpitz*, *Scharnhorst* and *Lützow* using midget submarines known as X-craft as they lay behind their anti-torpedo nets in Kåfjord. Under the codename Operation Source, six X-craft were to be towed by submarines to the mouth of Altafjord whereupon they would cast off before the X-craft proceeded independently up the fjord system to their respective targets. Three X-craft—the *X-5*, *X-6*, and *X-7*, commanded by Lieutenants Henty Henty-Creer, Donald Cameron, and Godfrey Place—were to attack *Tirpitz*. *X-8* commanded by Lieutenant Brian McFarlane was to attack the *Lützow* while *X-9* and *X-10* commanded by Lieutenants Thomas Martin and Kenneth Hudsperth were to attack *Scharnhorst*.

Initially, the submarines and X-craft were to sail together from Loch Cairnbawn until they reached the Shetlands where they were divided into two groups and proceed to Norway. The X-craft had an operational range of 1,500 miles (2,400 km) at 4 knots, which was just sufficient to make the journey into Kåfjord and back, however, living conditions inside the X-craft were so uncomfortable that it was decided that each of the midget submarines would be manned by a passage crew while they were

Above: Scharnhorst in a Norwegian fjord during 1943. (*World War Photos*)

Right: A RAF reconnaissance photograph taken on 10 September 1943 of Altafjord. *Scharnhorst* is visible surrounded by anti-torpedo nets in the top left of the image. The other vessels visible in the image include destroyers, supply ships and small Norwegian trawlers requisitioned by the German occupation forces. (*P02511.004, Australian War Memorial*)

towed to Norway before the operational crew took over. The operation got underway during the afternoon of 11 September when the submarines *Thrasher*, *Truculent*, and *Stubborn* towing X-5, X-6, and X-7 departed Loch Cairnbawn. They were followed to sea by the *Seanymph*, *Syrtis*, and *Sceptre* towing X-8, X-9, and X-10.

During the course of the journey to Altafjord, the crews of the X-craft and submarines experienced a variety of problems, handicaps and hazards. On 15 September, the tow between the *Stubborn* and X-7 broke. Contact was maintained which allowed for an auxiliary hawser to be passed to resume the tow. The day previous, X-8 had become detached from *Seanymph*. Contact between X-8 and *Seanymph* was lost for thirty-six hours before the submarine finally located the X-craft. It was soon found that problems existed with the two amatol charges being carried by the X-craft which led to it being withdrawn from the operation. A more unfortunate episode occurred on 16 September. The commanding officer of the *Syrtis*, Lieutenant-Commander M. H Jupp sent a signal to X-9 requesting that the X-craft surface. Jupp received no reply to his request and it soon became evident that the hawser had failed. The *Syrtis* reversed course and conducted a search for X-9, but the X-craft was never found. When the *Syrtis* reached a suitable distance from the Norwegian coast Jupp informed the Admiralty of this latest development. X-5, X-6 and X-10, meanwhile, enjoyed fairly uneventful voyages and all reached the Norwegian coast between 17 and 19 September where they were soon joined by X-7. During the evening of 19 September, the passage crews began to exchange positions with the operational crews who would conduct the attack.[9]

Aboard the *Tirpitz* and *Scharnhorst*, a mood of celebration was to be found. Before the stores lining Gronfjord and Adventfjord had been burned to the ground they were systematically searched and 'liberated' of large quantities of butter, chocolate, canned goods, and cigarettes. Much of this loot was exchanged, won and lost in poker schools which assembled across the ships. In addition to this, beer and schnapps flowed freely to celebrate the many decorations that were awarded following the attack. Nevertheless, while a mood of celebration existed, aboard the *Scharnhorst*, which was to be found anchored alone at the head of the Langfjord, four hours sailing from the *Tirpitz*, dissatisfaction was also widespread. A total of 500 Iron Cross Second Class decorations were awarded following Operation Silzien to crewmen from the *Tirpitz* while 162 were awarded to members of the *Scharnhorst*'s crew.

While neither ship had played a particularly large role in the attack on Spitsbergen, the fighting having been largely carried out by the destroyers, those aboard the *Scharnhorst* felt that the decorations that were awarded to those aboard the *Tirpitz* were largely unmerited. The *Scharnhorst* had seen much more war service than the *Tirpitz* and this fact was a sticking point between the ships.

There had always been a great deal of rivalry between the capital ships of the *Kriegsmarine*. An interrogation report compiled by the director of naval intelligence in London dated 23 February 1944 noted, 'That the ship's company was proud of *Scharnhorst* and had immense faith in the ship's capabilities and fighting qualities has been only too apparent. Even *Gneisenau*, the sister-ship was looked upon as a poor relation and relations with the crew of the *Tirpitz* were far from cordial, probably

Scharnhorst at anchor at Sopnes Bay at the end of Langfjord. (*Author's Collection*)

as the result of a feeling of rivalry'.[10] The report went on to describe the view of the *Tirpitz* held by those aboard the *Scharnhorst* in more detail:

> Discipline in *Tirpitz* was said to be much stricter than in *Scharnhorst* and the ship's company [was] very much younger and more inexperienced. The commanding officer, Captain Meyer, was always referred to in derogatory terms and many of the *Scharnhorst* survivors said that nothing would induce them to transfer to *Tirpitz*. They described her men as having a hang-dog look about them.
>
> Some leading stokers who had been transferred to *Tirpitz* from *Scharnhorst* used to meet their former shipmates and bewail their fate, complaining that their new ship was run like a detention barracks.
>
> Some of the scathing comments by the *Scharnhorst* survivors concerning *Tirpitz* and her men may well be due to the fact that they considered the crew of the flagship received better treatment than they did.
>
> In the matter of counting 'points' for the award of Iron Cross Second Class, *Tirpitz* was considered especially favoured … *Tirpitz* was strongly suspected of cheating the necessary conditions.[11]

While the crews of the *Tirpitz* in Kåfjord and *Scharnhorst* in Langfjord basked in the afterglow of the raid on Spitsbergen and harboured discontent over the award of decorations, they had no inclination that a handful of midget submarines were making their way along Altafjord to attack them. The X-craft ran the gauntlet of defences, which included a 15.5-mile-long (25km) minefield at the entrance to Sørøysundet, and prepared to launch the attack on 22 September. As it made the passage along Altafjord, *X-10* was plagued by a number of minor defects which included a leaking periscope and issues with the pump of the wet-and-dry compartment.

Aboard the X-craft Hudsperth did his utmost to repair his malfunctioning equipment. *X-10*'s periscope was virtually useless as a result of the leak while both of the submarine's compasses were found to also be virtually useless. It was almost inconceivable to enter Kåfjord under such circumstances. At the time, it was believed by those aboard *X-10* that *Scharnhorst* was anchored at her berth in Kåfjord. If *X-10* carried on and the equipment could not be repaired, it was likely that she would reveal the operation prematurely. In fact, during the time that the X-craft were journeying through to Kåfjord, *Scharnhorst* had weighed anchor in Langfjord and was at large in Altafjord.

Geoffrey Place in *X-7* sighted the battleship on 21 September as he made his way along the fjord as she lay off Arøya Island at the northern end of Altafjord. Disappointed at the proficiency of his crew during Operation Silizen, Hüffmeier had decided to sail into Altafjord to conduct firing exercises. Place considered attacking *Scharnhorst* when he saw her but decided against it. Ultimately Place had no way of informing Hudsperth of the whereabouts of the *Scharnhorst*.[12] The Admiralty too, by this time, had learned that *Scharnhorst* would not be found in Kåfjord and that the ship would be in Altafjord but had no way of notifying Hudsperth aboard *X-10*.

Around 7 a.m. on 22 September, *X-6* and *X-7* launched their attacks. Despite having been sighted prompting gunners aboard *Tirpitz* to open fire, the two X-craft succeeded in placing their charges beneath the battleship before they were abandoned with the crews becoming prisoners of war as the X-craft sank. *X-5* did not succeed in making an attack against *Tirpitz* and vanished. It is thought that *X-5* was sighted as it approached *Tirpitz* and was sunk with the loss of all hands. At approximately 8.10 a.m., *Tirpitz* was rocked by explosions as the charges laid by *X-7* detonated and set off those laid by *X-6*.

Scharnhorst behind anti-submarine nets in Kåfjord where she was to be the target of *X-10*. When the X-craft reached Kåfjord, *Scharnhorst* was to be found off Arøya Island in Altafjord conducting gunnery exercises. (*World War Photos*)

The damage was bad but it could have been much worse had *Kapitän* Meyer not realised the danger that his ship was in. Meyer ordered the bow to be swung away from the area where two of the charges had been laid using the anchor chains leaving just the stern over two charges. The detonation of the charges put the propulsion system out of action and flooded one generator room, leaving almost the entire ship without electricity. The ship's hydrophones and radio equipment were left inoperable and precious fuel leaked into the fjord. Much of the machinery had been shocked on its mounting and was damaged to such an extent that it could not be used while the propeller shafts could not be rotated.

In addition to this, the port rudder was damaged to such an extent that it could not be used. Twenty minutes following the detonation of the charges, 300 tons of water had entered the ship. Despite the desperate efforts to pump it out, thirty minutes after the charges had detonated 500 tons of water had flooded into the ship. With each damage report, the number of wounded increased although there was only one fatality – a seaman who had been thrown into the air and was killed when he landed on one of the anchor chains.[13]

Aboard *X-10*, Hudsperth and his crew heard the detonations erupting in Kåfjord and knew that the attack on the *Tirpitz* was underway. Despite their best efforts, they had not been able to repair any of their X-craft's malfunctioning components. With the attack on the *Tirpitz* the crew of *X-10* knew that the German defences had been alerted. Hudsperth had no option but to break off the attack. Over the next six days, Hudsperth and his crew would play hide-and-seek in the fjords. Poor weather helped the crew of *X-10* to avoid the German patrols. Shortly after midnight on 28 September, they located the *Stubborn*, which took the X-craft under tow. Following permission from Admiral Barry, the following day *X-10* was scuttled.

In the wake of the detonation of the charges, as *X-10* reversed course and began to make her way out of the fjord system, the first reports of the incident were being made by those aboard the *Tirpitz* via signal lamp to the destroyers *Z27* and *Erich Steinbrink*. The *Lützow* was ordered to release the *Watt* to provide *Tirpitz* with power while *Scharnhorst* was refused permission to return to her enclosure off Auskar Point as a hydrophone operator had detected suspicious noises close to the anchorage. Instead, the ship was ordered to keep moving at any cost.

It soon became apparent to the British by way of Ultra decrypts that the *Tirpitz* had received considerable damage. On 25 September, with Hitler's approval, the German naval staff decided that *Tirpitz* should be repaired at anchor in northern Norway. The ship would be out of commission for six months while she was repaired. Following the return of the *Lützow* to Germany on 1 October, *Scharnhorst* was left as the sole remaining capital ship possessed by the *Kriegsmarine* in northern waters.

Prior to the launching of Operation Source, around the time of Operation Silzien, on 7 September, during a visit to Washington D.C., Admiral Sir Dudley Pound, the first sea lord, caught a quiet moment with Churchill and told the prime minister of his intention to resign owing to suffering a stroke, stating that he was no longer fit for duty. Pound died on 21 October at the age of sixty-six. His replacement as first sea lord was Admiral Sir Andrew Cunningham, who had made his reputation as

Above left: Scharnhorst in Altafjord between March and December 1943. (*NH 71392, US Naval History and Heritage Command Center*)

Above right: Scharnhorst seen from the bow with a merchant ship sited on either side to offer protection against torpedo attack, 1943. (*World War Photos*)

commander-in-chief of the Royal Navy's Mediterranean Fleet. Before Cunningham was appointed to the position, Admiral Sir Bruce Fraser was offered the position but declined, telling Churchill, 'if one day I should sink the *Scharnhorst*, I might feel differently'.

On 25 September, the vice chief of the naval staff, Sir Neville Syfret, who oversaw operations during the interim period between Pound's resignation and Cunningham's appointment as first sea lord, received orders asserting his duty to resume the sailing of the Arctic convoys. The Admiralty, meanwhile, held reservations regarding the resumption of the convoys, remaining unconvinced of the benefits that the Arctic route merited compared to the risks involved. Furthermore, it was still not clear that the Battle of the Atlantic had been won. Nevertheless, the resistance of the Admiralty could not be sustained against Churchill's will and the fact that the single most powerful German ship in northern waters did not, for the moment, constitute a threat to the Arctic route. So it was that on 1 October Churchill wrote a long telegram to Stalin in which he informed the Soviet leader that the Arctic convoys would resume in November.

The first convoys of this renewed effort to set sail were the outward-bound JW-54A and the homeward bound RA-54A. These convoys succeeded in reaching their respective destinations without interference from German forces. The reason for the lack of activity by the Germans against these two convoys and for those that followed over the following weeks has been put down to a lack of reconnaissance. The Germans did, however, soon learn of the resumption of the convoys and renewed their efforts to cut this supply line to the Soviet Union.

Scharnhorst in late 1943. (*World War Photos*)

Above left: (*World War Photos*)

Above right: Scharnhorst at anchor somewhere in Norway during the winter of 1943. (*World War Photos*)

12

Ostfront

On 25 November 1943, *Scharnhorst* weighed anchor and conducted a two-hour-long full power trial during which she achieved a speed of 29.6 knots. During her 1940 trials, the ship had attained 31.1 knots.[1] It was also found, as a result of the trial, that the ship's draught had increased by 1.6 feet (0.5 m). A month earlier, the ship had received a new commanding officer in *Kapitän zur See* Fritz Hintze as Hüffmeier was promoted to a new position as *Kommandant* of the Channel Islands.[2] Shortly after Hintze had taken over command of the *Scharnhorst*, on 8 November, Kummetz left Norway for Germany for a period of extended leave and to receive treatment for medical conditions.

On the recommendations of *Flottenchef* (chief of the fleet) *Generaladmiral* Otto Schniewind, Dönitz appointed *Konteradmiral* Erich Bey as a temporary replacement. Of Bey, Dönitz wrote, 'Like Kummetz, he had grown up in destroyers and had received a comprehensive tactical training in both peace and war. He was an extremely efficient officer of very considerable war experience, and he had done well in all the appointments he had held'.[3]

Known as 'Achmed' Bey, he had begun the war as a noteworthy destroyer officer. Holding the rank of *Fregattenkapitän*, Bey commanded the 4th Destroyer Flotilla and conducted a daring minelaying sortie in the *Erich Steinbrink* off the Humber Estuary in November 1939. In February 1940, his flotilla laid more mines off Cromer Knoll. Promoted to *Kapitän zur See*, Bey commanded the 4th Flotilla under *Kommodore* Bonte at Narvik in 1940. When Bonte was killed in action on 10 April 1940 against HMS *Hardy*, Bey took over command. Three days later, all of his destroyers would be sunk or scuttled during the second battle of Narvik. Nevertheless, his reputation survived this setback and he was soon at sea once more. Promoted to *Konteradmiral*, flying his flag in *Z29*, Bey commanded the escorting destroyers during the Channel Dash in February 1942.[4] The crew of the *Scharnhorst* knew of Bey's background as a commander of destroyers and openly stated that he 'had no business commanding the battle group'.[5] It was not, however, their decision to make.

Before he returned to Germany, Kummetz advised Bey to wait until the *Tirpitz* was operational again before conducting sorties so that both ships could operate together. On her own, Kummetz advised, *Scharnhorst* would be vulnerable to enemy destroyers

Scharnhorst in one of the Norwegian fjords during late 1943. (*World War Photos*)

Above Scharnhorst underway sometime between July and December 1943. It is possible that this photograph was taken during her full-power trials of 25 November. (*Author's Collection*)

Right: Konteradmiral *Erich Bey.*

with their superior radar. Kummetz also reminded Bey that he could not rely on the Luftwaffe to undertake action against enemy surface ships and recommended that the new commander of the northern task force should ask for destroyers to be sent north as they were the most effective means of attacking a convoy.

On 20 November, the naval general staff considered the likely course of fleet operations during the winter of 1943–44 and issued a directive. It was a cautiously worded document that laid down no hard intentions and was somewhat woolly. None of the general staff knew quite what to do with the *Scharnhorst*. The directive stated that the ship and U-boats should be employed against convoy traffic, but, at the same time, as far as the *Scharnhorst* was concerned, the directive stated, 'operations must be compatible with our small strength, and the use of *Scharnhorst* during the winter is to be considered'.[6] The directive would appear to have confirmed Kummetz's belief that until the *Tirpitz* was repaired nothing more was realistically possible than a sortie by destroyers.

Two days later, Bey had prepared his own appreciation of the situation. Having consulted with *Kapitän zur See* Rolf Johannesson, the then commander of the 4th Destroyer Flotilla, in his opinion, the decision that had been made to send the 6th Destroyer Flotilla back to Germany was equivalent to giving the initiative to the enemy. Bey concluded that during the winter months, *Scharnhorst* was particularly vulnerable and that it was better to use destroyers to attack the convoys, possibly with the battleship in support. He noted, however, that the five destroyers of the 4th Destroyer Flotilla were not nearly enough to prevent the flow of supplies to the Soviet Union and that *Scharnhorst* would not be able to make up the difference in effective strength. Besides, *Scharnhorst* herself would require protection. Bey reasoned that two destroyers would be required to provide escort to *Scharnhorst*. Thus by his reasoning, *Scharnhorst* and two destroyers would be required to support the three attacking destroyers. In this *Scharnhorst* appeared to be more of a liability than an asset and she could hardly be said to be supporting the destroyers if two of their number were required to support her.

Flottenchef Schniewind, perhaps, offered the most pessimistic assessment of them all when he completed his appreciation on 5 December. To Schniewind's mind, the successive withdrawal of destroyers from Northern Waters, along with the withdrawal of some of the U-boats and Luftwaffe strength in the region combined with the crippling of the *Tirpitz* seemed to leave almost no chance at all of any success against the Arctic convoys. Claiming that the already weakened forces that were available would be less effective than they could potentially be because they would be forced to operate in the polar darkness, Schniewind insisted on accurate knowledge of the enemy's position as an absolute prerequisite. Thus it was that the chief of the fleet, the task force commander, and the destroyer commander in the north all considered there to be little chance of any action being successful. While the Germans deliberated and decided upon little in particular, the convoys to the Soviet Union continued to sail.

The first December convoy, JW-55A, departed Loch Ewe on 12 December. A few days into its journey, the convoy was sighted by a Luftwaffe reconnaissance aircraft, which prompted Fraser, flying his flag in the battleship HMS *Duke of York*, to put to sea with the Home Fleet in anticipation of the *Scharnhorst* emerging from her Norwegian refuge to attack the convoy. *Scharnhorst* did not put to sea and it was thus that the *Duke of York*, the cruiser *Jamaica* plus their destroyer screen composed of HMS *Saumarez, Savage, Scorpion,* and HnoMS *Stord* sailed through to Kola near Murmansk, where they arrived on 16 December, four days ahead of the convoy.

At Kola, Fraser called upon Admiral Arseniy Golovko, the commander of the Red Banner Northern Fleet and over the course of two days did much to thaw some of the Soviet resistance to full co-operation with the Royal Navy. On 18 December, Fraser weighed anchor and departed Kola so as to be at sea at the time that the next convoy bound for the Soviet Union departed Britain. As JW-55A approached the Murman coast, Fraser dashed west to Akureyri, Iceland, in order to refuel.[7]

At a meeting at the *Wolfschanze* with Hitler held on 19 and 20 December, Dönitz informed the *Führer* that under the codename Operation Ostfront, 'the *Scharnhorst* and the destroyers of the task force will attack the next Allied convoy headed from England to Russia via the northern route, if a successful operation seems assured'.[8] The next convoy, JW-55B, was comprised of twenty merchant ships and departed Loch Ewe on 20 December with a close escort provided by the corvettes *Borage* and *Wallflower*, and the minesweepers *Hydra* and *Hound*. Having departed Loch Ewe, the escort force was bolstered by the arrival of HMS *Wanderer, Wrestler, Whitehall, Oxlip, Honeysuckle,* and *Gleaner*, whereupon it set a course north to rendezvous with its ocean escort of seven destroyers commanded by Captain James McCoy in HMS *Onslow*. As it proceeded north to join the ocean escort force off Iceland, JW-55B and its close escort ran through fine weather, though the journey did not pass without incident. Aboard the *Wanderer*, the watch were cleaning the guns when an ordinary seaman who was servicing an Oerlikon slipped and fell overboard. A sea boat was quickly launched, which pulled the seaman from the icy water. Although he was in the hands of *Wanderer*'s doctor within seven minutes of falling overboard, the seaman succumbed to the extreme cold.[9]

Meanwhile, at Akureyri, as his ships took on fuel, Fraser summoned his captains and announced his intentions. The journey from Kola to Akureyri had given Fraser's ships the opportunity to exercise, and having practiced night exercises, Fraser outlined his intentions. Fraser's plan relied on an initial limitation of speed to 15 knots in order to conserve fuel. If and when a general action ensued, HMS *Jamaica* was to remain in support of *Duke of York* while the destroyers were to divide into two subdivisions and mount a torpedo attack.[10]

On 22 December, a Blohm and Voss BV 138 reconnaissance aircraft sighted JW-55B and commenced shadowing the convoy while the first attack against the convoy was launched by a group of Ju 88s the following day. As the Ju 88s launched their attacks against the convoy, Fraser received information from Ultra decrypts informing him that a group of U-boats was being assembled to attack the convoy. The decrypt also suggested that the *Scharnhorst* was being brought to three hours' readiness to sail. At 11 p.m., Fraser's ships left Akureyri. The initial report from the BV 138 that sighted JW-55B was inaccurate as it suggested that the convoy was comprised of troop transports, which led some within the German high command to conclude that the Allies were launching the much-feared invasion of Norway. It was, however, soon realised that the convoy was not the vanguard of an Allied invasion armada but

Fraser's flagship, HMS *Duke of York*, off Iceland during the summer of 1943. (*Author's Collection*)

Scharnhorst shortly before Operation Ostfront. (*Author's Collection*)

merely an ordinary munitions convoy. Further reports on the convoy were made by Ju 88s and another BV 138 during the course of 23 December.

While the convoy had been located, one detail caused uncertainty for the Germans—whether or not there was a British heavy covering force sailing in support of the convoy. The presence of such a force would have a crucial effect on whether and how the *Scharnhorst* was deployed. During the course of 24 December, staff officers at both Narvik and Kiel discussed by teleprinter the possibility of a heavy covering force being at sea, referring to 'a British unit located yesterday by its transmissions [that] may well be the covering force closing'.[11] The German staff officers discussed 'the supposed enemy squadron' and noted that 'complete reconnaissance and security from the enemy ... [is] not guaranteed', while also noting that the operation of the task force centred around the *Scharnhorst* carried an element of risk.[12] *Generaladmiral* Schniewind thought that there was 'no proof as of yet of a cover force being at sea'.[13] Schniewind's thoughts were backed by the report from a reconnaissance aircraft shadowing the convoy which reported the convoy as being composed of '12 merchant ships, up to 5,000 tons, three destroyers, far apart. Nothing further made out owing to bad visibility. Defence by medium and light flak'.

At 11.45 p.m., the *Fliegerführer* Lofotens signalled his intentions for the reconnaissance flights to be flown during the course of Christmas Day. Two BV 138s were to be dispatched to look for the British 'battle group approaching from the south-west'. *Konteradmiral* Otto Klüber, the admiral commanding Northern Waters, was on leave when the signals began to come in and was therefore not present at his headquarters in Narvik. Nevertheless, his staff assumed that the signals that had been picked up originated from a British heavy covering force. The only man who never had any doubts about a potential British heavy cover force was Dönitz. Indeed, Dönitz demanded much more definitive evidence of the presence of a heavy covering force as in his view, all of the evidence that had been compiled indicated that a heavy covering force was not sailing in company with the convoy. So it was that Dönitz decided that *Scharnhorst* would put to sea against JW-55B.

Taking into consideration the last reported position of the convoy, Schniewind issued orders to Bey to weigh anchor at 5 p.m. on Christmas Day and to sail in the *Scharnhorst* to intercept the convoy.

On 25 December 1943, as *Scharnhorst* lay at anchor in Langfjord, a south-westerly gale swept over the snow-covered mountains and hurled down the steep cliffs, whipping up the normally calm waters. Lying at anchor near the *Scharnhorst* were three destroyers of the 4th Destroyer Flotilla—Z29, Z34, and Z38—while two other destroyers from the flotilla—Z30 and Z33—lay alongside the *Tirpitz* in Kåfjord. Aboard *Scharnhorst*, an atmosphere of relaxed discipline reigned. *Kapitän zur See* Hintze made informal rounds of the ship, complimenting the men on the decorations that adorned their messes and issuing full rations of cigarettes to any man who had failed to receive his full ration.

Christmas mail was on board and the crew were to be found opening their mail and parcels from home. One party of sailors had gone ashore to ski while the ship's choir sang Christmas carols. The Christmas peace aboard the battleship was shattered at 10.55 a.m. when a signal from Bey arrived which stated 'Battle Group

Above left: Scharnhorst at anchor in Langfjord during the winter of 1943. In the foreground is a vessel of the 4th Destroyer Flotilla painted in a dazzle camouflage scheme. (Author's Collection)

Above right: Scharnhorst seen from astern in Langfjord, winter 1943. (Author's Collection)

is to be at 1 hours readiness from 1300/25/12. *Scharnhorst* and the 4th Z-Flotilla to acknowledge'.[14]

Meanwhile, Dönitz continued to cling to his belief that the *Scharnhorst* should put to sea. As meteorologists pointed out that the weather was bad and was getting increasingly worse and that in the gloom *Scharnhorst* would be at a disadvantage, Dönitz felt that if the weather was bad then so much the better for the *Scharnhorst*. In short, he believed that a great opportunity was being presented for a swift 'hit and run' raid by the *Scharnhorst*; she could get in and close on the convoy, do untold damage, and retire in the gloom long before any covering force could arrive on the scene. Adamant that the operation must go ahead, at 2.12 p.m. on 25 December, the naval general staff issued orders for the battle group to put to sea. Three minutes after the orders were issued from the naval general staff, Naval Group North signalled the code word 'Ostfront'. This was followed at 3.27 p.m. by orders from the headquarters of the admiral commanding Northern Waters which signalled to the Battle Group, 'Most Immediate. Ostfront 1700/25/12'.

For the sailors aboard the *Scharnhorst*, the order to stand by at an hour's notice to sail from Bey alongside the orders received from the naval general staff and Naval Group North was nothing more than they expected from the high command. Some of the more cynical members of the ship's company believed that it was all an exercise designed by the high command to ruin Christmas. To the north-east of Altafjord, at Hammerfest, two vessels of the 5th Minesweeper Flotilla—*R56* and *R58*—were at anchor when they received a wireless order at 3 p.m. to 'proceed at once to *Scharnhorst*. Mine-Sweeping escort to Point Lucie'.[15]

Point Lucie lay to the north-west of Hasvik, to the west of Söröya Island, and was part of a declared mined area through which the *Scharnhorst* and her destroyers would have to pass on their way to the open sea. With the faint spectral of the Northern Lights visible in the north-western sky, the two minesweepers proceeded to Langfjord. The sky was tolerably clear and starlit but with no moon it was extremely dark. Having entered Langfjord a wave of relief swept over *Oberleutnant zur See* Werner Hauss of the *R58* when the great shadow of the *Scharnhorst* rose ghost-like out of the darkness. The two minesweepers berthed alongside the battleship whereupon Hauss and *Oberleutnant zur See* Wilhelm Maclot, the commanding officer of *R56*, clambered up the flimsy ladder to the deck of the battleship. Both men were ill at ease; they had never set foot aboard a ship the size of *Scharnhorst* before, monstrous in her proportions and confusing in her complexity. Feeling a little embarrassed by their surroundings, they reported to the officer on duty and the officer of the watch who summoned an *Oberleutnant*.

Guided by an *Oberleutnant*, Maclot and Hauss were taken across the quarterdeck, which seemed to them to be endless, hustled down companionways, along narrow passages, past a row of officer's cabins, and along more passages before arriving at the cabin of *Kapitän* Hintze, by which time the two minesweeper commanders had lost all sense of direction. The *Oberleutnant* that had led them through the ship knocked on the door and then opened it. Stepping inside, they saluted and remained unobtrusively in the background, wondering what was in store for them. Hintze, the first officer, and the chief engineer were standing in the centre of the room while an adjutant hovered around holding a signal in his hand. On Hintze's desk, near to where the officers were gathered, the battle order from Bey, which was to be handed to the leader of the destroyer flotilla when anchors were weighed, lay. The *Scharnhorst* had already received her battle orders, which were contained in a sealed envelope and not to be opened until the ship had slipped her moorings. In accordance with previous orders, this set of orders stated:

a) Action of the First Battle Group, consisting of the *Scharnhorst* and five destroyers, against the convoy on December 26th at dawn, i.e. at about 1000 hours.

b) Battle line in close order only if battle conditions are favourable, i.e. tolerable weather conditions with good visibility, permitting a full appreciation of the enemy's dispositions.

c) If the tactical situation was not favourable for the *Scharnhorst*, the destroyers were to attack alone, the battleship standing by to pick up the destroyers while remaining herself at a distance from the target area. If necessary she was to withdraw to the outer fjord.[16]

As Hintze gave instructions to two of his ship's other officers who had entered the cabin, Maclot and Hauss took a discreet look around. The room was festooned with comfortable armchairs, paintings hung on the walls, and framed photographs sat atop a desk on which there was a bowl of fruit and nuts decorated with small pieces of tinsel. It was only then that it dawned on Hauss that it was Christmas Day. If he had not noticed the bowl, he would have quite forgotten. Hauss was still immersed in nostalgic thoughts of Christmas when he suddenly realised that Hintze was approaching.

The two *Leutnants* introduced themselves, whereupon Hintze enquired whether the two men were the commanding officers of the minesweepers before stating that the first officer, *Fregattenkapitän* Ernst Dominik, who had been on board *Scharnhorst* ever since she had been commissioned, would provide them with details. Dominik was an experienced gunnery expert who had risen from the captain of anti-aircraft armament to first gunnery officer before being appointed first officer. A man of unshakable composure, throughout his years of service aboard *Scharnhorst*, he had taken a personal interest in his men and had gained their deep-rooted respect and confidence.

Taken to another cabin, the two minesweeper commanders were asked what their top speed was. '16 knots' came the reply before the first officer followed up with another question, enquiring as to their maximum speed while conducting sweeps. '14 knots,' Maclot replied after a brief moment of hesitation. He pondered whether he should qualify his statement by adding the caveat that the stated speeds held good for normal conditions but that they would be quite out of the question in the prevailing storm outside. He decided to say nothing. It appeared to him almost certain that the operation would have to be called off and that the minesweepers could not put to sea. Dominik broke upon his thoughts, 'Further details will follow. As you can see, I've a great deal to attend to before sailing. Would you please see the Signals Officer now?' A messenger soon entered who was asked to take Maclot and Hauss to the signals officer. As they hurried after the messenger, Maclot murmured to Hauss, 'They don't seem to have much time for us in this old tub'.[17]

Led along a labyrinth of passages, past workshops, up and down stairways, past control posts and a torrent of compartments, the two *Leutnants* were struck by the hectic rush that engulfed the *Scharnhorst*. In the hectic rush on board, every man that they met looked as though he was on a vital errand and in a race against time. What the minesweeper commanders did not realise, however, was that while the ship may have looked like a disturbed ant hill, this was quite a normal state of affairs aboard a battleship preparing for sea.

Eventually, they ended up at the signals office where they were introduced to *Kapitänleutnant* Heinz-Günther Behr, the signals officer. As before, a brief conversation ensued before they were guided back to the upper deck. Taking their leave, Maclot and Hauss descended from the *Scharnhorst* to their respective ships. They had been on board the battleship for little more than half an hour. Around 5 p.m., while Maclot and Hauss were on board, Bey and his staff arrived aboard from the *Tirpitz*.[18]

At 7 p.m., later than had been planned, the minesweepers began to cast off from the *Scharnhorst* as the squadron began to put to sea. The minesweepers cleared the battleship and began to proceed seaward. As they did so, two small tugs approached the battleship out of the darkness. With the ship lying head into the wind and athwart the fjord, the tugs had to swing the battleship around in the narrow confines of the anchorage before she could make for the boom under her own power. Shortly after casting off, the loudspeaker system of the *Scharnhorst* had blared into life ordering the crew to the quarterdeck. The trampling of sea boots reverberated as crewmen scurried from living quarters, store rooms, wardrooms, and other locations to report to their respective officers. Gradually, the murmuring and trampling subsided leaving the crew assembled in silence in two long dark blocks. It was then that *Fregattenkapitän* Dominik approached. As the crew looked on expectant, he began a short address, removing the veil of secrecy, prompting a wave of spontaneous jubilation to break out. As cheers echoed around the fjord, some men, who moments earlier had been disciplined, gave in to the enthusiasm and excitement of the moment whereupon they lifted Dominik upon their shoulders and carried him forward. The crew quickly hurried to their action stations, and within three minutes of the crew being dismissed, all stations reported being cleared for action.

As Dominik went to the forecastle to oversee the weighing of the anchor, a motor launch glided across the water carrying the last group of men to join the *Scharnhorst*. They were the depth charge crew who had been on standby in the outer fjord in an effort to guard against midget submarines. With the depth charge crew back on board, Hintze gave the order to weigh anchor. The capstan began to revolve while the heavy anchor chain rattled through the hawsepipe. The two tugs that the crews of *R56* and *R58* had watched approach now nosed the ship at the bow and stern before cutting free as the waters of the fjord bubbled up as the ship's propellers rotated into life. Having been swung around, *Scharnhorst* proceeded down Langsfjord. *Scharnhorst* thundered past the two minesweepers which formed up astern. As they did so signal lamps flashed messages to the destroyers. *Z29*, the destroyer leader, signalled in reply. *Z38* swept in ahead of the *Scharnhorst* and dropped into station six cables ahead of the battleship to assist in navigating through the fjord network. Meanwhile, *Z29* and *Z34* took up station in the *Scharnhorst*'s wake.

Orders were signalled from the *Scharnhorst* to the destroyers, ordering an increase in speed to 17 knots. With no orders having been received to detach from the battle group, *R56* and *R58* (which had been joined by *R121*) maintained their respective courses and maximum speeds. Nevertheless, unable to attain 17 knots, they began to fall considerably behind the battleship. At 7.55 p.m., *Scharnhorst* and her destroyers swept through the inner Langfjord barrage trailed by the minesweepers. The battle group was now joined by two destroyers, which had sailed from Kåfjord and turned into the Stjernsundet. As the northern lights continued to dance in the sky, the battle group was swallowed by the darkness. Unable to see the battle group and unable to keep up with the ordered 17 knots, *R56* and *R58* eventually detached and returned to Hammerfest.

Cruising at 17 knots, from 9.10 p.m., the battle group steered through Stjernsundet and Stoeroeysund before steering through Lappahavet at 25 knots towards the open sea. At approximately 10 p.m., Bey ordered two of the destroyers to flank *Scharnhorst* in order to form an anti-submarine screen while *Z29* was ordered to the van of the formation. Point Lucie was passed at 11.04 p.m., whereupon the squadron took up a course of 10 degrees and made for the point where it was calculated that JW-55B could be intercepted.

Seven U-boats had been ordered to take up specific attack positions by 6 p.m. on 24 December. At 9 a.m. on 25 December, one of the seven U-boats, *U-601*, under the command of *Oberleutnant zur See* Otto Hansen, reported JW-55B as being on a course of 60 degrees in position 72° 25'N, 12° 30'E. At 10.45 a.m., the other U-boats were ordered to operate against the convoy on the basis of Hansen's report. *U-601* maintained contact with the convoy until around 6 p.m. During the course of the evening, *U-716* closed on the convoy and launched an unsuccessful attack against one of the escorting destroyers before being driven away by a depth charge attack.

Meanwhile, Fraser's heavy covering force, known as Force 2, continued eastward at 17 knots. So rough were the sea conditions that Fraser would later note that 'conditions in *Duke of York* were most uncomfortable, few people obtaining any sleep'.[19] Few people were asleep on Fraser's staff when an emergency Ultra signal was received at 2.16 a.m., which stated: '*Scharnhorst* probably sailed 6 pm. 25th December'.[20] This was followed at once by a further Ultra signal which provided Fraser with more details and a reconnaissance reports from a German reconnaissance aircraft operating to the north of the 72nd Parallel which put the convoy at 20 miles distant.

Intelligence from Ultra decrypts had allowed the Admiralty and Fraser to build up a fairly accurate picture of the strategic situation and of German intentions. At 11.58 a.m., an Enigma message transmitted to an unidentified vessel stating: 'Emergency proceed to *Scharnhorst* in Langsfjord. Further orders there', was intercepted. The decrypt for this message was sent to the Operational Intelligence Centre within the Admiralty at 8.50 p.m. on 25 December, before the signal was passed on to Fraser at 9.42 p.m.

An even clearer indication would have been provided by another intercepted signal at 12.43 a.m. on 26 December, which contained the following order that was sent out to U-boats operating in the Arctic: 'Own battle group consisting of *Scharnhorst* and 5 new destroyers left Lopphavet 2300/25 with the intention of attacking the convoy at about 0900/26'. While intercepted, this particular signal was ultimately not decrypted until it was too late.

Shortly before 12.30 a.m. on 26 December, the Enigma settings that had been used with effect since midday on 25 December were broken. One of the first decrypted messages that was sent through to Paymaster Commander Norman Denning in the Operational Intelligence Centre was the signal stating 'Ostfront 1700/25/12'. After the message was sent, the cryptanalyst Harry Hinsley telephoned Denning and told him that in future he would refer to 'Ostfront' by its British codename, 'Epilepsy'.[21] At 1.30 a.m. on 26 December, the Admiralty had transmitted the following message to Fraser aboard *Duke of York*:

At 1530A 25 December Admiral Commanding Northern Waters informed Battle Group and Admiral Polar Coast 'codeword EPILEPSY 1700A/25 December'. Comment. Meaning not yet evident ULTRA information will be available with a delay of some hours until 1200A/26 December but will not necessarily be complete for the North Norway area.[22]

Within minutes of this message being sent to Fraser, Denning received a further decrypt of a signal sent from the *Scharnhorst* to another vessel, which stated '*Scharnhorst* will pass outward bound as from 1800'. This particular decrypt was sent from the Government Code and Cipher School at Bletchley Park to the Operational

Intelligence Centre at 1.33 a.m. and prompted the Admiralty to send the signal to Fraser, notifying him of the likely sailing of the *Scharnhorst*. Shortly thereafter, Fraser received an explanation from the Admiralty: 'A patrol vessel presumably in the Altenfjord [*sic.*] area was informed at 1715 that *Scharnhorst* would pass outward bound from 1800A/25th December'.[23]

During the night of 25–26 December, Richard Pendered was one of the young code breakers on duty. Pendered recalled deciphering one signal around 3 a.m. addressed to the German Naval Command 'Von Kampfgruppe' (from Battle Group) which read: 'JSCHARNHORSTJ MIT FUENE NEUE ZERSTOERER ZWO DREI NULL NULL UHR LOPPHAUET AUS' ('*Scharnhorst* with five destroyers 2300 hours out of Lopphavet'.) If Pendered recalled this incident correctly (Hugh Seabag-Montefiore has raised doubts regarding whether Pendered's recollection is correct), then this was the first confirmation that the *Scharnhorst* was at sea.[24] Pendered's recollection is, nevertheless, consistent with a note included in Fraser's report, which stated, 'At 3.39 [26 December] Admiralty message 260319 was received in which Admiralty appreciated that *Scharnhorst* was at sea'.[25]

This recollection of events correlates with the recollection of a telegraphist who was serving aboard HMS *Onslow*, Derek Wellman. During the early morning watch of 26 December, Wellman was listening to the U-boat frequencies when he heard a series of mysterious clicks in his headphones, which prompted him to retune his radio. Having retuned the radio set, Wellman picked up a Morse signal on a different frequency, which was not coming from a U-boat as he knew that the sound of Morse code transmitted from a U-boat was much different from what he was hearing. The pitch of U-boat signals was far higher than those from shore installations and surface assets. The signal heard by Wellman was normal in pitch. After working out the bearing of the transmitter using his direction-finding apparatus, Wellman could see that the signal was originating from a point between the Norwegian coast and the convoy, which combined with the unusual way in which the transmission began, led Wellman to conclude that the signal was being given high priority by the transmitter. All of this suggested to the telegraphist, who had been told that *Scharnhorst* could potentially venture out from her Norwegian lair at any moment, that this was perhaps the crucial message announcing that the ship was at sea. Wellman immediately reported what he had heard to the officers gathered on the bridge of the destroyer.[26]

The news that it was highly probable that the *Scharnhorst* was at sea left Fraser in a quandary. If the battleship attacked at dawn and immediately retired, Force 2 was not yet in a position suitable to cut her off on her return to Norway. Fraser decided to make a crucial decision and elected to break radio silence and ordered the convoy to alter course to the north, away from the approaching raider, in the hope that the alteration of course would make the convoy more difficult to locate. Fraser was also lucky for his signal was picked up by the Germans, however, for reasons unknown, they failed to recall the *Scharnhorst*.

While having informed Fraser, the Admiralty also wanted McCoy to know of the *Scharnhorst*'s sailing so as to avoid him being surprised should he encounter the German battleship. McCoy was not, however, privy to Ultra intelligence. It was therefore better for the Admiralty to inform McCoy as opposed to Fraser or Vice Admiral Robert Burnett, whose squadron of three cruisers comprised the cruiser covering force known as Force 1, in order to avoid them breaking radio silence. Thus, at 3.19 a.m., a signal was sent to the Admiralty addressed to McCoy and repeated to Fraser and Burnett: 'Admiralty appreciate *Scharnhorst* is probably at sea'.

This signal was received aboard the *Duke of York* at 3.39 a.m. and has been incorrectly given by some as the time that the news that the *Scharnhorst* was at sea first reached the attention of Fraser. As the signal came through during the middle of the night, it was decided to inform the crews when the watches were changing and the men were having breakfast. Lieutenant Bryce Ramsden, a Royal Marine aboard HMS *Jamaica* whose action station was controlling the port 4-inch high-angle gun director, recalled the moment that the news was broadcast through the cruiser:

> For a second my heart stopped beating, and I tried to digest it. The *Scharnhorst* is at sea. The *Scharnhorst* is at sea. Then it had happened at last. No one said anything much, except for a momentary exclamation at the news. It was too big a thing, this sudden realisation of weeks, months of sea-time covering convoys, cruisers plodding away near Norway and Bear Island. Russia to Iceland, Iceland to Russia, hours of patient watch-keeping in foul weather and freezing seas, guarding against the possibility of this one thing. And suddenly, in the middle of one such watch, the news had been flung at us. I telephoned down to the control position below to find out if they had heard the pipes. Yes, they had heard it, and that seemed that. A sense of the inevitable came over me. I was embroiled in a great machine of movement and purpose. Something big was going to happen.[27]

Musician Ernie Heather—a member of the Royal Marine Band of the *Duke of York* whose action station was in the transmission station deep inside the battleship's armoured citadel where all of the information on the target was collated and fed to the guns, and who, if *Scharnhorst* did put to sea, would never see her—later said:

> We had our confidence in the ship we were sailing in, our confidence in our officers, and—though nobody would ever speak about it—our confidence in each other. So that should we come into contact with that enemy, then we were going to do our utmost and our level best to *annihilate* it.[28]

Aboard the *Scharnhorst*, her crew was finding the weather to be worse than had been forecast. The ships were sailing into a quartering sea with the effect that every now and again, the ship would seem to slip uneasily sideways into the side of a huge wave before struggling up and out in an unpleasant movement that left many of the crew from raw cadets to experienced sailors seasick. The destroyers, meanwhile, were sailing at the limits of their seaworthiness. Their bows plunged into the troughs and would occasionally rear into the air showing the forefoot of the ship and exposing the keel as far aft as the forward turret. All the while, the decks were washed down from bow to stern with crashing waves.

At sea, the ship's company of the *Scharnhorst* was divided into two watches—four hours on and four hours off. When the ship had weighed anchor, the starboard watch had gone on watch immediately while the port watch set about clearing the ship, stowing away sacks of potatoes, hundreds of boxes, and packing cases. The port watch relieved the starboard watch at midnight. At 4 a.m., the port watch were themselves relieved and slung their hammocks for the first time. The rest period for the port watch was short as they were soon back on duty. Around 7 a.m., an hour after breakfast had been served, all hands were called to action stations. Earlier, at 4.25 a.m., Hintze had left the bridge and made his way to the chart house, where he found Bey and the navigation officer, *Korvettenkapitän* Edgar Lanz. Bey was, at the time, comparing the reported position and track of the convoy with his own. Looking up at Hintze, he stated: 'If the convoy continues on the assumed course and we maintain our present course, we should, at 0630 be within about 30 miles'.

Hintze agreed. 'The only trouble is that visibility is deteriorating all the time,' the captain added.

'That can't be helped,' Bey retorted with a shrug of the shoulders, 'but I imagine our radar will pick it up when we get that far'.

Turning back to the chart, Bey worked with course triangles and compasses to mark points with a pencil for a while before scribbling a note on a piece of paper, which he handed to the signals officer: 'Put this through by W/T to *Z29* at 0700 hours!'[29]

What Bey handed the signals officer was an order for Johannesson to deploy the 4th Destroyer Flotilla in a reconnaissance sweep astride the assumed approach route of the convoy at 10 knots on a course of 250 degrees with *Scharnhorst* following roughly 10 miles behind the destroyer line. As the men of the *Scharnhorst* went to action stations, the destroyers took up their positions until 7.55 a.m., when Bey ordered them to alter course to 230 degrees. Bey was not aware of it, but he was almost within gunnery range of the convoy and within forty minutes would likely have been able to see the convoy. Indeed, at 8.40 a.m., McCoy estimated that *Scharnhorst* was somewhere in the region of 36 miles to the south-east of JW-55B. It was, however, at this point that Ostfront started to unravel.

13

'*Scharnhorst* Will Ever Reign Supreme'

At 4 a.m. on 26 December, JW-55B was to be found approximately 50 miles to the south of Bear Island, sailing east-north-east at 8 knots. The homeward bound RA-55B, meanwhile, was 220 miles to the west of Bear Island, and although it would be somewhat scattered by gales during 27 and 28 December, all of its ships would reach Loch Ewe unmolested on New Year's Day 1944. At the same time, Burnett and Force 1 were approximately 150 miles to the east of JW-55B and 45 miles east-south-east of Bear Island. Sailing at 18 knots, Burnett intended to be approximately 30 miles due east of the convoy by the time of the Arctic twilight on the morning of the 26th. Fraser and Force 2, meanwhile, were to be found sailing at 24 knots, 280 miles west of North Cape and 210 miles south-east of the convoy. At the time, Fraser was still far out from the scene of any potential engagement and needed to sail much further eastwards in order to cut the *Scharnhorst* off from her Norwegian refuge. He was, however, satisfied from the plot in the chart house of the *Duke of York* that the stage was well set.

Having received the signal that *Scharnhorst* had likely put to sea, at 3.44 a.m., he had ordered Force 2 to raise steam for full speed and at 4.01 a.m. had signalled McCoy to turn the convoy due north, although this order would not actually be completed until 6.25 a.m. At 6.28 a.m., Fraser made another series of signals in which he ordered McCoy to turn the convoy on to a bearing of 45 degrees and Burnett to close on the convoy so that the two covering forces could provide mutual support. Further signals were exchanged in which Fraser gave his own position while requesting those of Burnett and McCoy.

At 7.12 a.m., Burnett reckoned that Force 1 had sailed far enough southwards so ordered his ships to take up a westerly course. A south-westerly gale was blowing and with the heavy seas, Burnett wanted to approach the convoy from well to the south so as to avoid heading directly into the wind and heavy sea. At 8.15 a.m., Burnett received the latest position, course, and speed update from JW-55B, which prompted him to alter course to 305 degrees and increase speed to 24 knots.

By now Fraser, Burnett and McCoy were all aware of one another's position and what to expect. As a precaution against interception at 8.14 a.m., McCoy positioned four destroyers of the 36th Division on a line of bearing of 165 degrees on the starboard (and most vulnerable) side of the convoy. At 9.25 a.m., as he looked out across the sea, McCoy noted the intermittent glows of star shells to the south-east.[1]

The Germans were aware that their radar sets were largely inferior to those of the British and that their sets did not have the range, echo definition, or reliability of the British sets. They also maintained almost obsessive fears of the dangers of radar transmissions being located and seemed always to be wary of using radar. Many German officers tended to discount the efficiency of radar just as many British officers had done earlier in the war. Standing orders were maintained that radar should never be switched on without a specific order; such an order was only given in exceptional circumstances. As she approached JW-55B on the morning of 26 December, it seems unlikely that *Scharnhorst* was using her air-warning radar. Incredibly, however, it seems highly likely that she was not using her Seetakt radar either. At 8.20 a.m., Bey ordered *Scharnhorst* to take up a northerly course, an action which was not reported to Johannesson aboard *Z29* whose destroyers continued on their way. Soon, *Scharnhorst* would be sailing at a right angle to her destroyers and would lose contact with them which was ultimately never to be regained.

While *Scharnhorst*, it would appear, was not using radar, *Z29* was. Around 9.30 a.m., *Z29* sighted a vessel by radar, and five minutes later, visual contact was made. The vessel was off the starboard bow, sailing a parallel course. *Z30*, stationed on the starboard beam of *Z29*, also reported the vessel and assumed it to be an enemy vessel. The ship, which was only visible as a vague silhouette, was challenged and replied with the correct recognition signal. The flotilla then realised that the mysterious vessel was in fact one of their own, the *Z38*, which on taking up her position in the reconnaissance sweep had taken up the wrong course and headed too far north. *Z38*, upon realising this, had increased speed and altered course to assume her correct position. When *Z38* was challenged, Johannesson had signalled Bey that an enemy destroyer had been sighted, which prompted Hintze to broadcast to all stations: 'Wireless messages from the destroyers: Destroyers are in action!' Having correctly identified *Z38*, Johannesson corrected his signal to Bey which led to the announcement aboard the *Scharnhorst* being retracted. As the corrected signal was made to Bey, 12 miles astern the destroyers began to sight star shells.[2]

At 8.40 a.m., the forward Type 273 surface warning radar of HMS *Belfast* (Burnett's flagship) picked up a radar contact and four minutes later a signal was sent to HMS *Norfolk* and *Sheffield* reporting an unidentified contact bearing 295 degrees at a range of 16 miles. Burnett had estimated that the convoy was sailing on a bearing of 287 degrees from the *Belfast* at a range of 48 miles. He therefore came to the conclusion that if the unidentified contact picked up on the radar of the *Belfast* was the *Scharnhorst*, then she was squarely between the convoy and Force 1.

At 9.01 a.m., Burnett formed his cruisers on a line of bearing of 180 degrees. At 9.06 a.m., the Type 273 radar of HMS *Norfolk* picked up the contact at a range of 12 miles, and a minute later, the contact was picked up by the *Sheffield* at a range of 10 miles. The contact would turn out to be the *Scharnhorst*. When picked up on the radar sets of the *Norfolk* and *Sheffield*, *Scharnhorst* was sailing almost due south which means that Bey must have, at some point, decided that he had sailed far enough north and had altered course south to continue the search for the convoy.

As the clock struck 09.21 *Sheffield* transmitted the signal that everyone had been anxiously awaiting: 'Enemy in sight. Bearing 222°, range 13,000 yards'. Three minutes later, *Belfast* opened fire with four star shells but failed to spot the enemy. At 9.27 a.m., Burnett issued orders for *Norfolk* to open fire.

Matrosenfeldwebel Willie Gödde was at his position at the port forward searchlight control column on lookout duty as he had been throughout all of 26 December. Gödde could not be relieved during the watch changes as the petty officer who normally took over from him was away on leave. Wearing his telephone apparatus around his neck, which allowed him to be in constant communication with the ship's command, Gödde was able to listen to everything that was discussed at the control positions. Suddenly, columns of water 9 feet in diameter erupted out of the darkness around 500 yards abeam of his position. Clearly visible through the drifting snow that had started to fall and reduced visibility still further, a thought immediately darted through his mind: 'Shell splashes. Eight-inch shells at least'. As he switched his telephone apparatus to broadcast, all hell broke loose. The forward radar reported a contact whereupon alarm bells rang out. Through his equipment, Gödde hear a confusion of voices as orders and commands filled the air.[3]

Two minutes after *Norfolk* had opened fire, Burnett discovered that the heavy cruiser was obscuring *Belfast*'s range to the target so ordered her to drop back to clear the range. Those aboard the *Belfast* wondered why their own 6-inch guns had not opened fire. With the crew impatient for news, Captain Frederick Parham, the commanding officer of the *Belfast*, broadcast to the crew what was happening: 'After a few broadsides from the *Norfolk*, the enemy, whoever she may be, has turned away and we are now chasing her'. At 9.30 a.m., Burnett ordered all ships of Force 1 to open fire with their main armament, and less than a minute later, *Norfolk* fired a salvo of 8-inch shells. Lacking flashless cordite for her main armament, the flash of the *Norfolk*'s 8-inch guns almost temporarily blinded everyone above deck. The fire from the *Norfolk* was rapid and accurate with the ship firing six full broadsides in ten minutes before checking fire at 9.40 a.m. At 9.32 a.m., *Belfast*'s executive officer, Commander Philip Welby-Everard, who was watching from the bridge, felt fairly certain that *Norfolk* scored a hit on the enemy. As *Norfolk* engaged, Burnett ordered an alteration of course that saw Force 1 sail around the *Scharnhorst* to a position between the enemy and the convoy.

Scharnhorst had been taken completely by surprise. Nevertheless, despite being caught by surprise, amid the confusion and flurry of orders on board, turret 'Caesar' was soon returning fire. From his position, Gödde could see quite clearly the snowflakes falling in the orange-red flame of the enemy's gunfire. As he looked on, Gödde was 'momentarily dazzled by the long sheets of flame which burst from the *Scharnhorst*'s own armament, while the ship was wrapped in a cloud of warm acrid fumes'.[4] Pressing his eyes against the rubber-cushioned lenses of his binoculars, Gödde could not see anything of the ships that *Scharnhorst* was engaging. There were at least two ships—possibly three, but he could not be sure. *Steursmannsgefreiter* (navigator's yeoman) Wilhelm Kruse later claimed that three enemy cruisers were positively identified. The one thing that Gödde was certain of was that the first ship which was hidden and continued to fire salvo after salvo must be a heavy cruiser, with star shells also being fired obviously from another ship to observe the fall of shot. Shortly after opening fire against Force 1, *Scharnhorst* altered course to 150 degrees, almost a complete reversal of course, and increased speed to 30 knots.

With *Scharnhorst* sailing at 30 knots, the range between her and Force 1 began to increase which led Burnett to decide to break off contact with the enemy. At 10 a.m., he brought Force 1 on to a course of 305 degrees before, at 10.14, altering course once more, heading towards the convoy. Contact with the *Scharnhorst* was lost at 10.20 a.m. Burnett was later criticised for his decision to break off contact with the enemy. He would defend his decision by stating that he was convinced that *Scharnhorst* would try and work around to the north of the convoy and, believing his ships to be 4–6 knots slower than the German battleship, decided to place his cruisers between the enemy and the convoy. Detesters of Burnett's decision would point out that when contact was lost *Belfast* was eighteen miles nearer the convoy than *Scharnhorst* was and that it was mathematically impossible for the *Scharnhorst* to have reached the convoy before Force 1 did. They also argued that if *Belfast* had sailed north at 17 knots then she could have shadowed the *Scharnhorst* for much longer and remained in a position between the enemy and the convoy. Nevertheless, Burnett's decision was one which was ultimately supported by Fraser.[5]

At 10.35 a.m., Burnett signalled to Fraser that he had lost contact with the enemy, which was sailing north, and that he was closing on the convoy. Burnett's signal marked the beginning of a very anxious few hours for Fraser during which time he appeared, on occasion, to hold doubts about the outcome of the day.[6]

The engagement with Force 1 had been short, but it had left *Scharnhorst* wounded. Welby-Everand likely did witness a hit being sustained by the *Scharnhorst* as *Norfolk* managed to score two hits on the battleship. The first hit saw an 8-inch shell land between the third 5.9-inch gun on the port side and the port side torpedo tubes where it penetrated the upper deck and finished up in the technical petty officer's office without exploding. The shell caused a fire, which was quickly brought under control. According to *Matrosengefreiter* Günter Sträter, this shell from the *Norfolk* was measured and found to be 5 inches in diameter, which suggested that the *Scharnhorst* had been in an engagement with nothing large than a destroyer. Given that *Norfolk* was the only ship to be firing at the *Scharnhorst* when this shell landed and that she was firing her main armament, the shell had to be 8 inches. The second 8-inch shell caused much more serious damage, striking the Seetakt radar and tearing away the aerial. The shell also put the port high-angle director out of action. Shell fragments wounded *Leutnant* Schramm, the officer in charge of the gunnery range finder, while two radar ratings sustained serious leg wounds.

Having disengaged, at 9.55 a.m., Bey transmitted a signal to Group North: 'Under fire from believed cruisers with radar'. The news that the Seetakt was out of action made it around the ship fairly quickly, nevertheless, the crew were encouraged by a message broadcast over the ship's loudspeakers which told them that they were trying to get at the convoy from the north. Johannesson and his destroyers were now over 50 miles south-west of the flagship and had been out of contact with *Scharnhorst* for an hour. Despite having witnessed the star shell fired by *Belfast* to the north-east, Johannesson continued his search for the convoy to the south-west.

As he tried to sail around Burnett's cruisers and approach the convoy from the north, Bey issued signals to Johannesson in an effort to draw the destroyers towards his position. At 11.35 Bey issued another signal to the destroyers in which he gave the position of the *Scharnhorst*, her course and speed. It seems highly likely that Bey intended for Johannesson's destroyers to re-join him or at least to have the 4th Destroyer Flotilla take part in a joint attack, a pincer move in which the destroyers attacked the convoy from the south while *Scharnhorst* approached from the north. Shortly after he issued this signal, Bey received a sighting report of the convoy from *U-277*, which had been made at 9.45 a.m. and transmitted at 10 a.m., which placed JW-55B in square AB 6365, which prompted him, at 11.58, to send another signal to the 4th Destroyer flotilla to alter course to as to operate in square AB 6365.

During the forenoon, the destroyers HMS *Musketeer*, *Matchless*, *Opportune*, and *Virago* were detached from the convoy to join Force 1. As the clock ticked towards noon, Fraser began to show concern about the fuel situation of his ships, particularly his destroyers. At 8 a.m., the destroyers had reported that they possessed 70 per cent fuel, but since then, they had been sailing at high speed. Fraser knew that he would soon have to decide whether to return to Iceland or to make for the Kola Inlet. He began to also think that if *Scharnhorst* had turned for home after encountering Force 1 then there would be no chance of catching her. More appallingly, *Scharnhorst* may have slipped past Force 1 and could at that very moment have been sailing westward towards the Atlantic while he was sailing east.

While Allied control of the Atlantic was more powerful than it had been in the previous years of the war, *Scharnhorst* was a fast and powerful ship. What is more, she had always been a lucky ship and every possibility existed that she may have been lucky enough to run into and sink one of the large liners such as the RMS *Queen Mary*, which were regularly crossing the Atlantic loaded with up to 15,000 American troops in preparation for the invasion of Europe. At 12.03 p.m., Fraser decided to reverse course and signalled this by lamp to the other ships of Force 2. Force 2 had not settled on to their new course when a signal was received from Force 1, reporting an unidentified radar contact at a range of 13 miles. It was an electrifying moment on the admiral's bridge of the *Duke of York*; Force 2 immediately reversed course once more to close on Force 1.[7]

Sheffield was the first to pick up the *Scharnhorst* on radar. Three minutes later, *Norfolk* also picked up the contact. Burnett had been correct all along—there could be no doubt that this was the *Scharnhorst*. Bey had wasted three precious hours. At 12.20 p.m., Burnett issued the order to open fire, and one minute later, *Sheffield* once again made the signal 'Enemy in Sight'. Once *Sheffield* made the enemy in sight signal, Force 1 opened fire. To the crews of the British cruisers it appeared as though *Scharnhorst* had once again been caught by surprise. That was not, however, entirely the case. Around 12.20 p.m., radar contact was made by the *Scharnhorst* with Burnett's cruisers whereupon alarm bells rang out across the ship. Looking out into the midday twilight, Gödde saw three shadows off the port and starboard bow. Similar reports came in from across the ship. As initial orders were issued to the main guns and as the directors set about acquiring the targets, star shells burst in the air before shells began to crash into the sea all around. As the first shells from the British cruisers splashed down, sending up columns of water, the forward turrets of the *Scharnhorst* thundered the battleship's reply.

As the action got underway, Bey stood openly on the bridge, observing the enemy fire while Hintze and the first gunnery officer rushed to the control station. Having briefly observed fire from the cruisers, Bey stepped into the port armoured bulkhead of the control position where he ordered a turn to port in order to break off the action. *Scharnhorst* began to heel over heavily to starboard as she turned to take up an easterly course while the fire control directors of the main and secondary armaments held steadily on their targets. When *Scharnhorst* embarked on her turn to port, she was under fire not only from the three cruisers but also from HMS *Musketeer*. At approximately 12.24 p.m., *Norfolk* scored at least one hit on the *Scharnhorst*, which was observed from *Belfast* before *Sheffield* scored another hit approximately a minute later. *Scharnhorst* was not only taking punishment, however, she was also giving it out. From the beginning of the engagement, *Norfolk* appears to have been the main target of the German gunners as, lacking flashless cordite, the brilliant flash of her 8-inch gun offered the perfect aiming point.[8]

One early salvo from *Scharnhorst* landed between *Sheffield* and *Norfolk*, close to the starboard side of *Sheffield* which swept her upper deck with a storm of shrapnel. One piece of shrapnel, which was described as being the size of a man's head, penetrated the starboard side just below and aft the bridge where it severed electrical cables and caused a leak in a steam pipe. No one was injured but lookouts on the starboard side had very narrow escapes. At 12.33 p.m., *Scharnhorst* straddled the *Norfolk*. Of this salvo, one 11-inch shell struck the barbette of 'X' turret, knocking it out of action.

Looking out from his action station above the port hanger of the *Sheffield*, Commander Walker, *Sheffield*'s paymaster commander, saw that *Norfolk* had been hit and watched 'a sickening column of fire which hung for about ten seconds over "X" turret before subsiding'.[9] As a precaution, the magazine of 'X' turret was flooded. A second shell hit *Norfolk* on the starboard side amidships and penetrated the main deck before exploding beside the ship's secondary damage control headquarters, killing seven members of the crew and wounding others.[10] Fires broke out above the engine room, which blazed out of control, yet the cruiser continued to fight.

At 12.22 p.m., Burnett signalled to the destroyers sailing in his company to attack with torpedoes. Commander Ralph Fisher, the commanding officer of HMS *Musketeer*, failed to receive Burnett's signal to conduct torpedo attacks. It would later transpire that the signal was received but that in the heat of the moment it was not passed to the bridge by the signals staff. Fisher would later write in his after-action report that at the time *Scharnhorst* did not present a useful torpedo target. As Burnett made his signal to attack with torpedoes, *Musketeer* opened fire with her forward dual 4.7-inch guns. She would continue to keep up a steady stream of fire until 12.36 p.m. and fired no less than fifty-two rounds. At one stage, *Musketeer* was close enough to the *Scharnhorst* (2.5 miles distant) to observe hits on the battleship.

At 12.41 p.m., the British ships ceased firing as the range to *Scharnhorst* began to increase. The engagement had lasted around twenty minutes during which time *Sheffield* had fired ninety-seven rounds of 6-inch shells in twenty-six salvos visually as her Type 284 gunnery control radar was unserviceable. The Type 273 radar of the *Norfolk* was put out of action by *Scharnhorst* while her Type 284 was damaged. Nevertheless, *Norfolk* managed to fire thirty-one broadsides during the engagement. *Belfast*, meanwhile, fired thirty-eight broadsides during the engagement, fourteen of them visually, and also managed to fire seventy-seven rounds of 4-inch shells. With *Scharnhorst* increasing the range, Burnett decided to shadow the enemy with Force 1 until Force 2 was in a position to engage. As the destroyers settled down to give chase, the *Belfast*, *Norfolk*, and *Sheffield* took up station on the port quarter at a range of 7.5 miles, just out of visible range where they held station. Increasing speed to 28 knots in order to maintain station, at 12.56 p.m., Burnett signalled to Fraser the first of many shadowing reports.

At 1 p.m., Hintze broadcast to all crew members that the action had reached a lull, whereupon the gun crews set to work salvaging what brass cartridges from spent shells that they could while throwing others overboard. The main battery guns from which cordite gasses could not always be drawn off quickly enough were briefly traversed into the wind to be ventilated as munitions hoists rattled as racks were replenished. Meanwhile, Bey stood in the chart house discussing the strategic situation with his staff, Hintze and Lanz.

'We're not getting at the convoy at all,' the admiral grunted. 'The cruisers are always just where we want to strike. They were the same ones as this morning, weren't they, Hintze?'

Hintze remained thoughtful for a moment before replying: 'I'm inclined to agree, *Herr* Admiral. The artillery officer thinks so too. It was impossible to see the cruisers this morning, but the shell splashes, which I observed myself, were of the same calibre. The artillery officer thinks they were 8-inch and 5.9-inch'.

'Apparently, we're still being shadowed,' Bey continued. 'According to the aft radar reports at any rate. There's nothing actually to be seen. Let's hope we can shake her off in due course. I can see no point in making a third attempt to get at the convoy'. Bey paused, and as everyone stood silently, approached the chart table. Glancing at the distance to the north Norwegian coast before looking at the ship's then speed and course, he turned to Hintze:

'Return to Norway, Hintze. Altafjord. What is the course?'

Korvettenkapitän Lanz picked up the course triangles and drew a fine pencil line across the chart before informing Bey of the course whereupon the admiral gave a nod to Hintze.

'Course 155 degrees. Speed 28 knots. You may tell the men that we are returning to base. Thank you, gentlemen'.[11]

As *Scharnhorst* settled on to her new course and began to run south, the crew relaxed somewhat from their action stations as an intensified lookout was ordered. The short period of twilight was already over and darkness had descended around the ship. As *Scharnhorst* made for Altafjord, at 1.45 p.m., the 4th Destroyer Flotilla received an unsigned signal calling on them to break off the operation. This was followed by another signal from *Scharnhorst* timed at 2.20 p.m., which simply stated, 'Return to base'. Johannesson complied, turning his destroyers on to a southerly course and made for Point Lucie at a speed of 12 knots.

At 3 p.m., *Scharnhorst*'s crew were ordered to initiate action messing. As the crew of the battleship undertook action messing, from Fraser's point of view, the situation could not have been developing more satisfactorily. Fraser recognised that there was nothing that he could do if *Scharnhorst* broke away to the south-west for the *Duke of York*, *Jamaica*, and the destroyers could not have caught up with her. As things were, however, *Scharnhorst* was proceeding on an advantageous course of action so far as Fraser was concerned; three cruisers were just out of visual range on her port quarter, four destroyers were 10 miles away off her starboard quarter, and his own battleship with an escort was steadily approaching from wide on her starboard bow. At 3.15 p.m., Fraser was able to signal to the ships of Force 2 that they were an estimated 56 miles from the enemy. This news, when it filtered around the ships, caused hearts to thump and mouths to go dry for at the then-present closing rates, an engagement was only around forty-five minutes away.

Meanwhile, Burnett continued to shadow. At 3.45 p.m., Captain Donald Bain of the *Norfolk* signalled to Burnett that a fire was blazing in a wing compartment above one of the ship's fuel tanks that could not be controlled unless he could stop the ship from rolling. No sooner had the signal been received than it was noted from the bridge of the *Belfast* that *Sheffield* was also dropping astern. At 4.11 p.m., a signal reached Burnett from the *Sheffield*, which reported that the port inner shaft was out of action and that the ship's maximum speed was 8 knots. Owing to the continued high speed at which the cruiser had been travelling, the port inner turbine gearing had failed. The shaft was stopped and locked into position to prevent excessive vibration before, at 4.20 p.m., those on board the *Sheffield* were able to report to Burnett that the ship was once again underway at 23 knots.

As *Norfolk* and *Sheffield* dropped out of station, *Belfast* continued on alone. It would appear that the after radar that equipped *Scharnhorst* was still operational as Bey and Hintze were aware that they were being shadowed by cruisers, yet no action was taken to dispose of them. It is a source of wonder why *Scharnhorst* did not turn to attack the solitary *Belfast*, especially given that her radar must have disclosed that the three shadowing cruisers had dwindled to just one.

Meanwhile, Force 2 proceeded at 25 knots. In the large waves of the following sea it was difficult for the destroyers to keep up with the *Duke of York* even as she ploughed into the waves. A number of 20mm and 40mm anti-aircraft guns had been fitted on to the forecastle. However, as the battleship dove forward and ploughed headlong into the waves, the sudden rush of water over the foredeck and upper deck and as far aft as the quarterdeck, ripped some of the guns from their mounts along with ready-use lockers. At 16.17, *Duke of York*'s Type 273 radar picked up the first echoes of the enemy bearing 20 degrees at a range of 26 miles (41.8 km). Fraser and his staff were jubilant. The range between the *Duke of York* and *Scharnhorst* now began to decrease rapidly to such an extent that by 4.32 p.m., the range was approximately 17 miles (27.5 km).[12]

Having received confirmation from Burnett that only one heavy enemy unit was present, Fraser intended to close to within 6.5 miles (10.4 km) before issuing the order to open fire while detaching the destroyers to make a torpedo attack. As Force 2 closed in imperturbably, ahead and to port of the *Duke of York* were the destroyers HMS *Savage* and *Saumarez* while ahead and to starboard were the *Scorpion* and *Stord*. At 4.37 p.m., Fraser sent a signal to the destroyers ordering them to take up the most advantageous position for launching torpedoes while awaiting his signal to commence their respective attacks. Meanwhile, HMS *Jamaica* held station astern of the *Duke of York*. As they closed, *Scharnhorst* became visible to the British sailors. From the gunnery spotting position of the British flagship, *Scharnhorst* 'appeared of enormous length and silver grey in colour'. Meanwhile, Lieutenant-Commander James Crawford, the gunnery officer of the British battleship, stared at his target through a pair of high-power optics. 'To see this incredible sight about seven or eight miles away, like a silver ghost coming at you … It was a gunnery officer's dream come true'.[13]

At the same time that Fraser was issuing orders to his destroyers to move into a position in preparation for launching a torpedo attack, *Belfast*'s radar picked up the *Duke of York* at a range of 22.7 miles (36.5 km). Eight minutes later, Fraser signalled *Belfast* to open fire with star shells while transmitting an order to Force 2 to increase speed to 27 knots. Shortly before Fraser signalled *Belfast* to open fire with star shell, *Scharnhorst* altered course slightly to port. Upon receiving a report on this alteration of course, aboard the British flagship Fraser requested Captain Guy Russell, the commanding officer of *Duke of York*, to come to the voice pipes which connected the admiral's bridge to the ship's bridge below. When Russell reported to the voice pipe, Fraser issued his orders:

'In two minutes Force 2 will turn 080°, Russell. You can bring all heavy guns to bear at once'.[14] At 4.47 p.m., *Belfast* opened fire with star shells at a range of 10.5 miles. The star shells failed to illuminate *Scharnhorst*, or at least the star shells and the *Scharnhorst* were not seen from the flagship. At 4.48 p.m., *Duke of York* fired a salvo of four star shells from two of her port side 5.25-inch guns. The four star shells burst perfectly behind the target and hung in the sky, lighting up *Scharnhorst* perfectly. Reports of enemy in sight flooded in. As they watched the star shell burst, Fraser, Russell, and Crawford, among others aboard the *Duke of York*, Parham aboard the *Belfast*, and others on the closing warships who saw the *Scharnhorst* at that moment were all struck by the same thought: 'Good Lord! She's still got her turrets trained fore and aft'.[15]

For the 14-inch gun crews of the *Duke of York*, the waiting was over. Lieutenant Henry Leach, the man in charge of 'A' turret, later recalled events:

> 'All guns load with armour-piercing and full charge, load, load, LOAD!'; the clatter of the hoists as they brought up the shells and cordite charges from the magazines, the rattle of the rammers as they drove them into the chambers of the guns and the slam of the breeches as they closed were music to all. Then a great stillness for seemingly endless minutes, disturbed only by the squelch of the hydraulics as layers and trainers followed the pointers in their receivers from the director. 'Broadsides' and the interceptors, completing the firing circuit right up to the director layer's trigger, were closed; a glance at the range receiver whose counters were steadily, inexorably ticking down until … 12,000 yards … the fire gong rang and crash, all guns fired and the Battle of North Cape had started.[16]

The first broadside from *Duke of York* splashed down, sending up towering geysers of water that completely obliterated *Scharnhorst* from view. Astern, those aboard the *Jamaica* heard the roar and felt the concussion of, and watched on as, the ten 14-inch guns of the *Duke of York* fired their first salvo at the enemy. The firing of the guns momentarily lit up the flagship and left a great drift of cordite smoke hanging in the air. Before the first salvo from the flagship had landed, *Jamaica* too let loose with her own 6-inch broadside. As he watched from the admiral's bridge, Fraser almost became the ship's first casualty. On the wall of the bridge was a large clock that was used for timing course changes while zig-zagging. The clock was normally unshipped before the guns were fired, but on this occasion, it had been forgotten. When the flagship fired her first broadside, the clock was shaken off the wall and crashed to the floor just beside the admiral. After watching the firing of the first salvo, he made his way to the plot to handle the coordination of the attacks and would not set eyes on the *Scharnhorst* again.[17]

For a ship that was taken by surprise, *Scharnhorst* reacted quickly. At 4.56 p.m., she fired her first salvo. Still manning his position, Wilhelm Gödde watched as *Scharnhorst* returned fire before hearing *Kapitänleutnant* Wieting, the ship's second gunnery officer, order single guns of the starboard secondary batteries to fire star shells in between the main battery salvos with the idea of enabling the visual rangefinders to pick up the enemy. Gödde also heard an exchange between the first and secondary gunnery officers in which the first gunnery officer expressed his thoughts that it was inadvisable to use guns from the secondary armament to fire star shells as this reduced the number of guns that could be brought to bear and that this thus weakened the ship's defensive fire. Accordingly, Wieting ceased firing star shells and ordered the guns to be unloaded. As *Scharnhorst* had prepared to return fire, one of *Duke of York*'s salvos found its mark and crashed down on the starboard bow abreast turret 'Anton', putting the turret out of action.[18] Shortly after this hit was sustained, a second hit was sustained amidships. At this time, it began to be reported that turret 'Anton' had ceased reporting while fire and smoke were engulfing the area around the turret preventing entry.

In the wake of turret 'Anton' being knocked out of action, turrets 'Bruno' and 'Caesar' stepped up their rate of fire to a quick succession of salvos. Salvos from *Scharnhorst* at first fell short, but quickly, the ship's gunners found the range and began to regularly straddle the *Duke of York*. Any shells that fell over *Duke of York* served to straddle *Jamaica*. The science of spotting the impact of shells by radar was still a science that was in its infancy at the time, nevertheless, the return fire from *Scharnhorst* could be detected on the radar screen of the *Jamaica*. Lieutenant Bryce Ramsden, a Royal Marine aboard the cruiser, noted:

> Our radar operators and their colleagues in the main armament control centre were *distinctly* perturbed when on this their first experience, they saw on the radar tube the enemy shells coming towards *us* with every appearance of accuracy. Fortunately, we were not hit, but the whole ship shook and those on the bridge were drenched from a *very* near miss.[19]

HMS *Belfast* opened fire against *Scharnhorst* at 4.57 p.m., however, only one salvo was fired before the target disappeared into the gloom and was lost. Shortly afterwards, contact was regained and the cruiser opened fire once more from 5.05 p.m. Over a period of seven minutes, *Belfast* proceeded to fire five salvos from 'A' and 'B' turrets along with two twelve-gun broadsides by radar but guided by the gun flashes of the German battleship.[20]

As *Scharnhorst* began to alter course eastward, *Belfast* and *Norfolk*, which had joined the fray at 5 p.m., conformed. In his position, in the 4-inch director of the *Belfast*, Lieutenant Brook Smith and his men were comforting themselves with the thought that capital ships like the *Scharnhorst* rarely fired on mere cruisers when they received an awakening from their thoughts. '[S]uddeny my layer called out, "Look at that, Sir!" and I saw great columns of water rising in our wake, a cable length away. My crew's reaction was comical: "The ROTTEN swine! They're firing at us!" they said with great indignation'.[21]

The salvos might well have hit *Belfast* had she not altered course. Nevertheless, within seconds, the German gunners had adjusted their sights and fired another salvo. At this, Brooke Smith's petty officer took out his watch and counted the seconds as they passed by following seeing the flash of the *Scharnhorst*'s guns. 'If she's made the right correction, the next salvo should hit—now'. Fortunately for those aboard the *Belfast*, the gunners aboard the *Scharnhorst* had not made the right correction and the shells splashed down well astern.[22] Owing to the short range, *Duke of York*'s 5.25-inch guns had also been trained and had opened fire. These turrets lacked flashless cordite and after a time would be ordered to cease firing so as to not provide a point of aiming.[23]

It would appear that while Fraser had caught *Scharnhorst* by surprise and had succeeded in knocking out one-third of her main armament, the battle was not progressing quite as he had hoped as at 5.02 p.m., he signalled Burnett, 'Any more news?', hoping to hear of more hits being sustained by the enemy but was left disappointed by the negative reply. Despite being caught by surprise, *Scharnhorst* recovered well and showed herself to be a more than able opponent. It is suspected that she may have fired a salvo of torpedoes during her first turn away to port following the beginning of the engagement as Force 2 altered course in order to comb possible tracks. The ship turned to 55 degrees and then south-east on to a course of 110 degrees pursued by *Duke of York*. Her mean course was eastwards, but Bey and Hintze were not content with merely retreating back to Altafjord. Turret 'Caesar' kept up a rapid and accurate stream of fire while the ship altered course south-west from time to time in order to open the firing arc for turret 'Bruno', before resuming her easterly course.

At 5.13 p.m., Fraser issued orders to the destroyers to close and attack the German battleship with torpedoes. For the time being, it was already too late for such an order as the great opportunity for a destroyer attack had already passed.

As the battle raged, it was almost inevitable that sooner or later, at least one 11-inch shell from the *Scharnhorst* would strike the British flagship. Wing Commander Robin Compston, the RAF liaison officer attached to Fraser's staff, watched the exchange of fire between the two battleships with great interest:

Waiting to go over the top will convey the feeling that I personally experienced on the admiral's bridge between 4.30 and 4.50 pm. when the flagship's first shattering broadside thundered on its way. We hadn't long to wait before the enemy's reply came, the shots short at first and then suddenly the most perfect straddle on our forecastle. Had one of those eleven-inch shells scored a lucky hit inboard, how different might have been the outcome of the battle. Shortly after the straddle a salvo pitched in the sea just ahead of us and the *Duke of York*'s stem ran through the swirl some seven seconds after the spurts of water had subsided.

On our port bow we saw the flashes from the guns of the cruiser *Belfast* as she engaged the enemy yet again that day, while the brilliant flash of the *Scharnhorst*'s guns, firing broadsides at the flagship enabled us to mark her position in the darkness. During this amazing fireworks display the officers on the bridge were calmly going about their duties, sending vital signals and even finding time between our broadsides and those of the enemy to give their men a running commentary on events over the loudspeaker. Star shells from both sides lit up the scene continuously. It is curious how naked one feels when a very bright light descends in one's vicinity—'now we shall catch it' is the feeling.

A sudden rattle of bits and pieces falling proved, on examination after the battle, that an eleven-inch shell had severed rope and steel stays on the foremast just abaft the bridge.[24]

Two 11-inch shells from the *Scharnhorst* passed through the masts of the *Duke of York* severing all of the wireless aerials and wires to the gunnery radar. One of the 11-inch shells tore away some two-thirds of the strut of the tripod mast. Lieutenant H. Bates, who operated the Type 273 surface warning radar of the *Duke of York*, climbed the mast and found the aerials had been jarred so that they were pointing skyward. Operating the appropriate controls in the aerial compartment, Bates repositioned the aerials so that they were horizontal and stabilised again, restoring use of the radar set.[25] The after receiving aerial of the Type 281 air warning radar was, however, damaged to such an extent that it would remain out of action until the ship reached port. As Bates began the process of bringing the Type 273 radar back online, a 5.9-inch shell from *Scharnhorst* struck the *Duke of York* destroying the Admiral's barge. By this time Fraser had more pressing concerns than the loss of his barge for it appeared that, despite being caught off guard and incurring some damage, *Scharnhorst* was going to get away.

Since 5.08 p.m., *Scharnhorst* had settled on to her easterly course with short deviations to allow turret 'Bruno' to fire, and had from then steadily opened the range to her pursuers. At 17.20 Burnett was forced to inform Fraser that his ships had lost touch with *Scharnhorst*. *Duke of York* meanwhile continued to fire, first at fleeting targets and, as the range opened, blindly by radar control. *Duke of York* began firing by radar at 17.17 when the range had opened up to 7.61 miles (12.25 km) and maintained a steady stream of blind fire for another forty-four broadsides, twenty-five of which were judged to be straddles. A further sixteen salvos were judged to have splashed down within 200 yards of the target.

During this time, at least three hits were observed, one of which started a fairly considerable fire on the superstructure aft, which provided a useful aiming point until it was extinguished much to the disappointment of the gun layer. HMS *Jamaica* had, during this time, been moving from one quarter to another behind the *Duke of York* and fired at *Scharnhorst* whenever she was presented with an opportunity. By 5.42 p.m., the range between *Jamaica* and *Scharnhorst* had opened up to 10.2 miles (16.45 km) whereupon Captain John Hughes-Hallett ordered the cruiser to cease fire, having decided that blind firing was of doubtful value and that *Jamaica*'s fire would likely confuse the radar spotting on board the flagship. As the slogging match between the *Duke of York* and *Scharnhorst* ensued, at 5.32 p.m., the Admiral Northern Waters received a signal from *Scharnhorst* that stated 'Surrounded by heavy units', and at 6.02 p.m., Dönitz received a signal from the battleship, which stated: 'Most Immediate. *Scharnhorst* will ever reign supreme. The commanding officer'. It was followed at 6.25 p.m. by a second signal, 'Flag Officer Cruisers and CO of *Scharnhorst* report: To the *Führer*. We shall fight to the last shell'.

By 6.08 p.m., the range between the *Duke of York* and *Scharnhorst* was such that Fraser signalled to the destroyers requesting them to report his fall of shot. At 6.13 p.m., *Scorpion* reported that the fire from *Duke of York* was falling approximately 200 yards short. Three minutes later, *Scorpion* reported that only occasional shell splashes could be identified owing to smoke. At 6.20 p.m., *Scharnhorst* ceased fire with the range at 11.3 miles (18.2 km). Four minutes later, the Type 284 radar of the *Duke of York* developed a defect which caused her to check fire.

The decision aboard *Duke of York* to check fire created a distinct atmosphere of gloom and disappointment in the ship's director control tower for it appeared that despite being hit and straddled, *Scharnhorst* would use her superior speed to escape. Even the destroyers, over 6 miles closer to the enemy than the *Duke of York*, were 6 miles (9.8 km) from *Scharnhorst* and were hardly gaining any ground. A feeling of bitter frustration and disappointment descended on the bridge.[26]

At 6.40 p.m., Fraser signalled to Burnett: 'I see little hope of catching *Scharnhorst* and am proceeding to support convoy'.[27] Fire had been checked because the Type 284 blind fire control radar had developed a fault and the 14-inch director could no longer see the target. Work commenced to repair the radar from 6.24 p.m. Shortly after Fraser had signalled his intention to Burnett to return to support the convoy, the radar was repaired, by which time the situation had changed. On the radar screen Fraser could see that the destroyers were gaining ground on the German battleship and so decided to reverse course to re-engage.

One minute before ceasing fire, *Scharnhorst* transmitted what would ultimately prove to be one of her last signals, 'Opponent is firing by radar location at more than 18,000 yards. My position AC 4965 (70° 09' N, 28° 30' E). Course 110 degrees, speed 26 knots'. Debate exists as to whether *Scharnhorst* was operating her aft radar set. Years after the war the former Executive Officer of the *Scharnhorst*, *Kapitän zur See* Helmuth Giessler who left the ship during the summer of 1943 was asked about the use of radar aboard the ship. According to Giessler, both Bey and Hintze were obsessed with the risk of radar transmissions being intercepted by direction-finding equipment that they believed all British ships possessed. Both men held considerable faith in the effectiveness of the radar equipment of the *Scharnhorst* but preferred not to use it owing to transmissions being intercepted.

Wilhelm Gödde, however, has referred to more than one occasion to a shadower of the *Scharnhorst* which could only have been detected through the use of radar. It is presumed that until she ceased firing at 6.20 p.m. that *Scharnhorst* had been firing under radar control. Until 6.20 p.m., the *Duke of York*'s 5.25-inch secondary armament, which had been providing the gunners of the *Scharnhorst* with an aiming point, was still firing, although they were nearing their maximum range and it seems highly unlikely that the flashes of these guns could have still been observed from aboard the *Scharnhorst* given the poor visibility.

At 6.20 p.m., just after *Scharnhorst*'s guns fell silent, a salvo from *Duke of York* crashed down and scored what would prove to be a crucial hit. A shell penetrated the ship's armour on the starboard side, crashed through the machinery spaces and put the starboard boiler room out of action.[28] *Matrosenobergefreiter* Hubert Witte, a messenger on the admiral's bridge watched as the speedometer on the bulkhead in front of him dropped to 22 knots as reports arrived of a shell hit aft. Other accounts of the action claim that speed was reduced to 8 knots. Whatever the case may be with regards to the exact reduction in speed, at one point *Korvettenkapitän* Otto König, the engineering officer, was heard to report to Hintze that 22 knots could be maintained. Clearly, König and the other members of the ship's engineering department managed to carry out admirably efficient damage control work and isolated the damaged boiler room before cross-connecting the remaining machinery to allow the ship to pick up speed to maintain 22 knots. It was, however, not enough; *Scharnhorst*'s vital superiority in speed was lost.

By 6.30 p.m., the shadows of the destroyers approaching on either beam could be seen. Ten minutes later the four destroyers had split into two subdivisions in preparation for a torpedo attack. As the destroyers approached, *Scharnhorst* did her best to drive off them off with gunfire but to no avail. In response, the four destroyers returned fire with their respective main armaments. HNoMS *Stord* was the first to launch an attack, Lieutenant-Commander Skule Storheill, the commanding officer of the *Stord*, took his ship in so close to the *Scharnhorst* while conducting his attack run that to observers on board the *Scorpion* it appeared as though Storheill was hell-bent on ramming the enemy battleship. *Scorpion* was next to launch an attack run.

As *Scorpion* attacked, star shells from *Savage* and *Saumarez* fell between her and the *Scharnhorst*. Far from illuminating *Scharnhorst*, the star shells blinded those on board the *Scorpion* from seeing their target, obliging them to press on in order to sight their target. The star shell also blinded those aboard *Scharnhorst* to the approach of the *Scorpion* for she made no attempt to concentrate fire on the destroyer. As *Scorpion* and *Stord* returned fire with their respective main armaments, those aboard *Scharnhorst* gained full appreciation for the impending danger that the ship was in, prompting the helm to be thrown over hard to starboard. Presented with a beam target, simultaneously with the *Stord*, *Scorpion* fired a full salvo of eight torpedoes at the *Scharnhorst*.

The violent turn to starboard executed by the *Scharnhorst* altered the situation for the *Savage* and *Saumarez*, for rather than chasing the stern of the battleship, the destroyers now found themselves on a converging course with their target. As *Scorpion* and *Stord* hauled off to the north, their attacks complete, at 6.53 p.m., seconds after *Scorpion* had let loose her salvo of torpedoes, *Savage* fired a salvo of eight torpedoes followed by a volley of four torpedoes from the *Saumarez*. As *Saumarez* approached to launch her torpedoes, an 11-inch shell from *Scharnhorst* passed through her director control tower without exploding. Nevertheless, the passage of the shell killed ten men in the tower and mortally wounded another who would later die of his wounds in hospital. A further eleven men were wounded.

Another shell exploded in the water close to the ship's starboard side where it sprayed the entire starboard side and upper deck with a storm of shrapnel. Splinters penetrated the side of the destroyer and damaged the forced lubrication system for the starboard main engines. The shaft had to be stopped to prevent further damage meaning that the *Saumarez* could only limp onwards using her port shaft at 8 knots. Aboard *Duke of York*, three heavy underwater explosions were heard while those aboard the *Belfast* reported hearing a total of six explosions. It seems certain that between them *Scorpion* and *Stord* scored at least one hit on the starboard side while *Savage* and *Saumarez*, it is believed, scored at least three hits on the port side.

One torpedo appears to have struck *Scharnhorst* in a boiler room, a second appears to have hit aft, and a third forward. Günter Sträter reported that he heard a message broadcast that a torpedo had struck boiler room I, which caused an involuntary reduction in speed to 8 knots and then heard the welcoming news that the ship was making 22 knots once more. As the destroyers launched their attacks, the *Duke of York* began tracking *Scharnhorst* on her Type 284 radar, and from 6.42 until 7 p.m., the ship made changes between blind and visual control as the glow in the smoke and the flashes from the guns of the *Scharnhorst* afforded fleeting points of aim.

For a time, in her efforts to avoid the torpedo tracks from the destroyers, *Scharnhorst* was steering south-west, almost towards *Duke of York* allowing the range between the two battleships to decrease rapidly. Shortly before 7 p.m., *Duke of York* and *Jamaica* turned 90 degrees to starboard to open 'A'-arcs, and to administer the *coup de grâce*. As they did so, a curious lull in the battle emerged before at 7.01 p.m., *Duke of York* opened fire once more at a range of 6 miles. The first broadside fired by the *Duke of York* in this re-engagement struck the *Scharnhorst* on the quarter deck. With direct fire now possible, twenty-five broadsides were fired, of which twenty-one were straddles while many hits were observed. From on board HMS *Belfast*, Ordinary Seaman Richard Wilson watched the destroyer attacks and then the re-engagement of the *Duke of York*:

> The destroyer attack was a glorious muddle of starshells, pom-pom tracer, great deep and red flashes and what not, then there was another long pause, with occasionally a sudden flash from somewhere. Then suddenly everything happened at once. Everybody started shooting, the whole scene was lit up by starshell and there was the *Scharnhorst* steaming down our starboard side with smoke pouring out amidships. She fired a single starshell which landed right overhead, and there we were, lit up like Piccadilly and waiting for it. Then the shells came, but the big salvo fell aft and the tracer ones went overhead like cricket balls. I expect their gunnery was all to bits.[29]

From on board the *Scharnhorst*, Gödde later recalled the confusion that began to reign at this time:

> I gathered from the telephone reports that more and more enemy units were joining the attack. Meanwhile came the report that a shell had landed on the plane handler deck and that the place was in flames. Because a destroyer had approached us from our wake to within 400 meters, the after 15-cm turret and the after 10.5 flak guns

had to be turned to defend against these enemy attacks. I have a poor recollection of the times and of certain incidents, but the ship at this point took several hits from heavy guns.[30]

As the *Duke of York* re-engaged, Gödde heard new contacts being reported followed by Hintze requesting a bearing and the ranges which were given. Shortly afterwards, turret 'Caesar' opened fire on the shadowy opponents, one of which was quickly identified as a battleship. As turret 'Caesar' returned fire against *Duke of York*, *Kapitänleutnant* Wieting ordered the ship's secondary armament to join in the fire against the British battleship and to also fire against the second opponent, which, from the calibre of its shells, was judged to be a cruiser.

Shell after shell slammed into the *Scharnhorst*. Heavy explosions followed one another and as each bout of violent explosions subsided it was succeeded by a slow vibration which was as if the hull itself was trembling. Steel crashed upon steel, fires broke out while billowing smoke from the rapidly spreading flames mingled with the acrid cordite fumes. Between the thunder of the *Scharnhorst*'s salvos, the crew could hear the dull rumbling of star shells exploding, the crash of incoming shells, and the rattle as splinters peppered the upper works. Among the fearful din of the battle in which *Scharnhorst* was now enveloped, none but those with a well-trained ear could distinguish voices and interpret orders picked up on the ship's telephone system. As Gödde listened to the cacophony around him, a heavy explosion shook the ship. Gritting his teeth, Gödde realised that the bow of the ship had run straight into the path of a shell. The blast flung Gödde into the air before violently depositing him on the deck. Momentarily losing consciousness, when he wearily opened his eyes as he came to, he saw Hintze.

Hintze had left the control position through the port door opposite Gödde's action station in order to take a quick look around. The lenses of the optical instruments in the control position had all either been destroyed by flying shrapnel or made temporarily unserviceable by clinging snow and water that had begun to freeze.[31] Just as Hintze was making his way through the armoured door, a 14-inch shell hit the bow. Splinters grazed Hintze's face but the *Kapitän* seemed hardly to notice. His only feeling was of something slowly trickling down his forehead to his cheeks which he dabbed with a handkerchief. As he did so, he noticed Gödde lying crumpled on the deck. Hintze helped the crumpled man to his feet who was then dispatched to see why the starboard control was not answering. As he did so, Hintze withdrew once more into the control position. Making his way to the starboard control, against the light of a star shell, Gödde could see that all of the men at the position were dead while all that remained of the actual control position was a mass of twisted metal, cables, and shattered instruments.

The report was sent to the captain that the crewmen at the station were dead.[32] Shortly after making his report, a 6-inch shell struck *Scharnhorst* forward whereupon fragments of shell tore into the position around where Gödde was standing. A Quartermaster who was sent by Hintze to report on the situation ordered Gödde to move into the command station as there was no need for him to remain outside any longer. Inside the command position, Gödde was given a new appreciation of the struggle that his ship was in against overwhelming odds. *Scharnhorst* was making

20 knots, the third engine was out of action owing to a damaged steam line and was locked into position. All the while damage control parties and parties of engineers were working desperately to repair the damage. *Korvettenkapitän* König reported that he was hopeful of getting everything in order once more within twenty to thirty minutes as the ship altered course to the north to escape her pursuers.

For *Scharnhorst*, there was to be no escape. From the north, HMS *Norfolk* opened fire once more but checked after two salvos due to the confusion of the situation and because she had difficulty in distinguishing friend from foe. *Belfast* also opened fire at 7.15 p.m. under visual control at a range of 9.5 miles and claimed two hits. Under local control, turret 'Caesar' continued to fire at the closing British warships. Of this time in the battle, Fraser himself noted, 'Little information … [was] forthcoming from this part of the action as they [the German sailors] were not unnaturally stunned by the success of our destroyer attacks and the pounding which their ship was receiving'.[33] With both the *Duke of York* and *Jamaica* having closed the range and opened 'A'-arcs, to Bryce Ramsden, the tracer now appeared almost horizontal, so flat was the trajectory. Recalling the scene, Ramsden noted:

> Suddenly—a bright-red glow, and in it the enemy was to be clearly seen for a brief moment. 'She's hit! My God, we've got her!' I was yelling like one possessed. We were cheering in the director. All over the ship a cheer went up, audible above the gun-fire. I had risen half standing in my seat as the wild thrill took hold of me. Again the dull glow, and in its light the sea was alive with shell-splashes from an out-pouring of shells. Great columns of water stood out clearly in the brief instant of light, and I could see smoke hanging above her. I was mad with excitement until I realised that my ravings must have been an incoherent babble of enthusiasm to those below, as the telephones were still hanging around my head. I straightened my tin hat, sat down and told them as calmly as I could that we could see that our shells had set her on fire, and that both the *Duke of York* and ourselves were hitting, and hitting hard. She must have been hell on earth.[34]

Matrosengefreiter Helmut Boekhoff, a loader in one of the *Scharnhorst*'s starboard 1.5-inch guns was one member of the ship's crew who was taking shelter inside the superstructure from the hail of shellfire.

> A star shot came right across us. We were lit up from stern onwards and they landed on the deck and I was in the tower and I was certain that armament had hit and the armour plate was absolutely red and there was something whistling round in the middle of it, like it [was] coming through … I thought 'Oh here it comes', but it didn't come through, it went outside and there was haywire all over.[35]

Inside the control position, a flood of reports was streaming in without a break. From the light of gun flashes through the periscopes that illuminated the relative darkness of the position, Gödde recognised the tall figure of *Fregattenkapitän* Dominik, who had come up from the commander's office to report to Hintze. As he did so, Gödde also recognised the figure of Bey leaning upright against the starboard wall. As he looked around recognising figures, Gödde heard some of the incoming reports.

'First officer to Captain: Forward dressing-station destroyed. Ship's doctor, chaplain and entire personnel killed'.[36]

'Starboard II – 5.9-inch reports: hit; gun can be trained to a limited extent only', which was followed shortly thereafter by, 'Starboard II—5.9-inch: out of action from another hit'.[37]

None of the 14-inch shells from the *Duke of York* penetrated the armoured deck which remained intact, instead, they exploded on contact with the deck wreaking havoc and causing significant numbers of casualties. The port forward SK C/28 was hit whereupon the guns and their hoists were put out of action. The aircraft hangar sustained a hit, and the Arado inside was destroyed while ruptured fuel tanks sparked a large fire, which the crew managed to extinguish within around ten minutes. A number of the Luftwaffe personnel on board tried to launch the remaining Ar 196s but there was no compressed air to operate the catapult. The remaining aircraft were destroyed over the following few minutes. Further hits landed on the starboard side forward 4.1-inch gun and near the funnel. One 0.79-inch gun of the starboard side was seen to receive a hit and was ripped from its mount and flung through the air to crash down on the deck.

Around this time, *Scharnhorst* was struck with unprecedented force and trembled violently along her entire length. Emergency lamps fell from their mountings. As crew members set to and replaced them, further heavy explosions occurred. All eyes turned to *Kapitänleutnant* Behr who shook his head with the words, 'Nothing's come through yet'.

'That was a torpedo hit', proclaimed *Korvettenkapitän* Walter Bredenbreuker, the first gunnery officer, 'It couldn't have been anything else'.[38]

Suddenly, Behr delivered a bulletin: '"B" turret to damage control party: order to flood! Magazine chamber "B" turret to be flooded'.[39] The men listened aghast. Turret 'Anton' had been out of action since the first engagement with the *Duke of York* and now it appeared that they had lost turret 'Bruno' also. As the men retreated to their thoughts, turret 'Bruno' could be heard firing again, distant and subdued, but firing nevertheless. Enveloped in smoke and fumes, the turret was to continue to fire in defiance. The violent explosion was not a torpedo hit as Bredenbreuker thought, rather, it was the result of turret 'Anton' receiving a second hit in the magazine chamber. The ship trembled and the smoke enveloped turret 'Bruno' as hot splinters penetrated the bulkhead protecting the magazines. The precaution of flooding the magazine of turret 'Bruno' was taken before it was decided to pump out both of the forward magazines a few minutes later.

According to *Matrosengefreiter* Rudi Birke, who served in turret 'Bruno', every time the breeches were opened, thick black smoke belched out, which blinded and choked the gun crew. This, combined with the motion of the ship, served to make almost every member of the gun crew violently seasick. A slight alteration of course to the north was made by the ship which prevented the turret from bearing on the British ships, which brought the gun crew temporary respite as the hatches were opened exposing the turret to fresh air.

As all of this was occurring, *Oberleutnant* Bosse, the ship's torpedo officer, departed the control position and was seen to be running along the upper deck among the hail of shrapnel to train the port side triple torpedo tubes on their aftermost bearing. Bosse succeeded in firing all three torpedoes, although only two went over the side as the third remained frozen in the tube. Shells, meanwhile, continued to crash down. One shell carried away the starboard anchor while another parted the anchor cable on the forecastle.

Behr soon reported, 'Heavy guns report: Ammunition exhausted: "B" turret has three shots left, "C" turret none'.

An order was passed to carry ammunition astern to turret 'Caesar' from the magazine of turret 'Anton'. The 5.9-inch guns continued to fire alone before under the guidance of *Kapitänleutnant* Fügner, the third gunnery officer, turret 'Caesar' was brought back into action, the thunder of its guns heard above the barking of the secondary armament. As Fügner directed the fire of the turret, a message crackled throughout the ship: 'From the Captain to all stations: Wireless signal to Supreme Command. The *Scharnhorst* will go on fighting to the last shell. Long live the *Führer*! Long live Germany!'[40] Everyone knew that the end was near.

Watching from his vantage point on the *Duke of York*, Wing Commander Compston noticed that *Scharnhorst* was glowing on the bridge and quarterdeck as she continued to return fire. The *Duke of York* fired another broadside at the target now less than three miles away. The tracer bands of the ship's 14-inch shell enabled the observers to follow the little circles of light to the glowing target. As each shell registered, flames and sparks flew up as the high explosives disintegrated. The flag lieutenant, Vernon Merry, who was also looking out at the target from beside Compston, noted the same effect:

> Every time we hit her, it was just like stoking up a huge fire, with flames and sparks flying up the chimney. Every time a salvo landed, there was this great gust of flame roaring up into the air, just as though we were prodding a huge fire with a poker. Tremendous, [an] unforgettable sight.[41]

At 7.19 p.m., Fraser ordered *Jamaica* and, a minute later, *Belfast* to close on the *Scharnhorst*, which appeared almost stationary and to sink the battleship with torpedoes.[42] Hughes-Hallett complied and began to close. As the *Jamaica* closed, *Scharnhorst* turned north and then sharply to port to take up a south-westerly course. This sudden movement likely disconcerted the torpedo crew of the cruiser, who fired three torpedoes to port at 7.25 p.m. One of the torpedoes misfired while no hits were observed from the other two. Burnett, meanwhile, upon receiving Fraser's signal to attack *Scharnhorst* with torpedoes, swung his cruisers to starboard to expose the target to the portside torpedo tubes of his ships. As he did so he also unleashed his four destroyers, which divided into two subsections. HMS *Matchless* and *Musketeer* began to make for the port side of the *Scharnhorst* where her bilge was exposed while the *Opportune* and *Virago* headed around to starboard.[43]

With *Scharnhorst* a blazing wreck, at 7.29 p.m., following unleashing eighty broadsides, the *Duke of York* checked fire. Two minutes before the *Duke of York* checked fire, *Belfast* fired three torpedoes, and claimed one hit, although no one saw it and Fraser would say that the hit was 'considered unlikely'. Burnett, on the other hand, hotly disputed this and would forever remain convinced that *Belfast* struck *Scharnhorst* with a torpedo and that it was his flagship that delivered the decisive final blow. The *Belfast* turned to fire another salvo of torpedoes at the *Scharnhorst* at 7.35 p.m. but found such a melee of ships and fire around the target that she was forced to round the German battleship to the southward and await a more favourable opportunity to attack which would not come. As the destroyers closed in, the torpedo crew of HMS *Matchless*, which had been damaged amidships by a green sea that destroyed her voice pipes, missed the order to open fire with torpedoes as the other destroyers struck the mortally wounded enemy.[44]

At 7.37 p.m., *Musketeer* fired four torpedoes to starboard at a range of half a mile. Columns of spray were seen erupting between the funnel and main mast as two, possibly three, hits were observed. Meanwhile the *Opportune* fired four torpedoes at a range of a mile and claimed one hit. Turning, the destroyer made a second run and fired another four torpedoes and claimed another hit. HMS *Virago*, a new destroyer, which was less than two months out of the builder's yard and with a ship's company 70 per cent of whom were raw and had never been at sea before, took its opportunity to attack. Following *Opportune*, the *Virago* fired four torpedoes at a range of 1.5 miles and observed two hits. As the destroyer retired westward, the gun crews opened fire with the ship's 4.7-inch guns.

With three cruisers and eight destroyers in the vicinity, the *Duke of York* began to clear away to the north in order to avoid the melee. Owing to the scrum of cruisers and destroyers that launched attacks, it has been difficult to determine which ships scored hits with their torpedoes. It would appear, however, that in this latest assault, five torpedoes found their mark. In all of the torpedoes attacks conducted against the *Scharnhorst*, the *Savage*, *Scorpion Opportune*, and *Stord* each fired eight torpedoes; *Virago* fired seven; *Jamaica* five with one misfire; *Musketeer* and *Saumarez* fired four each; and *Belfast* three totalling fifty-five torpedoes in all of which eleven are considered to have hit.

The torpedo hits had a cumulative effect and aggravated the damage caused by the gunfire and internal explosions. One torpedo struck aft in Section III when the after damage control party was already fully engaged. The midships damage control party was ordered to control the situation but found the section so badly damaged that the passageway was impassable which led to the watertight bulkheads being closed as they tried to reach the area from the port side. Access via the port side also proved impossible so the section was fully cut off, trapping twenty-five men in the aft portion of the ship. A torpedo also finally knocked turret 'Bruno' out of action, the detonation jamming the elevating and training mechanisms of the turret.

As the torpedoes hit, the *Scharnhorst* took on an increasing list. According to Fritz-Otto Busch, as the torpedoes from the destroyers slammed into the *Scharnhorst*, the order was issued: 'From the Captain to all stations. Destroy all secret papers and installations. To damage control party: prepare for scuttling: All men detailed for scuttling to their stations!'[45] Busch goes on to describe how the damage control parties complied with Hintze's order and proceeded to fit scuttling charges throughout the ship where they were detonated one by one. That the order was issued to set scuttling charges and was carried out, however, is something that is unlikely given that efforts were underway to close the watertight bulkhead and shore up the damaged positions in an effort to keep the ship afloat. Busch goes on to state that while this supposed order was being carried out, Hintze beckoned the navigation officer over to him, 'Pass to the Action Information Centre, a last report of our position in clear text. Quickly Lanz. Time is running out'.

Hintze then gripped the arm of Behr: 'To all stations, from the Captain: Abandon ship. Every man to the upper deck. Life-jackets on. Prepare to jump overboard'.[46] As Hintze urged the twenty-five men in the control position to leave, the order to abandon ship began to filter through the ship. In the port 4.1-inch gun, Staff Chief Gunner *Stabsoberstückmeister* Johann Wibbelhoff rose from his seat and ordered every man to leave the turret. The gun crew hesitated as throughout the action, the turret had suffered neither damage nor casualties.

'Leave the turret boys,' Wibbelhoff repeated, raising his voice, 'I'm staying where I belong'.

'I'm staying too,' stated *Obermaat* Werner Moritz as he moved to Wibbelhoff's side.

Not another word was spoken as the men began to file out of the turret, returning the battery commander's final salute as they went. *Matrosenobergefreiter* Günter Sträter, one of the last men to leave the turret, watched as Wibbelhoff put his hand in his pocket and produced a packet of cigarettes. In the calm and deliberate manner so familiar to his men, Wibbelhoff lit one up and proceeded to swing back in his seat. Moritz, likewise, lowered himself into his seat as Sträter left the turret.[47]

Despite being ordered to leave, most of those in the command station refused to leave the position and abandon ship without Hintze and Bey. A young seaman shook his head and simply stated, 'We're staying with you'. Another young rating stated that he had no life jacket and that he too was staying in the position. To this, Hintze responded by unfastening his own life jacket and took it off.

'Here you are,' Hintze replied, handing the young seaman his life jacket, 'You have mine. I'm a good swimmer. But now off with you. I'll come afterwards, never fear'.[48]

The combined efforts of Hintze and Bey succeeded at length in getting the men out of the position. Every man received a parting handshake from the admiral and captain, who then moved out onto the wings of the bridge. From this vantage point, Hintze looked silently down on the upper deck, which was swarming with men who continued to flood the deck from companionways and hatches before assembling in silent groups. Not a sound was heard above the roar of the sea and the howl of the wind save the dull explosion of a single star shell as it came over from one of the British ships as the crew assembled among the dead who were strewn all around. Nowhere on deck was there the slightest panic. Holding a megaphone, Hintze began to give instructions to the assembled men for leaving the ship: 'Don't go overboard to starboard, my friends. Go over from the port side, and slide from the rail into the water'.

Dominik, meanwhile, stood below the bridge to pass on Hintze's instructions for going overboard. *Scharnhorst* was now rolling heavily in the rough sea and was enveloped in dense smoke, but was still slowly moving. Her starboard side lay in the water practically to the wings of the bridge while waves began to wash the main mast. Many of those who proceeded to enter the water were sucked under or knocked out by falling debris. Some men jumped from the searchlight tower. By the time they hit the water, however, they were already dead, having hit the side of the ship first. At 7.45 p.m., *Scharnhorst* heeled over on her side and sank by the bow. As she capsized and sank, two of the three propeller screws were observed to still be turning by those who had entered the water.

The last moments of the *Scharnhorst* were obscured from the view of the British ships by a dense cloud of smoke so that no one was sure when exactly the ship sank. A dull underwater explosion was reported by some as marking the ship sinking. Looking at the radar screen of the *Duke of York*, Lieutenant Vivian Cox, a member of Fraser's personal staff, reported that the echo of the *Scharnhorst* was fading, inferring that the German battleship was sinking.[49] The last British ships to sight the *Scharnhorst* were the *Jamaica*, *Matchless*, and *Virago* at 7.38 p.m.[50] With no view of the *Scharnhorst* owing to the smoke, it was by no means clear at the time that she had sunk. Fraser became quite uncharacteristically perturbed over the lack of hard news that the German battleship had definitely slipped beneath the waves. Normally, the most unruffled of men, he began to pace the admiral's bridge impatiently, firing off a volley of signals. The nearest destroyer was ordered to illuminate the enemy while Burnett was requested to keep him informed of the *Scharnhorst*'s position while a signal was made to HMS *Scorpion* stating: 'Has *Scharnhorst* sunk?'[51]

At 7.48 p.m., *Belfast* closed in on the suspected location of the *Scharnhorst* to deliver a second torpedo attack but saw nothing of the battleship. A star shell was fired by the cruiser to locate the target, but as Burnett later wrote, 'to the chagrin of the torpedomen, the affair was complete'.[52] Instead of the battleship, Burnett's flagship found debris, oil, and rafts—almost all that was left of one of the proudest ships in the *Kriegsmarine*. Of the sinking of the *Scharnhorst* at the Battle of North Cape, the official British historian Stephen Roskill later wrote, 'Thus did a ship which had caused us immense trouble since the beginning of the war meet her end'.[53]

14

'On the Field of Honour'

For those in the water, it now became a struggle of life and death. For those who had a mind to live, they now found themselves fighting to do so. One such individual was Helmut Boekhoff:

> By the time I was lying on a raft, I had somebody got hold of my boot which I let go, because if you don't let the boot go you go with them. And you couldn't save anybody because the moment you were in the water all you think about was yourself.[1]

As they were making their preparations to enter the water, Gödde and another sailor, *Maat* Johann Deierling, lost their footing and were swept from the ship by a receding wave. Gödde was drawn down by the suction. An unbearable pressure increased in his eardrums before he was shot to the surface, whereupon he desperately tried to get clear of the whirling waters that eddied around the ship as she capsized and began to sink. In front of him, Gödde saw a float that formed part of the ship's minesweeping equipment, on which another member of the crew was sitting astride. Swimming over to the float, the crewman attempted to pull Gödde up, but the float overturned, depositing both men into the water. Gödde then saw a brass cartridge from one of the 11-inch shells bobbing in the water. Upon reaching the shell casing, he attempted to grab hold of it, but its smooth surface and the water caused it to slip away from his grip before it then filled with water and sank. Pieces of wood washed away from the ship floated all around. Gödde succeeded in pushing one piece under his body, but despite clinging on for dear life, he fell off.

Lifted onto the crest of a wave, Gödde was confronted by what he would later call 'a gruesome sight'. Star shells and searchlights still illuminated the scene. *Scharnhorst* was just visible lying on her side. Gödde sighted the light of a raft flickering close by and swam over to it. The raft contained a young officer and several other men. As he swam towards the raft, the officer suddenly stood up and, through the raging storm, shouted, 'Three cheers for the *Scharnhorst*!' Gödde and everyone in the vicinity who heard the shout joined in the cheering.[2]

Suddenly, Gödde heard shouts from men who were swimming closer to the ship: 'It's the Captain. He's swimming near the ship; he can't hold out; he's got no life jacket'.[3] Gödde knew at that moment that the last man who could leave and who could make it to the upper deck to abandon ship had done so, allowing Hintze to fulfil his duty as the last man to abandon ship. As *Scharnhorst* began to capsize and sink, fuel oil began to pour out of the hull and spread across the water. While nauseating, the fuel oil had the effect of cushioning the violence of the breaking sea.

Gödde now tried to reach the raft that was near him but in the few moments that had elapsed it had by now filled. Abandoning his attempt to reach the raft, he swam towards wooden props which were used by the damage control parties to shore up damaged sections of the hull. Reaching one such prop, Gödde hauled himself up onto the piece of wood, which offered him some support.

Of the ship's lifeboats and rafts, only a few were in the water. Most of the rafts and boats had been cut free and lowered into the water in good time, but splinters and fragments of shells had riddled them with holes, making a large proportion of them useless. Gradually, the sound of firing died away and as the last star shell burned out, darkness reclaimed the sea. The small groups of survivors that huddled together on the rafts could hardly see each other, not to mention the isolated swimmers in the water. They were completely exhausted, incapable now of feeling, numbed by weariness and the cold.

As the time approached 8 p.m., Fraser was still not satisfied that the *Scharnhorst* had actually sunk. At 7.57 p.m., he signalled to all ships, 'Clear the area of the target except those ships with torpedoes and one destroyer with searchlight'. As *Belfast* closed to comply with Fraser's order and launch her second torpedo attack, thick oil was seen on the surface of the water and the smell of burnt oil became increasingly noticeable. Looking down from the bridge, Captain Parham sighted German sailors in the water. 'We came across a raft full of shouting, if not screaming, German sailors. Rather a horrid sight, really'.[4] Another ship with torpedoes was HMS *Matchless*, the crew of which was hopeful of making another attack. As the ship closed, the crew was ordered from action stations to rescue stations. A large scrambling net was hung over the side of the ship as members of the crew stood ready with lines, boat hooks, and life jackets.

Among the German sailors in the water, cheering for the *Scharnhorst* and for Germany along with singing had broken out. It would appear to be the case that what Parham and other British seamen thought was shouting and screaming was in fact cheering and singing. Suddenly, the German sailors were aware of a flash and the thunder of guns. The apparent whizzing of shells overhead broke the darkness but then came the dull crack as star shells burst and lit up the area. For a moment, the men in the water thought that their rafts were being fired upon, but they quickly realised their mistake as the thin fingers of the searchlight beam began to pierce the darkness.

As *Matchless* edged forward and began to search for survivors, wreckage and bodies littered the sea. Six ratings were pulled from the water, soaked through, frozen with the cold, and covered with oil. Glad that they had been rescued, the six men were treated like any other survivors who were pulled from the water, taken to a mess deck and given rum to fetch up any oil that they may have ingested. Issued with dry clothing, they were put into hammocks slung in the forward mess. Approximately a cable away from the *Matchless*, the searchlight of HMS *Scorpion* was sweeping the scene. Close to HMS *Scorpion*, Hintze was reportedly seen in the water along with

Dominik. Both men were reportedly badly wounded. It would appear that Hintze died before he could be rescued while Dominik managed to grab hold of a line but that it slipped through his fingers as he succumbed to the perishing cold.[5]

Coder Farr, a member of *Scorpion*'s crew, saw in the searchlight beam a red German flag spread out into the water over some wreckage to which a group of men were clinging. The crew of the *Scorpion* also heard chilling screams in the darkness, some of them despairing because many of the men who had escaped the *Scharnhorst* realised that they would not be rescued as they would succumb to the cold before one of the destroyers reached them. According to Lieutenant-Commander William Clouston, the commanding officer of the *Scorpion*, there were approximately 100 members of the *Scharnhorst*'s crew around his destroyer at one point, but many of them drifted away out of sight and out of reach. HMS *Scorpion* succeeded in rescuing thirty men from the water including Wilhelm Gödde and Günter Sträter. In total, out of *Scharnhorst*'s company of 1,968, only thirty-six men were rescued from the waters off North Cape. Of the survivors, Gödde was the most senior survivor.

Now, at last, an exchange of signals convinced Fraser that the *Scharnhorst* had been sunk. At 8.04 p.m., *Scorpion* signalled: 'Am picking up German survivors'. At 8.18 p.m., over half an hour after the *Scharnhorst* had slipped beneath the waves, Fraser signalled, 'Has *Scharnhorst* sunk?' A reply was forthcoming from Burnett, which stated 'Satisfied that *Scharnhorst* is sunk'. This signal was followed by another signal from the *Scorpion* at 8.30 p.m.: 'Survivors state that *Scharnhorst* has sunk'.[6] HMS *Matchless* and *Scorpion* continued their search for survivors until 8.40 p.m. Shortly after 9 p.m., HMS *Sheffield* rejoined Force 1 whereupon Fraser ordered all ships in the area to proceed independently to the Kola Inlet.[7]

As the ships made for Murmansk, Fraser gathered his officers on board his flagship and briefed them on the events that had unfolded before paying tribute to the German sailors:

> Gentlemen, the battle against *Scharnhorst* has ended in victory for us. I hope that if any of you are ever called upon to lead a ship into action against an opponent many times superior, you will command your ship as gallantly as *Scharnhorst* was commanded today.[8]

A signal was sent by Fraser to the Admiralty that simply stated '*Scharnhorst* sunk', to which he received the reply, 'Grand, well done'.[9] For Henry Leach, the elation at the victory that had been achieved was soon overcome by the significance of the moment:

> There's one's feelings at the end of this. There's an affinity between seamen, and you felt a note of nostalgia to an extent. We were also very tired and I suppose when you're very tired and short of sleep you are more emotional. I think there's no question about that. So it was with a feeling, not of gloating, but of intense relief that it was us that had won and not them—not the enemy. And of course, the convoy was saved from the raider attack.[10]

Fraser's ships arrived at Murmansk on 27 December, where they began to replenish their fuel stocks. Upon their arrival in Murmansk, Admiral Golvoko was as grudging as ever with his praise:

Admiral Sir Bruce Fraser greeting Admiral Arseniy Golovko, the commander of the Red Banner Northern Fleet, aboard HMS *Duke of York* while refuelling at Murmansk following the Battle of North Cape. (*Author's Collection*)

> The destruction of the German warship is, indisputably, a major success for the British. It should be added that they were assisted by preliminary basing on the Kola Inlet and the fact that their journey here and visit went undiscovered by the enemy.[11]

At Kola, the *Duke of York* was refuelled while the Type 281 radar, which had been damaged during the course of the battle was repaired. During the afternoon of 27 December, while *Matchless* and *Scorpion* were anchored at the roadstead, the German sailors who had been pulled from the water were put on to a Soviet tug to be transferred to the *Duke of York*. The transfer to the tug greatly alarmed a large number of the German sailors who thought that they were being turned over to the Soviets. Some of the sailors went so far as to state that they would jump overboard. They were calmed by a German-speaking British officer who reassured them that Fraser had ordered that all of the sailors were to be taken on board the *Duke of York* so as to be taken back to England in the flagship.

As the tug drew alongside the British flagship, Johnnie Merkel, a German-Canadian by birth, went up to the senior British destroyer officer on board who was assisting with the transfer and, addressing him in English, on behalf of his comrades, thanked the destroyer crews for their selfless care. Turning to his fellow survivors, Merkel called for three cheers for the crews of the British destroyers. All of the German sailors joined in. Afterwards, Gödde could not help but reflect on how strange an event it was—German cheers for British sailors in a Soviet port.[12]

With the refuelling completed, *Duke of York* departed Murmansk and set a course for Scapa Flow. During the passage, the survivors were allowed to exercise on the upper deck of the battleship and between the hangers where they were much photographed by members of the crew. Once back in Britain, the survivors were transferred from the *Duke of York* to the merchant ship SS *St Ninian* before being landed and interned for the remainder of the war. Early on New Year's Day 1944, the *Duke of York* arrived back at Scapa Flow. War correspondents, who were not permitted to sail with the ships, had been waiting since before dawn at the entrance to the fleet anchorage in fishing trawlers. As the correspondents looked on:

Survivors for the *Scharnhorst* on the catapult deck of the *Duke of York* during the passage to Scapa Flow.

[S]uddenly out of the murk to the norrard appeared the *Duke of York* with smoke-blackened fourteen-inch guns flying her shell-torn [sic.] battle ensign and cramming on almost every piece of bunting in the ship. Astern of her came the cruiser *Jamaica* and then the long line of destroyers all flying battle ensigns and bunting and over their torpedo tubes turned outboard the 'Affirmative' signal and beneath it the numeral signals showing the number of hits on the *Scharnhorst*.[13]

A flood of congratulations poured into the ships of the Home Fleet from various quarters. To Fraser, King George VI sent the message, 'Well done, *Duke of York*, and all of you. I am proud of you'. From Churchill came the message, 'Heartiest congratulations to you and the Home Fleet on your brilliant action. All comes to him who knows how to wait'.[14] At the time of the battle Churchill was in Carthage preparing to fly to Marrakesh. On the morning of 27 December, he was preparing to leave for his aircraft when he was handed a telegram giving the fateful news of the sinking of the *Scharnhorst*. He stopped to dictate a telegram to Stalin:

The Arctic Convoys to Russia have brought us luck. Yesterday enemy attempted to intercept with battle-cruiser *Scharnhorst*. Commander-in-Chief Admiral Fraser with the *Duke of York* (35,000-ton battleship) cut off *Scharnhorst*'s retreat, and after an action sunk her.[15]

A few days later, a cordial reply was received from Stalin, which ended with the words, 'I shake your hand firmly'.[16]

Congratulations were also forthcoming from the War Cabinet, the first lord of the Admiralty, the first sea lord, President Roosevelt, and Abdul Ilah, the regent of Iraq. Salutes were received from Crown Prince Paul of Greece; Admiral Douglas Fisher in Russia; Rear Admiral Royal Ingersoll, the commander-in-chief of the US Atlantic Fleet; Rear Admiral Elias Corneliussen, the commander-in-chief of the Royal Norwegian Navy; as well as from Fraser's peers in the Royal Navy: Rear Admiral Sir

HMS *Duke of York* entering Scapa Flow, New Year's Day 1944. (*Robert Henderson*)

John Cunningham, the commander-in-chief Mediterranean Fleet; Admiral Sir James Somerville, commander-in-chief Eastern Fleet; and Vice Admiral Sir Algernon Willis, commander-in-chief Levant among others. Signals were also received from the French battleship *Richelieu*, the USS *Ranger*, and the air officer commanding 18 Group RAF, the officers and men of the Orkneys and Shetlands Defence Force, the president of the Merchant Navy Officers Association, and the Barge Owners of London.

The loss of the *Scharnhorst* shook the *Kriegsmarine*. Dönitz struggled to understand why Bey had broken off the first encounter with Force 1 when in his judgement, Bey had it in his power to overwhelm the British cruisers:

> The correct thing to have done ... would have been to continue the fight and finish off the weaker British forces, particularly as it was plain that they had already been hard hit.... Had this been done an excellent opportunity would ... have been created for a successful attack on the convoy.[17]

As *Duke of York* sailed to Scapa Flow, Dönitz promulgated his conclusions in a directive to the *Kriegsmarine* on 29 December that, incidentally, was intercepted, decoded, and redistributed to authorised recipients of Ultra that same day. Dönitz began his directive by stressing how imperative it was for the *Scharnhorst* to make an intervention against the Arctic Convoys in an effort to attempt to relieve the pressure on the *Wehrmacht* forces fighting on the Eastern Front. Dönitz went on to state that the prospects for the attack had been favourable and that aerial reconnaissance had established that the convoy was escorted by only light units while any limitations imposed by the weather were to the *Scharnhorst*'s advantage. Dönitz emphasised that the most important lesson that could be drawn from the battle was that the British had been able to detect *Scharnhorst* at a range of thirty miles with radar and that they could use their radar to bombard her while remaining unseen. Meanwhile, Dönitz's summary also highlighted that the Germans had no indication of how much damage the *Scharnhorst* had inflicted on HMS *Norfolk*, *Sheffield*, or *Duke of York*.

Above left: Blindfolded survivors from the *Scharnhorst* aboard the SS *St. Ninian*.

Above right: The survivors are seen here walking down a gangplank from the SS *St. Ninian* into internment for the remainder of the war.

The same day that Dönitz produced his directive, Admiral Friedrich Lützow, the head of the propaganda department of the *Kriegsmarine*, delivered an address on German radio in which he stated, 'We pay tribute to our comrades who died the death of seamen in the heroic battle against enemy superiority. The *Scharnhorst* is now on the field of honour'.[18] In Altafjord, the crew of the *Tirpitz* heard the news of the sinking of the *Scharnhorst* and shuddered. According to one member of the *Tirpitz*'s crew, the sinking of the *Scharnhorst* 'cast a long shadow over the ship's company'.

Among those lost on board the *Scharnhorst* were some members of the *Tirpitz*'s crew who had been sent to *Scharnhorst* to fill positions left vacant by men on leave.[19] One such individual was *Korvettenkapitän* Rolf Woytschekowski-Emden, an English-speaking intelligence officer who interrogated the men of the *X-6* following the X-craft's attack on the *Tirpitz* during Operation Source.[20] The sinking of the *Scharnhorst* left the *Tirpitz* as the sole remaining German capital ship in northern waters. Dubbed 'The Lonely Queen of the North', she too would eventually be sunk, but not until 12 November 1944 as the result of an air raid launched by RAF Bomber Command.

In his memoirs of the Second World War, Winston Churchill summarised the sinking of the *Scharnhorst* as thus:

[T]he sinking of the *Scharnhorst* not only removed the worst menace to our Arctic Convoys, but gave new freedom to our Home Fleet. We no longer had to be prepared at our average moment against German heavy ships breaking out into the Atlantic at their selected moment. This was an important relief.[21]

15

The Fate of the *Gneisenau*

Since detailing the events of the Channel Dash, this book has focused on the subsequent career of the *Scharnhorst* up to her sinking at the battle of North Cape. It is now necessary to look at the fate that befell the *Gneisenau*. The repair work on the damage that was incurred during Operation Cerberus had been completed by 26 February 1942 and the ship was scheduled to be deployed to Norway on 6 March. On 26 February, the ship was still in dry dock, nevertheless, her ammunition stores were restocked and preparations were underway for a short round of sea trials before the ship departed Germany for Norway. On the night of 26–27 February, the RAF launched a heavy air raid against Kiel.[1] A single bomb struck the forecastle and penetrated the armoured deck before exploding.[2] Hot fragments from the bomb ignited the propellant charges in the forward turret, which caused an enormous explosion that served to throw turret 'Anton' off its mount and burned out the entire bow section.[3] The remainder of the crew managed to partially flood the forward magazines, preventing a more catastrophic explosion the likes of which had destroyed HMS *Hood*, HMS *Barham*, and the USS *Arizona*. The explosion in turret 'Anton' killed 112 members of the crew and wounded a further twenty-one others.[4]

The extensive damage that was sustained by the *Gneisenau* from the explosion of the forward turret convinced the *Oberkommando der Marine* to rebuild *Gneisenau* in order to mount six 15-inch guns as had originally been planned, as opposed to simply repairing the ship. The damaged bow section was removed so that a lengthened bow could be constructed, which would serve to correct the decrease in freeboard that would have been caused by the heavier 15-inch guns and new turrets.[5] On 4 April, escorted by the training ship *Schlesien* and the icebreaker *Castor*, the *Gneisenau* sailed to Gotenhafen.[6] On 1 July, the ship was formally decommissioned with her crew being paid off and redeployed in the U-boat arm of the *Kriegsmarine*.[7]

By early 1943, the ship had been sufficiently repaired for the process of converting the ship to be armed with 15-inch guns to begin. Events conspired against the *Gneisenau*, however, as Hitler, angered at the performance of the *Admiral Hipper* and *Lützow* during the Battle of the Barents Sea, decided to scrap the entire surface fleet of the *Kriegsmarine*. While Dönitz managed to save a significant number of vessels

Above: Turret 'Anton' following being thrown off its mount by the explosion of the bomb which struck the forecastle and ignited the propellant charges. Some 112 members of the crew were killed when the turret exploded and burnt out the bow section. (*Author's Collection*)

Below: A close-up view of *Gneisenau* in the dry dock at Kiel following the RAF raid of 26–27 February. (*Author's Collection*)

from being decommissioned and sent to the breakers yard, the cessation of work on the *Gneisenau* was ordered.[8]

In the wake of this decision, *Gneisenau* was disarmed and used for spare parts. Reusable parts of the ship were scavenged and used to repair and keep the remaining elements of the *Kriegsmarine*'s surface assets operational, one such example being the removal of oil pumps which were sent to Norway to be fitted to the damaged *Tirpitz* in early 1944.[9] The main and secondary armament of the ship were removed in order to be used as gun batteries.[10] Two of the ship's SK C/34 guns were used to construct Battery Fjell and Battery Ørland (now known as the Austrått fortress). Construction work on Battery Fjell began in the late summer of 1942 and was completed in July 1943. When constructed, the battery was to protect the seaward approach to Bergen, nevertheless, the guns were often fired against approaching aircraft.

In order to mount the SK C/34 turret, which was originally turret 'Bruno', at the fortress, it was necessary to dig around 55 feet (17 m) vertically into the mountainside.

Right: Gneisenau photographed from an RAF reconnaissance at Gotenhafen in June 1942. The arrows are as follows: B—Turret 'Bruno' with guns removed, C—Turret 'Caesar', D—Camouflage netting, E—the base of turret 'Anton' on the pier, and F—the roller path bearings for turret 'Anton' on the dockside. (*NH 91654, US Naval History and Heritage Command Center*)

Below: Taken by a RAF reconnaissance aircraft on 1 August 1942, Gneisenau can be seen undergoing repair and refit work. The three main armament turrets have been removed by this time. The incomplete aircraft carrier *Graf Zeppelin* can be seen at the top of the photograph. (*NH 91657, US Naval History and Heritage Command Center*)

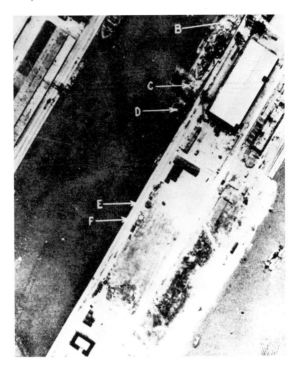

This was considered a time-consuming task. Rather than blasting a tunnel into the mountain, the turret was lifted into a depression over which concrete was poured. The construction work was mainly carried out by prisoners from Eastern Europe, although it is worth noting that some Norwegian prisoners were also employed. The gun turret, when fitted to the *Gneisenau*, had weighed approximately 600 tons. As a gun battery, additional armour plating was added to the turret giving it a weight of 1,000 tons. When the turret first fired a salvo, the firing produced a minor earthquake while the concussion flattened some barns in the surrounding area and shattered all of the windows in Fjell. Subsequently, full salvos were never fired again.

Turret 'Caesar' meanwhile went on to form the Austrått fortress. The battery was constructed in 1942 to protect Trondheimsfjord. Approximately 650 Yugoslavian slave labourers were employed in cutting bunkers and tunnels into the hillside in order to fit and serve the turret. By August 1943, the gun turret had been fitted and was fired for the first time. The battery would see no engagements during the remainder of the war. After the war, the Norwegian military took over the fortress.

Turret 'Caesar' was fired for the last time in 1953 while the site remained operational until finally being decommissioned in 1968. As a result, the site remains in a good state of preservation today. Today, the site is a museum with the underground barracks, the turret shaft, and ammunition rooms open to the public. The site is one of the most complete examples of Second World War German coastal batteries in existence. Turret 'Anton' was also removed from the hull of the *Gneisenau* and the individual guns were fitted at sites in Denmark and Holland. The secondary armament from the *Gneisenau*, the 5.9-inch SK C/28 guns, were also re-employed as coastal batteries; one gun turret was sited on the Danish Island of Fanø while another was sited at Blåvand as part of the Tirpitz Battery which was sited to protect the entrance to Esbjerg. In 1951, the gun turrets were removed from Fanø and Blåvand to the Stevnsfort where they remain today. The Stevnsfort was built between 1950 and 1953 to help defend against Soviet naval forces from the Baltic. With the end of the Cold War, the fort lost its strategic importance and was closed in 2000. The site was reopened in 2008 as a museum.

The hull of the *Gneisenau* remained in Gotenhafen until the end of the war. As the Red Army advanced on the city, the remains of the ship were taken out to the entrance of the harbour and scuttled as a blockship on 27 March 1945. The following day, the city fell to Soviet forces and was assigned to the Gdańsk Voivodeship, who renamed the city Gdynia. In 1947, the Polish government ordered that the remains of the *Gneisenau* be removed from the harbour entrance, prompting salvage operations to begin.[11] The hull was sealed and re-floated on 12 September 1951 before being towed away to be scrapped.[12] It is believed that some of the steel from the *Gneisenau* was subsequently used in the construction of Polish merchant vessels.[13] When she was re-floated on 12 September 1951, the *Gneisenau* was the largest ship to ever be raised.

One of the three gun barrels from turret 'Bruno' being unloaded at Bergen prior to being installed at Battery Fjell. (*Museum Vest, avdeling Fjell Festning*)

Taken shortly after the end of the war in 1945, the hull of the *Gneisenau* is seen here in Gotenhafen harbour having been sunk as a blockship. (*NH 83613, US Naval History and Heritage Command Center*)

Above left: Gneisenau in Gotenhafen following being sunk as a blockship. Note the camouflage netting on the forward parts of the superstructure. (*Author's Collection*)

Above right: The remains of the hull in position at the entrance of Gdynia harbour, seen here in 1946. Note the lighthouse in the foreground on the left. (*Author's Collection*)

The hull of the *Gneisenau* while being broken up. (*Michał Banach*)

16

The Wreck of the *Scharnhorst*

In September 2000, a joint expedition was launched by the BBC, Narvik Rikskringkasting AS (NRK), and the Royal Norwegian Navy to locate the wreck of the *Scharnhorst*. Prior to this, a search of the sea floor for signs of the sunken battleship had been undertaken—9.6 square miles (25 square km) of the seabed around the official sinking position was searched without any sign of the wreck being found. Research conducted at the National Archives in Kew revealed that the navigation log of HMS *Duke of York* recorded a different sinking position to those that were recorded by Admiral Fraser in his official dispatches. Crucially for the researchers, none of the other ships that took part in the Battle of North Cape noted any positions for the location of the sinking position of the *Scharnhorst*.

Armed with this information from the navigation log of the *Duke of York*, simulations were made at the Royal Norwegian Navy's naval academy. At the academy, computers were loaded with the navigational data from the log of the *Duke of York* along with her documented performance data, whereupon a virtual battle of North Cape was fought. The simulator at the naval academy was similar to an aircraft simulator but with the bridge of a ship replacing the cockpit of an aircraft. Beginning at noon on 26 December 1943, the simulator recreated every movement of the *Duke of York* until the *Scharnhorst* was sunk. After several hours, the simulator had concluded the battle. This completed, the simulator's computer system downloaded data showing a different location of the *Scharnhorst*'s sinking, approximately 20 miles to the north of the position given by Fraser in his official dispatches.

So it was that in September 2000, the underwater survey vessel *Sverdrup II* operated by the Norwegian Defence Research Establishment departed Hammerfest in arctic Norway to conduct surveys of the new location. On one occasion during her regular seabed mapping operations, the *Sverdrup II* had already surveyed the area indicated as the sinking location by the logbook of the *Duke of York* and the simulator where a large object had been detected. Now *Sverdrup II* played host as the sonar platform for a joint expedition by the BBC, NRK, and the Royal Norwegian Navy.

Arriving at the indicated location, the *Sverdrup II* again picked up a large object lying on the seabed. Having identified an object on the seabed that was consistent with the approximate dimensions of a ship like the *Scharnhorst*, the expedition transferred to the mine control and underwater search and recovery vessel HNoMS *Tyr*. On 10 September, from the *Tyr*, a Scorpio 21 remotely operated vehicle (ROV) was prepared and deployed in order to visually examine the object.

When the ROV reached the seabed, part of the mystery was immediately solved as it became clear that the expedition had come across the wreck of a ship lying in approximately 950 feet (290 metres) of water.[1] Whether or not the wreck was that of the *Scharnhorst*, however, remained to be determined. As the ROV manoeuvred its way around the wreck the presence of gun turrets and torpedo tubes consistent with those of the *Scharnhorst* were located leaving no doubt as to the identification of the ship.[2]

Sunk at 72° 16' N, 28° 41' E, the hull lies upside down on the seabed in two pieces. Some distance from the bulk of the hull the bow lies among a twisted mass of steel having been blown off as a result of an explosion in the barbette of turret 'Anton'. The hull lies surrounded by various pieces of debris. A short distance from the hull among the debris field, the ship's main mast and rangefinders stand the correct way up on the seafloor. The stern anchor remains in position on the stern. The hull shows extensive damage from both shellfire and torpedoes.[3]

Today, outside of Wilhelmshaven stands a memorial stone to all of those who lost their lives aboard the *Scharnhorst*.

Epilogue

A memorandum that was written by Ludwig Cordes, a noted authority on the German Navy, after the war made the following point:

> When war broke out in 1939 it was clear that the majority of warships either in commission or building, and especially the larger surface units, were not suitable for the war at sea against enemy commerce irrespective of whether the enemy was Poland, France or Britain. This had been a lesson of the First World War which should logically have been taken to heart when rebuilding the Fleet. In fact it had been one of the decisive lessons of the First World War that the German High Seas Fleet, though outstanding technically, was so limited in its range as to present no effective threat to Britain's lines of supply.
>
> When rebuilding the Fleet, the dictum to have been borne in mind when planning any German surface warship was 'great range'. This had been realised in 1928 when the *Deutschland* class Panzerschiffe were designed with diesel drive. All the more incomprehensible, then, was the reversion in 1934 to steam-driven battleships such as *Scharnhorst* and *Gneisenau*, and later *Bismarck* and *Tirpitz*. This cut the 20,000nm radius of action of the armoured ships to less than half that for battleships. It was in that fact that the German surface navy ceased to be an effective opposition to any sea power.[1]

The *Scharnhorst* and *Gneisenau* were very much products of their time. After the First World War, the *Reichsmarine* had little opportunity to carry out a thorough and intensive programme of experiments aimed at developing such things as diesel drive, which could have potentially prevented a reversion to steam propulsion. The construction of the *Scharnhorst* and *Gneisenau* as part of the German rearmament programme was politically motivated and only partly motivated on naval grounds. Their construction was completed against the backdrop of momentous political change in Germany and Europe, which heavily influenced their design.

From the inception of the design, planning, and construction, the Scharnhorst-class were subject to several limitations, first and foremost of which were the provisions and restrictions of the Treaty of Versailles. The ships represented a compromise on political grounds. Their design was ultimately not thought through from a military point of view.

Despite this, *Scharnhorst* and *Gneisenau* met with great success, especially when compared with the *Bismarck* and *Tirpitz* and the other German surface vessels. They successfully sank the armed merchant cruiser *Rawalpindi* and sank the destroyers HMS *Ardent* and *Acasta* along with the aircraft carrier *Glorious*. In addition to this, they sank twenty-two merchant vessels totalling 113,690 gross registered tons. Further to this, they helped to humiliate the Royal Navy, RAF, and Britain in general with their daring dash up the English Channel.

While being the most successful German capital ships of the war, taken as part of the German war machine as a whole, the accomplishments of the *Scharnhorst* and *Gneisenau* were none too impressive. By the beginning of March 1942, U-boats had sunk a total of 5.5 million tons of Allied merchant shipping while aircraft had sunk almost 2 million tons. Surface raiders, by contrast, had succeeded only in sinking 363,146 tons.[2] In addition to this, U-boats and aircraft had shown themselves to pose a bigger threat to the Royal Navy's capital ships than were the battleships of the *Kriegsmarine*. Only two capital ships of the Royal Navy, the aircraft carrier HMS *Glorious* and the battlecruiser HMS *Hood* were sunk by capital ships of the *Kriegsmarine*. The six other Royal Navy capital ships lost up to the beginning of March 1942, which numbered three battleships, one battlecruiser, and two aircraft carriers, were all sunk by aircraft or U-boats.[3]

Scharnhorst and *Gneisenau* could, without doubt, have been better used by the *Kriegsmarine*, perhaps in co-ordination with the *Bismarck* had she not been sent on her ill-fated voyage of May 1941 and had Raeder waited for at least one of the ships at Brest to be brought back into operation. Ultimately, the surface fleet of the *Kriegsmarine* lost out to the U-boat fleet. To compound matters, there was little experience at the top levels of the German naval high command on how best to use the ships of the *Kriegsmarine*.[4] Ships like the *Scharnhorst* and *Gneisenau* took up vast quantities of steel, took many man hours to construct, and cost millions of Reichsmarks, not to mention that 1,600 to 2,000 officers and sailors were required to crew the vessels, and the vast quantity (6,200 tons) of fuel oil required to fill the bunkers of each of the ships. This does not, however, detract from the resources that the Royal Navy and RAF had to divert to attacks on the ships in attempts to destroy them. While *Gneisenau* met with what may be deemed to be an inglorious end, *Scharnhorst* holds a special place in history for fighting the last battleship engagement between British and German naval forces, which would also prove to be the penultimate battleship engagement in history.

APPENDIX I
Commanding Officers

Below are listed the names of the commanding officers of the *Scharnhorst* and *Gneisenau*.

Scharnhorst

Kapitän zur See Otto Ciliax	7 January 1939–20 September 1939
Kapitän zur See Kurt Hoffmann	21 September 1939–28 March 1942
Kapitän zur See Friedrich Hüffmeier	29 March 1942–17 October 1943
Kapitän zur See Fritz Hintze	18 October 1943–26 December 1943

Gneisenau

Kapitän zur See Erich Förste	21 May 1938–25 November 1939
Kapitän zur See Harald Netzbrandt	26 November 1939–1 August 1940
Kapitän zur See Otto Fein	20 August 1940–14 April 1942
Kapitän zur See Rudolf Peters	15 April 1942–May 1942
Kapitän zur See Wolfgang Kähler	May 1942–July 1942

APPENDIX II

Ships Sunk by the *Gneisenau* and *Scharnhorst* During Operation Berlin

Name	Nationality	Type of Vessel	Date of Sinking/Capture	Position	Dead	POWs	GRT
Kantara	British	Passenger-Cargo Ship	22 February	47-12N/40-13W	Unknown	Unknown	3,237
Trelawny	British	Passenger-Cargo Ship	22 February	47-12N/40-13W	1	39	4,689
Lustrous	British	Tanker	22 February	47-12N/40-13W	0	37	6,156
A. D. Huff	British	Freighter	22 February	47-12N/40-13W	0	42	5,866
Harlesden	British	Passenger-Cargo Ship	22 February	47-12N/40-18W	7	34	5,483
Marathon	Greek	Freighter	9 March	21N/25W	0	38	6,352
Athelfoam	British	Motor Tanker	15 March	42N/43-25W	2	45	6,554
British Strength	British	Motor Tanker	15 March	42N/43W	2	Unknown	7,139
Simnia	British	Motor Tanker	15 March	40-28N/43-30W	3	54	6,197
Bianca	Norwegian	Motor Tanker	15 March	40N/43W	0 (Captured)	N/A	5,688
San Casimiro	British	Motor Tanker	15 March	39-58N/43-19W	0 (Captured)	3	8,046
Polykarp	Norwegian	Motor Tanker	15 March	45-40N/23-26W	Unknown	Unknown	6,405
Rio Dorado	British	Passenger-Cargo Ship	16 March	42N/43W	39	0	4,507
Empire Industry	British	Freighter	16 March	43-28N/45-24W	0	38	4,507
Granli	Norwegian	Passenger-Cargo Ship	16 March	300 miles E of Newfoundland	0	18	1,577
Mangkai	Dutch	Freighter	16 March	43-15N/43-05W	36	9	8,298
Myson	British	Passenger-Cargo Ship	16 March	44N/43W	0	43	4,564
Royal Crown	British	Passenger-Cargo Ship	16 March	44N/43W	0	39	4,364
Silverfir	British	Freighter	16 March	44N/43W	1	40	4,347
Sardinian Prince	British	Passenger-Cargo Ship	16 March	44N/43W	0	44	3,491
Demeterton	British	Freighter	16 March	46-30N/43-40W	0	Unknown	5,251
Chilean Reefer	British	Cargo Ship	16 March	46-12N/44-45W	9	3	1,831

Note: All vessel nationalities are given as they were at the time that they were sunk or captured.

APPENDIX III

Survivors of the *Scharnhorst*

Achilles, Johann	*Matrosenobergefreiter*
Alsen, Willi	*Matrosenobergefreiter*
Backhaus, Helmut	*Matrosenobergefreiter*
Birke, Rudi	*Matrosengefreiter*
Boekhoff, Helmut	*Matrosengefreiter*
Bohle, Günter	*Matrosenobergefreiter*
Feifer, Helmut	*Maschinenobergefreiter*
Gödde, Wilhelm	*Oberbootsmannsmaat*
Groenewond, Heinz	*Matrosenobergefreiter*
Hager, Hans	*Matrosengefreiter*
Hovedesbrunken, Wilhelm	*Matrosenhauptgefreiter*
Kastenholz, Johann	*Oberbootsmannmaat*
Koster, Wilhelm	*Matrosengefreiter*
Kruse, Wilhelm	*Steursmannsgefreiter*
Laisz, Franz	*Maschinenobergefreiter*
Lobin, Gerhard	*Matrose*
Loffenholz, Heinrich	*Bootsmannmaat*
Lorke, Günter	*Matrose*
Marko, Franz	*Maschinenobergefreiter*
Merkle, Johann	*Mechanikergefreiter*
Pfeil, Heinz	*Matrosenobergefreiter*
Rauschert, Max	*Maschinenhauptgefreiter*
Reimann, Ernst	*Mechanikergefreiter*
Schaffrati, Paul	*Maschinenobergefreiter*
Schafer, Max	*Matrosengefreiter*
Scherer, Franz	*Bootsmannmaat*
Schutz, Hermann	*Matrosenobergefreiter*
Steiniganz, Hans	*Maschinenhauptgefreiter*
Strater, Günter	*Matrosengefreiter*
Trzembiatowski, Hans	*Matrosenobergefreiter*
Wallek, Martin	*Zimmermannobergefreiter*
Wiebusch, Nicolaus	*Matrosenobergefreiter*
Wiest, Johann	*Mahanikergefrater*
Witte, Hubert	*Matrosenobergefreiter*
Zanger, Rolf	*Maschinenhauptgefreiter*
Zaubitzer, Horst	*Mechanikergefreiter*

APPENDIX IV
Scharnhorst Roll of Honour

Below can be found the most complete list of names of those who lost their lives in the sinking of the *Scharnhorst* on 26 December 1943.

Abel, Harry
 Matrosenhauptgefreiter
Abele, Alfred
 Obermaschinist
Abraham, Günter
 Matrosengefreiter
Acker, Albrecht
 Obermaschinist
Ackermann, Friedrich
 Matrosenobergefreiter
Adam, Alfred
 Matrosenhauptgefreiter
Adamski, Stanislaus
 Matrosenobergefreiter
Adler, Erich
 Leutnant zur See
Ahlemann, Kurt
 Kapitänleutnant
Ahlemeyer, Josef
 Matrosenobergefreiter
Albrecht, Karl
 Matrosengefreiter
Alexander, Hermann
 Matrosenobergefreiter
Altmann, Walter
 Matrosenobergefreiter
Ammermann, Bernhard
 Matrosengefreiter
Andexer, Georg
 Matrosenobergefreiter
Angermann, Rudolf
 Matrosenobergefreiter
Anhalf, August
 Matrosenobergefreiter
Anschütz, Albert-Ernst
 Matrose
Anton, Hans   *Maat*
Appel, Walter
 Matrosenobergefreiter
Arenz, Peter
 Matrosenobergefreiter
Arndt, Bruno
 Matrosenobergefreiter
Arnold, Josef
 Matrosenobergefreiter

Arns, Werner
 Matrosenobergefreiter
Artelt, Hugo
 Matrosenobergefreiter
Arzt, Helmut
 Matrosenobergefreiter
Auerswald, Rudi
 Matrosenobergefreiter
Babucke, Rudolf
 Obermaat
Bach, Gerhard
 Matrosenobergefreiter
Bach, Stefan
 Matrosenobergefreiter
Bachmann, Alois
 Matrosenobergefreiter
Backhaus, Lothar
 Matrosengefreiter
Badberg, Harm
 Matrosenhauptgefreiter
Bade, Herbert
 Matrosenobergefreiter
Bader, Erich   *Matrose*
Baier, Jürgen
 Seekadett
Bajohr, Horst
 Matrosenobergefreiter
Balla, Wilhelm
 Obermaat
Ballerstädt, Alwin
 Obermaschinist
Balzer, Karl
 Obergefreiter
Balzer, Kurt
 Matrosenobergefreiter
Bandemer, Erich
 Matrosenobergefreiter
Bandlow, Heinz
 Matrosenobergefreiter
Bär, Erwin
 Matrose
Barbe, Ernst
 Matrose
Bargfleth, Hermann
 Matrosenobergefreiter

Barnahl, Heinz
 Obermaat
Barnett, Kurt
 Matrosenobergefreiter
Barth, Joachim
 Matrosengefreiter
Bartoszynski, Bruno
 Matrosenobergefreiter
Bassa, Bronislaw
 Matrosenobergefreiter
Bast, Walter
 Matrosenobergefreiter
Bastgen, Gustav
 Matrosenobergefreiter
Baucke, Gustav
 Matrosenobergefreiter
Bauer, Friedrich
 Matrosenobergefreiter
Bauer, Heinrich
 Matrosenobergefreiter
Bauer, Josef
 Matrosenobergefreiter
Bauer, Willy
 Matrosenobergefreiter
Bäuerle, Erwin
 Matrosenobergefreiter
Bauherr, Heinz
 Matrosenobergefreiter
Baule, Hans
 Matrosenobergefreiter
Baum, Hans
 Matrosenhauptgefreiter
Baum, Josef
 Matrosenobergefreiter
Baumann, Gottfried
 Matrose
Baumann, Willi
 Matrosengefreiter
Baumgärtner, Hugo
 Matrosengefreiter
Baums, Jakob-Peter
 Obersteuermann
 (Navigator)
Baur, Benedikt
 Matrosenobergefreiter

Bauser, Bernhard
 Matrosengefreiter
Bazant, Franz
 Matrosenhauptgefreiter
Bechstein, Ernst
Beckel, Wolfgang
 Matrosengefreiter
Beckenbauer, Ludwig
 Obermaat
Becker, Erwin
 Obermaat
Becker, Franz
 Matrosenobergefreiter
Becker, Gerhard
 Matrosenobergefreiter
Becker, Helmut
 Matrosengefreiter
Becker, Johannes
 Matrosenobergefreiter
Becker, Josef
 Maat
Becker, Karl
 Seekadett
Bercker, Werner
 Matrosenobergefreiter
Beckert, Gerhard
 Matrosenobergefreiter
Beelke, Rudolf
 Matrosengefreiter
Behm, Werner
 Matrosenobergefreiter
Behne, Ernst
 Matrosengefreiter
Behr, Heinz-Günther
 Kapitänleutnant
Behrendt, Alfred
 Matrose
Behrendt, Friedrich
 Matrosenhauptgefreiter
Behrendt, Otto
 Matrosenobergefreiter
Behrens, Karl
 Matrosenobergefreiter
Behrens, Norbert
 Matose

Beier, Franz
    Matrosengefreiter
Belger, Erich
    Matrosenobergefreiter
Benorden, Johann
    Matrosengefreiter
Bensch, Walter
    Matrosenobergefreiter
Benscheidt, Julius
    Obermaat
Benthein, Rolf
    Matrosenobergefreiter
Berg, Oskar-Heinz
    Maat
Berg, Werner
    Matrosenobergefreiter
Berger, Ernst
    Matrosenobergefreiter
Berger, Hans   *Maat*
Berger, Johannes
    Matrose
Berger, Werner
    Matrosenobergefreiter
Bergh, Erich
    Obermaschinist
Bergholz, Heinz
    Matrosenobergefreiter
Bergk, Erich
    Obermaschinist
Bergs, Gottfried
    Obermaat
Bernhardt, Heinrich
    Matrose
Bernhart, Heinrich
    Matrosengefreiter
Berres, Erwin
    Matrosenobergefreiter
Bertram, Erich
    Matrosenobergefreiter
Bertram, Heinz
    Matrosengefreiter
Bertram, Lothar
    Matrose
Besier, Kurt
    Matrosenobergefreiter
Betsche, Helmut
    Matrosenobergefreiter
Betten, Erwin
    Matrosenobergefreiter
Beuchelt, Heinz
    Matrosenobergefreiter
Bey, Erich
    Konteradmiral
Beyer, Helmut
    Matrosenobergefreiter
Bezler, Walter
    Matrosenobergefreiter
Bieberneit, Heinz
    Matrosengefreiter
Biemann, Walter
    Matrosenobergefreiter
Biensch, Adolf
    Matrose
Biermann, Franz
    Matrosengefreiter
Biermann, Heinz
    Matrosengefreiter
Bierschenk, Horst
    Matrosenobergefreiter
Bilstein, Alfons
    Matrosenhauptgefreiter
Binder, Alois
    Matrosenobergefreiter
Birkelbach, Herbert
    Matrosengefreiter

Birkenhauer, Karl
    Maat
Bischoff, Rudolf
    Maat
Bitter, Alfons
    Matrosenhauptgefreiter
Blahsmann, Karl
    Matrosenobergefreiter
Blanke, Berthold
    Matrosengefreiter
Blanke, Rolf
    Maat
Bley, Joachim
    Matrosengefreiter
Bley, Werner
    Matrosenobergefreiter
Blöcher, Gottfried
    Seekadett
Bludau, Hans
    Matrose
Blümchen, Kurt
    Matrosengefreiter
Blume, Alfred
    Maat
Blume, Hubert
    Matrosengefreiter
Blume, Robert
    Matrosenobergefreiter
Blumenberg, Karl
    Matrosengefreiter
Blümle, Rudolf
    Obermaschinist
Bock, Bernhard
Bock, Johannes
    Matrosengefreiter
Bockel, Fritz
    Maat
Böckler, Gustav
    Matrosengefreiter
Böggering, Josef
    Matrosengefreiter
Böhle, Gustav
    Maat
Böhm, Heinz
    Matrosengefreiter
Böhme, Gerhard
    Matrosenobergefreiter
Böhme, Heinz
    Matrosenobergefreiter
Böhmer-Fellis, Johannes
    Matrosengefreiter
Böhne, Gerhard
    Matrosengefreiter
Bohte, Karl-Heinz
    Matrosengefreiter
Böll, Karl
    Matrosengefreiter
Bölz, Wilhelm
    Obermaat
Borchmann, Helmut
    Obermaat
Borkowski, Werner
    Matrosenobergefreiter
Bormann, Rainer
    Kadett
Born, Paul
    Matrosenobergefreiter
Börner, Walter
    Obermaat
Bornschein, Otto
    Matrosenobergefreiter
Bornschein, Werner
    Matrosenhauptgefreiter
Börste, Josef
    Matrosenobergefreiter

Bosacki, Edmund
    Matrosenobergefreiter
Bosch, Friedrich
    Matrosenobergefreiter
Boßmeier, Johannes
    Matrosenobergefreiter
Bossau, Heinrich-Hans
    Matrosenobergefreiter
Bosse, Günter
    Matrose
Bosse, Walter
    Oberleutnant zur See
Bösser, Wilhelm
    Matrosenobergefreiter
Bothe, Helmut
Bothe, Karl-Heinz
    Matrosengefreiter
Böthig, Rudolf
    Obermaschinist
Brähler, August-Wilhelm
    Matrosenobergefreiter
Brandl, Rudolf
    Matrosenobergefreiter
Bradner, Franz
    Matrosenobergefreiter
Brankatsch, Rudolf
    Matrosenobergefreiter
Branse, Heinrich
    Matrosengefreiter
Braschoss, Kasper
    Matrose
Brathauer, Heinrich
    Obermaat
Bratke, Erwin
    Matrosenobergefreiter
Bräuer, Helmut
    Matrosenobergefreiter
Bräuking, Rudolf
    Matrose
Braun, Georg
    Matrosengefreiter
Braun, Gerhard
    Seekadett
Braun, Wilhelm
    Matrosenhauptgefreiter
Braunschweig, Wilhelm
    Matrosenobergefreiter
Bredenbreuker, Walter
    Korvettenkapitän
Bregulla, Heinrich
    Matrosenhauptgefreiter
Breit, Josef
    Matrosenobergefreiter
Brenk, Friedrich
    Obermaat
Brenscheidt, Julius
    Obermaat
Breuer, Josef
    Matrosenobergefreiter
Breuer, Theodor
    Maat
Brieler, Bernhard
    Matrosenobergefreiter
Brix, Ottokar
    Matrosengefreiter
Brockfeld, Ernst
    Matrose
Brockob, Willi
    Matrosenobergefreiter
Brose, Siegfried
    Matrosengefreiter
Brose, Walter
    Matrosenobergefreiter
Brosig, Alfred
    Matrosenobergefreiter

Brouwer, Günter
    Matrosengefreiter
Brüchmann, Johannes
    Matrose
Brückner, Helmut
    Obermaat
Bruder, Fritz
    Obermaat
Brüggehoff, Hans
    Matrosenobergefreiter
Brühmann, Wilhelm
    Matrosengefreiter
Bruhn, Erwin
    Matrosenobergefreiter
Brümmer, Rudolf
    Matrosenobergefreiter
Brüning, Fritz
    Matrosenhauptgefreiter
Brunke, Heinz
Brunn, Fredi
    Matrosenobergefreiter
Brzozowski, Ludwig
    Obermaat
Buchau, Horst
    Matrosengefreiter
Buchholz, Kurt
    Matrosenobergefreiter
Buchholz, Rudi
    Matrose
Buchhorn, Hans
    Matrosenhauptgefreiter
Buchmann, Heinz
    Matrosenobergefreiter
Buquoy, Johannes
    Seekadett
Busche, Severinus
    Matrosenobergefreiter
Camin, Walter
    Maat
Castorf, Wilhelm
    Obermaat
Celback, Paul
    Matrosengefreiter
Chrambach, Hans
    Fähnrich zur See
Christkauz, Albert
    Matrosenobergefreiter
Colmsee, Gerhard
    Matrosenobergefreiter
Conrad, Richard
    Matrosenobergefreiter
Conrad, Walter
    Oberbootsmaat
Conrads, Heinrich
    Maat
Cottmann, Heinrich
    Matrosenhauptgefreiter
Cravatzo, Heinrich
    Matrosenobergefreiter
Curback, Werner
    Matrosengefreiter
Czaikowski, Joachim
    Matrosengefreiter
Dabow, Gerhard
    Matrosenhauptgefreiter
Dahmen, Peter
    Matrosengefreiter
Dahms, Hans-Joachim
    Oberleutnant zur See
Damaschun, Horst
    Matrosenobergefreiter
Danelak, Heinz
    Matrosenobergefreiter
Danisch, Dietrich
    Seekadett

Dänner, Albert
    Matrosenobergefreiter
Därr, Ernst
    Kapitänleutnant
Daubner, Daniel
    Matrosengefreiter
Daum, Heinrich
    Matrose
Dausch, Alfred
    Matrose
Decken, Heinrich
    Matrosenobergefreiter
Dederky, Wolf
    Matrose
Degenbeck, Josef
    Matrosenobergefreiter
Degenhardt, Heinrich
    Oberstückmeister
Degn, Sören
    Oberleutnant zur See
Deierling, Johann
    Maat
Deitrich, Wilhelm
    Matrosenobergefreiter
Deklerski, Johannes
    Matrosenobergefreiter
Demuth, Josef
    Kadett
Dendler, Karsten
    Matrosengefreiter
Dewitz, Erwin
    Matrosenobergefreiter
Dickmanns, Johann
    Matrosenobergefreiter
Dickmayer, Gotthard
    Maat
Diehl, Heinrich
    Matrosenobergefreiter
Dielsschneider, Christian
    Matrosenobergefreiter
Dierks, Walter
    Obermaat
Dietrich, Gerhard
    Matrosenobergefreiter
Dietrich, Walter
    Matrosenobergefreiter
Dille, Wilhelm
    Matrosenobergefreiter
Dimke, Harry   *Maat*
Distel, Heinz
    Matrosengefreiter
Distler, Franz
    Matrosengefreiter
Dölling, Günter
    Seekadett
Dominik, Ernst
    Fregattenkapitän
Doneis, Johann
    Maat
Döpfner, Adolf
    Matrosenobergefreiter
Dörge, Werner
    Matrosenobergefreiter
Döring, Kurt
    Matrosenobergefreiter
Dornbluth, Karl-Heinz
    Obermaat
Dorner, Rupert
    Matrosenobergefreiter
Draeger, Wolfgang
    Matrosenobergefreiter
Draese, Dietrich
    Oberstarzt
Dräger, Albert
    Matrosenobergefreiter

Dräger, Otto
Drees, Fritz
    Matrosengefreiter
Dreßler, Heinz
    Matrosengefreiter
Drevermann, Johannes
    Matrosenhauptgefreiter
Dries, Walter
    Obermaat
Dröge, Werner
    Matrosenobergefreiter
Drsese, Dietrich
    Oberstabarzt
Druschki, Ernst
    Oberleutnant zur See
Dubber, Hermann
    Matrosenobergefreiter
Duffrenne, Herbert
    Oberfähnrich zur See
Dunemann, Walter
    Matrosenobergefreiter
Ebert, Fritz
    Matrosenobergefreiter
Ebert, Willy
    Matrosenhauptgefreiter
Eckert, Rudolf
    Matrosenobergefreiter
Eden, Johann
    Matrosenobergefreiter
Eden, Johannes
    Matrosen
Eggers, Otto
    Matrosenobergefreiter
Ehlke, Herbert
    Matrosenobergefreiter
Ehm, Werner
    Obermaat
Eichermüller, Georg
    Matrosen
Einfalt, Wilhelm
    Matrosenobergefreiter
Einöder, Anton
    Matrosenobergefreiter
Eiser, Karl
    Matrosenobergefreiter
Eisl, Josef
    Matrosenobergefreiter
Eissler, Eugen
    Matrosengefreiter
Ellerbrock, Günter
    Matrosenobergefreiter
Elser, Walter
    Matrosenobergefreiter
Elzmann, Wilhelm
    Obermaat
Entinger, Richard
    Matrose
Eppmann, Günter
    Matrosenobergefreiter
Erb, Hermann
    Maat
Erbach, Hans
    Kadett
Erdel, Reinhard
    Matrosenobergefreiter
Erlemeyer, Kurt
    Oberbootsmaat
Ermlich, Georg
    Matrosenobergefreiter
Ernst, Heinz
    Matrosenobergefreiter
Ernst, Helmut
    Matrosenhauptgefreiter
Eschenlohr, Adolf
    Maschinengefreiter

Escher, Helmut
    Obermaat
Esser, Georg
    Obermaat
Etgeton, Erwin
    Matrosenobergefreiter
Falke, Günter
    Matrosenobergefreiter
Falkenberg, Heinz
    Matrosenobergefreiter
Falkenberg, Wilhelm
    Matrosengefreiter
Färber, Richard
    Ingenieusr
Farthmann, Paul
    Matrosengefreiter
Fäseke, Friedrich-Wilhelm
    Matrosenobergefreiter
Faust, Bruno
    Matrosenobergefreiter
Fegbeitel, Johann
    Matrosenobergefreiter
Fehn ter, Hermann
    Matrosenobergefreiter
Feige, Erwin
    Obermaat
Feldkamp, Ernst
    Obermaat
Felske, Franz
    Matrosenobergefreiter
Feser, Anton
    Matrosenobergefreiter
Fichtner, Otto
    Matrosenobergefreiter
Ficker, Oskar
    Matrosenobergefreiter
Fieberling, Konrad
    Matrosenobergefreiter
Fiedler, Gerhard
    Leutnant zur See
Fiehn, Willi-Max
    Obermaat
Fingerle, Rudolf   *Maat*
Finke, Herbert
    Matrosenobergefreiter
Finze, Heinrich
    Matrosenobergefreiter
Firnkäs, Otto
    Matrose
Firsching, Otto-Alfred
    Matrosenhauptgefreiter
Fischer, Georg
    Matrosenobergefreiter
Fischer, Heinz-Ernst
    Matrosenobergefreiter
Fischer, Herbert
    Matrosenobergefreiter
Fischer, Rudolf
    Matrosenobergefreiter
Fleischmann, Konrad
    Matrosenobergefreiter
Flesch, Robert
    Matrosenobergefreiter
Fliessgarten, Rolf
    Matrosenobergefreiter
Flinsch, Fritz
    Oberbootsmannsmaat
Flügge, Wilhelm
    Matrosengefreiter
Förster, Erich
    Matrosenobergefreiter
Förster, Helmut
    Seekadett
Förster, Ludwig
    Matrosenhauptgefreiter

Fottner, Georg
    Matrosenobergefreiter
Franke, Gerhard
    Obermaat
Franke, Heinz
    Obermaat
Franz, Eberhard
    Matrosengefreiter
Fräsdorf, Paul
    Obermaat
Fredersdorf, Helmut
    Matrosenhauptgefreiter
Freese, Johann
    Maat
Freiheit, Walter
    Obermaat
Frein, Karl
    Maat
Freitag, Johann
    Matrosenobergefreiter
Frey, Herbert
    Matrosengefreiter
Frey, Rudolf-Hubert
    Matrosenobergefreiter
Frey, Willi
    Matrosenobergefreiter
Freyberg, Heinrich
    Bootsmannsmaat
Friedmann, Konrad
    Matrosenobergefreiter
Friedrich, Otto
    Matrosenobergefreiter
Friedrichs, Herbert
Frische, Hans
    Matrosengefreiter
Fritz, Otto
    Feldwebel
Fritzsche, Erich
    Matrosenobergefreiter
Fritzsche, Heinz
    Obermaat
Froese, Hans
    Matrosengefreiter
Frohberg, Manfred
    Obermaat
Fröhlich, Gerhard-Kurt
    Matrosenobergefreiter
Fromme, Walter
    Matrosenobergefreiter
Frommlet, Maximilian
    Matrosenobergefreiter
Fuegner, Friedrich
    Kapitänleutnant
Füller, Alexander
    Matrosenobergefreiter
Gade, Karl
    Matrosenobergefreiter
Gaida, Franz
    Matrosengefreiter
Galli, Franz
    Matrosenobergefreiter
Gallmeier, Emil
    Matrosengefreiter
Gäpler, Otto
    Maat
Gardoll, Walter
    Obermaat
Garmatz, Fritz
    Matrosenobergefreiter
Garten, Wiegand
    Leutnant zur See
Gaßner, Adolf
    Mechanikersgefreiter
Gassmann, Hugo
    Matrosenobergefreiter

Gehlen, Heinz
  Maat
Gehm, Karl
  Matrosengefreiter
Gehrig, Kurt
  Matrosenobergefreiter
Geiger, Walter
  Obermaat
Geissdorf, Walter
  Matrosenobergefreiter
Geithner, Heinz
  Matrosenobergefreiter
Gekeler, Heinz
  Matrosenobergefreiter
Gerisch, Erhard
  Maat
Geuss, Ernst
  Matrosenhauptgefreiter
Gierhard, Kurt
  Maschinengefreiter
Gierl, Anton
  Matrose
Gies, Hans
  Matrosenobergefreiter
Gilly, Helmut
  Maat
Gisser, Alfred
  Matrosenobergefreiter
Glaß, Günther
  Korvettenkapitän
Glass, Otto
  Matrosengefreiter
Glogger, Michael
  Matrosengefreiter
Glöver, Richard
  Matrosenhauptgefreiter
Gnosa, Franz
  Matrosengefreiter
Göbel, Heinz
  Matrosenobergefreiter
Gogolock, Walter
  Matrosenobergefreiter
Göhler, Robert
  Matrose
Gold, Ernst
  Maat
Goldammer, Curt
  Bootsmannsmaat
Golicki, Leo
  Maat
Gölitzer, Erich
  Matrose
Goller, Leopold
  Maat
Golomski, Siegmund
  Matrosengefreiter
Goosfeld, Heinz
  Matrosenobergefreiter
Göpel, Wilhelm
  Matrosengefreiter
Göpfert, Max
  Matrosenhauptgefreiter
Görner, Harry
  Matrosengefreiter
Görten, Willi
  Matrosenobergefreiter
Görtz, Gustav
Goschinger, Karl-Heinz
  Matrosengefreiter
Gosebrock, Max
  Steuermannsgefreiter
Goss, Werner
  Oberfähnrich zur See
Gottmann, Heinrich
  Matrosenhauptgefreiter

Gottschalk, Harald
  Obermaat
Götz, Anton
  Unteroffizer
Götz, Erhard
  Matrosenobergefreiter
Grahl, Melchlor
  Matrosenobergefreiter
Grahn, Heinz
  Matrosengefreiter
Grasemann, Friedrich
  Matrosenobergefreiter
Grässner, Fritz
  Matrose
Grauel, Ewald
  Matrosenobergefreiter
Greier, Joachim
  Kapitänleutnant
Greil, Rudolf
  Matrosenobergefreiter
Griebel, Theodor
  Matrose
Griese, Albert
  Obermaat
Gritschke, Werner
  Matrosengefreiter
Grögerchen, Helmut
  Matrose
Gromatka, Heinz
  Obermaat
Gromowski, Karl
  Matrosenobergefreiter
Gröning, Ernst
  Obermaat
Gross, Alfred
Gross, Kurt
  Oberfeldwebel
Grösser, Adam
  Obermaschinist
Grossmann, Willi
  Matrosengefreiter
Grube, Helmut
  Matrosenobergefreiter
Grube, Joachim
  Fähnrich zur See
Gruber, Otto
  Steuermannsgefreiter
Grund, Georg
  Obermaat
Grunert, Erich
  Oberleutnant zur See
Grunert, Günter
  Matrosengefreiter
Grünert, Walter
  Matrosenhauptgefreiter
Grunewald, Walter
  Matrosenobergefreiter
Grünhofer, Georg
  Matrosenobergefreiter
Grusa, Fritz
  Matrosengefreiter
Grzyb, Alois
  Matrosenobergefreiter
Gsottberger, Johann
  Matrosenobergefreiter
Guhe, Josef
  Maat
Gunder, Heinrich
  Obermaat
Günther, Ludwig
  Matrosengefreiter
Gustafik, Franz
  Matrosenobergefreiter
Haak, Walter
  Matrosenobergefreiter

Haas, Otto
  Steuermannsgefreiter
Haase, Heinz
  Obermaat
Habben, Erich
  Maat
Haberl, Franz
  Obermaat
Häberle, Wilhelm
  Matrosenobergefreiter
Habermann, Harry
  Matrosenobergefreiter
Haering, Gotthard
  Oberfähnrich zur See
Hage, Rudolf
  Obermaat
Hahlen, Heinrich
  Obermaat
Hahn, Herbert
  Matrosenobergefreiter
Halbig, Werner
  Matrosenobergefreiter
Hambitzer, Heinrich
  Matrosenobergefreiter
Hammen, Emil
  Matrosengefreiter
Hammer, Johann
  Matrosenobergefreiter
Hammer, Ludwig
  Unteroffizer
Hänecke, Horst
Haneke, Helmut
  Matrosenobergefreiter
Hanke, Rudi
  Matrosenobergefreiter
Hansen, Heinrich
  Obermaat
Hansen, Helmut
  Matrosenobergefreiter
Hansen, Peter
  Matrosenobergefreiter
Hanstein von, Jobst-Burgh
  Oberleutnant zur See
Hanues, Josef
  Matrosenobergefreiter
Harck, Wilhelm
  Matrosenobergefreiter
Harms, Enno
  Oberbootsmaat
Harms, Ferdinand
  Obermaat
Harnisch, Richard
  Obermaat
Harter, Otto
  Matrosenobergefreiter
Härtl, Rudolf
  Matrosenobergefreiter
Hartung, Horst
  Matrosengefreiter
Hartwig, Fritz
  Obermaat
Harz, Fritz
  Matrosenobergefreiter
Haslinger, Heribert
  Matrosengefreiter
Haub, Erwin
  Matrosengefreiter
Haubensak, Alfred
  Matrosenobergefreiter
Haubold, Arno
  Maat
Haufe, Helmut
  Obermaat
Haumann, Ewald
  Obermaat

Haupt, Gustav
  Matrosengefreiter
Hauseux, Franz
  Matrosengefreiter
Hebbel, Maximilian
  Matrosenhauptgefreiter
Hebner, Herbert
  Matrosengefreiter
Hechler, Kurt
Hecht, Werner
  Matrosenobergefreiter
Heck, Emil   *Maat*
Heck, Georg
  Matrosenobergefreiter
Heckers, Otto
  Matrosenobergefreiter
Heckmann, Karl-Heinz
  Matrosenobergefreiter
Heckmann, Werner
  Obermaat
Heid, Walter
  Matrosenobergefreiter
Heidenreich, Kurt
  Matrose
Heider, Siegfried
  Maat
Heidl, Rudi
Heidorn, Gustav
  Matrosenobergefreiter
Heinen, Eugen
  Maat
Heini, Kurt
  Matrosenobergefreiter
Heinz, Adolf
  Obermaat
Heinz, Hans
  Matrose
Heinz, Otto
  Obermaat
Heinze, Horst
  Matrosenobergefreiter
Held, Wilhelm
  Obermaat
Hellendahl, Karl
  Oberbootsmaat
Hellhammer, Heinrich
  Matrosenobergefreiter
Helsborg, Emil
  Matrosengefreiter
Hemersch, Josef
  Matrosenobergefreiter
Henkel, Wilhelm
  Matrosenobergefreiter
Henn, Leopold
  Oberfeldwebel
Hennig, Ernst
  Matrosengefreiter
Henninger, Arno
  Matrosenobergefreiter
Hennings, Peter
  Leutnant zur See
Hentschel, Paul
  Matrosenobergefreiter
Herden, Franz
  Matrosenobergefreiter
Herden, Georg
  Matrosenobergefreiter
Herfort, Richard
  Matrosenobergefreiter
Hering, Fritz
  Matrosenobergefreiter
Hermann, Alfons
  Matrosenobergefreiter
Hermann, Erich
  Matrosenobergefreiter

Hermes, Ehrhardt
  Matrosenobergefreiter
Herrlein, Josef
  Matrosenhauptgefreiter
Herrndorf, Harald
  Matrosenobergefreiter
Herscher, Hermann
  Matrosenobergefreiter
Hertel, Friedrich
  Matrosenobergefreiter
Herth, Werner
  Matrosengefreiter
Heyden, Heribert
  Matrosenobergefreiter
Heyder, Heribert
  Matrosenhauptgefreiter
Heyer, Martin
  Matrose
Heymann, Heinz
  Matrosenobergefreiter
Heyne, Waldemar
  Matrosengefreiter
Hillmann, Kurt
  Matrosenobergefreiter
Hilpert, Franz
  Matrosenobergefreiter
Himken, Georg
  Matrosengefreiter
Himly, Ewald
  Matrosenobergefreiter
Hindahl, Emil
  Matrosengefreiter
Hinsche, Richard
  Obermaat
Hintze, Fritz
  Kapitän zur See
Hirsch, Anton
  Matrosengefreiter
Hirsch, Georg
  Matrosenobergefreiter
Hirt, Heinz
  Matrosengefreiter
Hitzholer, Heinrich
  Matrosenobergefreiter
Hobza, Ernst
  Matrose
Hochfeldt, Edmund
  Matrosenobergefreiter
Hockauf, Horst *Maat*
Hockling, Antoniao
  Matrosenobergefreiter
Höfel, Walter
  Matrosenobergefreiter
Hofer, Josef
  Matrosenobergefreiter
Hofer, Martin
  Matrosengefreiter
Hoffmann, Erich-Friedl
  Seekadett
Hoffmann, Erik
  Unteroffizer
Hoffmann, Heinz
  Matrosenhauptgefreiter
Hoffmann, Leonard
  Matrose
Hoffmann, Paul
  Bootsmannsmaat
Hoffmann, Wilhelm
  Matrosenobergefreiter
Hofius, Karl
  Matrosenobergefreiter
Hofmann, Anton
  Matrosenobergefreiter
Hofmann, Leonard
  Matrosengefreiter

Hofmeister, Jakob
  Matrosengefreiter
Hofner, Franz
  Matrose
Hofstetter, Fritz
  Leutnant zur See
Hohl, Paul
  Matrosenobergefreiter
Hohlmann, Hermann
  Matrosenobergefreiter
Hohmann, Johann
  Matrose
Hohmann, Theodor
  Matrosengefreiter
Höhn, Alfred
  Matrosenobergefreiter
Hohs, Josef
  Funkmeister
Holeczek, Wilhelm
Holl, Josef
  Maat
Hollands, Heinrich
  Obermaat
Holob, Friedrich
  Matrosengefreiter
Holz, Helmut
  Matrosenobergefreiter
Holzbrecher, Alfons
  Matrose
Holzhausen, Wilhelm
  Obermaschinist
Honigmann, Joachim
  Obermaat
Hönle, Adalbert
  Matrosenhauptgefreiter
Höpflinger, Leo
  Matrosengefreiter
Hoppe, Hans
  Obermaat
Hoppe, Heinz
  Matrose
Hörentrup, Oskar
  Matrosengefreiter
Horzer, Alfred
  Matrosenhauptgefreiter
Hostermann, Wilhelm
  Obermaat
Hoyer, Benno
  Seekadett
Hoyer, Heinz-Helmut
  Matrosenobergefreiter
Huber, Jakob
  Matrosenobergefreiter
Huber, Wilhelm
  Matrosenobergefreiter
Hubler, Friedrich
  Matrosengefreiter
Hübner, Herbert
  Matrosenobergefreiter
Humburg, Emil
  Matrosenhauptgefreiter
Humkamp, Johann
  Obermaat
Hummler, Erich
  Matrosenobergefreiter
Hunger, Johannes
  Matrosengefreiter
Hunnkamp, Johann
  Obermaat
Hüsken, Heinrich
  Matrosengefreiter
Hütter, Josef
  Matrosenobergefreiter
Ibels, Helmut
  Matrosengefreiter

Ideus, Albert-Georg
  Matrosenobergefreiter
Iffinger, Jacob-Johann
  Matrosenobergefreiter
Illig, Jakob
  Matrosenobergefreiter
Imhorst, Emil
  Maat
Ingenohl, Otto
  Matrosenobergefreiter
Issel, Paul
  Matrosenobergefreiter
Jaax, Wilhelm
  Matrosenobergefreiter
Jablonski, Max
  Matrose
Jacobsen, Erhard
  Matrose
Jäger, Erich
  Obermaat
Jäger, Herbert
  Obermaat
Jäger, Kurt-Hans
  Obermaat
Jäger, Willi
  Matrosenobergefreiter
Jahn, Albert
  Obermaat
Jahn, Oswald
  Obermaat
Jahnke, Franz
  Matrosengefreiter
Jakomeit, Georg
  Matrosenobergefreiter
Jankowski, Johann
  Matrosenobergefreiter
Jansen, Konrad
  Matrose
Jansen, Rudolf
  Matrosenobergefreiter
Janssen, Heinrich
  Matrosengefreiter
Jantzen, Helmut
  Maat
Jarsen, Kurt
  Matrose
Jenkel, Walter-Erwin
  Matrosenobergefreiter
Jensen, Karl
  Matrosengefreiter
Jerga, Oskar
  Matrosenobergefreiter
Jeschawitz, Max
  Matrose
Joachim, Franz
  Matrosengefreiter
Jobmann, Ernst
  Matrosenobergefreiter
Jöckle, Fred
  Matrosenobergefreiter
John, Willi
  Matrosengefreiter
Jöhnk, Hans *Maat*
Jonisch, Adolf-Erich
  Matrosenhauptgefreiter
Joseph, Erwin
  Matrosenhauptgefreiter
Jost, Heinz
  Matrosenobergefreiter
Josten, Heinz
  Matrosengefreiter
Jouck, Albert
  Matrosenhauptgefreiter
Jülicher, Hans
  Matrosenhauptgefreiter

Jung, Eduard
  Maat
Jung, Erich
  Obermaat
Junghans, Günther
  Matrosengefreiter
Junghans, Karl-Eduard
Jürgens, Janssen
  Obersteuermann
Jürges, Joachim
  Matrosengefreiter
Jürn, Willi
  Matrosengefreiter
Jurschina, Karl
  Matrosenobergefreiter
Kabbe, Paul
  Obermaschinemaat
Kahl, Ernst
  Matrosenhauptgefreiter
Kähler, Horst
  Matrosengefreiter
Kalkowski, Erich
  Matrosengefreiter
Kamp, Franz
  Seekadett
Kämpf, Heinz
  Matrosenobergefreiter
Kapitza, Bernhard
  Maat
Kassel, Johann
  Matrosengefreiter
Kastner, Herbert
  Matrosenhauptgefreiter
Kaufmann, Gerhard
  Obermaat
Kauper, Herbert
  Matrosenobergefreiter
Keckstein, Wenzel
  Matrosenobergefreiter
Kehr, Werner
  Obermaat
Keidel, Andreas
  Matrosenobergefreiter
Keiger, Hermann
  Matrosenobergefreiter
Kelle, Heinz
  Matrosenobergefreiter
Keller, Herbert
  Matrosengefreiter
Keller, Max
  Oberleutnant zur See
Kelling, Werner
  Maat
Kelz, Rudolf
  Matrose
Kempe, Martin
  Matrosengefreiter
Kempf, Gerhard
  Seekadett
Kempinski, Hans-Joachim
  Matrosenobergefreiter
Kern, Arno
  Feldwebel
Kern, Ernst
  Maat
Kerschke, Günter
  Matrosenobergefreiter
Kerstions, Josef
  Seekadett
Kienbaum, Heinz
  Matrosenobergefreiter
Kiessler, Hans
  Maschinengefreiter
Kimmerle, Gotthiff
  Matrosenhauptgefreiter

Kimmig, Friedrich
  Matrosenhauptgefreiter
Kindler, Rolf
  Matrose
Kipp, Johann
  Obermaschinemaat
Kirsch, Heinz
  Matrosenobergefreiter
Kirschbaum, Walter
  Maat
Kissel, Heinrich
  Maat
Klaahsen, Hermann
  Matrosenobergefreiter
Klaas, Erwin
  Matrosenhauptgefreiter
Klanthe, Friedrich
  Unteroffizer
Klarwasser, Ignatz
  Matrosenhauptgefreiter
Klein, Adolf
  Matrosengefreiter
Klein, Gerhard
  Matrosengefreiter
Klein, Hans
  Matrosenobergefreiter
Klein, Wilhelm
  Matrosenobergefreiter
Kleine, Friedrich
  Matrosenobergefreiter
Kleineidam, Erich
  Matrosenobergefreiter
Kleinjung, Karl
  Matrosenobergefreiter
Kliem, Johann-Rudolf
  Matrosenobergefreiter
Klimek, Otto
  Matrosenobergefreiter
Klingler, Walter-Ernst
  Matrosengefreiter
Klubberg, Heinz
  Matrosenobergefreiter
Klubescheidt, Leo
  Matrosenobergefreiter
Kluge, Heinz
  Matrosenobergefreiter
Klumps, Josef
  Obermaat
Klüter, Reinhard
  Matrose
Knoblauch, Ernst
  Matrosenobergefreiter
Knöfler, Bruno
  Matrosenobergefreiter
Knoll, Siegfried
  Matrosengefreiter
Knoop, Willi
  Matrosenobergefreiter
Köchling, Friedrich
  Matrosengefreiter
Köhl, Helmut
  Matrosenobergefreiter
Köhler, Ernst
  Obermaat
Köhler, Friedrich
  Matrose
Köhler, Hans
  Matrose
Köhler, Werner
  Obermaschinist
Köhler, Wilhelm *Maat*
Kolasse, We
  Oberleutnant zur See
Kolecki, Artur
  Matrosenobergefreiter
Koleske, Erwin
  Matrosenobergefreiter
Koll, Karl
  Matrosenobergefreiter
Kollmann, Konrad
  Matrosenobergefreiter
Kolter, Ferdinand
  Maat
Komorek, Josef
  Matrose
Köner, Rudolf
  Matrosenobergefreiter
König, Otto
  Korvettenkapitän
König, Rolf
  Matrosengefreiter
Königdorf, Johann
  Matrosenobergefreiter
Könnecke, Hans
  Matrose
Kopatz, Wilhelm
  Matrosenobergefreiter
Kopke, Manfred
  Matrosenobergefreiter
Kopmann, Karl
  Matrosenobergefreiter
Koppmann, Artur
  Matrosenobergefreiter
Korbas, Wilhelm
  Matrosenobergefreiter
Korehnke, Fritz
  Obermaat
Körner, Philipp
  Matrosenobergefreiter
Kornher, Franz
  Matrosenobergefreiter
Korth, Friedrich
  Matrose
Kosak, Johannes
  Matrosenobergefreiter
Kosche, Günter
  Matrosenobergefreiter
Koschek, Gerhard
  Matrosenobergefreiter
Koschnicke, Walter
  Matrosengefreiter
Koslowski, Fritz
  Matrosenobergefreiter
Kosse, Wilhelm
  Obermaschinist
Köster, Heinrich
  Matrosenobergefreiter
Köstermann, Johann
  Matrosenobergefreiter
Kostrzewa, Ernst
  Matrosenobergefreiter
Kotthaus, Günter
  Bootsmannsmaat
Köttler, August
  Matrosenobergefreiter
Kötz, Erich
  Obermaat
Kowalski, Georg
  Matrosenobergefreiter
Kowalzik, Heinz
  Obermaat
Koziol, Richard
  Matrose
Kraatz, Wilhelm
  Matrosenobergefreiter
Kracht, Rudi
  Matrosenhauptgefreiter
Krafczyk, Georg
  Matrosenobergefreiter
Kraft, Wilhelm
  Matrosenhauptgefreiter
Krahforst, Walter
  Oberbootsmaat
Krahforst, Wilhelm
  Matrosenobergefreiter
Krämer, Erich
  Matrosenobergefreiter
Kramer, Hans
  Obermaat
Kramer, Heinrich
  Matrosenobergefreiter
Krämer, Ludwig
  Obermaat
Krämer, Reinhard
  Maat
Kramer, Valentin
  Matrosenhauptgefreiter
Kraska, Kurt
  Matrose
Krause, Alfred
  Matrosengefreiter
Krause, Egon
  Matrosengefreiter
Krause, Erich
  Matrose
Krause, Gerhard-Wilhelm
  Matrosenobergefreiter
Krause, Rudolf
  Matrosenobergefreiter
Krause, Werner
  Oberleutnant zur See
Krausse, Heinz
  Matrosenobergefreiter
Kray, Kurt
  Maat
Krebs, Egon
  Obermeister
Kreiner, Alois
  Matrosenobergefreiter
Kreis, Paul-Rudolf
  Matrosenobergefreiter
Kreitner, Herbert
  Matrose
Krejci, Heinrich
  Matrose
Krenz, Ferdinand
  Matrosenhauptgefreiter
Krenzlin, Helmut
  Obermaat
Kress, Hans-Günter
  Seekadett
Kreussel, Heinrich
  Matrosengefreiter
Kreutzer, Rudolf
  Maat
Krimmling, Werner
  Matrosenobergefreiter
Kronenberg, Mathias
  Matrose
Kröner, Gottfried
  Matrose
Krönig, Gustav
  Matrosenobergefreiter
Krüger, Heinz
  Matrosenobergefreiter
Krüger, Heinz
  Maat
Krüger, Herbert
  Matrosengefreiter
Krüger, Hugo
Krüger, Siegfried
  Matrosenobergefreiter
Krüning, Heinz
  Matrosenhauptgefreiter
Krupop, Edmund
  Matrosenobergefreiter
Kruppe, Herbert
  Matrosenobergefreiter
Krürwel, Herbert
  Matrosenobergefreiter
Kruse, Heinrich
  Matrose
Kufner, Hans *Maat*
Kühlwein, Günther
  Kapitänleutnant
Kühn, Hans
  Matrosenobergefreiter
Kuhne, Eberhard
  Matrosenobergefreiter
Kuhställer, Helmut
  Matrosenobergefreiter
Kuklick, Walter
  Matrosenobergefreiter
Künne, Rudolf
  Matrosenhauptgefreiter
Kuntzsch, Gerhard
  Matrosenobergefreiter
Kurkowski, Leo
  Matrosenobergefreiter
Kurz, Karl
  Matrosenhauptgefreiter
Kuschke, Heinz
  Matrose
Kutscha, Karl
  Matrosengefreiter
Kutschbach, Kurt-Heinz
  Matrosenobergefreiter
Kutschera, Werner
  Obermaschinist
Kutschik, Kurt
  Matrosengefreiter
Kutzner, Willi
  Matrosenobergefreiter
Laar, Gustav
  Matrosenobergefreiter
Labaj, Otto
  Matrose
Laggies, Albert
  Matrosenobergefreiter
Lahmer, Rupert
  Matrosenobergefreiter
Lampe, Herbert
  Matrosenobergefreiter
Landsberger, Karl
  Matrosenobergefreiter
Lang, Walter
  Oberfähnrich zur See
Langbarthel, Hans
  Matrosenobergefreiter
Lange, Emil
  Obermaat
Langenbach, Wilhelm
  Maat
Langer, Günter
  Matrosengefreiter
Langer, Siegfried
  Obermaat
Lanz, Edgar
  Korvettenkapitän
Lasch, Karl
  Matrose
Laschat, Heinz
  Matrosenobergefreiter
Laschke, Adolf
  Maat
Laube, Karl
  Obermaat
Lauer, Robert
  Matrosenobergefreiter
Lauterbach, Heinz
  Obermaat

Lawrenz, Karl
 Matrosenobergefreiter
Lebinski, Willi
 Matrosenobergefreiter
Ledule, Friedrich
 Matrosenobergefreiter
Lehbrink, Emil
 Obermaat
Lehmann, Willi
 Matrosenobergefreiter
Lehne, Josef
 Matrosenobergefreiter
Leidig, Egon
 Obermaat
Leidl, Georg
 Obermaat
Leinenbach, Erich
 Signalobergefreiter
Leinert, Karl
 Matrosenobergefreiter
Lemke, Kurt
 Matrosengefreiter
Lendzian, Kurt
 Matrosengefreiter
Leng, Gerhard
 Matrosengefreiter
Lenger, Stefan
 Obermaat
Lenski, Alfred
 Matrose
Lentz, Karl
 Matrosenobergefreiter
Lenz, Alfred
 Matrosengefreiter
Leonhardt, Werner
 Matrose
Lepkejus, Bruno
 Maat
Leptien, Wilf
 Obermaat
Lickfeld, Werner
 Matrosenobergefreiter
Lidowski, Lidifons
 Matrosenobergefreiter
Liebilen, Werner
 Matrose
Liebscher, Werner
 Matrose
Lieder, Emil
 Matrosenobergefreiter
Liese, Friedhelm
 Matrosengefreiter
Lietzau, Fritz
 Matrosenhauptgefreiter
Limbach, Friedl
Limbach, Werner
 Oberleutnant zur See
Limper, Fritz
 Matrosenobergefreiter
Linde, Axel
 Matrosenobergefreiter
Lindemann, Friedrich
 Matrosenobergefreiter
Lindemann, Horst
 Matrose
Linge, Josef
 Maat
Linnemann, Josef
 Maat
Linsdorf, Fritz
 Matrosenobergefreiter
Lippelt, Otto
 Matrose
Lippowitsch, August
 Matrosenobergefreiter

Lohkämper, Wilhelm
 Matrosengefreiter
Lommatzsch, Helmut
 Matrosenobergefreiter
Löscher, Werner
 Obermaat
Lublow, Erwin
 Matrosengefreiter
Lück, Alois
 Matrosenobergefreiter
Ludewig, Hans
 Matrose
Ludziarczyk, Rudolf
 Matrosenobergefreiter
Lüker, Heinrich
 Matrosengefreiter
Maass, Rudolf
 Matrosenhauptgefreiter
Mach, Gerhard
 Fähnrich zur See
Mader, Leopold
 Matrose
Maderthaner, Karl   *Maat*
Mahlmann, Walter
 Matrosenobergefreiter
Mainz, Wilhelm
 Matrosenobergefreiter
Mair, Georg
 Matrosenobergefreiter
Maisel, Siegfried
 Fähnrich zur See
Maiwald, Werner
 Matrose
Maiweg, Günther
 Matrosenobergefreiter
Malyska, Werner
 Matrosenobergefreiter
Manig, Rudolf
 Matrosenobergefreiter
Mantel, Karl
 Matrosengefreiter
Marczyk, Erwin
 Matrosengefreiter
Marenbach, Heinrich
 Maat
Markert, Helmut
 Matrosenobergefreiter
Markmann, Hermann
 Obermaschinist
Marsiske, Paul
 Matrosengefreiter
Marten, Johannes
 Oberleutnant zur See
Martens, Karl
 Matrosengefreiter
Marter, Erich
 Obermaat
Martin, Erich
 Matrosenobergefreiter
Martini, Helmut
 Matrosengefreiter
Masekowitz, Heinz
 Matrosengefreiter
Masjosthusmann, Josef
 Matrosenhauptgefreiter
Matern, Horst
 Matrose
Matuszcak, Albert
 Matrosengefreiter
Matz, Wendelin
 Matrose
Matzat, Rudolf
 Matrosengefreiter
Maurer, Hermann
 Matrosengefreiter

Mauruschat, Walter
 Obermaat
Mausolf, Kurt
 Matrosenobergefreiter
Meidhof, Johann
 Matrosenobergefreiter
Meidt, Karl
 Matrosenobergefreiter
Meier, Emil
 Matrosengefreiter
Meinunger, Walter
 Matrosenobergefreiter
Meissner, Friedrich
 Seekadett
Meister, Heinz
 Matrosenobergefreiter
Menhofer, Hermann
 Obermaat
Menn, Werner
 Matrosenobergefreiter
Mentrup, Josef
 Matrose
Menze, Fred
 Matrosenobergefreiter
Merk, Werner
 Matrosengefreiter
Merten, Horst
 Matrosenobergefreiter
Merten, Paul
 Matrosenobergefreiter
Mess, Hans
 Matrose
Mester, Heinz-Johann
 Maat
Mette, Herbert
 Matrosenobergefreiter
Metz, Konstantin
 Oberleutnant zur See
Meumair, Georg
 Matrosenobergefreiter
Meyer, Friedrich
 Matrosengefreiter
Meyer, Günther
 Matrosenobergefreiter
Meyer, Helmut
 Maat
Meyer, Karl
 Matrosenhauptgefreiter
Meyer, Werner
 Matrosenobergefreiter
Meyer, Wolfgang
 Seekadett
Michaelis, Johann
 Matrosenobergefreiter
Michalczak, Herbert
 Matrosenobergefreiter
Miebenthaler, Wilhelm
 Matrosenobergefreiter
Miethe, Erwin
 Obermaat
Mindt, Erwin
 Matrosengefreiter
Miotke, Günther
 Matrosenobergefreiter
Mirsberger, Walter
 Matrosenobergefreiter
Mitzscherlich, Eberhard
 Matrosenhauptgefreiter
Mocek, Franz
 Obermaat
Mocek, Fritz
 Matrosenobergefreiter
Mock, Helmut
 Matrosengefreiter
Mölich, Karl   *Maat*

Mönig, Herbert
 Kapitänleutnant
Monka, Herbert
 Matrosenhauptgefreiter
Morenz, Paul
 Matrosengefreiter
Morgenthum, Anton
 Matrosenobergefreiter
Moritz, Werner
 Obermaat
Morscheiser, Erich
 Matrosenobergefreiter
Mozek, Franz
 Obermaat
Mühlbauer, Franz
 Matrosenobergefreiter
Mulch, Heinrich
 Matrosenobergefreiter
Müllenelsen, Johann
 Matrosengefreiter
Müller, Albert
 Matrosenobergefreiter
Müller, Albert
 Matrosenobergefreiter
Müller, Franz
 Maat
Müller, Fritz
 Matrose
Müller, Georg
 Matrosenobergefreiter
Müller, Gerhard
Müller, Günther
 Matrosengefreiter
Müller, Heinrich
Müller, Heinrich
 Matrosenobergefreiter
Müller, Heinz
Müller, Heinz
 Matrosenobergefreiter
Müller, Helmut
 Matrose
Müller, Herbert
 Obermaschinist
Müller, Joachim
 Matrosenobergefreiter
Müller, Karl
 Matrosenobergefreiter
Müller, Karl
 Matrosenhauptgefreiter
Müller, Karl
 Matrosenhauptgefreiter
Müller, Karl-Heinz
 Matrosenobergefreiter
Müller, Kurt
 Matrosengefreiter
Müller, Max
 Matrosenobergefreiter
Müller, Waldemar
 Matrosenhauptgefreiter
Müller, Walter
 Matrosengefreiter
Müller, Werner
 Matrosenobergefreiter
Naarmann, Friedrich
 Obermaat
Nagel, Walter
 Matrosenhauptgefreiter
Nauheimer, Peter-Philipp
 Matrosenobergefreiter
Naumann, Kurt
 Maat
Neff, Wilhelm
 Matrosenobergefreiter
Nehrke, Heinz
 Matrosengefreiter

Neitzert, Erich
 Matrosenobergefreiter
Nell, Kurt
 Seekadett
Nell, Willi
 Matrosengefreiter
Nessler, Heinrich
 Matrosenobergefreiter
Neumann, Erich
 Matrosenobergefreiter
Neumann, Karl-Heinz
 Matrosengefreiter
Neumann, Otto
 Matrosenobergefreiter
Neumann, Walter
 Matrosenobergefreiter
Neumann, Hans
 Regierungsrat
Neumayer, Josef
 Matrosenobergefreiter
Nicklisch, Werner
 Matrosenobergefreiter
Niecke, Alexander
 Obermaat
Niele, Johann
 Matrosengefreiter
Niemann, Kurt
 Maat
Niemeyer, Günter
 Seekadett
Nienaber, Heinrich
 Matrosenobergefreiter
Nimse, Siegfried
 Matrosenobergefreiter
Ningelgen, Franz
 Matrose
Nipperdey, Alfred
 Matrosenhauptgefreiter
Nitschke, Fritz
 Obermaat
Noack, Werner
 Obermaat
Noe, Walter
 Matrose
Nolte, Hermann
 Matrosengefreiter
Nousch, Willy
 Matrosenobergefreiter
Nowak, Karl-Heinz
 Matrosenobergefreiter
Nowak, Wilfrid
 Matrosenobergefreiter
Nütz, Josef
 Matrosenobergefreiter
Obertreis, Gerd
 Seekadett
Oetken, August
 Matrosenobergefreiter
Ortner, Anton
 Matrosenhauptgefreiter
Ortner, Johann
 Matrose
Ortner, Richard
 Matrosengefreiter
Ostendorp, Otto
 Matrosenobergefreiter
Osthus, Herbert
 Matrosengefreiter
Ostromienski, Paul
 Matrosenobergefreiter
Pahnke, Otto *Maat*
Palicki, Heinrich
 Matrosengefreiter
Pallasch, Reinhold
 Matrosenobergefreiter
Pancke, Heinrich
 Matrosenobergefreiter
Parker, Joachim
 Matrosenobergefreiter
Partsch, Walter
 Matrosenobergefreiter
Pascher, Johann
 Matrosenhauptgefreiter
Paschold, Helmut
 Matrosenobergefreiter
Päsler, Hans
 Matrosenobergefreiter
Pastejrik, Karl
 Matrosengefreiter
Pätz, Horst
 Matrosengefreiter
Paul, Günther
 Matrosengefreiter
Pauschert, Heinrich
 Matrosengefreiter
Paustian, Max
 Oberbootsmannsmaat
Pawelczyk, Heinrich
 Matrosengefreiter
Pawletko, Gerhard
 Matrose
Pawlitzky, Ernst
 Matrosenobergefreiter
Pehrs, Johann
 Matrosenobergefreiter
Pelzer, Egon
 Matrosenobergefreiter
Pense, Werner *Maat*
Penzel, Werner
 Matrosengefreiter
Penzel, Werner
 Matrosenobergefreiter
Peper, Wilhelm
 Maat
Perlet, Rudolf
 Matrosenobergefreiter
Pernak, Karl
 Matrosenobergefreiter
Peters, Jürgen
 Matrosenobergefreiter
Peters, Louis
 Matrosengefreiter
Petersen, Rudi
 Obermaschinist
Petruschke, Helmut
 Matrosenobergefreiter
Petsch, Ernst
 Matrosenobergefreiter
Petzner, Franz
 Matrosenobergefreiter
Pfaff, Heinz
 Matrosenhauptgefreiter
Pfaff, Robert
 Matrosengefreiter
Pfeifer, Helmut-Kurt
 Obermaat
Pfeifer, Johann
 Matrosenobergefreiter
Pfeiffer, Werner
 Matrosengefreiter
Pfister, Willi
 Matrosengefreiter
Philipp, Willi
 Matrosenobergefreiter
Pilger, Paul
 Matrosenobergefreiter
Pingel, Fritz
 Matrosenobergefreiter
Piontek, Heinz
 Matrosenobergefreiter
Pisarsky, Adalbert
 Matrosenobergefreiter
Pister, Johann
 Maat
Plank, Johann
 Matrosenobergefreiter
Plate, Heinz
 Obermaat
Plate, Karl-Heinz
 Matrosenobergefreiter
Platen, Theodor
 Matrosengefreiter
Podwojewski, Alfred
 Matrosenobergefreiter
Pohl, Rudi
 Matrosenobergefreiter
Pohland, Alfons
 Maat
Pöhler, Horst
 Matrosenobergefreiter
Pohlitz, Hans
 Matrosenhauptgefreiter
Polak, Johann
 Matrosenobergefreiter
Pölk, Günter-Werner
 Matrosenobergefreiter
Pollak, Otto
 Seekadett
Pollei, Wilhelm
 Matrosengefreiter
Pollinger, Johann
 Mechanikersgefreiter
Pongratz, Josef
 Matrosenobergefreiter
Poppe, Kurt
 Matrosengefreiter
Pörschmann, Fritz
 Matrosenobergefreiter
Pott, Heinrich
 Matrosenobergefreiter
Prehm, Walter
 Matrose
Preis, Karl
 Matrosenobergefreiter
Przyborowski, Ottokar
 Matrosenobergefreiter
Przybyl, Bruno
 Matrosenhauptgefreiter
Püchner, Herbert-Bruno
 Matrosengefreiter
Pütz, Andreas
 Matrose
Putzke, Paul
 Matrosenobergefreiter
Querbach, Anton
 Matrosenobergefreiter
Quinten, Hubert
 Matrosenobergefreiter
Raab, Karl *Maat*
Rabbel, Hubert
 Matrosenobergefreiter
Rabe, Heinrich
 Feldwebel
Rabsahl, Hans
 Matrosenobergefreiter
Radeck, Georg
 Matrosenobergefreiter
Radigk, Alfred
 Obermaat
Rahm, Helmut
 Matrosengefreiter
Rakowski, Klaus
 Seekadett
Rannacher, Hermann
 Matrosengefreiter
Rasch, Werner
 Matrose
Rateiski, Gerhard
 Mechanikersgefreiter
Rau, Rudi
 Matrosenobergefreiter
Rauch, Karl
 Matrosenobergefreiter
Rauh, Rudolf
 Matrosenobergefreiter
Rauh, Walter
 Oberfähnrich zur See
Rauhut, Walter
 Matrosenobergefreiter
Rauschhardt, August
 Matrosenobergefreiter
Razer, Harti
 Maat
Reckert, Jacob
 Obermaat
Reddig, Hans
 Matrosenobergefreiter
Redecker, Horst
 Matrosenobergefreiter
Redix, August
 Obermaat
Rehberg, Alfred
 Obermaschinist
Reichel, Herbert
 Matrose
Reichelt, Gerhard
 Matrosengefreiter
Reil, Michael
 Matrosenobergefreiter
Reimann, Günter
 Obermaat
Reimers, Hans
 Matrose
Reinartz, Wilhelm
 Matrosenhauptgefreiter
Reinecke, Theodor
 Matrosenobergefreiter
Reiser, Herbert
 Matrosenobergefreiter
Reising, Paul
 Matrosengefreiter
Reisinger, August
Reithermann, Oskar
 Matrosenobergefreiter
Reitz, Heinrich
 Matrosenobergefreiter
Renner, Erwin
 Maat
Reschke, Erich
 Obermaat
Ress, Adolf
 Matrosenobergefreiter
Rettmer, Wilhelm
 Matrose
Richter, Anton
 Matrosenobergefreiter
Richter, Herbert
 Matrosenobergefreiter
Richter, Hermann
 Matrosenhauptgefreiter
Richter, Kurt
 Matrosenobergefreiter
Richter, Kurt
 Matrosenobergefreiter
Riebe, Gerhard
 Matrosenobergefreiter
Riebel, Otto
 Obermaat
Riedel, Rudi
 Obermaat

Riegel, Willy
Matrosenobergefreiter
Rieger, Helmut
Matrosenobergefreiter
Rieger, Hermann
Feldwebel
Riegler, Karl
Matrosenobergefreiter
Riemann, Georg
Matrose
Ritschel, Martin
Sekadett
Ritter, Horst
Obermaat
Ritter, Rudolf   *Maat*
Ritz, Konrad
Matrosengefreiter
Rodemann, Helmut
Matrosengefreiter
Rödiger, Walter
Obermaat
Rogen, Georg
Matrosengefreiter
Rohde, Werner
Matrosenobergefreiter
Rohloff, Erwin
Matrosenobergefreiter
Rohn, Karl
Matrosenobergefreiter
Rohr, Franz
Matrosenobergefreiter
Rohspeintner, Albin
Matrosenobergefreiter
Roisch, Erich
Matrosenobergefreiter
Rölleke, Alfred
Obermaat
Roloff, Hermann
Matrosenobergefreiter
Römisch, Gerhard
Matrosenobergefreiter
Ronge, Eduard
Maat
Roppel, Heinz
Matrose
Rösch, Otto
Matrosenobergefreiter
Röschke, Werner
Matrosenobergefreiter
Rösel, Walter
Matrosenobergefreiter
Rosenow, Gerhard
Matrosenobergefreiter
Rosenthal, Hans
Stabsarzt
Ross, Karl
Matrosenobergefreiter
Rossetto, Günter
Matrosengefreiter
Rössler, Gregor
Matrose
Rostin, Otto
Matrosenhauptgefreiter
Roth, Alfred
Obermaschinist
Roth, Jakob
Matrosenhauptgefreiter
Roth, Waldemar
Matrosenobergefreiter
Rothmund, Friedrich
Matrose
Ruchay, Heinrich
Matrosenobergefreiter
Rückert, Paul
Matrosenobergefreiter

Rüdiger, Heinz
Matrosenhauptgefreiter
Rudner, Theodor
Matrosenobergefreiter
Rudolph, Werner
Maat
Ruge, Hugo
Matrosenobergefreiter
Ruhl, Leopold
Matrosenobergefreiter
Rühl, Paul
Matrosenobergefreiter
Ruhl, Willi
Matrosengefreiter
Rühle, Walter
Matrosenobergefreiter
Rühlemann, Otto
Matrosengefreiter
Rupp, Hermann
Maat
Rüschoff, Wilhelm
Matrosenobergefreiter
Ruser, Walter
Matrosenobergefreiter
Rüstemeyer, Friedrich
Obermaat
Rüter, Johann
Matrose
Ruthe, Alfred
Matrosenobergefreiter
Sandbrink, August
Matrosenobergefreiter
Sander, Gerhard
Matrosenobergefreiter
Sänger, Oskar
Matrosenobergefreiter
Sappeck, Walter
Matrosenobergefreiter
Sasse, Alfons
Matrosenobergefreiter
Scale, August
Obermaat
Schaeblen, Heinz
Matrosenobergefreiter
Schäfer, Karl
Matrosengefreiter
Schäfers, Willi
Matrosenobergefreiter
Schäffer-Röhl, Harry
Matrosenobergefreiter
Schaffrath, Walter
Matrosenhauptgefreiter
Schallenberg, Georg
Matrosenobergefreiter
Schappert, Wilhelm
Matrosengefreiter
Scharf, Johannes
Matrosenobergefreiter
Scharf, Siegfried
Matrosenobergefreiter
Scharrer, August
Matrosengefreiter
Schartmer, Johann
Matrosenobergefreiter
Schätzgen, Hans
Matrosenobergefreiter
Schaube, Werner
Matrosenobergefreiter
Schaukellis, Kurt
Matrosenobergefreiter
Schaumann, Ewald
Matrosenhauptgefreiter
Scheele, Reinhard
Sekadett
Scheffler, Karl
Matrosengefreiter

Scheffler, Walter
Matrosenobergefreiter
Scheidemann, Helmut
Matrosenobergefreiter
Schelle, Friedrich
Matrosenobergefreiter
Schenkl, Ernst
Obermaat
Schepers, Gerhard
Matrose
Scherer, Karl-Heinz
Matrosenobergefreiter
Scherkus, Hans
Matrosenobergefreiter
Scheugenflug, Max
Matrosenobergefreiter
Schian, Walter
Matrosenobergefreiter
Schiel, Edgar
Matrosengefreiter
Schieritz, Hans
Seekadett
Schieritz, Heinz
Matrosenobergefreiter
Schildknecht, Rolf
Maat
Schilling, Hans
Oberbootsmannsmaat
Schimak, Hermann
Seekadett
Schindler, Richard
Matrosenobergefreiter
Schink, Paul
Matrosenobergefreiter
Schink, Rudolf
Matrosenobergefreiter
Schläger, Kurt
Matrosengefreiter
Schlemmert, Walter
Matrosengefreiter
Schlenger, Sebald
Matrosenobergefreiter
Schliebeck, Josef
Matrosenobergefreiter
Schlitter, Reinhard
Matrosenobergefreiter
Schmager, Karl
Maat
Schmalz, Werner
Matrosenobergefreiter
Schmalzried-Rüsch, Siegfried
Matrosengefreiter
Schmelter, Paul
Matrosenobergefreiter
Schmelz, Heinz
Schmerbeck, Eugen
Matrosengefreiter
Schmid, Friedrich
Matrosenobergefreiter
Schmid, Heinrich
Matrosenobergefreiter
Schmid-Burgk, Johannes
Seekadett
Schmidt, Erich-Franz
Matrosenobergefreiter
Schmidt, Ernst-Otto
Matrosenobergefreiter
Schmidt, Heinrich
Matrosenhauptgefreiter
Schmidt, Heinz
Matrosengefreiter
Schmidt, Horst
Matrosenobergefreiter
Schmidt, Karl

Schmidt, Philipp
Matrosengefreiter
Schmidt, Willi
Matrosenobergefreiter
Schmidt, Willi
Matrosenobergefreiter
Schmidt, Willibald
Seekadett
Schmitt, Walter   *Matrose*
Schmitz, Heinz
Matrosengefreiter
Schmitz, Johann
Matrosenhauptgefreiter
Schmude, Walter
Matrosengefreiter
Schnabel, Robert
Matrosenobergefreiter
Schnarre, Heinrich
Matrosenobergefreiter
Schneeberg, Heinz
Matrosengefreiter
Schneider, Adolf
Matrosengefreiter
Schneider, August
Obermaat
Schneider, Erich
Matrosenobergefreiter
Schneider, Heinrich
Matrosenobergefreiter
Schneider, Jakob
Signalobergefreiter
Schneider, Kurt
Matrosengefreiter
Schnellbacher, Ludwig
Matrose
Schnitzler, Walter
Matrosengefreiter
Schoch, Kurt
Matrosenhauptgefreiter
Schock, Heinrich
Matrosenhauptgefreiter
Schödel, Rudolf
Matrosengefreiter
Schöffel, Karl
Feldwebel
Scholtyssek, Servatius
Matrosenobergefreiter
Scholz, Engelbert
Matrose
Schönbach, Alfred
Matrosenobergefreiter
Schöne, Werner-Max
Matrosenobergefreiter
Schöneberger, Wilhelm
Matrosenhauptgefreiter
Schönfeld, Harry
Obermaat
Schönfelder, Bernhard
Matrosenobergefreiter
Schönfelder, Heinz
Matrosenobergefreiter
Schönrock, Walter
Matrosengefreiter
Schoster, Anton
Matrosenobergefreiter
Schotte, Hansjörg
Seekadett
Schottke, Harald
Oberleutnant zur See
Schramm, Heinz
Bootsmannsmaat
Schrank, Simon
Matrosengefreiter
Schreier, Fritz
Matrosenhauptgefreiter

Schreiner, Ludwig
Obermaat
Schrock, Paul
Matrosenobergefreiter
Schröder, Andreas
Matrosenobergefreiter
Schröder, Erich
Schröder, Erich
Matrosenobergefreiter
Schröder, Jans-Hansen
Obermaat
Schröder, Rudolf   *Maat*
Schröter, Hubert
Matrosenobergefreiter
Schubert, Kurt
Matrose
Schubert, Ludwig
Matrosenobergefreiter
Schubert, Rudolf
Matrose
Schuberth, Andreas
Matrosenobergefreiter
Schuch, Georg
Obermaat
Schuhmacher, Heinz
Matrosenobergefreiter
Schuhmann, Heinz
Matrosenobergefreiter
Schüler, Bernhard
Maat
Schüler, Friedrich
Matrosenobergefreiter
Schülke, Heinz
Matrosengefreiter
Schulte, Hans-Günther
Matrosengefreiter
Schulte, Heinz
Matrosengefreiter
Schulte, Willi
Schulte-Gahmen, Heinz
Oberleutnant zur See
Schultze, Heinrich
Obermaat
Schulz, Bruno
Oberleutnant zur See
Schulz, Paul
Matrosenobergefreiter
Schulz, Rigowald
Matrose
Schulz, Werner
Matrosengefreiter
Schulz, Wolfgang
Matrosenhauptgefreiter
Schulze, Egon
Matrosengefreiter
Schulze, Richard
Matrosenobergefreiter
Schulze, Wilhelm
Matrosenobergefreiter
Schumacher, Ernst
Matrosengefreiter
Schumacher, Heinrich
Matrosengefreiter
Schumacher, Hermann
Matrosengefreiter
Schumann, Emil
Matrosenobergefreiter
Schumann, Gerhard
Matrosenobergefreiter
Schurat, Horst
Seekadett
Schust, Karl
Oberleutnant zur See
Schuster, Ewald
Matrosengefreiter

Schuster, Karl
Maat
Schütze, Kurt
Obermaat
Schwäbbken, Heinrich
Matrosenobergefreiter
Schwaiger, Johann
Matrosengefreiter
Schwanke, Kurt
Matrosenobergefreiter
Schwanz, Kurt
Matrosenobergefreiter
Schwaps, Georg
Matrosenobergefreiter
Schwarz, Gerhard
Matrosengefreiter
Schweika, Richard
Matrosenobergefreiter
Schweitzer, Ludwig
Matrosenobergefreiter
Schwend, Walter
Matrosengefreiter
Schwenk, Hans
Oberleutnant zur See
Schwenter, Maximilian
Maschinengefreiter
Sczymzak, Harry
Matrosengefreiter
Seeland, Heinz-Günter
Matrosenobergefreiter
Seelemeier, Wilhelm
Matrosenhauptgefreiter
Sehl, Edwin
Maat
Sehl, Ludwig
Maat
Sehon, Rudolf
Matrosenhauptgefreiter
Seibt, Günter
Seekadett
Seidelmann, Reinhard
Matrosenobergefreiter
Seiler, Erwin
Matrosenobergefreiter
Seng, Karl
Obermaschinist
Severin, Bruno
Matrosenobergefreiter
Sichler, Kurt
Matrosenobergefreiter
Sidow, Wilhelm
Siebert, Kurt
Matrosenobergefreiter
Siedelmann, Horst
Matrose
Sieg, Hans
Matrosenobergefreiter
Sievers, Hans
Matrose
Silbermann, Fritz
Obermaat
Silwian, Joseph
Matrosenhauptgefreiter
Simonides, Ernst
Matrosengefreiter
Singer, Willy
Matrosenobergefreiter
Siodlaczek, Heinrich
Matrosenobergefreiter
Sistenich, Josef
Matrosenobergefreiter
Sitek, Karl
Matrose
Skrzippek, Walter

Spamer, Heinrich
Signalobermaat
Spanfelner, Max
Matrosenobergefreiter
Späth, Hans
Matrosenobergefreiter
Specht, Ernst
Obermaat
Specowius, Otto
Matrosenobergefreiter
Spengler, Walter
Obermaat
Spenner, Werner
Matrosenobergefreiter
Sperling, Heinz
Matrosenobergefreiter
Sperzel, Heinz
Matrosenobergefreiter
Spicher, Karl
Matrosenobergefreiter
Spies, Eduard
Matrosenobergefreiter
Spies, Willi
Obermaat
Spille, Friedrich
Obermaat
Spohn, Josef
Matrosenobergefreiter
Spörer, Ernst
Matrosenobergefreiter
Spuzel, Heinz
Matrosenobergefreiter
Staats, Friedrich
Matrosenobergefreiter
Stadermann, Hermann
Matrosenobergefreiter
Stadler, Josef
Matrosenobergefreiter
Stahl, Alfred
Matrosenobergefreiter
Stahl, Gerhard
Matrosenobergefreiter
Stapel, Kurt
Matrosengefreiter
Stark, Heinz
Matrosenobergefreiter
Starke, Gustav   *Obermaat*
Statz, Herbert
Matrosenobergefreiter
Stauder, Max
Matrosenobergefreiter
Stawitzki, Günter
Matrosenobergefreiter
Stawowski, Paul
Matrosengefreiter
Stefan, Josef
Matrosengefreiter
Steffen, Franz
Matrosenobergefreiter
Stegbauer, Johann
Matrosengefreiter
Stegemann, Erwin
Matrose
Steiger, Ludwig
Matrosenobergefreiter
Steinert, Kurt
Matrosengefreiter
Steiniger, Günther
Matrosengefreiter
Steinke, Max
Matrosenobergefreiter
Steinke, Willi
Matrosenobergefreiter
Steinmeyer, Helmut
Matrosenobergefreiter

Steinweg, Kurt
Matrose
Steireif, Andreas
Matrosenobergefreiter
Stelzmüller, Franz
Matrosenobergefreiter
Stender, Ernst
Matrosenobergefreiter
Stenger, Emil
Matrosenobergefreiter
Stenzel, Erich
Matrosenobergefreiter
Steppa, Wilhelm
Obermaat
Stetenbuhr, Erwin
Matrosenobergefreiter
Stiehl, Herbert
Obermaat
Stiep, Wilhelm
Matrosenhauptgefreiter
Still, Hans
Matrosengefreiter
Stille, Günter
Matrosenobergefreiter
Stineker, Erich
Maat
Stinski, Walter
Matrosenobergefreiter
Stobbe, Walter
Matrose
Stöber, Ernst
Matrosenobergefreiter
Stock, Heinrich
Obermaat
Stockey, Hans
Matrosenobergefreiter
Stöckler, Hans
Matrosenobergefreiter
Stog, Rudi   *Maat*
Stollfuß, Johann
Maat
Stolorz, Gerhard
Matrosengefreiter
Stolte, Erich
Matrosenobergefreiter
Stoltze, Hans
Matrosenobergefreiter
Stolz, Hermann
Matrosengefreiter
Stolze, Heinz
Matrosenobergefreiter
Störbrock, Josef
Matrosenobergefreiter
Storde, Karl-Heinz
Matrosengefreiter
Strauch, Erich
Matrose
Strauhs, Ludwig
Matrosenobergefreiter
Streihs, Ulrich
Kadett
Strodtkötter, Martin
Matrosenobergefreiter
Strotmann, August
Matrosenhauptgefreiter
Stubauer, Ferdinand
Matrose
Stüdemann, Fritz
Matrosenobergefreiter
Sügling, Helmut
Matrosengefreiter
Sühs, Willi
Matrosenobergefreiter
Sühs, Wolfgang
Matrosenobergefreiter

Sunke, Herbert
   Matrosenobergefreiter
Süss, Karl
   Matrosenobergefreiter
Swiniartzki, Kurt
   Matrose
Treuter, Max
   Matrosenobergefreiter
Ueberall, Erwin
   Matrosenobergefreiter
Uhl, Erich
   Matrosenobergefreiter
Uhlhorn, Heinrich
   Matrosenobergefreiter
Uhlig, Kurt
   Matrosenobergefreiter
Uhlig, Werner
   Matrose
Uhlig, Witolf
   Matrosenobergefreiter
Ulbrich, Gerhard
   Obermaat
Ulrich, Josef
   Matrosenobergefreiter
Unglaube, Herbert
   Matrosengefreiter
Urbach, Friedrich
   Matrose
Urlhart, Alois
   Matrosenobergefreiter
Vagt, Karl-Heinrich
   Korvettenkapitän
Vallentin, Walter
   Oberfeldwebel
Van Riet, Franz
   Matrosengefreiter
Van Scharrel, Weert
   Matrosenobergefreiter
Vanek, Rudolf
   Matrosenobergefreiter
Vanhofen, Hermann
   Matrosenobergefreiter
Verhoven, Heinz
   Obermaat
Vetterlein, Werner
   Matrosenobergefreiter
Vielkind, Franz
   Matrosenobergefreiter
Vierjahn, Adolf
   Oberfunker
Vieth, Johannes
Vietheer, Walter
   Feldwebel
Vogel, Emil
   Matrosenobergefreiter
Vogel, Ernst
   Matrosengefreiter
Vogt, Werner
   Matrosenobergefreiter
Vohs, Herbert
   Matrose
Voigt, Hans
   Matrosenobergefreiter
Voigt, Werner
   Matrosenobergefreiter
Völkel, Herbert
   Obermaat
Völkner, Heinz
   Matrosengefreiter
Völkner, Willi
   Matrosenobergefreiter
Voll, Hermann
   Matrose
Völskow, Heinz
   Matrose
Von Berkel, Bernhard *Maat*
Von Darl, Johannes
   Obermaat
Von Der Reith, Walter
   Feldwebel
Von Der Mosel, Werner
   Obermaat
Von Lattorf, Kuno
   Oberleutnant zur See
Von Livonius, Gerhard
   Leutnant zur See
Von Restorff, Burkhard
   Oberleutnant zur See
Von Sierakowski, Kurt
   Obermaat
Vormbaum, Friedrich
   Matrosenobergefreiter
Voß, Hans
   Matrosenobergefreiter
Voß, Karl-Heinz
   Matrosengefreiter
Voß, Rudolf
   Matrosenobergefreiter
Wagener, Anton
   Matrosenhauptgefreiter
Wagner, Alfred
   Matrosenobergefreiter
Wagner, Fritz
   Matrosenobergefreiter
Wagner, Georg
   Matrosenobergefreiter
Wagner, Heinz
   Matrosenobergefreiter
Wagner, Horst
   Matrose
Wagner, Otto
   Matrosenobergefreiter
Wagner, Rolf
   Matrosenobergefreiter
Wagner, Rudolf
   Matrosengefreiter
Wahl, Richard
   Matrosenobergefreiter
Wahl, Willi
   Matrosenobergefreiter
Wahler, Franz
   Obermaat
Wahsner, Herbert
   Matrosenobergefreiter
Walburg, Heinz
   Seekadett
Walczuch, Paul
   Matrosenobergefreiter
Walderbach, Antonius
   Matrosenobergefreiter
Waldmann, Walter
   Matrosenhauptgefreiter
Waldschmidt, Hans
   Mechanikersgefreiter
Wallacher, Wilhelm
   Matrosenobergefreiter
Wallbrecht, Paul
   Matrosengefreiter
Wallraff, Günther
   Matrosengefreiter
Walsthöwi, Richard
   Matrosenobergefreiter
Walter, Alfred
   Matrosenobergefreiter
Walter, Friedrich
   Obermaat
Walter, Heinrich
   Matrosengefreiter
Walter, Heinz
   Matrosenobergefreiter
Walther, Richard
   Matrosengefreiter
Wanders, Rudolf
   Matrosenobergefreiter
Wappler, Leopold
   Matrosengefreiter
Warmann, Gerhard
   Matrosenhauptgefreiter
Warnkens, Hermann
   Maat
Waskow, Friedrich
   Matrosenobergefreiter
Weber, Fenno
   Matrosenobergefreiter
Weber, Heinz
   Obermaat
Weber, Jakob
   Matrosenobergefreiter
Weber, Johann
   Maschinengefreiter
Weber, Karl-Heinz
   Matrosenobergefreiter
Weber, Siegfried
   Seekadett
Wecker, Gregor
   Matrosenobergefreiter
Weder, Heinz *Matrose*
Wegener, Anton
   Oberbootsmannsmaat
Wegner, Otto
   Matrosenobergefreiter
Wehren, Theodor
   Matrosenobergefreiter
Weidenhaupt, Rudolf
   Matrosenhauptgefreiter
Weingart, Hans
   Matrosenobergefreiter
Weinhold, Rolf-Karl
   Matrosenobergefreiter
Weise, Fritz
   Matrosenobergefreiter
Weishäupl, Josef
   Matrosenobergefreiter
Weißhaupt, Eugen
   Bootsmannsmaat
Weiss, Franz
   Matrosenobergefreiter
Weiss, Heinz
   Matrose
Weiss, Heinz
   Mechanikersgefreiter
Welle, Josef
   Obermaat
Welslau, Fritz
   Matrosenhauptgefreiter
Welters, Johannes
   Matrosenobergefreiter
Wende, Friedrich
   Matrosenhauptgefreiter
Wendler, Werner
   Matrosenobergefreiter
Werle, Alfred
   Matrosengefreiter
Wermann, Oskar
   Matrosenobergefreiter
Werner, Heinz
   Matrosenobergefreiter
Werner, Otto
   Oberfeldwebel
Werther, Wilhelm
   Leutnant zur See
Wessels, Georg
   Matrosenobergefreiter
Wettengel, Helmut
   Matrosenobergefreiter
Weynans, Joseph
   Obermaat
Wibbelhoff, Johann
   Stabsoberstückmeister
Wickert, Otto-Emil
   Matrosenobergefreiter
Widenhaupt, Rudolf
Widmann, Wilhelm
   Matrosenobergefreiter
Wiedemeier, Kurt
   Matrosenobergefreiter
Wiegand, Gottfried
   Matrosenobergefreiter
Wiese, Hans
   Matrose
Wiesner, Bernhard
   Matrosenobergefreiter
Wieting, Dietrich
   Korvettenkapitän
Wildhagen, Heinz
   Matrosenobergefreiter
Wilhelmi, Wilhelm
   Matrose
Wilke, Fritz *Seekadett*
Wilke, Gerhard
   Maschinenmaat
Wilke, Paul
   Matrosenobergefreiter
Wilkening, Friedrich
   Obermaat
Will, Friedrich
   Matrose
Wille, Günther
   Matrosenobergefreiter
Willer, Karl-Heinz
   Matrosenobergefreiter
Willmer, Erwin
   Matrosengefreiter
Windhorst, Heinz
   Matrosengefreiter
Windmüller, Paul
   Kapitänleutnant
Winkler, Rudolf
   Matrosenobergefreiter
Winter, Erich
   Matrosenobergefreiter
Wionzeck, Herbert
   Maschinengefreiter
Wippich, Gottfried
Wirth, Franz
   Matrosengefreiter
Wirzfeld, Anton
   Matrosenobergefreiter
Wischermann, Paul
   Maat
Witt, Siegward
   Seekadett
Witt, Walter
   Matrosengefreiter
Witt, Willi
   Obermaat
Witte, Bernhard
   Obermaat
Wittelbecher, Heinz
   Matrosenhauptgefreiter
Wittenberg, Friedrich
   Matrosenobergefreiter
Witthöft, Werner
   Matrosenobergefreiter
Wittich, Iwo
   Matrosenobergefreiter
Wittig, Helmut
   Obermaat
Witting, Gernot
   Leutnant zur See

Wittka, Walter
 Matrosenobergefreiter
Wittkopf, Friedrich-Augus
 Oberfeuerwerksmaat
Witzki, Ernst-Johann
 Maat
Wogersin, Albert
 Obermaat
Wohlers, Willi
 Matrosenhauptgefreiter
Wohlgemuth, Ewald
 Matrosenobergefreiter
Woigk, Bernhard
 Matrosenobergefreiter
Woinzeck, Herbert
 Matrosenobergefreiter
Wolf, Alfred
 Obermaat
Wolf, Hermann
 Matrosenobergefreiter
Wolf, Horst
 Matrosengefreiter
Wolf, Johann
 Matrosengefreiter
Wolf, Karl-Heinz
 Matrosengefreiter
Wolfer, Friedrich
 Obermaschinist
Wolff, Fritz
 Oberfunker
Wolff, Helmuth
 Matrosengefreiter
Wollek, Erwin
 Matrosenobergefreiter
Wolter, Erich
 Matrosenobergefreiter
Worbs, Paul
 Matrosengefreiter
Woßmann, Hans
 Matrose
Wötzen, Herbert
 Matrosenobergefreiter
Woytschekowski-Emden, Rolf
 Korvettenkapitän
Wucherpfenig, Paul
 Matrosenobergefreiter
Wulf, Erich
 Matrose
Wulf, Ernst
 Matrosenobergefreiter
Wulf, Gustav
 Matrosenobergefreiter
Würz, Günther
 Maat
Wyssocki, Hubert
 Obermaschinist
Zahora, Josef
 Matrosenobergefreiter
Zntarra, Karl-Heinz
 Matrosenobergefreiter
Zausch, Walter
 Matrosenhauptgefreiter
Zellner, Karl
 Matrosengefreiter
Zerdak, Thomas
 Matrosengefreiter
Zeuner, Sigurd
 Obermaat
Ziegler, Georg
 Matrosenobergefreiter
Ziegler, Ludwig
 Seekadett
Zierau, Heinz
 Matrosengefreiter
Zieschank, Johann
 Matrosenobergefreiter
Zietlow, Heinz
 Matrosenobergefreiter
Zimmermann, Gustav
 Matrosenobergefreiter
Zimmermann, Maximilian
 Matrosenobergefreiter
Zimmermann, Walter
 Matrosengefreiter
Zindler, Heinz
 Matrosenobergefreiter
Zippel, Kurt
 Matrosenobergefreiter
Zipser, Kurt
 Matrose
Zorn, Julius
 Maat
Zschiegner, Paul
 Marineassistenzarzt
Zufall, Heinrich
 Matrosenobergefreiter
Zulbeck, Fritz
 Matrosenobergefreiter
Zwigard, Alfred
 Matrosenobergefreiter

APPENDIX V
Gneisenau Roll of Honour

Below are the list of names of those known to have been killed aboard the *Gneisenau* between 1940 and 1942.

Ahrens, Karl
  Matrose
Ancker, Wilhelm
  Seekadett
Anhelm, Fritz
  Matrosenobergefreiter
Appelt, Ernst
  Matrose
Aulich, Erich
  Maschinengefreiter
Bachmann, Heinrich
  Matrosenobergefreiter
Balke, Werner
  Matrose
Bauer, Johann
  Kadett
Bauschinger, Willi
  Maschinenmaat
Beck, Karl
  Matrosengefreiter
Becker, Hugo
  Matrosenobergefreiter
Bennewitz, Karl
  Matrose
Bergbauer, Erwin
  Matroseobergefreiter
Bickel, Richard
  Matrose
Biersack, Rudolf
  Matrose
Bloch, Wolfgang
  Fähnrich zur See
Bobsien, Jochim
  Seekadett
Böhme, Heinz
  Matrose
Bolay, Arthur
  Bootsmannsmaat
Boller, Alfred
  Feldwebelgefreiter
Bornhake, Werner
  Matrosengefreiter
Bösch, Hans
  Matrosengefreiter

Brabandt, Bernhard
  Matrosenhauptgefreiter
Brand, Walter-Günter
  Matrose
Brieger, Walter
  Matrosengefreiter
Brzoska, Karl
  Matrosenobergefreiter
Buchka, Hans-Georg
  Fregattenkapitän
Büscher, Karl
  Oberbootsmannsmaat
Christensen, Willi
  Hauptgefreiter
Dieckmann, Hans
  Matrosengefreiter
Diehm, Herbert
  Kadett
Dobbelfeld, Anton
  Maat
Dommer, Erwin
  Matrosenobergefreiter
Doose, Ernst
  Matrose
Dörfler, Leo
  Matrosenobergefreiter
Dreber, Albert
  Feldwebelgefreiter
Eckardt, Ernst
  Matrosenobergefreiter
Ehlers, Johannes
  Schuhmacher
Eichler, Erich
  Matrosenobergefreiter
Eisert, Helmut
  Maschinenmaat
Emberger, Kurt
  Matrosengefreiter
Falk, Friedrich
  Feldwebelmaat
Fannrich, Theodor
  Matrose
Fetdkamp, Herbert
  Matrosengefreiter

Fock, Hans-Heinrich
  Verwaltungefreiter
Frank, Herbert
  Matrosengefreiter
Frick, Wolfgang
  Matrose
Friedrich, Herbert
  Oberfeldwebel
Fritsche, Werner
  Leutnant zur See
Gallun, Wilhelm
  Maschinenhauptgefreiter
Geßner, Helmut
  Matrose
Giese, Gerhard
  Seekadett
Gleichmann, Herbert
  Matrosengefreiter
Graf Lanjus, Anton
  Matrose
Gundel, Andreas
  Maschinenmaat
Güth, Fritz
  Maschinengefreiter
Gutschmidt, Heinz
  Maschinengefreiter
Haase, Johannes
  Matrosenhauptgefreiter
Haefner, Harry
  Matrosenobergefreiter
Hähnel, Wilhelm
  Matrose
Hammer, Siegfried
  Matrosengefreiter
Hansen, Hermann
  Friseur
Hartmann, Norbert
  Maschinengefreiter
Heber, Heinz
  Maschinenobergefreiter
Heckert, Heinz
  Matrosenobergefreiter
Heidrich, Herbert
  Matrose

Heine, Walter
Matrosengefreiter
Hempel, Herbert
Matrosenobergefreiter
Hentges, Nikolaus
Matrose
Hirsch, Jofef
Maschinengefreiter
Hoyer, Martin
Matrosengefreiter
Jakobsen, Oskar
Matrosenobergefreiter
Jänisch, Heinz
Matrosengefreiter
Jennewein, Willy
Matrosenobergefreiter
Jensen, Artur
Verwaltungobergefreiter
John, Heinz
Matrose
Kannegießer, Eugen
Korvettenkapitän
Karlisch, Richard
Maschinenobergefreiter
Klein, Willi
Maschinenmaat
Klepsch, Herbert
Matrose
Klick, Karl
Matrosengefreiter
Knauß, Walter
Matrosengefreiter
Knust, Werner
Matrosenobergefreiter
Köhler, Rudolf
Matrosengefreiter
Kricke, Heinz
Matrosenobergefreiter
Krieger, Robert
Matrose
Kuballa, Gottfried
Matrose
Kügler, Alois
Matrose
Kühl, Hans
Obermaat
Kühne, Rolf
Matrosengefreiter
Laube, Hans-Joachim
Signalgefreiter
Lehmann, Alfred
Matrose
Lehmann, Heinz
Matrose
Lenz, Erich
Matrose
Lettermann, Willi
Matrose
Licht, Richard
Mechanikermaat
Liesecke, Artur
Matrosenobergefreiter
Lindner, Günter
Musikobergefreiter
Lischka, Gerhard
Musikobergefreiter
Lötzich, Werner
Matrose
Maag, Eugen
Mechanikerobergefreiter
Marascheck, Rolf
Matrose
Marschall, Erhard
Matrose

Mathis, Paul
Matrose
Matthies, Fritz
Maschinenobergefreiter
Mayr, Max
Matrose
Meyer, Alfred
Matrosengefreiter
Meyer, Erich
Maschinenmaat
Michalski, Fritz
Matrosengefreiter
Miene, Johannes
Matrose
Möllers, Paul
Matrosengefreiter
Müller, Friedrich
Matrose
Müller, Heinrich
Matrosenhauptgefreiter
Müller, Helmut
Matrose
Müller, Rudolf
Matrose
Münch, Heinz
Matrose
Narten, Rolf
Matrose
Naurath, Emil
Bootsmannsmaat
Neubacher, Paul
Bootsmann
Nickolaus, Hermann
Matrosenobergefreiter
Nöbel, Lothar
Maschinengefreiter
Oelrichs, Gerd
Bootsmannsmaat
Oertel, Erich
Matrosenobergefreiter
Oesterling, Günther
Matrosenobergefreiter
Olofsson, Nils
Schneider
Ordnung, Otto
Matrose
Ottens, Otto
Maschinenhauptgefreiter
Paddags, Hans
Matrose
Paephe, Karl-Heinz
Signalgefreiter
Pahlke, Erich
Sanitätsgefreiter
Palzer, Paul
Matrosengefreiter
Parchmann, Gerhard
Matrosengefreiter
Piotrowski, Ottohar
Matrosengefreiter
Plagmann, Karl-Heinz
Maschinenobergefreiter
Postel, Jonny
Matrosenobergefreiter
Quaß, Ulrich
Matrosenobergefreiter
Quindeau, Theodor
Obermaschinist
Remmele, Karl
Bootsmannsmaat
Rink, Ewald
Bootsmannsmaat
Röder, Johannes
Matrose

Roelen, Peter
Musikgefreiter
Rohde, Emil
Matrosenobergefreiter
Rosengarten, Martin
Matrose
Roth, Hans
Fähnrich zur See
Roth, Heinz
Kadett
Rüdiger, Hans
Mechanikermaat
Rutenberg, Alexander
Musikmaat
Sangerhausen, Werner
Matrosengefreiter
Schacht, Ulrich
Maschinenobergefreiter
Schade, Wolfgang
Seekadett
Scheel, Gustav
Oberfeldwebelmaat
Schenk, Gerhard
Musikobermaat
Schiebold, Werner
Matrose
Schmidtke, Otto
Feldwebel
Schmitz, Erwin
Kantinenverkäufer
Schmitz, Karl
Mechanikergefreiter
Schneider, Alfred
Mechanikergefreiter
Schneider, Artur
Schneider
Schneider, Rudolf
Maschinengefreiter
Schober, Paul
Obergefreiter
Scholl, Franz
Maschinengefreiter
Schubert, Rudolf
Matrose
Schumacher, Klaus
Leutnant zur See
Schütz, Otto
Matrosengefreiter
Schwarz, Reinhold
Matrosenhauptgefreiter
Schweizer, Wilhelm
Bootsmannsmaat
Sdunnek, Wilhelm
Matrose
Seeger, Horst
Matrose
Seifert, Werner
Matrose
Siefert, Karl
Maschinenmaat
Sievers, Helmut
Matrose
Simon, Harry
Matrose
Skoda, Wilhelm
Matrose
Skowroniki, Günter
Maschinenmaat
Sodenkamp, Erich
Maschinengefreiter
Sonnabend, Otto
Matrosengefreiter
Sonnenburg, Gerhard
Matrosengefreiter

Sperber, Gerhard
Matrose
Stawowsky, Paul
Matrose
Stein, Walfried
Matrose
Steiner, Ernst
Maschinengefreiter
Stelzer, Hans
Matrosengefreiter
Stiegel, Harald
Seekadett
Strasser, Günter
Matrose
Struck, Fritz
Matrosenobergefreiter
Tetzlaff, Reinhold
Matrosengefreiter
Thum, Franz
Maschinenobergefreiter
Tschernach, Wilhelm
Bootsmannsm
Van Meegen, Franz
Matrosengefreiter
Vogel, Günter
Matrose
Von Coelln, Gerd
Matrose
Von Froenau, Abalbert *Leutnant zur See*
Voß, Heinrich
Matrosengefreiter
Walder, Johann
Matrose
Wannek, Ernst
Bootsmannsmaat
Wendt, Johannes
Matrosenobergefreiter
Wichert, Paul
Matrosengefreiter
Wildenhain, Günther
Matrose
Wriege, Karl
Mechanikerobergefreiter
Zagel, Hans
Maschinenmaat
Zehfuß, Alois
Matrosengefreiter
Zeil, Fritz
Matrose
Zimmer, Uno
Matrosengefreiter
Zschocke, Erich
Assistenzarzt (Second Lieutenant Doctor)
Zuckermann, Adalbert
Sanitätshauptgefreiter
Zywek, Kurt
Maschinenobergefreiter

Endnotes

Introduction
1. Moffat, J., *I Sank the Bismarck: Memoirs of a Second World War Navy Pilot* (London: Corgi Books, 2010), p. 217.
2. Roskill, S. W., *War at Sea 1939–1945 Volume I: The Defensive* (London: Her Majesty's Stationary Office, 1954), p. 496.
3. The final battleship engagement in history was the Battle of Surigao Straight which was fought on 25 October 1944 as part of the Battle of Leyte Gulf. For additional information on this engagement see Howard Sauer, *The Last Big-Gun Naval Battle: The Battle of Surigao Strait* (Palo Alto: The Glencannon Press, 1999) and Kenneth I. Friedman, *Afternoon of the Rising Sun: The Battle of Leyte Gulf* (Novato: Presidio Press Inc., 2001).

Chapter 1
1. Gröner, E., *German Warships: 1815–1945* (Annapolis: Naval Institute Press, 1990), p. 31.
2. Churchill, W., *The Second World War: Volume V Closing the Ring* (London: Folio Society, 2003), p. 245; Dan Van Der Vat, *The Atlantic Campaign* (New York: Harper and Row, 1988), p. 82; BR 1736 (48) (2) Naval Staff History of the Second World War, *Home Waters and the Atlantic Volume II, 9th April 1940–6th December 1941* (1961), pp. 14-15.
3. McMurtri, F. E. (ed.), *Jane's Fighting Ships 1940* (London: Sampson Low, Marston & Co, 1940), pp. 212–213.
4. Article 190, Treaty of Versailles (1919).
5. Knowles, D., *Tirpitz: The Life and Death of Germany's Last Great Battleship* (Stroud: Fonthill Media, 2018), p. 16.
6. Parker, J., *Task Force: Untold Stories of the Royal Navy* (London: Headline Book Publishing, 2003), pp. 95–102.
7. Johnston, I. and McAuley, R., *The Battleships* (London: Channel 4 Books, 2000), pp. 110–111.
8. Kennedy, P., *The Rise and Fall of British Naval Mastery* (London: Macmillan, 1983), p. 274; Elmer B. Potter (ed.), *Sea Power: A Naval History* (Annapolis: Naval Institute Press, 1981), p. 233.
9. Kennedy, *op. cit.*, pp. 275–276.
10. Marriott, L., *Treaty Cruisers: The First international Warship Building Competition* (Barnsley: Pen and Sword, 2005), p. 11.
11. Garzke, W. H. and Dulin, R. O., *Battleships: Axis and Neutral Battleships in World War II* (Annapolis: Naval Institute press, 1985), pp. 4-5; Norman Friedman, *U.S. Battleships: An illustrated Design History* (Annapolis: Naval Institute Press, 1985), p. 182.
12. Muir, M., 'Gun Calibers and Battle Zones: The United States Navy's Foremost Concern During the 1930s', *Warship International*, No. 1 (1980), p. 25.
13. Knowles, *op. cit.*, p. 18; Antony Preston, *The World's Worst Warships* (London: Conway Maritime Press, 2002), p. 117.
14. Garzke and Dulin, *op. cit.*, p. 128.
15. *Ibid.*, p. 130.
16. Gardiner, R., *Conway's All the World's Fighting Ships, 1922–1946* (Annapolis: Naval Institute Press, 1980), p. 225.
17. Garzke and Dulin, *op. cit.*, p. 130.
18. Weinberg, G., *The Foreign policy of Hitler's Germany: Diplomatic Revolution in Europe, 1933–36* (Chicago: University of Chicago Press, 1970), p. 212.
19. Kershaw, I., *Hitler 1889–1936: Hubris* (New York: W.W. Norton, 1998), p. 556.
20. Bloch, M., *Ribbentrop* (New York: Crown publishers Inc., 1992), pp. 73–74.
21. Kershaw, *op. cit.*, p. 558; Klaus Hildebrand, *The Foreign Policy of the Third Reich* (London: Batsford, 1973), p. 39.
22. Garzke and Dulin, *op. cit.*, p. 130.
23. Breyer, S., *Battleships and Battlecruisers, 1905–1970* (New York: Doubleday & Company, 1974), p. 294.
24. *Ibid.*
25. Knowles, *op. cit.*, pp. 21–23.

Chapter 2

1. Gröner, *German Warships*, p. 31.
2. *Ibid.*, p. 99.
3. Breyer, *Battleships and Battlecruisers*, p. 294.
4. Campbell, J., *Naval Weapons of World War Two* (London: Conway Maritime Press, 2002), p. 241.
5. Knowles, *Tirpitz*, p. 32.
6. Gröner, *op. cit.*, p. 31.
7. Garzke and Dulin, *Battleships*, p. 182.
8. *Ibid.*, p. 183.
9. Woton Hard (*Woton Hart*) armour possessed a breaking strength of 85–96 kg/sq. mm and would expand up to 20 per cent. See Gröner, *op. cit.*, p. x.
10. Gröner, *op. cit.*, p. 31.
11. Garzke and Dulin, *op. cit.*, p. 185.
12. Wotan *Weich* had a breaking strength of 65–75 kg/sq. mm and expanded up to 25 per cent.
13. Garzke and Dulin, *op. cit.*, pp. 185-186.
14. *Ibid.*, p. 186.
15. *Ibid.*, pp. 188–189.
16. Breyer, 1974, *op. cit.*, p. 295.
17. Gröner, *op. cit.*, p. 31.
18. *Ibid.*
19. Donald, D. (ed.), *Warplanes of the Luftwaffe* (London: Aerospace, 1994), p. 107; J. R. Smith, Anthony Kay, *German Aircraft of the Second World War* (London: Putnam & Company Ltd, 1972), p. 268.
20. Knowles, *op. cit.*, pp. 42–43.

Chapter 3

1. Koop, G. and Schmolke, K-P., *Battleships of the Scharnhorst Class* (Barnsley: Pen and Sword, 2014), p. 36.
2. *Ibid.*

Chapter 4

1. Williamson, G., *German Battleships 1939–45* (Oxford: Osprey Publishing Limited, 2003), p. 8.
2. *Ibid.*
3. Gröner, *German Warships*, p. 32.

Chapter 5

1. Hastings, M., *Bomber Command* (London: Pan Books, 2010), p. 4.
2. Williamson, *German Battleships 1939–45*, p. 8.
3. Jurgen Rohwer, *Chronology of the War at Sea 1939–1945: The Naval History of World War Two* (Annapolis: Naval Institute Press, 2005), p. 6.
4. Hampshire, A. C., *The Blockaders* (London: William Kimber, 1980), p. 17.
5. *Ibid.*, p. 93.
6. Roskill, *War at Sea 1939–1945 Volume I*, pp. 82–83.
7. Afflerbach, H, Strachan, H. (Eds.) *How Fighting Ends: A History of Surrender* (Oxford: Oxford University press, 2012), p. 204; Duskin, G., Segman, R., *If the Gods are Good: The Epic Sacrifice of HMS Jervis Bay* (Annapolis: Naval Institute Press, 2004), p. 66; Poolman, K., *Armed Merchant Cruisers* (London: Leo Cooper, 1985), p. 122.
8. *London Gazette*, 9 July 1940.
9. Roskill, 1954, *op. cit.*, p. 84.
10. *Ibid.*, p. 85.
11. *Ibid.*, p. 86.
12. *Ibid.*
13. Dildy, D. C., *Battles of World War II Denmark and Norway 1940: Hitler's Boldest Operation* (Oxford: Osprey Publishing Limited, 2009), p. 7.
14. *Ibid.*, pp. 7–9.
15. *Ibid.*, p. 12.
16. Garzke and Dulin, *Battleships*, p. 154.
17. Williamson, *op. cit.*, p. 9.
18. Smith, P. C., *The Battle-Cruiser Renown 1916–1948* (Barnsley: Pen and Sword, 2008), p. 66.
19. Garzke and Dulin, *op. cit.*, p. 135.
20. Smith, *op. cit.*, p. 67.
21. *Ibid.*, p. 68.
22. *Ibid.*
23. *Ibid.*, p. 69.
24. *Ibid.*
25. Garzke and Dulin, *op. cit.*, p. 135.
26. Smith, *op. cit.*, p. 69.
27. *Ibid.*, p. 70.
28. Garzke and Dulin, *op. cit.*, p. 154.
29. *Ibid.*, pp. 154 and 157.
30. Williamson, *op. cit.*, p. 10.
31. Garzke and Dulin, *op. cit.*, p. 137.

Chapter 6

1. Garzke and Dulin, *Battleships*, p. 157.
2. Rhys-Jones, G., *Churchill and the Norway Campaign* (Barnsley: Pen and Sword, 2008), p. 189.
3. Maier, K. A. (et al.), *Germany and the Second World War Volume II: Germany's Initial Conquests in Europe* (Oxford: Clarendon Press, 1991), p. 215.

4. Garzke and Dulin, *op. cit.*, p. 137.
5. BR 1840(1), The German Campaign in Norway (Portsmouth: Naval Historical Branch).
6. Rhys-Jones, *op. cit.*, p. 189.
7. BR 1840(1).
8. Humble, R., *Hitler's High Seas Fleet* (New York: Ballantyne Books, 1971), p. 57.
9. Howland, V. W., 'The Loss of HMS Glorious: An Analysis of the Action', *Warship International*, Vol. 31, No.1 (1994), p. 61.
10. Asmussen, J., 'Operation "Juno"', Scharnhorst-class.*dk*, Scharnhorst-class.dk/scharnhorst/history/scharnjuno.html (2010), Accessed 14/04/2019.
11. Rossiter, M., *Ark Royal: The Life, Death and Rediscovery of the Legendary Second World War Aircraft carrier* (London: Corgi Books, 2007), pp. 121-122.
12. Haarr, G. H., *The Battle for Norway: April–June 1940* (Annapolis: Naval Institute Press, 2010), p. 336.
13. Howland, *op. cit.*, p. 52; Rohwer, *Chronology of the War at Sea 1939–1945*, p. 26.
14. English, J., *Amazon to Ivanhoe: British Standard Destroyers of the 1930s* (Kendal: World Ship Society, 1993), p. 17.
15. Haarr, *op. cit.*, pp. 349 and 443.
16. Rhys-Jones, *op. cit.*, p. 191.
17. Ballantyne, I., *HMS Rodney: Slayer of the Bismarck and D-Day Saviour* (Barnsley: Pen and Sword, 2016), p. 111
18. Dildy, *Battles of World War II Denmark and Norway 1940*, p. 88.
19. Rossiter, *op. cit.*, p. 124.
20. *Ibid.*, pp. 124–125.
21. Dildy, *op. cit.*, pp. 88–89.
22. Rossiter, *op. cit.*, p. 125.
23. Garzke and Dulin, *op. cit.*, pp. 138–139.
24. *Ibid.*, p. 158.
25. *Ibid.*, p. 139.

Chapter 7

1. Garzke and Dulin, *Battleships*, p. 140.
2. See Arnold Hague, *The Allied Convoy System 1939–1945: Its Organization, Defence and Operation* (Annapolis: Naval Institute Press, 2000).
3. Hague, *The Allied Convoy System 1939–1945*, p. 127.
4. Knowles, *Tirpitz*, p. 104.
5. Nathan Miller, *War at Sea: A Naval History of World War II* (Oxford: Oxford University Press, 1996), p. 147.
6. *Ibid*.
7. Garzke and Dulin, *op. cit.*, p. 140.
8. *Ibid.*, p. 140–142.
9. Ballantyne, *HMS Rodney*, p. 123.
10. *Ibid*.
11. *Ibid.*, p. 124.
12. *Ibid.*, p. 125.
13. *Ibid.*, p. 126.
14. *Ibid*.
15. *Ibid*.
16. Smith, *The Battle-Cruiser Renown 1916–1948*, p. 129.
17. *Ibid*.
18. Rossiter, *Ark Royal*, p. 242.

Chapter 8

1. Garzke and Dulin, *Battleships*, p. 143.
2. Jacobs, P., *Daring Raids of World War Two: Heroic Land, Sea and Air Attacks* (Barnsley: Pen and Sword, 2015), p. 18.
3. *Ibid.*, p. 19.
4. *Ibid.*, p. 20.
5. *Ibid*.
6. Hastings, *Bomber Command*, p. 151.
7. *Ibid.*, p. 119.
8. *Ibid.*, pp. 130–131; Stephen Roskill, *Churchill and the Admirals* (London: Collins, 1977), p. 139.
9. Hastings, *op. cit.*, p. 116.
10. Kriegstagebuch Des Kreuzers *Prinz Eugen*, 18 May–1 June 1941; Paul Schmalenbach, 'KM Prinz Eugen', *Warship Profile 6* (Windsor: Profile Publications, 1971), p. 141; Fritz-Otto Busch, *Prinz Eugen* (London: Fist Futura Publications, 1975), pp. 108–109.
11. Ward, C., *4 Group Bomber Command: An Operational Record* (Barnsley: Pen and Sword, 2012), p. 548.
12. John Asmussen, 'The Scharnhorst at Brest, France (22 March 1941–11 February 1942', Scharnhorst-class.*dk* (2010), Scharnhorst-class.dk/scharnhorst/history/scharnbrest.html, Accessed 24/05/2019.

Chapter 9

1. Kemp, R., *Raiders: WWII Britain's Most Daring Special Operations* (London: Century, 2012), pp. 55–56.
2. *Ibid.*, p. 63.
3. Jacobs, *Daring Raids of World War Two*, p. 53.
4. Knowles, *Tirpitz*, p. 88.
5. Woodman, R., *Arctic Convoys 1941–1945* (Barnsley: Pen and Sword, 2013), pp. 33–53.
6. Bishop, P., *Target Tirpitz: X-Craft, Agents and Dambusters—The Epic Quest to Destroy Hitler's Mightiest Warship* (London: Harper Press, 2012), p. 49.
7. Ford, K., *Run the Gauntlet: The Channel Dash 1942* (Oxford: Osprey publishing, 2012), p. 17.

8   Denis Richards, *The Royal Air Force 1939–1945 Volume I: The Fight at Odds* (London: Her Majesty's Stationary Office, 1953), pp. 358–360.
9   Sebag-Montefiore, H., *Enigma: The Battle for the Code* (London: Phoenix, 2011), p. 208.
10 *Ibid*.
11 Hinsley, F. H., *British Intelligence in the Second World War: Its Influence on Strategy and Operations* (London: Her Majesty's Stationary Office, 1994), p. 135.
12 Ford, *op. cit.*, pp. 34–35.
13 *Ibid.*, p. 36.
14 Roskill, S. W., *War at Sea 1939–1945 Volume II: The Period of Balance* (London: Her Majesty's Stationary Office, 1956), p. 156.
15 Ford, *op. cit.*, p. 56.
16 *Ibid.*, p. 57.
17 Roskill, 1956, *op. cit.*, pp. 155–156; Richards, *op. cit.*, pp. 368–370.
18 Jacobs, *op. cit.*, p. 68.
19 Ford, *op. cit.*, p. 66.
20 *Ibid.*, p. 69.
21 *Ibid.*, p. 70.
22 Roskill, 1956, *op. cit.*, p. 159.
23 *Ibid*.
24 Breyer, S., *The German Battleship Gneisenau* (West Chester: Schiffer Publishing, 1990), p. 34.

Chapter 10
1   Admiralty Intelligence Division, *U523 Interrogation of Survivors*, October 1943, p. 14.
2   *Ibid.*, p. 12.
3   *Ibid*.
4   Williamson, *German Battleships 1939–45.*, p. 14.
5   Knowles, *Tirpitz*, pp. 130–134.
6   Woodman, *Arctic Convoys 1941–1945*, pp. 298–299.
7   *Ibid.*, p. 299.
8   For a more in-depth look at the Battle of the Barents Sea, see Michael Pearson *Red Sky in the Morning: The Battle of the Barents Sea 1942* (Barnsley: Pen & Sword Books Ltd, 2007).
9   Bishop, *Target Tirpitz*, p. 194.
10 *Ibid.*, p. 198.
11 Roskill, *War at Sea 1939–1945 Volume II*, pp. 398–399.
12 Knowles, *op. cit.*, p. 174; Bishop, *op. cit.*, p. 199.
13 Dönitz, K., *Memoirs: Ten Years and Twenty Days* (New York: Weidenfeld & Nicolson, 1959), pp. 310–311.
14 Roskill, 1956, *op. cit.*, p. 400.
15 Garzke and Dulin, *Battleships.*, p. 164.
16 Alf R. Jacobsen, *X-Craft Verses Tirpitz: The Mystery of the Missing X-5* (Stroud: Sutton Publishing, 2006), p. 94.
17 Knowles, *op. cit.*, p. 180.
18 Jacobsen, *op. cit.*, p. 94.
19 *Ibid*.
20 *Ibid.*, p. 113.
21 *Ibid*; Bishop, *op. cit.*, p. 205.

Chapter 11
1   US War Department, 'Commando Operations: Section II British Task Force, Spitsbergen Operation', *British Commandos, Military Intelligence Service*, Special Series No. 1 (1942), available at: lonesentry.com/manuals/commandos/spitsbergen.html, Accessed 03/05/2019.
2   Knowles, *Tirpitz*, p. 182.
3   Zetterling, N. and Tamelander, M., *Tirpitz: The Life and Death of Germany's Last Super Battleship* (Oxford: Casemate Publishers, 2009), p. 208.
4   Jacobsen, *X-Craft Verses Tirpitz*, p. 109.
5   Zetterling and Tamelander, *op. cit.*, pp. 209–210.
6   Knowles, *op. cit.*, p. 185.
7   Jacobsen, *op. cit.*, p. 126.
8   *Ibid*.
9   Knowles, *op. cit.*, pp. 191–193.
10 Jacobsen, *op. cit.*, p. 126.
11 *Ibid.*, p. 126–127.
12 Gallagher, T., *Against All Odds* (London: Pan Books, 1973) pp. 103–105.
13 Knowles, *op. cit.*, p. 208.

Chapter 12
1   Jacobsen, A., *Scharnhorst* (Stroud: Sutton publishing, 2003), p. 88.
2   Jacobsen, *X-Craft Verses Tirpitz*, p. 182; Williamson, *German Battleships 1939–45*, p. 14.
3   John Winton, *Death of the Scharnhorst* (London: Cassell, 2001), p. 49.
4   *Ibid*.
5   *Ibid.*, p. 50.
6   *Ibid*.
7   Knowles, *Tirpitz*, p. 214.
8   *Ibid*.
9   Woodman, *Arctic Convoys 1941–1945*, p. 356.
10 *Ibid.*, p. 355.
11 Knowles, *op. cit.*, p. 215.

12 *Ibid.*
13 *Ibid.*
14 Winton, *Death of the Scharnhorst*, p. 75.
15 Busch, F-O., *The Drama of the Scharnhorst* (Ware: Wordsworth, 2001), p. 55.
16 *Ibid.*, pp. 60–61.
17 *Ibid.*, p. 63.
18 Bishop, *Target Tirpitz*, p. 284.
19 Winton, *op. cit.*, p. 69.
20 *Ibid.*
21 Sebag-Montefiore, *Enigma*, p. 298; Patrick Beesly, *Very Special Intelligence: The Story of the Admiralty's Operational Intelligence Centre, 1939–1945* (London: Hamish Hamilton, 1977), p. 215.
22 Seabag-Montefiore, *op. cit.*, pp. 298–299.
23 *Ibid.*, p. 299.
24 Hugh Seabag-Montefiore has raised doubts over whether Pendered has recalled the signal deciphered at 03.00 correctly. Neither the original German message nor the decrypt appear in the National Archives. Furthermore, Seabag-Montefiore has noted that the content of this message is similar to one initiated at 0043 on 26 December which was sent to U-boats operating in the Arctic.
25 *Ibid.*
26 *Ibid.*, p. 300.
27 Winton, *op. cit.*, p. 70.
28 *Ibid.*
29 Busch, 2001, *op. cit.*, pp. 98–99.

Chapter 13
1   Winton, *Death of the Scharnhorst*, p. 84.
2   Busch, *The Drama of the Scharnhorst*, p. 101.
3   *Ibid.*, pp. 103–104.
4   *Ibid.*, p. 104.
5   Knowles, *Tirpitz*, p. 217.
6   Daniel Knowles, *King George V-class Battleships* (Stroud: Fonthill Media, 2022), p. 226.
7   *Ibid.*
8   *Ibid.*
9   Winton, *op. cit.*, p. 99.
10 Knowles, 2018, *op. cit.*, p. 217.
11 Busch, 2001, *op. cit.*, pp. 119–120.
12 Knowles, 2018, *op. cit.*, p. 217.
13 Winton, *op. cit.*, p. 111; Bryce Ramsden, 'Sinking the *Scharnhorst*', *Blackwood's Magazine*, No. 1549 (1944), pp. 345–346.
14 Busch, 2001, *op. cit.*, p. 132.
15 Winton, *op. cit.*, p. 113.
16 *Ibid.*, pp. 114–115.
17 Knowles, 2022, *op. cit.*, pp. 228-229.
18 Knowles, 2018, *op. cit.*, p. 218.
19 Ramsden, *op. cit.*, p. 347.
20 Brian Lavery, *The Last Big Gun: At War and at Sea with HMS Belfast* (Oxford: The Pool of London Press, 2015), p. 178.
21 *Ibid.*, p. 179.
22 *Ibid.*
23 Knowles, 2022, *op. cit.*, p. 229.
24 Winton, *op. cit.*, p. 118.
25 Knowles, 2022, *op. cit.*, p. 230.
26 *Ibid.*, p. 231.
27 Winton, *op. cit.*, p. 120.
28 Knowles, 2018, *op. cit.*, p. 128.
29 Lavery, *op. cit.*, p. 181.
30 Gödde, USN 1 Proc, p. 52.
31 Busch, 2001, *op. cit.*, p. 146.
32 *Ibid.*
33 Admiral Sir Bruce Fraser, 'Sinking of the German Battle-Cruiser *Scharnhorst* on the 26th December, 1943', *Supplement to the London Gazette*, No. 38038, 7 August 1947, p. 3709.
34 Winton, *op. cit.*, p. 132.
35 *Ibid.*, p. 133.
36 Busch, 2001, *op. cit.*, p. 150.
37 *Ibid.*
38 *Ibid*, p. 151.
39 *Ibid.*
40 *Ibid.*, p. 153.
41 Winton, *op. cit.*, p. 134.
42 Fraser, *op. cit*, p. 3709.
43 Woodman, *Arctic Convoys 1941–1945*, p. 372.
44 *Ibid.*
45 Busch, 2001, *op. cit.*, p. 154.
46 *Ibid.*, p. 157.
47 *Ibid.*, pp. 154–155.

48   *Ibid.*, p. 158.
49   Woodman, *op. cit.*, p. 373.
50   Fraser, *op. cit.*, p. 3710.
51   Knowles, 2022, *op. cit.*, p. 233.
52   Winton, *op. cit.*, p. 142.
53   Roskill, S., *The Navy at War 1939–1945* (London: Collins, 1960), p. 324.

Chapter 14

1   BBC Documentary with Ludovic Kennedy.
2   Busch, *The Drama of the Scharnhorst*, pp. 163–165.
3   *Ibid.*, p. 165.
4   Winton, *Death of the Scharnhorst*, p. 142.
5   Fraser, 'Sinking of the German Battle-Cruiser *Scharnhorst* on the 26th December, 1943', p. 3710.
6   Winton, *op. cit.*, pp. 146–147; Woodman, *Arctic Convoys 1941–1945*, p. 373.
7   Fraser, *op. cit.*, p. 3710.
8   Knowles, *Tirpitz*, p. 219.
9   *Ibid.*, p. 218.
10   Johnston, McAuley, *The Battleships*, pp. 168–169.
11   Arseni Golvoko, *With the Red Fleet* (London: Putnam, 1965), p. 187.
12   Busch, 2001, *op. cit.*, p. 170.
13   Winton, *op. cit.*, p. 157.
14   *Ibid.*, pp. 157–158.
15   Churchill, *The Second World War Volume V*, p. 349.
16   *Ibid.*
17   Dönitz, *Memoirs*, pp. 383–384.
18   Winton, *op. cit.*, p. 160.
19   Bishop, *Target Tirpitz*, p. 291.
20   Knowles, *op. cit.*, p. 205.
21   Churchill, *op. cit.*, p. 222.

Chapter 15

1   Garzke and Dulin, *Battleships*, pp. 149–150.
2   Williamson, *German Battleships 1939–45*, p. 18.
3   Breyer, *The German Battleship Gneisenau*, p. 34.
4   Garzke and Dulin, *op. cit.*, p. 150.
5   *Ibid.*, pp. 150–151.
6   Breyer, 1990, *op. cit.*, p. 34.
7   Williamson, *op. cit.*, p. 18; Richard Garrett, *Scharnhorst and Gneisenau: The Elusive Sisters* (London: Hippocrene Books, 1978), pp. 120 and 122.
8   Garzke and Dulin, *op. cit.*, p. 153.
9   Knowles, *Tirpitz*, p. 221.
10   Garzke and Dulin, *op. cit.*, p. 161.
11   Gröner, *German Warships*, p. 32; Garzke and Dulin, *op. cit.*, p. 153.
12   Breyer, 1990, *op. cit.*, p. 34.
13   Garrett, *op. cit.*, p. 121.

Chapter 16

1   Williamson, *German Battleships 1939–45*, p. 14.
2   *Ibid*; Fenton, 'The Sinking of the "Scharnhorst"', *BBC* (17 February 2011), bbc.co.uk/history/worldwars/wwtwo/scharnhorst_01.shtml, Accessed 06/05/2019.
3   Fenton, *op. cit.*

Epilogue

1   Koop and Schmolke, *Battleships of the Scharnhorst Class*, Conclusion page 1.
2   Knowles, *Target Tirpitz*, pp. 96–99.
3   *Ibid.*, p. 99.
4   *Ibid.*, p. 281.

Bibliography

Archival Material

ADM 119/620 Destroyer Attempts to Intercept German Battlecruisers Gneisenau, Scharnhorst and Prinz Eugen (Kew: The National Archives)
ADM 234/328 Passage of Enemy Fleet Through English Channel and Report of Operation in Battle Summary 11 (Kew: The National Archives)
Admiralty Intelligence Division, *U523 Interrogation of Survivors* (October 1943)
AIR 2/7912 Passage of Scharnhorst, Gneisenau and Prinz Eugen Through the Straits of Dover (Board of Inquiry Evidence) (Kew: The National Archives)
AIR 8/614 RAF Attacks on Scharnhorst, Gneisenau and Prinz Eugen (Kew: The National Archives)
BR 1840(1), The German Campaign in Norway (Portsmouth: Naval Historical Branch)
Kriegstagebuch Des Kreuzers *Prinz Eugen*, 18 May-1 June 1941

Literature

'Article 190', *Treaty of Versailles* (1919)
Afflerbach, H, Strachan, H. (eds.), *How Fighting Ends: A History of Surrender* (Oxford: Oxford University Press, 2012)
Ashworth, C., *RAF Coastal Command 1936–1939* (London: Patrick Stephens Ltd, 1992)
Ballantyne, I., *HMS Rodney: Slayer of the Bismarck and D-Day Saviour* (Barnsley: Pen and Sword, 2016)
Beesly, P., *Very Special Intelligence: The Story of the Admiralty's Operational Intelligence Centre, 1939–1945* (London: Hamish Hamilton, 1977)
Bennett, G. H. (ed.) *Hitler's Ghost Ships: Graf Spee, Scharnhorst and Disguised German Raiders* (Plymouth: University of Plymouth Press, 2012)
Bishop, P., *Target Tirpitz: X-Craft, Agents and Dambusters – The Epic Quest to Destroy Hitler's Mightiest Warship* (London: Harper Press, 2012)
Bloch, M., *Ribbentrop* (New York: Crown publishers Inc., 1992))
BR 1736 (48) (2) Admiralty, Naval Staff History of the Second World War, *Home Waters and the Atlantic Volume II, 9th April 1940–6th December 1941* (1961)
Breyer, S., *Battleships and Battlecruisers, 1905–1970* (New York: Doubleday & Company, 1974)
Breyer, S., *The German Battleship Gneisenau* (West Chester: Schiffer Publishing, 1990)
Busch, F. O., *The Drama of the Scharnhorst* (Ware: Wordsworth, 2001)
Busch, F. O., *Prinz Eugen* (London: Fist Futura Publications, 1975)
Campbell, J., *Naval Weapons of World War Two* (London: Conway Maritime Press, 2002)
Churchill, W. S., *The Second World War Volume V: Closing the Ring* (London: Folio Society, 2003)
Dildy, D. C., *Battles of World War II Denmark and Norway 1940: Hitler's Boldest Operation* (Oxford: Osprey Publishing Limited, 2009)
Donald, D. (ed.), *Warplanes of the Luftwaffe* (London: Aerospace, 1994)
Dönitz, K., *Memoirs: Ten Years and Twenty Days* (New York: Weidenfeld & Nicolson, 1959)
Duskin, G., Segman, R., *If the Gods are Good: The Epic Sacrifice of HMS Jervis Bay* (Annapolis: Naval Institute Press, 2004)
English, J., *Amazon to Ivanhoe: British Standard Destroyers of the 1930s* (Kendal: World Ship Society, 1993)
Ford, K., *Run the Gauntlet: The Channel Dash 1942* (Oxford: Osprey Publishing, 2012)
Fraser, B., 'Sinking of the German Battle-Cruiser *Scharnhorst* on the 26th December, 1943', *Supplement to the London Gazette*, No. 38038 (7 August 1947), pp. 3703-3714.
Friedman, K. I., *Afternoon of the Rising Sun: The Battle of Leyte Gulf* (Novato: Presidio Press Inc., 2001)
Friedman, N., *U.S. Battleships: An illustrated Design History* (Annapolis: Naval Institute Press, 1985)
Gallagher, T., *Against All Odds* (London: Pan Books, 1973)
Gardiner, R., *Conway's All the World's Fighting Ships, 1922–1946* (Annapolis: Naval Institute Press, 1980)
Garrett, R., *Scharnhorst and Gneisenau: The Elusive Sisters* (London: Hippocrene Books, 1978)
Garzke, W. H., Dulin, R. O., *Battleships: Axis and Neutral Battleships in World War II* (Annapolis: Naval Institute press, 1985)

Golvoko, A., *With the Red Fleet* (London: Putnam, 1965)
Gröner, E., *German Warships: 1815–1945* (Annapolis: Naval Institute Press, 1990)
Grove, E., *German Capital Ships and Raiders in World War II: From Scharnhorst to Tirpitz, 1942–1944* (London: Routledge, 2002)
Haarr, G. H., *The Battle for Norway: April-June 1940* (Annapolis: Naval Institute Press, 2010)
Hague, A., *The Allied Convoy System 1939–1945: Its Organization, Defence and Operation* (Annapolis: Naval Institute Press, 2000)
Hampshire, A. C., *The Blockaders* (London: William Kimber, 1980)
Harding, D., *Sink the Scharnhorst* (York: Benchmark Publishing, 2016)
Haslop, D., *Britain, Germany and the Battle of the Atlantic: A Comparative Study* (London: Bloomsbury, 2013)
Hastings, M., *Bomber Command* (London: Pan Books, 2010)
Hellwinkel, L., *Hitler's Gateway to the Atlantic: German Naval Bases in France 1940–1945* (Barnsley: Seaforth Publishing, 2014)
Hildebrand, K., *The Foreign Policy of the Third Reich* (London: Batsford, 1973)
Hinsley, F. H., *British Intelligence in the Second World War: Its Influence on Strategy and Operations* (London: Her Majesty's Stationary Office, 1994)
Howland, V. W., 'The Loss of HMS Glorious: An Analysis of the Action', *Warship International*, Vol. 31, No.1 (1994), pp. 47-62.
Humble, R., *Hitler's High Seas Fleet* (New York: Ballantyne Books, 1971)
Jackson, R., *The Royal Navy in World War II* (Annapolis: Naval Institute Press, 1997)
Jacobs, P., *Daring Raids of World War Two: Heroic Land, Sea and Air Attacks* (Barnsley: Pen and Sword, 2015)
Jacobsen, A. R., *Scharnhorst* (Stroud: Sutton publishing, 2003)
Jacobsen, A. R., *X-Craft Verses Tirpitz: The Mystery of the Missing X-5* (Stroud: Sutton Publishing, 2006)
Johnston, I, McAuley, R., *The Battleships* (London: Channel 4 Books, 2000)
Kemp, P., *Escape of the Scharnhorst and Gneisenau* (London: Ian Allen, 1975)
Kemp, R., *Raiders: WWII Britain's Most Daring Special Operations* (London: Century, 2012)
Kennedy, P., *The Rise and Fall of British Naval Mastery* (London: Macmillan, 1983)
Kershaw, I., *Hitler 1889–1936: Hubris* (New York: W.W. Norton, 1998)
Knowles, D., *King George V-class Battleships* (Stroud: Fonthill Media, 2022)
Knowles, D., *Tirpitz: The Life and Death of Germany's Last Great Battleship* (Stroud: Fonthill Media, 2018)
Konstam, A., *The Battle of North Cape: The Death Ride of the Scharnhorst 1943* (Barnsley: Pen and Sword, 2011)
Konstam, A., *British Battlecruisers 1939–1945* (Oxford: Osprey publishing Limited, 2003)
Koop, G., Schmolke, K. P., *Battleships of the Scharnhorst Class* (Barnsley: Pen and Sword, 2014)
Lavery, B., *The Last Big Gun: At War and at Sea with HMS Belfast* (Oxford: The Pool of London Press, 2015)
Marriott, L., *Treaty Cruisers: The First international Warship Building Competition* (Barnsley: Pen and Sword, 2005)
Maier, K. A., (et. al.), *Germany and the Second World War Volume II: Germany's Initial Conquests in Europe* (Oxford: Clarendon Press, 1991)
Martienssen, A., *Hitler and His Admirals* (London: Secker, 1948)
McMurtri, F. E., (ed.), *Jane's Fighting Ships 1940* (London: Sampson Low, Marston & Co, 1940)
Miller, N., *War at Sea: A Naval History of World War II* (Oxford: Oxford University Press, 1996)
Moffat, J., *I Sank the Bismarck: Memoirs of a Second World War Navy Pilot* (London: Corgi Books, 2010)
Muir, M., 'Gun Calibers and Battle Zones: The United States Navy's Foremost Concern During the 1930s', *Warship International*, No. 1 (1980)
Parker, J., *Task Force: Untold Stories of the Royal Navy* (London: Headline Book Publishing, 2003)
Pearson, M., *Red Sky in the Morning: The Battle of the Barents Sea 1942* (Barnsley: Pen & Sword Books Ltd, 2007)
Poolman, K., *Armed Merchant Cruisers* (London: Leo Cooper, 1985)
Potter, E. B. (ed.), *Sea Power: A Naval History* (Annapolis: Naval Institute Press, 1981)
Preston, A., *The World's Worst Warships* (London: Conway Maritime Press, 2002)
Ramsden, B., 'Sinking the Scharnhorst', *Blackwood's Magazine*, No. 1549 (1944)
Rhys-Jones, G., *Churchill and the Norway Campaign* (Barnsley: Pen and Sword, 2008)
Richards, D., *The Royal Air Force 1939–1945: Volume I The Fight at Odds* (London: Her Majesty's Stationary Office, 1953)
Robertson, T., *Channel Dash* (London: Evans, 1958)
Rohwer, J., *Chronology of the War at Sea 1939–1945: The Naval History of World War Two* (Annapolis: Naval Institute Press, 2005)
Roskill, S. W., *Churchill and the Admirals* (London: Collins, 1977)
Roskill, S. W., *The Navy at War 1939–1945* (London: Collins, 1960)
Roskill, S. W., *War at Sea 1939–1945 Volume I: The Defensive* (London: Her Majesty's Stationary Office, 1954)
Roskill, S. W., *War at Sea 1939–1945 Volume II: The Period of Balance* (London: Her Majesty's Stationary Office, 1956)
Rossiter, M., *Ark Royal: The Life, Death and Rediscovery of the Legendary Second World War Aircraft carrier* (London: Corgi Books, 2007)
Sauer, H., *The Last Big-Gun Naval Battle: The Battle of Surigao Strait* (Palo Alto: The Glencannon Press, 1999)
Schmalenbach, P., 'KM Prinz Eugen', *Warship Profile* 6 (Windsor: Profile Publications, 1971)
Sebag-Montefiore, H., *Enigma: The Battle for the Code* (London: Phoenix, 2011)
Smith, P. C., *The Battle-Cruiser Renown 1916–1948* (Barnsley: Pen and Sword, 2008)
Smith, R. J., Kay, A., *German Aircraft of the Second World War* (London: Putnam & Company Ltd, 1972)
Van Der Vat, D., *The Atlantic Campaign: The Great Struggle at Sea, 1939–1945* (London: Hodder and Stoughton, 1988)
Vulliez, A., Mordal, J., *Battleship Scharnhorst* (London: Hutchinson, 1958)
Ward, C., *4 Group Bomber Command: An Operational Record* (Barnsley: Pen and Sword, 2012)
Weinberg, G., *The Foreign policy of Hitler's Germany: Diplomatic Revolution in Europe, 1933–36* (Chicago: University of Chicago Press, 1970)
Williamson, G., *German Battleships 1939-45* (Oxford: Osprey Publishing Limited, 2003)
Winton, J., *Death of the Scharnhorst* (London: Cassell, 2001)
Woodman, R., *Arctic Convoys 1941–1945* (Barnsley: Pen and Sword, 2013)

Zetterling, N., Tamelander, M., *Tirpitz: The Life and Death of Germany's Last Super Battleship* (Oxford: Casemate Publishers, 2009)

Webpages

Asmussen, J., 'Operation "Juno"', Scharnhorst-class.*dk*, Scharnhorst-class.dk/scharnhorst/history/scharnjuno.html (2010), Accessed 14/04/2019.
Asmussen, J., 'The Scharnhorst at Brest, France (22 March 1941-11 February 1942', Scharnhorst-class.*dk* (2010), Scharnhorst-class.dk/scharnhorst/history/scharnbrest.html, Accessed 24/05/2019.
Bowes, C., 'How Germany's Feared *Scharnhorst* Ship was Sunk in WW2', *BBC* (26 December 2011), bbc.co.uk/news/world-europe-16265665, Accessed 26/10/2019.
Fenton, N., 'The Sinking of the "Scharnhorst"', *BBC* (17 February 2011), bbc.co.uk/history/worldwars/wwtwo/scharnhorst_01.shtml, Accessed 06/05/2019.
Historische Marinearchiv, *Crew Lists of WWII* (2019), historisches-marinearchiv.de/index.php, Accessed 26/10/2019.
US War Department, 'Commando Operations: Section II British Task Force, Spitsbergen Operation', *British Commandos, Military Intelligence Service*, Special Series No. 1 (1942), available at: lonesentry.com/manuals/commandos/spitsbergen.html, Accessed 03/05/2019.

Other Sources

Kennedy, L., 'The Life and Death of the *Scharnhorst*', BBC (1971)

London Gazette, 9 July 1940

Index

Abyssinia 16
Acasta, HMS 91-93, 95-99, 224
Admiral Graf Spee 16-18, 21, 32, 34, 45, 47-48, 81
Admiral Hipper 72, 81-83, 86, 88, 90, 100, 102-105, 111-112, 114, 154, 156, 215
Admiral Hipper-class 22, 28, 84, 104
Admiral Scheer 16-18, 21, 47, 63, 112, 114
Adventfjord 163, 166
Akureyri 175
Altafjord 156-159, 161-162, 164-168, 170, 178, 192, 196, 214
Amagi-class 14
Andfjord 88
Anglo-German Naval Agreement 20-21
Arado Ar-95 34, 36-38
Arado Ar-196 34-35, 38-40, 111, 162, 164, 203
Archangel 132, 160
Arctic Ocean 9, 157, 160-161, 163, 182
Ardent, HMS 91-93, 96, 99, 224
Arizona, USS 215
Ark Royal, HMS 88, 91-92, 101-102, 119-120
Aurora, HMS 69
Austrått Fortress 216, 218
Avro Manchester 143
Azores 48, 111

BBC 151, 221
Bain, Donald 193
Barker, J. F. 91-92
Barry, Claude 164, 169
Baltic Sea 36, 72, 75, 77, 87, 105-106, 132, 152-153, 218
Barentsburg 160-161, 163
Barents Sea 154-155, 162, 215
Barham, HMS 215
Barnetsz, Willem 160
Bates, H. 197
Beamish, Victor 139
Bear Island 154, 157, 162, 184, 186

Beatty, David 11
Behr, Heinz-Günther 180, 203-204, 206, 228
Belfast, HMS 187-189, 191-197, 200, 202, 204-205, 207, 209
Bergen 82, 101, 156, 216, 219
Berlin 20, 154, 159
Bernd von Arnim 63, 83
Bey, Erich 145, 172-174, 177-181, 185, 187, 189-193, 196, 198, 203, 206, 213, 229
Birke, Rudi 203, 227
Bismarck 9, 21-23, 28, 120-121, 126-127, 141, 223-224
Bismarck-class 11, 22, 28, 41, 67
Blackburn Skua 101-102
Blåvand 218
Blohm & Voss BV-138 175, 177
Bodø 90
Boekhoff, Helmut 202, 208, 227
Bogen Bay 156-157
Boulogne 139, 144
Borage, HMS 175
Borah, William 13
Boudreaux 114, 119
Bredenbreuker, Walter 203, 229
Brest 39, 114, 118, 120-130, 132-136, 141, 144-145, 150, 224
Bristol Beaufighter 148
Bristol Beaufort 101-102, 105, 123-125, 143
Bristol Blenheim 63, 143
Brown, E. L. 101
Brunsbüttel 63, 149-150
Burnett, Robert 184, 186-193, 196-198, 204-205, 207, 210
Burrough, Harold 131
B-Dienst 110, 114, 118

Cain, William 119
Cameron, Donald 164
Campbell, HMS 146-147
Campbell, Kenneth 123-125
Cap Griz Nez 139, 141
Cape Farewell 107

Cape Verde 112, 118
Carls, Rolf 82, 115
Casson, John 101
Castor 215
Channel Islands 136, 172
Chitral, HMS 68
Churchill, Winston 169-170, 212, 214
Ciliax, Otto 51, 63, 133-136, 138-139, 141, 143-145, 148-150, 225
Clyde, HMS 102, 104
Colorado-class 14
Colvin, G. R. 135
Compston, Robin 196
Conning, G. 118
Convoys
  Dervish 132
  HN-12 81
  HX-106 110
  HX-111 110
  HX-114 114
  JW-51A 154
  JW-54A 170
  JW-55A 174-175
  JW-55B 175, 177, 181, 185-187, 190
  PQ-1 132
  PQ-2 132
  PQ-7B 132
  PQ-12 153
  PQ-13 153
  PQ-14 153
  PQ-15 153
  PQ-16 153
  PQ-17 153-154
  PQ-18 154
  QP-8 153
  QP-9 153
  QP-10 153
  QP-11 153
  QP-14 154
  QP-15 154
  RA-54A 170
  RA-55B 186

Cordes, Ludwig 223
Corneliussen, Elias 212
Cossack, HMS 81
Coulston, William 210
Cox, Vivian 207
Crawford, James 194
Cunningham, Andrew 169-170
Cunningham, John 213
C-class 69

Dalrymple-Hamilton, Frederick 117-118
Danae-class 69
Daring, HMS 81
Deal 142
Deierling, Johann 208, 230
Delaware-class 14
Delhi, HMS 69-70
Denmark 81-82, 115, 218
Denmark Strait 65-66, 69, 106-108, 126
Denning, Norman 182
Deutsche Werke 20, 43, 87, 150
Deutschland 12-13, 16-19, 21, 47, 66-67, 69
Deutschland-class 18-19, 21-22, 24, 28, 67, 223
Devonport 69
Devonshire, HMS 69
Diether von Roeder 63
Dominik, Ernst 180-181, 202, 206, 210, 230
Dönitz, Karl 155-156, 159, 172, 175, 177-178, 198, 213-215
Douglas Boston 143
Dover 134-136, 139, 141-142
Duke of York, HMS 174-176, 182, 184, 186, 190, 192-205, 207, 211-213, 221
Duke-Woolley, Raymond 142
Dunkerque 18-19, 69, 120
Dunkerque-class 18-21
Durston, Albert 130
D'Oyly-Hughes, Guy 91, 96

Eden, Anthony 20
Edinburgh, HMS 69, 153
Elkington, Robert 92
Emden 12
Emerald, HMS 117
Erbslöh, Paul-Günther 32
Erich Steinbrink 63, 88, 102, 156, 162, 169, 172
Esmonde, Eugene 141-142
E-Boat 139, 141

Fairey Fulmar 119-120
Fairey Swordfish 91-92, 102, 141-143
Falkland Island, Battle of 43-44, 51
Fanø 218
Faroe Islands 65-66, 69, 99
Fein, Otto 115, 117, 144, 148-150, 225
First World War 12-13, 15, 21, 63, 65, 68, 81, 223

Fisher, Douglas 212
Fisher, Ralph, 191
Fjell 216, 218-219
Focke-Wulf Fw-62 36
Focke-Wulf Fw-190 142
Forbes, Charles 69, 71-72, 83
Förste, Erich 43, 225
France 9, 13, 15-16, 18, 21-22, 59, 63, 72, 133, 223
  Marine Nationale 18
Fraser, Bruce 156, 170, 174-176, 182-184, 186, 189, 192-198, 202, 204-205, 207, 209-212, 221
Friedrich Eckoldt 63
Friedrich Ihn 105, 135
Furious, HMS 15, 69, 114

Galland, Adolf 136
Gdynia 218, 220
Geneva 15
  Disarmament Conference 15, 18
Germany 9, 11-13, 16, 18-20, 22, 34, 36, 59, 63, 65, 67, 71-72, 81-83, 86-87, 102, 110, 120, 126, 130, 132-134, 136, 150, 152-153, 155-156, 158-160, 164, 169, 172, 174, 204, 209, 215, 223
Gibraltar 107, 110, 114, 118-120, 135
Giessler, Helmuth 146, 148, 150, 198
Glasford, C. E. 91
Glasgow, HMS 69
Gleaner, HMS 175
Glorious, HMS 88, 90-97, 99-101, 224
Gloster Gladiator 90
Glowworm, HMS 83-84
Gneisenau 9, 11, 20, 22-34, 36-38, 40, 43-51, 59, 61, 63, 65-66, 68-72, 75, 81-82, 84-93, 95-96, 100, 102-108, 110-130, 132-133, 135-140, 144-150, 166, 215-220, 223-226, 240
Gneisenau, SMS 43-44
Gödde, Willie 188, 190, 195, 198, 200-202, 208-211, 227
Golovko, Arseniy 175, 211
Gotenhafen 105-106, 152, 156, 215, 217-220
Graf Zeppelin 34, 217
Gray, A. W. 86, 119
Great Britain 9, 13-16, 20-22, 59, 63, 65-66, 72, 81, 90, 99, 102, 107, 110, 112, 121, 125-126, 131-132, 135, 143, 161, 175, 211, 223-224
Greenland Sea 160
Greif 102
Greyhound, HMS 83
Gronfjord 163, 166

Halifax 69, 107, 110
Hammerfest 178, 181, 221

Handley Page Halifax 128, 130, 143
Hansen, Otto 181
Hans Lody 88, 102, 105, 162
Hans Lüdemann 83
Harding, Warren G. 13
Harstad 88, 90
Hauss, Werner 179-180
Hawker Hurricane 90
Heath, J. B. 91
Heather, Ernie 184
Heinkel He-60 36
Heinkel He-114 34, 36-37
Henty-Creer, Henty 164
Herbert, A. V. 84
Hermann Schoemann 72, 88, 102, 135, 148-149
Hermione, HMS 135
High Seas Fleet 11-12, 69, 223
Hillmann, Ralph 124-125
Hinsley, Harry 182
Hintze, Fritz 172, 177, 179-181, 185, 187, 191-193, 196, 198-199, 201-202, 206, 209, 225, 232
Hitler, Adolf 18-22, 43, 51, 54, 59-60, 81-82, 88, 131-134, 150, 154-156, 169, 175, 215
Hoffmann, Kurt 63-64, 68, 80, 91, 110, 143-146, 148, 150, 152, 225
Holland 148, 218
Hollmann, Hans 32
Honeysuckle, HMS 175
Hood, HMS 69, 119, 215, 224
Hound, HMS 175
Howaldtswerke 105
Huascaran 100, 102
Hudsperth, Kenneth 164, 168-169
Hüffmeier, Friedrich 152, 159, 163, 168, 172, 225
Hughes-Hallett, John 197, 204
Hvalfjord 132, 156
Hyde, John 123
Hydra, HMS 175

Ibel, Max 136
Iceland 65-66, 69, 106, 132-133, 153-154, 156, 175-176, 184, 190
Illah, Abdul 212
Iltis 120
Ingersoll, Royal 212
Ingram, David 102
Ireland 65
Isfjord 162-163
Italy 13-16

Jaguar 120
Jamaica, HMS 154, 175, 184, 192-195, 197, 200, 202, 204-205, 207, 212
Japan 13-16, 130
Jeanne d'Arc 126
Johannesson, Rolf 174, 185, 187, 189-190, 192, 206
Jordan, Ron 101

Juniper, HMT 90
Junkers Ju-88 135, 175, 177
Jupp, M. H. 166
Jutland, Battle of 13

Kåfjord 156, 158-159, 164, 167-169, 177, 181
Kaga-class 14
Karlsruhe 43
Karl Galster 63, 72, 88, 102, 105, 156, 162
Karl Junge 158
Kennelly, Bill 84-85
Kenya, HMS 131
Kiel 20, 25, 43, 45, 48, 64, 66, 72, 76-77, 81, 87, 102, 104-106, 149-151, 177, 215-216
Kii-class 14
King George V, HMS 41, 117
King George V-class 14, 41
King George VI 212
Kingcombe, Brian 142
Klüber, Otto 162, 177
Kola Inlet 190, 210-211
Köln 63, 156
Kondor 102
König, Otto 199, 202, 233
Königsberg 32, 101
Korth, Claus 81
Kretzschmar, Walther 145
Kriegsmarine 7, 9, 11, 19, 22-24, 28, 31-32, 43, 51, 59, 63, 66, 81-83, 100, 110, 121, 132-133, 154-157, 166, 169, 207, 213-216, 224
   2nd Destroyer Flotilla 72
   4th Destroyer Flotilla 172, 174, 177-178, 185, 190, 192
   5th Minesweeper Flotilla 178
Kriegsmarinewerft 20, 51, 59
Kristiansand 82
Krossfjorden 161
Kruse, Wilhelm 188, 227
Kummetz, Oskar 154, 156-158, 162-164, 172, 174
Kursk 159

La Roche 127
La Rochelle 120
Langfjord 166-168, 177-179, 181
Lanz, Edgar 185, 192, 206, 233
Las Palmas 48
Le Touquet 139-140
Leach, Henry 194, 210
League of Nations 15-16
Leberecht Maass 72
Leipzig 28, 129, 156
Littorio 41
Loch Ewe 69, 154, 174-175, 186
Loch Cairnbawn 164, 166
Lockheed Hudson 100, 135-136, 143
London 15-16, 20, 106, 125, 164, 166, 213
London Naval Treaty 15
Longyearbyen 161-163

Lovell, Ted 96
Löwisch, Wolf 91
Luchs 72
Luftwaffe 34, 63, 101, 120, 134, 136, 141-143, 145, 147, 153-155, 174, 203
Luth, Wolfgang 81
Lütjens, Günther 82-85, 100, 102, 104, 106-107, 110-112, 114-115, 117-120, 126, 133-134
Lützow 152, 154, 156-157, 164, 169, 215
Lützow, Friedrich 214

Mackay, HMS 146-147
Maclot, Wilhelm 179-180
Maerker, Julius 43-44
Malaya, HMS 112, 114, 118, 135
Måløy 131
Marinewerft 51
Marschall, Wilhelm 65, 70-72, 88, 90, 100
Martin, Thomas 164
Matchless, HMS 190, 204-205, 207, 209-211
Max Schulz 63
McCoy, James 175, 183-187
Mcfarlane, Brian 164
Mediterranean 14, 132
Merchant Ships
   Adria 106, 108
   A. D. Huff 111, 226
   Alsteror 100
   Altmark 34, 81-82
   Athelfoam 114, 226
   Atlantis 90
   Bianca 114, 119, 226
   Biarwood 154
   Borgund 99
   Bremen 69
   British Strength 114, 226
   Chilean Reefer 115-118, 226
   Daldorch 154
   Demerton 114
   Dithmarschen 88, 90
   Empire Gilbert 154
   Empire Industry 114, 226
   Ermland 111-112, 118, 120
   Esso Hamburg 110-111
   Friedrich Breme 111
   Granli 114, 226
   Gretafield 81
   Harlesden 111, 226
   Hugh Williamson 154
   John H. B. Latrobe 154
   John Walker 154
   Kantara 111, 226
   Mangkai 114, 226
   Myson 114, 226
   Liana 81
   Linda 81
   Loch Maddy 81
   Lustrious 111, 226
   Oil Pioneer 90
   Orama 90
   Osmed 81

   Polykarb 114, 119, 226
   Rhone 81
   Richard H. Alvey 154
   Rio Dorado 114-115, 226
   Royal Crown 114, 226
   Santos 81
   San Casimiro 114, 119, 226
   Sardinian Prince 114, 226
   Schlettsdat 107, 110-111
   Silverfir 114, 226
   Simnia 114, 226
   Sleipner 81
   Trelawny 111, 226
   Uckermark 112, 114, 117-118, 120
Merkel, Johnnie 211
Messerschmitt Me-109 101, 139, 142
Messerschmitt Me-110 101
Meyer, Hans 162, 167, 169
Molotov-Ribbentrop Pact 160
Montevideo 81
Mulliss, William 124-125
Murmansk 132, 175, 210-211
Musketeer, HMS 190-191, 204-205
Mussolini, Benito 159
Mutsu 14
M-class 16

Naiad, HMS 106, 110
Narvik 81-82, 84, 88, 90, 119, 156, 158, 162, 172, 177
Narvik rikskringkasting AS 221
Nelson, HMS 14, 69, 117
Netzbrandt, Harald 63, 225
Newcastle, HMS 69-71
Nicholl, Len 117
Norfolk, HMS 69, 187-193, 196, 202, 213
Northern Patrol 63, 65, 67
North Sea 9, 12, 22, 63, 65-66, 69, 71, 82-83, 104, 133, 143
Norway 9, 19, 65, 69, 72, 81-82, 88, 90, 99, 131-132, 150, 153-156, 160, 163-164, 166, 169, 171-172, 175, 182-184, 192, 215-216, 221
Norwegian Sea 160
Nürnberg 28, 129, 156

Onslow, HMS 175, 183
Opportune, HMS 190, 204-205
Orkney Islands 12, 213
Oslo 82
Oxlip, HMS 175

Parat 100
Parham, Frederick 188, 194, 209
Paris 12, 127
Partridge, R. T. 101
Paul Jacobi 63, 72, 105, 135, 156
Paul of Greece, Crown Prince 212
Pearl Harbor 133
Pendered, Richard 183
Persie, Richard 125
Pizey, Mark 144, 146-147

Place, Godfrey 164, 168
Poland 21-22, 59, 63, 81, 223
Portal, Charles 125-126
Portugal 48
Pound, Dudley 169-170
Preussen 31
Prince of Wales, HMS 133
Prinz Eugen 43, 126-128, 130, 133, 135-136, 138-149, 152, 155

Queen Mary, RMS 190
Quisling, Vidkun 82

Raeder, Erich 19, 22, 54, 59, 66, 82, 88, 132-134, 154-155, 224
Ramillies, HMS 110
Ramsay, Bertram 136
Ramsden, Bryce 184, 195, 202
Ranger, USS 213
Rawalpindi, HMS 66-71, 224
Reichsmarine 12, 16, 18, 21, 223
Renown, HMS 82-86, 119
Repulse, HMS 69, 114, 119, 133
Reykjavik 162
Richard Beitzen 135
Richelieu 41, 213
River Plate, Battle of 81
Rivers
    Clyde 69
    Elbe 87, 149
    Forth 69
    Jade 72, 150
    Maas 144, 146
    Scheldt 144-145
    Tyne 69
    Weser 72
Roberts, Philip Quellyn 132
Rodney, HMS 14, 41, 69, 101-102, 114-118, 135
Roope, Gerard B. 83
Roosevelt, Franklin D. 212
Royal Air Force 63, 82, 86-87, 90, 100-101, 121-122, 125-126, 128, 130, 134-136, 139, 143-144, 146, 151, 155, 165, 196, 213, 215-217, 224
    Bomber Command 63, 123, 125-126, 130, 143-146, 159, 214
    Coastal Command 72, 100, 102, 123, 135-136, 143-144, 146, 155
    Fighter Command 135, 138-139
    Hawkinge 139
    Kenley 139
    Manston 141-143
    North Coates 123
    St. Eval 123
    Uxbridge 139
    2 Group 63
    3 Group 63
    18 Group 213
    19 Group 135
    46 Squadron 90
    72 Squadron 142
    91 Squadron 139
    124 Squadron 142
    224 Squadron 135
    263 Squadron 90
    401 Squadron 142
Royal Navy 7, 9, 11, 14-15, 18, 20, 22, 34, 63, 69-70, 82-83, 99-100, 110, 117, 119, 126-127, 130, 132-133, 136, 139, 154, 160-164, 170, 175, 212, 224
    Force H 119-120
    Grand Fleet 11-12
    Home Fleet 63, 66, 69-70, 72, 83, 105-106, 133, 155-156, 162-164, 174, 212, 214
    Nore Command 135
    Reserve Fleet 65
    Volunteer Reserve 161
    8th Destroyer Flotilla 69
    20th Destroyer Flotilla 83
    21st Destroyer Flotilla 114, 146
    800 Squadron (FAA) 101
    803 Squadron (FAA) 101
    825 Squadron (FAA) 141
Royal Canadian Navy 132, 160
Royal Norwegian Navy 161, 212, 221
Russell, Guy 194
R56 178-179, 181
R58 178-179, 181
R121 181

Saalwächter, Alfred 133
Saint Nazaire 126-127
Saumarez, HMS 175, 193, 199-200, 205
Savage, HMS 175, 193, 199-200, 205
Scapa Flow 12, 64, 82, 91, 102, 106, 133, 162-163, 211-213
Sceptre, HMS 166
Scharnhorst 9, 11, 20, 22-30, 32-35, 38-39, 41-42, 51-56, 58-102, 104-107, 109-115, 118-123, 125-130, 132-141, 143-153, 155-159, 161-215, 221-228
Scharnhorst, SMS 51
Scharnhorst-class 11, 23-25, 28, 30, 32-34, 41, 67, 84, 110, 223
Schlesien 77
Schleswig-Holstein 156
Schniewind, Otto 172, 174, 177
Schultz, Felix 51
Scorpion, HMS 175, 193, 198-200, 205, 207, 209-211
Scotland 65, 72, 133
Scott, Jimmy 124-125
Sealion, HMS 135
Seanymph, HMS 166
Second London Naval Treaty 16
Seeadler 72
Seekriegsleitung 82
Shannon, Henry 85
Sheerness 144
Sheffield, HMS 69, 154, 187-188, 190-193, 210, 213
Short Stirling 143
Sicily 159
Sierra Leone 107, 135
Simon, John 20
Singapore 115
Skinner, Ron 102
Skudenesfjord 105
Smith, Brook 196
Somerville, James 119-120, 213
Sopocko, Eryk 115
Southampton, HMS 69
Soviet Union 132, 153, 156, 160, 170, 174-175
    Red Army 132, 218
Spain 48
Spitsbergen 160-164, 166-167
Spurway, Kenneth V. 101
St. Ninian, SS 211, 214
Stadtlandet 71
Stalin, Joseph 170, 212
Stavanger 105
Stevnsfort 218
Stord, HnoMS 175, 193, 199-200, 205
Storheill, Skule 199
Strasbourg 18
Sträter, Günter 189, 200, 206, 210, 227
Stubborn, HMS 166, 169
Suffolk, HMS 69
Supermarine Spitfire 121, 135, 139, 141-142, 162
Surcouf 16
Svalbard Archipelago 160-163
Svalbard II 99
Sverdrup II 221
Sweden 82
Switzerland 15
Syfret, Neville 170
Syrtis, HMS 166

Takoradi 114
Terschelling 148
Theodor Riedel 72, 156, 162
Thorshaven 99
Thrasher, HMS 166
Tirpitz 9, 21-23, 28, 49, 59-60, 132, 153, 156-158, 161-164, 166-169, 172, 174, 177, 180, 214, 216, 223-224
Tovey, John 106, 110, 155
Treaty of Versailles 9, 11-12, 18, 20-21, 224
Trondheim 81-83, 88, 90, 100-105, 156
Trondheimsfjord 102, 218
Truculent, HMS 166
Turkey 36
Tyr, NoMS 222
T13 146, 148
T15 148
T16 148
T17 148
T20 156
T21 156

U-boat 11, 63, 72, 112-113, 126, 152-155, 157, 161, 174-175, 181-183, 215, 224
   U-9 81
   U-14 81
   U-23 81
   U-47 64
   U-57 81
   U-61 81
   U-63 81
   U-105 112
   U-124 112-113
   U-251 153
   U-277 190
   U-456 153
   U-523 152
   U-586 170
   U-601 181
   U-716 182
United Kingdom (see Great Britain)
United States 13-16, 111
   Army Air Force 159
   Navy 7, 11, 18
Ushant 136

Vaernes 101
Vågsøy 131
Valiant, HMS 88
Vestfjord 82-84
Vian, Philip 81
Vickers Wellington 63, 136, 143

Victorious, HMS 141, 153
Virago, HMS 190, 204-205, 207
Vivacious, HMS 146-147
Von Blomberg, Werner 19, 51, 54
Von Fritsch, Werner 19, 43
Von Pufendorf, Rudolf 72
Von Reuter, Ludwig 12
Von Ribbentrop, Joachim 20
Von Schleicher, Kurt 18
Von Tirpitz, Alfred 59
Von Willisen, Hans-Karl 32

Wallflower, HMS 175
Walton, Eric 118
Wanderer, HMS 175
Warspite, HMS 69
Washington D.C. 13-14, 169
Washington Naval Treaty 14-16, 18
Washington, USS 41
Weimar Republic 12
Welby-Everard, Philip 188-189
Wellman, Derek 183
Wells-Cole, Peter 117-118
Whitehall, HMS 175
Whitshed, HMS 146-147
Whitworth, William 82, 84, 126
Wibbelhoff, Johann 206, 238
Wilhelmshaven 20, 43, 48, 51, 54, 58-60, 65-66, 71-72, 74, 81-82, 87-89, 149-150, 222
Wilhelm Bremen 158

Wilhelm Heidkamp 63, 72
Willis, Algernon 213
Wilson, Richard 200
Wilson, Woodrow 13
Witte, Hubert 199, 227
Wohlfarth, Herbert 81
Wolfgang Zenker 72
Worcester, HMS 146-147
Woytschekowski-Emden, Rolf 214, 239
Wrestler, HMS 175

X-5 164, 166, 168
X-6 164, 166, 168, 214
X-7 164, 166, 168
X-8 164, 166
X-9 164, 166
X-10 164, 166, 168-169

Zenker, Hans 16
Z25 135, 153
Z27 162, 169
Z28 156
Z29 135, 144-145, 148, 156, 162, 172, 177, 181, 185, 187
Z30 162, 177, 187
Z31 162
Z33 162, 177
Z34 177, 181
Z38 177, 181, 187